FACILITATING COMMUNITY RESEARCH FOR SOCIAL CHANGE

Facilitating Community Research for Social Change asks: what does ethical research facilitation look like in projects that seek to move toward social change? How can scholars weave political and social justice through multiple levels of the research process?

This edited collection presents chapters that investigate research facilitation in ways that specifically attempt to disrupt and challenge anti-Indigenous and anti-Black racism, ableism, homophobia, transphobia, patriarchy, and sexism to work toward social change. It also explores what it means to develop facilitation practices across multiple contexts and research settings, including specific facilitation methods considered by researchers working with visual and community-based methods with Black, Indigenous, and racialized communities. The complexities of how scholars negotiate decisions within their research with people and communities have an effect not only on how researchers construct their participants and communities, but also on the overall purpose of projects, the ways their projects are shared and disseminated, and what is learned in the doing of facilitation.

This book will be of great interest to both emerging and established researchers working within the social sciences. It specifically attends to diverse fields within the social sciences that include health, media studies, environmental studies, social work, sociology, education, participatory visual research methodologies, as well as the evolving field of digital humanities.

Casey Burkholder is an Associate Professor at the University of New Brunswick, Canada, interested in community-based and participatory visual research. In choosing a research path at the intersection of resistance and activism, gender, sexuality, DIY media-making, and pre-service teacher education, Casey's work engages participatory approaches to equity and social change. Her recent projects can be found at: www.caseyburkholder.com.

Funké Aladejebi is an Assistant Professor of history at the University of Toronto, Canada. She is the author of *Schooling the System: A History of Black Women Teachers* (2021), which explores the intersections of race, gender, and access in Canadian educational institutions. Her research interests are in oral history, the history of education in Canada, Black feminist thought, and transnationalism. Her current research projects can be found at www.funkealadejebi.com.

Joshua Schwab-Cartas is a mixed race Indigenous Binnizá-Austrian, father, filmmaker, and Indigenous language scholar-activist. He is currently a SSHRC Postdoctoral Fellow at the University of British Columbia in the department of Language and Literacy Education. His research seeks to explore how best to combine mobile technology, specifically cellphilms, into Indigenous practice and land-based education as means of fostering intergenerational knowledge transmission and language reclamation.

FACILITATING COMMUNITY RESEARCH FOR SOCIAL CHANGE

Case Studies in Qualitative, Arts-Based and Visual Research

Edited by Casey Burkholder, Funké Aladejebi and Joshua Schwab-Cartas

LONDON AND NEW YORK

Cover image: Alicia Arias-Camison Coella

First published 2022
by Routledge
4 Park Square, Milton Park, Abingdon, Oxon OX14 4RN

and by Routledge
605 Third Avenue, New York, NY 10158

Routledge is an imprint of the Taylor & Francis Group, an informa business

© 2022 selection and editorial matter, Casey Burkholder, Funké Aladejebi and Joshua Schwab-Cartas; individual chapters, the contributors

The right of Casey Burkholder, Funké Aladejebi and Joshua Schwab-Cartas to be identified as the authors of the editorial material, and of the authors for their individual chapters, has been asserted in accordance with sections 77 and 78 of the Copyright, Designs and Patents Act 1988.

All rights reserved. No part of this book may be reprinted or reproduced or utilised in any form or by any electronic, mechanical, or other means, now known or hereafter invented, including photocopying and recording, or in any information storage or retrieval system, without permission in writing from the publishers.

Trademark notice: Product or corporate names may be trademarks or registered trademarks, and are used only for identification and explanation without intent to infringe.

British Library Cataloguing-in-Publication Data
A catalogue record for this book is available from the British Library

Library of Congress Cataloging-in-Publication Data
A catalog record has been requested for this book

ISBN: 978-1-032-05800-9 (hbk)
ISBN: 978-1-032-05802-3 (pbk)
ISBN: 978-1-003-19923-6 (ebk)

DOI: 10.4324/9781003199236

Typeset in Bembo
by SPi Technologies India Pvt Ltd (Straive)

CONTENTS

List of Contributors   viii
Acknowledgements   xix

Thinking through Research Facilitation: An Introduction   1
Casey Burkholder, Funké Aladejebi, and Joshua Schwab-Cartas

PART I
Troubling Equity within Research Facilitation   15

1 "If You're Going to Work with Black People, You Have to
  Think About These Things!": A Case Study of Fostering an
  Ethical Research Process with a Black Canadian Community   17
  Sadie K. Goddard-Durant, Andrea Doucet, and Jane-Ann Sieunarine

2 Lessons Learned, Lessons Shared: Reflections on Doing
  Research in Collaboration with Sex Workers and Sex
  Worker-led Organizations   33
  Ryan T. Conrad and Emma McKenna

3 Researcher Don't Teach Me Nonsense: Engaging African
  Decolonial Practices in a Critical Mathematics
  Education Project   48
  Oyemolade Osibodu

4 Decolonizing from the Roots: A Community-led Approach
   to Critical Qualitative Health Research   63
   Tenzin Butsang

5 A Reflexive Account of Performing Facilitation in
   Participatory Visual Research for Social Change   76
   *Katie MacEntee, Jennifer Thompson, Milka Nyariro, and
   Claudia Mitchell*

PART II
Facilitating in the Digital Realm   93

6 "Nah You're My Sisters for Real!": Utilizing Instagram and
   Mobile Phones to Facilitate Feminist Conversations with
   Asian Migrant Women in Aotearoa   95
   Helen Yeung

7 Facilitation as Listening in Three Community-Based
   Media Projects   112
   Chloë Brushwood Rose, Bronwen Low, and Paula M. Salvio

8 Theorizing Non-Participation in a Mail-Based
   Participatory Visual Research Project with 2SLGBTQ+
   Youth in Atlantic Canada   127
   *Brody Weaver, Amelia Thorpe, April Mandrona, Katie MacEntee,
   Casey Burkholder, and Pride/Swell*

PART III
Ethics and Facilitation in Research Processes   143

9 Research Assistants as Knowledge Co-Producers:
   Reflections Beyond Fieldwork   145
   Nicole M.Y. Tang and Jan Gube

10 Injustice in Incentives? Facilitating Equitable Research with
   People Living with Poverty   161
   Tobin LeBlanc Haley and Laura Pin

11 Queering Pride Facilitation: An Autoethnography of
   Community Organizing   178
   Amelia Thorpe

PART IV
Art and Ethical Research Practices in Research Facilitation   193

12 Facilitating Queer Art in the Climate Crisis   195
    Sabine LeBel

13 Ethnodramatic Inqueery   208
    Patrick Tomczyk

14 Round and Round the Carousel Papers: Facilitating a Visual Interactive Dialogue with Young People   221
    Catherine Vanner, Yasmeen Shahzadeh, Allison Holloway, Claudia Mitchell, and Jennifer Altenberg

15 Screening Stories: Methodological Considerations for Facilitating Critical Audience Engagement   240
    Caterina Tess Kendrick, Katie MacEntee, and Sarah Flicker

16 "Becoming I/We" Together as Critical Performance Pedagogy: Facilitating Intra-Actions and Metissage from Inhabiting/Living Practice   258
    Genevieve Cloutier, Alison Shields, Lap-Xuan Do-Nguyen, Samira Jamouchi, and Yoriko Gillard

17 What We Think We Know for Sure: Some Concluding Thoughts on Facilitation   277
    Casey Burkholder, Funké Aladejebi, and Joshua Schwab-Cartas

Index   288

CONTRIBUTORS

Funké Aladejebi is an Assistant Professor in the Department of History at the University of Toronto. Her research and teaching interests focus on oral history, the history of education in Canada, Black Canadian women's history, and transnationalism. Her book, *Schooling the System: A History of Black Women Teachers* (MQUP, 2021), explores the importance of Black Canadian women in sustaining their communities and preserving a distinct Black identity within restrictive gender and racial barriers. Her articles on Black Canadian history and feminist pedagogies have appeared in *Education Matters*, *Ontario History*, and the *Southern Journal of Canadian Studies*. She is also currently co-editing with Dr. Michele Johnson, a collection of essays titled, *Unsettling the Great White North: African Canadian History* (UTP, 2022), which explores the histories of African Canadian, Canadian, and African Diasporic communities across chronological, regional, and thematic subjects.

Jennifer Altenberg is a Michif woman, mother, and educator in the Homeland of The Metis, Treaty 6, Saskatoon, SK. Anti-racist and resistance practices to colonial discourse inspire the work she does in the classroom and the Saskatoon community, specifically as a Co-Community Scholar supporting The Young Indigenous Women's Utopia, which engages girls in cultural reclamation, ceremony, storytelling and art-based activism and research. Jennifer is a graduate of the Saskatchewan Urban Native Teacher Education Program at the University of Saskatchewan and completed her Master's Degree in Anti-Racist, Anti-Oppressive Education in Educational Foundations at the University of Saskatchewan. Jennifer lives with her partner and their blended family of 4 children in Treaty 6 and has been in the classroom working with young people for over 15 years.

Contributors **ix**

Chloë Brushwood Rose (she/her) is an Associate Professor in the Faculty of Education at York University and settler in Tkaronto, Treaty 13 territory. Her research interests bridge several fields, including community-engaged visual research methods, media and arts-based education, and gender, feminist and queer studies. Chloë is also in practice as a child and adolescent psychotherapist. Her scholarly work has appeared in a range of journal publications representing diverse fields, including the *Psychoanalysis, Culture & Society*; *Qualitative Studies in Education*; *Visual Studies*; *Changing English*; *International Journal of Leadership in Education*; and, *Gender and Education*. Her books include the co-authored *Community-based Media Pedagogies: Relational Approaches to Listening in the Commons* (2016).

Casey Burkholder (she/her) is an Associate Professor at the University of New Brunswick's Faculty of Education. Her research program centers on work with 2SLGBTQ+ youth and pre-service teachers to agitate for social change through participatory visual research approaches, including DIY art production and participatory archiving. In choosing a research path at the intersection of resistance and activism, gender, sexuality, inclusion, DIY media-making, and Social Studies education, Casey seeks to work with community members to create solidarities, address oppressive systems and structures, and take collaborative social action from-the-ground-up. Casey previously co-edited *Fieldnotes in Qualitative Education and Social Science Research* with Dr. Jen Thompson (Routledge, 2020) and *What's a Cellphilm?: Integrating Mobile Phone Technology into Participatory Visual Research and Activism* (Brill/Sense, 2016) with Dr. Katie MacEntee and Dr. Josh Schwab-Cartas.

Tenzin Butsang is a PhD student in Social and Behavioural Health Sciences at the University of Toronto, where she also completed a Master of Public Health in Indigenous Health. She is a Tibetan settler born on unceded Coast Salish territory. Her research examines settler colonial violence, surveillance, and the carceral state.

Genevieve Cloutier (she/they) is a settler with mixed ancestry living on unceded and unsurrendered Anishinaabe territory. She has a Media Arts degree from Emily Carr University of Art and Design and a MA(Ed) from the University of Ottawa, where she received funding from the Social Science and Humanities Research Council to pursue her PhD on emergent, transdisciplinary, participatory, and relational artistic re-search. She is an artist, activist, and facilitator in her community and a part-time professor at the University of Ottawa, where she teaches How to Teach Senior Visual Art. She has been a guest-editor for Canadian Art Teacher, and her writing has been published in *Western Front Magazine*, the *Canadian Review of Art Education*, the *Journal of Canadian Association of Curriculum Studies*, and the *International Journal of Education & the Arts*. She recently contributed a chapter to *Perspectives on art education in Canada, Volume 1: Surveying the landscape (2019)*.

Ryan T. Conrad is a SSHRC postdoctoral fellow in Cinema & Media Studies with Archive/Counter-Archive at York University in Toronto. From 2017-2019 he was a postdoctoral fellow at the AIDS Activist History Project housed in the Sociology and Anthropology department at Carleton University. He holds a PhD from the Centre for the Interdisciplinary Study of Society and Culture at Concordia University and an MFA in interdisciplinary studio arts with a focus on film, video, and performance from the Maine College of Art.

Lap-Xuan Do-Nguyen is a visual artist and social practitioner born in Ho Chi Minh City, Vietnam. She holds a Bachelor in Visual Communication from Nanyang Academy of Fine Arts (Singapore) and a Master of Art from the University of New South Wales (Australia). Her works embody performative fragments—of words, visualization, movement, and sound—across the themes of identity, displacement, marginalization, and liminality. Since 2018, she has been awarded the UNSW Scientia PhD Scholarship to pursue her art-based research in art, pedagogy, and visual culture. Approaching socially-engaged and performative art practices as a personal philosophical quest, Lap-Xuan interrogates how language, silence and the in-between of institutional representations of communication, have driven some of the ways we perceive limitations of 'Voice'. She considers artistic experience as alternative socially experimental spaces to juggle variables of the individual voice. Thus, her works are not aiming to establish dichotomies, rather open the dialogical spaces.

Andrea Doucet is a Canada Research Chair in Gender, Work, and Care, Professor in the Department of Sociology and Centre for Gender and Women's Studies at Brock University, and Adjunct Research Professor in Sociology at Carleton University and the University of Victoria. She has published widely on care/work practices and responsibilities, feminist and ecological onto-epistemologies, narrative analysis, research ethics, and genealogies of concepts. She is the author of two editions of *Do Men Mother?* (University of Toronto Press, 2006, 2018), which was awarded the John Porter Tradition of Excellence Book Award from the Canadian Sociology Association, co-author of two editions of *Gender Relations: Intersectionality and Social Change* (with Janet Siltanen, Oxford, 2008, 2017), and co-editor of *Thinking Ecologically, Thinking Responsibly: The Legacies of Lorraine Code* (with Nancy Arden McHugh, SUNY Press, 2021).

Sarah Flicker is a York Research Chair in Community-Based Participatory Research and Full Professor in the Faculty of Environmental and Urban Change at York University. She is engaged in an exciting program of research that focuses on the engagement of youth and other actors in environmental, sexual and reproductive justice. More broadly, she is interested in community-based participatory methodologies and is active on a variety of research teams that focus on adolescent sexual and reproductive health and responding to gender-based violence in Canada and South Africa. Recently, she has published in the areas of health promotion, sexuality, ethics, decolonizing methodologies, participatory visual methods and community-based participatory research methods. Her research has informed policy at the municipal, provincial and federal levels. Her research teams have won a number of prestigious awards for youth engagement in health research. She is also an inaugural member of the Royal Society of Canada's College of New Scholars, Artists and Scientists.

Yoriko Gillard is a PhD candidate at the University of British Columbia and teaches at Capilano University and Simon Fraser University. She is a Japanese immigrant respectfully residing on the land of Coast Salish people: səlilwətaʔɬ təməxʷ (Tsleil-Waututh), šxʷməθkʷəy̓əmaʔɬ təməxʷ (Musqueam), Stz'uminus (Tsa-Mee-Nis), Qayqayt (Ka-kite), S'ólh Téméxw (Stó:lō), and kʷikʷəƛ̓əm (kwikwetlem). Her educational philosophy stems from the words of Carl Leggo, "live creatively and poetically." Her research initiatives include, *KIZUNA, Liminal Storytelling*, and *HEARTH Project: hear/heart/art/earth* and chapters in various edited books include, *I Hair You: Creative Acts as a Way of Communication*; *Living Practices of 'ma'*; *KIZUNA: Life as Art*; *KIZUNA: Gather for Nepal*; *Caught in the Middle: My Liminal Space*; *Living with a Liminal Mind*. Her latest solo performance was at Nikkei National Museum & Culture Centre, Burnaby, BC, Canada, *KIZUNA: Past-Present-Future: A Tribute to Japanese Canadian Community*, presented as part of *Hastings Park 1942*.

Sadie K. Goddard-Durant is an Adjunct Professor and Post-Doctoral Fellow with Professor Andrea Doucet in the Department of Sociology at Brock University. She develops programs and policies grounded in research she does *with* Black women in Canada and the Caribbean about how they are navigating gendered and racialized daily structures and systems, and what support they need for their wellbeing. In her research-practice, Sadie utilizes qualitative research methodologies informed by Black feminist, trauma, and decolonial frameworks, and provides training for persons in these methodologies. Her current work is shaped by her decade long experience providing psychotherapy in domestic violence shelters, crisis centers and the criminal justice system in North America and the Caribbean to women and girls who are survivors of gender-based violence.

Jan Gube is an Assistant Professor at the Department of Curriculum and Instruction, The Education University of Hong Kong. He initially trained in language studies and has since dedicated his career to understanding the lives and supporting the education of individuals from diverse cultural backgrounds. His research is concerned with larger questions about diversity, equity, race and ethnicity with an emphasis on the nexus between schooling and cultural identities, including the implications of these for curriculum and practice. This research has appeared in journals such as Integrative Psychological Behavioral Science, Identities, Visual Studies, Culture & Psychology, and Knowledge Cultures. He also co-edited *Education, Ethnicity and Equity in the Multilingual Asian Context* (Springer) and *Identities, Practices and Education of Evolving Multicultural Families in Asia-Pacific* (Routledge).

Samira Jamouchi is an artist, Assistant Professor in visual art and researcher. She holds an MA from the Académie Royale des Beaux-Arts in Brussels (1997, Belgium) and from the Oslo National Academy of the Arts (2001, Norway). Her artistic research includes textile, sculpture, immersive installation, video and performative events. Her arts-based research connects intimately her practices as artist, teacher and researcher. As an a/r/tographer she merges visual, pedagogical and philosophical perspectives. Her work on performative approaches takes the form of artistic exhibitions, pedagogical working tools, and scientific papers. Her artistic work has been exhibited in four continents, she has held lectures and workshops in different European Universities, and her articles have been published in several international scientific journals. Jamouchi's doctoral work at the University of Agder (Norway) is a material-discursive inquiry on performative approaches to art(istic) education, focussing on the phenomenon of wool felting from post-qualitative theories.

Sabine LeBel is an Assistant Professor in the Department of Culture and Media Studies at the University of New Brunswick. She does research in the area of environmental media studies. She investigates the representation of trash in visual culture, affective responses to planned obsolescence, and media materiality. She also works in the area of mobile media art, especially cellphilms as queer and feminist art practice. Alongside her academic work, Dr. LeBel has an art practice, primarily in video, as both a curator and a filmmaker. Her pieces typically deal with queer themes and environmental issues, often through scifi aesthetics and experimental narratives.

Tobin LeBlanc Haley is an Assistant Professor at the University of New Brunswick. She is a white settler and Mad woman living in Fredericton, NB (thanks COVID) on the unceded territory of the Wolastoqey. She is a community-engaged researcher who focuses on the impact of social policy for people living at the intersection of socio-economic poverty and disability.

Allison Holloway is a PhD Student in the Department of Integrated Studies of Education at McGill University. She is interested in how girls and women use social media platforms to challenge gender-based violence and inform sexual consent education. She is also interested in young people's experiences giving rise to new policy and resources in sex education curriculum. Her research explores how youth voices can shift the discourse of consent from anti-harm to a collaboration between active individuals in secondary sex education. Recently, she has worked on a project exploring student and teacher experiences of teaching and learning about gender-based violence in the classroom.

Caterina Tess Kendrick (she/her) recently graduated from York University with her Masters of Environmental Studies. She is interested in the role of education and art in intercultural relationship building. Caterina has had the honour and privilege to support community-based research projects related to youth sexual health, harm reduction, and participatory visual methodologies. She is of Italian-English-Irish descent and has lived most of her life on the territories covered by the Dish with One Spoon Wampum. She grew up in a household that was the meeting place of different worlds— deaf/hearing, immigrant/settler, and ability/disability— these influences inspire her relationship explorations.

Bronwen Low is an Associate Professor in the Department of Integrated Studies in Education at McGill University. Her research includes the implications and challenges of popular youth culture for curriculum theory, literacy studies, and school transformation; community digital media pedagogies; translanguaging and the multilingual Montreal hip-hop scene; and life stories and equity education. She has been leading and participating in research, knowledge dissemination, and program and curriculum development projects with a primary focus on how to best support socially marginalized young people underserved by traditional schooling models and practices. Recent articles have appeared in the International Journal of Art and Design Education, Research Studies in Music Education, Visual Studies, Urban Education, and the Journal of Curriculum Studies. Her books include *Slam school: Learning through conflict in the hip-hop and spoken word classroom* (2011), and co-author of *Community-based Media Pedagogies: Relational Approaches to Listening in the Commons* (2016).

Katie MacEntee's research focuses on the use of participatory visual methodologies to address HIV and AIDS, gender-based violence, LGBTQ2S youth homeless and for the study of sexual and reproductive health. She is the postdoctoral fellow on the CIHR funded project *"Adapting and Scaling-up 'Peer Navigators" to Targeted Populations of Street-Involved Youth in Canada and Kenya to Increase Linkage to HIV Prevention, Testing and Treatment"*, which is studying the adaptation and scale up of peer outreach workers to support youth who are experiencing housing insecurity in Canada and Kenya to access HIV testing, prevention, and treatment. Katie is also a research associate in the Faculty of Health at York University where she is developing an interactive, open-access video resource to support instructors and students navigate disability accommodations in clinical placement and practicum programs.

April Mandrona developed and directs NSCAD University's new graduate program in Art Education. She received a doctorate in Art Education from Concordia University and was a SSHRC postdoctoral fellow at McGill University in the Department of Integrated Studies in Education. She has published articles and book chapters on young people's visual culture, rurality, ethics, and participatory visual research. Recent co-edited volumes include *Visual Encounters in the Study of Rural Childhoods* (Rutgers, 2018), *Our Rural Selves: Memory, Place, and the Visual in Canadian Rural Childhoods* (MQUP, 2019), and *Ethical Practice in Participatory Visual Research with Girls: Transnational Approaches* (Berghahn, 2021). Dr. Mandrona is the current editor-in-chief of the *Canadian Art Teacher* Journal. Her recent SSHRC-funded community art education research with historically excluded groups focuses on the social roles of artistic production and innovative approaches to understanding narrative, belonging, well-being, and participation.

Emma McKenna (she/her) is a SSHRC postdoctoral fellow at the University of Ottawa in the Department of Criminology, and an Honorary Killam postdoctoral fellow at the University of Alberta in the Department of English and Film Studies. Emma earned her PhD in English and Cultural Studies (2019) from McMaster University, and her MA and Honours BA in Women's and Gender Studies from the University of British Columbia and the University of Toronto, respectively. Emma's research interests include critical feminisms, intersectionality, second wave feminist history, feminist criminology, archival studies, sexuality studies, labour studies, disability studies, and life writing in memoir and poetry. She serves as an Editorial Board Member of *Atlantis: Critical Studies in Gender, Culture and Social Justice*.

Claudia Mitchell is a Distinguished James McGill Professor in the Department of Integrated Studies in Education, McGill University and the Director of the Institute for Human Development and Well-being. As the founder of the Participatory Cultures Lab, a Canadian Foundation for Innovation funded unit, she is particularly interested in research and training related to participatory visual methodologies. She is the Editor-in-Chief of the award winning journal *Girlhood Studies: An Interdisciplinary Journal*.

Milka Nyariro is a Postdoctoral Fellow at McGill University's Department of Medicine. She received her PhD from McGill University's Department of Integrated Studies in Education in 2021. Her concentration is Gender and Women's studies. Prior to enrolling for the doctorate program, Milka worked with African Population and Health Research Center (APHRC) as a Research Officer in the Education Research Program. Part of her responsibilities included coordinating data collection and participating in data analysis, report writing and dissemination of research findings.

Oyemolade (Molade) Osibodu (she/her) is an Assistant Professor in the Faculty of Education at York University. She completed her doctorate at Michigan State University. Broadly, her research lies at the intersection of mathematics and social justice. More specifically, Molade explores equitable approaches to ensure Black students feel seen and valued in their learning; interrogates how mathematics can be leveraged as a space to discuss local and global issues of (in)justice in the classroom; and, as Canada continues to be a hub for many African immigrants and refugees, she examines how they negotiate learning in mathematics spaces while also navigating racialization often for the first time. Her scholarly work has appeared in the *National Council of Teachers of Mathematics Annual Perspectives in Mathematics Education*; *For the Learning of Mathematics*; and the *Comparative Education Review*

Laura Pin (she/her) is an Assistant Professor at Wilfrid Laurier University, on the territory of the Neutral, Anishnaabe and Haudenosaunee peoples, on the treaty territory of the Haldimand Tract. She received a PhD in Political Science from

York University. Prior to joining Laurier, she was a postdoctoral scholar at the University of Guelph, with a joint appointment to the Political Science Department and Community-Engaged Scholarship Institute. Her scholarship and pedagogy is at the intersection of critical policy studies, participatory democracy, and local politics, and she co-leads the community-engaged Housing on the Rural-Urban-Fringe (RUF) project with Dr. Tobin Leblanc Haley.

Pride/Swell is a SSHRC Connections Grant-funded social distance art & activism project with 2SLGBTQ+ youth from across Atlantic Canada. For one year, 50 2SLGBTQ+ youth from across Atlantic Canada received a package in the mail that contained 1) art supplies; and 2) a prompt. Through art making and collaborative approaches to archiving (on social media and in physical spaces), Pride/Swell is a group of 2SLGBTQ+ youth who share experiences creating queer-focused community around art, identities, and space during COVID-19.

Paula M. Salvio is a Professor of Education and Affiliate Professor of Classics, Humanities and Italian Studies at the University of New Hampshire. Her scholarship is grounded in the cultural and historical foundations of education with a specialization in psychoanalysis and post-colonial theory. Her research focuses on the impact that marginalization, trauma and war have on women, children and youth in formal and informal educational settings. She is the author of *The Story-Takers: Public Pedagogy, Transitional Justice, and Italy's Non-Violence Protest Against the Mafia* (2017) and *Anne Sexton: Teacher of Weird Abundance* (2007); co-author of *Community-based Media Pedagogies: Relational Approaches to Listening in the Commons* (2016); and, co-editor of *Love's Return: Psychoanalytic Essays on Childhood, Teaching and Learning* (2006). Her scholarly essays have appeared in a range of academic journals including *Curriculum Inquiry, Italian Studies, Educational Theory, The Journal of the American Psychoanalytic Association*, and *Gastronomica: The Journal of Food and Culture*.

Joshua Schwab-Cartas is a Postdoctoral Fellow at the University of British Columbia. He completed his PhD at McGill University where he was an active member of Dr. Claudia Mitchell's Participatory Cultures Lab. Dr. Schwab-Cartas uses cellphilms (or mobile technologies + film production) as an educational tool to explore Indigenous language revitalization strategies in the Isthmus Zapotec community of his maternal grandfather in Ranchu Gubiña, Oaxaca, Mexico. For many years he has worked with a Zapotec media collective, to create a series of initiatives aimed specifically at youth to revitalize language and culture. Some of these strategies have included Zapotec classes, recording elders, producing CDs in the Zapotec language with bilingual inserts, playing games like bingo, producing documentary films, and establishing a community radio station which broadcasts in the Zapotec language. Dr. Schwab-Cartas is a leading participatory visual researcher, having co-edited the book, *What's a Cellphilm? Integrating mobile phone technology into participatory visual research and activism* in 2016 with Brill/Sense.

Yasmeen Shahzadeh recently completed a M.A. in Education and Society in the Department of Integrated Studies in Education at McGill University, with a concentration in Gender and Women's Studies. Her research analyzed gender within secondary school textbooks in Jordan. She was a Research Assistant supporting the Time to Teach about Gender-Based Violence in Canada research project, and a researcher with the Local Engagement Refugee Research Network (LERRN). She is currently based in Jordan working in consulting on gender, education, and employment. Yasmeen holds a B.A. in International Development Studies from McGill University.

Alison Shields is an Assistant Professor in Art Education at the University of Victoria. She received a PhD in Art Education from the University of British Columbia and an MFA from the University of Waterloo. She has exhibited her paintings across Canada and abroad, including a solo exhibition entitled Studio as Portal at McClure Art Centre in Montreal (2020) and inclusion in a collaborative and participatory event about Arts-based Research at the Tate Exchange Gallery in Liverpool (2018). Her art practice and research focus on painting, artistic inquiry, studio practices and artist residencies.

Jane-Ann Sieunarine is a mother and community researcher who has collaborated with Andrea Doucet and Sadie Goddard-Durant on several community based studies on Black motherhood in the context of Ontario, Canada.

Nicole M.Y. Tang is a native Hong Konger who is currently pursuing a postgraduate degree in Human Rights and International Politics at the University of Glasgow. She completed her studies in philosophy at the University of Warwick and was formerly a research assistant at the Department of Curriculum and Instruction at The Education University of Hong Kong. Her work focused on the promotion of cultural inclusion and diversity in education, with an emphasis on teacher education and community-engagement. Since her involvement in this project, she has acquired an expanded interest in research topics such as social equity, diversity, and cultural identity. She is particularly interested in exploring the Hong Konger identity in both local and global contexts.

Jennifer Thompson (she/her) is a Postdoctoral Research Fellow in the Center for Public Health Research (CReSP) at Université de Montreal and working with MYRIAGONE, the McConnell-University of Montreal Chair in Youth Knowledge Mobilization. Her research interests include participatory visual methodologies, youth knowledge mobilization, and the relationships between water and society. Prior to her current position, Jen held a SSHRC postdoctoral fellowship in the Department of Anthropology at Durham University in the UK. Jen has a background across engineering, education, and international development, and has conducted fieldwork (either in person or virtually) with universities and non-profit organizations in Cameroon, Ethiopia, Kenya, Mali, Mozambique, Myanmar, and

Sierra Leone. Her co-edited book with Casey Burkholder, *Fieldnotes in Qualitative Education and Social Science Research*, was published by Routledge in 2020.

Amelia Thorpe is a PhD Candidate and Vanier Scholar, studying Critical Studies in Education at the University of New Brunswick. She holds a MEd in Social Justice Education (OISE) and has extensive experience working with queer, trans*, and non-binary youth and seniors. Amelia sits on the Board of Directors of the Canadian Professional Association for Transgender Health (CPATH) and is very active in several national research and education committees with a focus on gender identity and sexual orientation. Her research interests include identity making; community advocacy and education; feminist narrative ethics; and story-telling within minoritized communities.

Patrick Tomczyk completed his PhD at the University of Alberta. While there, he held a Doctoral Fellowship from the Social Sciences and Humanities Research Council of Canada. His research focuses on the intersections of queer theory, pedagogy and arts-based research, as they relate to lived experiences of sexual and gender minority youth, with particular focus on queering hetero/cisnormativity in schools through ethnodramatic inqueery. He is passionate about creating social change that fosters equity, diversity and inclusion in order to create safer learning environments for all students. Dr. Tomczyk is an elementary school principal, as well as a certified counsellor with the Canadian Counselling and Psychotherapy Association.

Catherine Vanner is an Assistant Professor of Educational Foundations at the University of Windsor. She uses qualitative and participatory methods to analyze the relationship between gender, violence, and education in North American and Sub-Saharan African contexts. She has worked as a Postdoctoral Fellow at McGill University and as an Education Advisor and Consultant for Plan International Canada, UNESCO, and the Canadian International Development Agency. She completed a Ph.D. in Education at the University of Ottawa and a M.A. in International Affairs from Carleton University. She lives in Windsor, Ontario with her partner and two children.

Brody Weaver (she/they) is a white-settler, trans* queer emerging artist, researcher, and writer currently living and studying in Kjipuktuk (Halifax, Nova Scotia). Currently studying media art, critical studies, curatorial studies and art education at NSCAD University, they believe in art as an alternative means of pedagogy and public space as a site for education. Interested in queer memory-keeping activities, this broad term referring to a spectrum of activities from DIY community-based engagements that resist documentation to the 21st century's institutional Queer Museum, she seeks to leverage the pedagogical potential of art through participatory, community-based, and research-based processes that make critical use of archives, historiographies, and collective lived experience.

Helen Yeung (she/they) is a feminist researcher, community organizer, activist and zine-maker in Aotearoa (New Zealand). Her work as an activist first began through grassroots organizing in domestic and family violence prevention for migrant women and youth of colour. She is passionate about violence-prevention, and building spaces for marginalized communities through organizing, conducting educational workshops, and designing culturally specific facilitation frameworks. Helen is currently completing her PhD at Auckland University of Technology under the School of Communications Studies. With an academic background in Politics and International Relations, her research centres on migrational and diasporic experiences, feminism and gender, digital activism, DIY media production, multimodality and alternative participatory methods. She is also the founder of Migrant Zine Collective, a zine collective which aims to amplify the voices of migrant communities through activism, self-publishing and arts-based practices.

ACKNOWLEDGEMENTS

Casey, Funké, and Joshua would like to thank the book's reviewers and Routledge's editorial board for their careful and thoughtful feedback on our manuscript.

We would also like to thank the chapter contributors for their critical scholarship, for pushing our thinking forward, for generously responding to feedback, and for expanding and shaping the ways we now think about facilitating community-based, qualitative, and participatory visual research.

Casey would like to thank her supportive partner and kid for facilitating the editing of this collection, and for always making her laugh. Thank you also to her wonderful and critically supportive colleagues, friends, students, and mentors: Alice Chan, Alicia Noreiga, Amanda Wuerth, Amelia Thorpe, Angela Tozer, Angie Lee, April Mandrona, Auralia Brooke, Brody Weaver, Claudia Mitchell, Darrah Beaver, Erin Morton, Javier Davila, Jen Thompson, Katie Hamill, Katie MacEntee, Katie Thorsteinson, Louise Lockhart, Matt Rogers, Percy Sacobie, Roger Saul, Starlit Simon, and Wendy Narvey. Thank you to the Pride/Swell research participants for co-facilitating art, activism, and archives amidst COVID-19. A special thank you to Lauren Cruikshank and Sabine LeBel for *Feminist Write Club*.

Funké would like to thank all of her family members for their unconditional love and support while we laboured to complete this collection. She is most especially thankful for Javon Gillam, Lisa Best, Francesca D'Amico-Cuthbert, Jenneillia Julius, Thomas Hooper, Pamela Fuentes, Katie Bausch, Rhonda George, Carlie Manners and Erica Weste, whose generosity and kindness has provided the space to think through the importance of community-based facilitation and research. She is also grateful for the mentorship and support to her colleagues and friends Michele A. Johnson, Barrington Walker, Molly Ladd-Taylor, Kate McPherson, Anne Rubenstein, Melanie Newton, Nhung Tuyet Tran, Sean Mills, Erin Morton, Karen Flynn, Tamara Walker, and Stefanie Hunt-Kennedy.

Josh would like to thank his ever supportive partner Toni and always inspiring Jelibean for always ensuring he had a right balance between editing/writing this collection and family time. He would like to thank his fellow colleagues, Elders, participants, and collaborators for their amazing support and critical conversations that helped shape his thinking around facilitation in community, Modesta Vicente, Adela Carrasco, Ruth Carrasco, Jennifer Thompson, Matthew Donovan, Morgan Phillips, José Arenas Lopez, Geoff Horner, Katie MacEntee and Sujaya Neupane. He is also incredibly grateful for the mentorship and endless support of Claudia Mitchell, Mela Sarkar and Candace Kaleimamoowahinekapu Galla. He also wants to thank Candace for all the critical conversation that helped further his thinking about community based Indigenous language revitalization and facilitation. And of course he wants to give a special thanks to Binni Cubi for keeping him grounded in Binniza life ways.

Finally, Casey, Funké, and Joshua would also like to thank our colleagues, friends, and families who have been endlessly supportive through the writing and editing of this collection.

THINKING THROUGH RESEARCH FACILITATION

An Introduction

Casey Burkholder, Funké Aladejebi and Joshua Schwab-Cartas

What does research facilitation look like? What are the decisions that researchers make in research? What are the on-the-ground ethics that researchers engage in while facilitating research projects in community-based research? What sociocultural factors should be considered when thinking through ethical and culturally responsive facilitation?

This edited collection was inspired by conversations that we have had about failures and stresses in our own facilitation practices as scholars of community-based research studies. In 2019, Funké gave a public talk about her research engaging in oral history production with Black female teachers and principals in Ontario, Canada. During this talk, she described her experiences driving to participants' homes, many of whom lived in rural communities, and feeling unsafe driving in these rural spaces as a Black woman who is not known in these communities. Funké considered her own positionality, alongside broader experiences of racialization and anti-Black racism in Canada; factors that stood outside of the institutional parameters and expectations of conducting ethical research. Ultimately, Funké's discussion considered the dangers of research facilitation as a Black woman within these spaces. After the talk, Casey—a white woman—expanded these discussions to consider what happens when we facilitate research that seeks to disrupt white supremacy, patriarchy, and centres participants' ways of knowing and how this work is taken on by research facilitators. What does facilitation really look like in action, she wondered? What about other researchers who have experienced challenges in facilitation, including travelling to participants, or within specific institutional spaces? Within her own work, especially through facilitating participatory visual research with 2SLGBTQ+ youth and pre-service teachers, Casey often has to facilitate in academic and institutional spaces that are not gender affirming. Her work often considers the ways in which research for social change and research facilitation also occur within

DOI: 10.4324/9781003199236-1

oppressive spaces (see also Burkholder & Thorpe, 2021). In thinking through these ideas, Casey also began to talk to her friend and colleague Josh—a mixed race Indigenous Binnizá-Austrian scholar activist—about what facilitation looks like in his research creating cellphilms to explore Indigenous practice (Cajete, 1993; Urrieta Jr., 2015) and land-based education (Simpson, 2016) as means of fostering intergenerational knowledge transmission and language reclamation. Together, we sought not only to confront but engage with the commonalities and tensions between our facilitation processes, while also wanting to learn what others were encountering in their research.

This introductory chapter establishes facilitation as an important yet underreported component of qualitative, community, arts-based, and visual research traditions. Through a review of the qualitative and community-based methodological literature on research facilitation and an examination of the role of the researcher within scholarship, we highlight and interrogate philosophical, historical, and political assumptions in the existing literature. Although institutional and regulatory ethics have been ingrained in university research settings, scholars such as Eve Tuck and K. Wayne Yang (2014) have asked us to consider the ways in which participants' and communities' refusal of research influence our ethical frameworks. Tuck and Yang contend,

> The regulatory ethical frames that now dominate the conversation about ethics in academe are only a recent provision, and they cannot do enough to ensure that social science research is deeply ethical, meaningful, or useful for the individual or community being researched.
> *(Guishard & Tuck, 2013) (p. 812)*

We take up Tuck and Yang's call to ask: What does ethical research facilitation look like beyond institutional guidelines? What might deep, ethical, meaningful, or useful facilitation look like in qualitative, participatory visual, and community-based research? Putting social justice and community concerns about power within research processes at the fore, the volume argues that thinking through research facilitation must go beyond researcher reflexivity and move towards action within the research settings in which we work.

What Is Facilitation?

Although facilitating ethical research has long been identified within medical research literatures (Reid, Brown, Smith, Cope, & Jamieson, 2018), there is a dearth of academic theorizing on facilitating ethical research in the social sciences (exceptions include Brown & Danaher, 2019; Graham, Powell, & Truscott, 2016; Groundwater-Smith et al., 2012; Milne, 2012; Nic Gabhainn & Sixsmith, 2006; Powell, Graham, & Truscott, 2016; Switzer, 2020; Tuck, 2009; Tuck & Yang, 2014). Theorizing the decisions made by the research facilitator within qualitative, arts-based, and participatory visual research has also been underreported.

Although researcher reflexivity has been well documented (Raheim et al., 2016), as well as the need for researchers to "suspend damage" (Tuck, 2009) to participants and communities, this collection speaks to the gaps in qualitative and participatory visual research literature on ethical research facilitation and explores the complex and incremental decisions made by researchers in response to unexpected moments during fieldwork and research. What does community-specific facilitation look like? What strategies might researchers engage in with communities in order to "do most good"? Or do the limitations of academic research always mitigate the potential to "do good"? The book seeks to respond to these questions by highlighting five central themes: 1) unrepresented perspectives on processes of facilitating research for social change within an emancipatory social justice framework; 2) negotiating unforeseen complications in facilitating research; 3) ethical practices in research facilitation; and calls specific attention to 4) facilitating research in the digital realm; and 5) facilitating arts-based and visual research. Taken together, the chapters in this collection theorize research facilitation within community-based approaches, participatory visual approaches, as well as specific methodologies including oral histories, cellphilm method, photovoice, and digital ethnography.

Why Talk about Facilitation Now?

Research facilitation is a central component of qualitative, ethnographic, participatory, and visual research, widely discussed but undertheorized in research methods courses. The collection draws on research case studies across numerous international contexts and considers interdisciplinary research methodologies. In particular, the collection includes an engaged focus on facilitating art-based and visual research, including within the digital realm, original contributions. Given increasing globalization and the desire for communities to tell their own stories, contributions in this collection consider the Canadian context, but position international experiences as one way to disrupt Western notions of knowledge production. Careful not to reproduce the "uneven global power relations and resource flows," we situate this analysis as a way to think critically and honestly about the politicized nature of research facilitation (Stein, 2017, p. 4). As a result, contributors attend critically to the structural relations of working across contexts in relation to researching within communities, including working with Black, Indigenous, people of colour, and 2SLGBTQ+ communities. Our hope is that this research will create new avenues for considering research facilitation and its impact on minority communities.

Facilitating during the COVID-19 Pandemic?

Perhaps most pointed in our global reflection of research facilitation is to consider the specific opportunities and challenges of this particular time and space, late 2021. During the COVID-19 pandemic, our research practices shifted drastically, as did the role of digital technology in this process, along with the rest of our lives. We also think there is something productive in thinking through how research for social change has been facilitated throughout the pandemic. We have been inspired by Sarah Switzer's postdoctoral project on facilitating community-engaged and participatory visual research amidst the COVID-19 pandemic. Switzer suggests that during the pandemic:

> As practitioners, we were encountering unique ethical and pedagogical challenges in adapting our work online, or to remote settings. There were also limited resources to guide this process. Resources for online learning in secondary or post-secondary institutions are guided by different goals, aims and institutional contexts. Similarly, research ethics boards are not attuned to the unique issues of participatory research, where there is a strong emphasis on the process of doing work together, in a good way.
>
> *(2021, para. 2)*

We bring this collection together in an effort to understand how community-based researchers have facilitated research for social change in the time before and the time during the COVID-19 pandemic. Paying particular attention to ongoing debates about the methods and goals of research facilitation, we consider the ways in which this work responds to current contexts, social location, and institutional affiliations. We organize the book into four sections, 1) Troubling Equity within Research Facilitation; 2) Facilitating in the Digital Realm; 3) Ethics and Facilitation in Research Processes; and 4) Art and Ethical Research Practices in Research Facilitation.

Organization of the Book

Part I: Troubling Equity within Research Facilitation

Scholars facilitating research with marginalized communities or facilitating across varying identities that include differences in relation to race, age, ability, class, sexuality, employment, and gender offers an important space for inquiry. What can we learn about facilitating research if we interrogate the concept and assumption of equity, or if we disrupt the notion that facilitation is a neutral and objective practice, or if we trouble the understanding of ethics as a universally shared concept/set of principles? The authors in this section take up a variety of facilitation practices, face different challenges, and offer several important suggestions about what has worked and what has failed in their facilitation contexts.

The book opens with a chapter from Sadie Goddard-Durant, Andrea Doucet, and Jane-Ann Sieunarine, "'If You're Going to Work with Black People, You Have to Think about These Things!' A Case Study of Fostering an Ethical Research Process with a Black Canadian Community." In this chapter, the authors discuss considerations and strategies which researchers can use towards facilitating ethical research processes with Black communities in urban areas in Canada. The authors draw on their experience as researchers conducting an investigation on young mothers who access two non-profit organizations in two urban settings in Canada. The authors discuss how, together, they thought through the implications of the Black mothers' daily lived experiences before implementing ethical practices in their research. The chapter discusses the authors' ethico-onto-epistemic responsibilities (Doucet, 2018) while navigating the challenges of working within the structural, temporal, and relational injustices which became a part of the research process. In so doing, this research contributes to efforts to honour and protect the full humanity of Black communities in the facilitation of research processes. The chapter also considers the intersections of race, gender, motherhood, and access to resources to understand the complexity of Black experiences in Canada, and how these intersections influence research facilitation.

The second chapter in the book, Emma McKenna and Ryan Conrad's "Lessons Learned, Lessons Shared: Reflections on Doing Research in Collaboration with Sex Workers and Sex Worker-led Organizations," takes up concerns with how to ethically approach research within marginalized communities. As activist academics, the authors seek to provide a "best practices guide" for researchers, students, and community workers doing collaborative research with sex worker-led organizations and individuals who do sex work. The chapter contributes to recent conversations in the social sciences and humanities examining: the criminalization of sex work, the impact of criminalization on sex workers and their clients, the stigmatization of sex workers, the inaccuracy of human trafficking frameworks on sex workers' lived realities, and sex worker-led community activism. Through this work, the authors highlight the first of its kind, longitudinal study in Canada that examines sex worker mutual aid strategies during crisis.

In Chapter Three, "Researcher Don't Teach Me Nonsense," Oyemolade Osibodu considers Fela Kuti's 1986 song titled, *Teacher Don't Teach Me Nonsense*, as a call for accountability and an examination of the responsibility the research has in ensuring that they did not *teach* or *do* nonsense. In this chapter, the author, a critical math educator, discusses the ways they attempt to disrupt the researcher-researched binary in their collaboration with five Sub-Saharan African youth. Employing decolonial frameworks and methodologies often not engaged with in critical mathematics education, Osibodu seeks to disrupt the impact of coloniality within the spheres of power, knowledge, and being. Throughout the research, Osibodu continuously reminded collaborators that they were not bound by the consent forms that they signed in order to shift the project's research design to reflect participants' desires. Ultimately, Osibodu argues that although scary and uncomfortable, co-managing the research design with participants can create spaces of deep, ethical, and meaningful facilitation in research spaces.

The fourth chapter in the section comes from Tenzin Butsang and is titled, "Decolonizing from the Roots. A Community-Led Approach to Qualitative Health Research." Situated in Tkaronto [Toronto], Ontario on the traditional lands of the Huron, Wendat, Anishinaabe, Haudenosaunee, and the Mississaugas of the Credit, this chapter describes a community-led project to facilitate family reunification and supports for urban Indigenous parents, particularly woman-identifying and Two-Spirit individuals, who have been in contact with the law. The chapter details the development process of a project both created by and accountable to, community members from inception to analysis. Using this project as an example and guided by Two-Eyed Seeing, a framework which brings together Western and Indigenous approaches (Bartlett et al., 2012), the author reflects on the meaning of decolonizing research within the confines of several interacting colonial systems. Butsang discusses the concept of knowledge co-creation in the context of Indigenous health research and argues its necessity for any sustainable move towards decolonial praxis. The chapter explores the use of oral storytelling as a decolonizing method, its relation to the emergence of podcasting in Indigenous health research, and the implications of podcasting as a collaborative research method for social change, particularly in the realm of criminal justice.

In Chapter Five, we offer Katie MacEntee, Jennifer Thompson, Milka Nyariro, and Claudia Mitchell's collaborative piece, "A Reflexive Account of Performing Facilitation in Participatory Visual Research for Social Change," which reflects on autoethnographic performances of facilitation at an international academic conference. Drawing on the collective memory-work of Frigga Haug (1987), they collectively explore how integrating cellphones and cameras in a researcher-facilitated manner impact both the form and outcomes of the intervention as a means of knowledge production and social action. By performing autoethnography at a conference, they engaged in the act of inquiry in situ. They describe how they have situated their inquiry in Burawoy's (2003) reflexive revisiting by re-examining four individual performances, and reflecting on moments of discomfort as well as moments of opportunities in seeking the transformative, decolonizing potential of this work.

Part II: Facilitating in the Digital Realm

Part Two of the book seeks to understand and unsettle strategies that researchers engage with while working in the digital realm. From embodied and online contexts stretching from New Zealand to Atlantic Canada, the authors share explorations into the affordances and tensions that exist when facilitating research in the digital realm. In the context of the COVID-19 pandemic, we note the importance of technology in facilitation strategies and the increased role that the postal service has played during the pandemic.

In Chapter Six, "'Nah You're My Sisters for Real!': Utilizing Instagram and Mobile Phones to Facilitate Feminist Conversations with Asian Migrant Women in Aotearoa," Helen Yeung explores the potential of creating feminist conversations with Asian women in the diaspora through their mobile devices in everyday spaces. Yeung's study was carried out using a set of interactive prompts on Instagram, which aims to encourage participants to engage in acts of storytelling, self-learning, and consciousness-raising in discussions on intersectionality and resisting patriarchal gender norms. Yeung argues that this practice is significant for Asian women in the diaspora who are "twice marginalized" in their existence through race and gender, reflecting larger structures of "transnational inequality, racial hierarchy, marginalization and exclusion" (Kim, 2011, pp. 88–89). Yeung draws attention to the existing knowledge gap featuring the unheard and invisible stories, voices, and experiences of Asian women which are often neglected in white-dominated, mainstream perspectives. Yeung also explores her positionality and explains the ways she sought to build meaningful relationships with participants through shared experiences of "institutionalized racism, of being othered and positioned as an outsider within white hegemonic spaces" (Voloder, 2013, p.13).

In chapter Seven, Chloe Brushwood Rose, Bronwen Low, and Paula Salvio's "Facilitation as Listening in Three Community-based Media Projects" takes up the notion of listening within community-based research. Central to the mandates of many community-based media projects is to give socially marginalized people the opportunity to tell their own stories and to find their own voices. However, a focus on voice can oversimplify processes of representation and action, and can neglect the vital role played by listening in pedagogies designed to sustain individual and community expression. This chapter draws upon data from a comparative study of three community-based media pedagogy and production projects based in New York, Toronto, and Montreal, in which listening was central to their storytelling—the listening of project facilitators to participants, of participants to each other, and of the participants to themselves as they mine and shape memory, experience, and observation into multimedia narrative. The authors work with data across the three sites to explore the particular strategies of listening adopted by the various project facilitators, drawing upon a cross-disciplinary theory of listening as an intersubjective process with social, ethical, and affective dimensions. These strategies include listening informed by curiosity rather than expertise, aesthetic listening, and listening that can tolerate discomfort and ambiguity

In Chapter Eight, "Theorizing Non-Participation in a Mail-based Participatory Visual Research Project with 2SLGBTQ+ Youth in Atlantic Canada," Brody Weaver, Amelia Thorpe, April Mandrona, Katie MacEntee, Casey Burkholder, and the Pride/Swell research group describe non-participation in a digital project facilitated during the COVID-19 pandemic. In this piece, the authors write together as members of Pride/Swell, a distance, mail-based art and activism project with 2SLGBTQ+ youth in Atlantic Canada. The project was launched in July 2020 and continued until July 2021. For one year, 50 2SLGBTQ+ youth from across Atlantic Canada received a package in the mail each month that contained 1) art supplies; and 2) a prompt. Through art-making and collaborative approaches to archiving (on social media and later in physical spaces, see Burkholder et al., 2021), the authors seek to share their experiences creating queer-focused community around art, identities, and space during the COVID-19 pandemic. In this chapter, Weaver and their colleagues specifically focus on what non-participation has looked like in this year-long art and activism project.

Part III: Ethics and Facilitation in Research Processes

In part three of the book, authors take up issues of power, privilege, and ethical responsibilities within research. From an exploration of the roles of research assistants in research facilitation to the practice of providing incentives and honoraria for research and troubling community facilitation, the contributions in this section explore the murkiness of facilitation in relation to participants and Principal Investigators (PIs).

In Chapter Nine, Nicole Tang and Jan Gube's, "Research Assistants as Knowledge Co-producers: Reflections Beyond Fieldwork" highlights key issues of power in research relationships. The contributions of research assistants are often overlooked in the production of research knowledge, yet they play an important role in supporting research projects to completion. This chapter examines the roles of research assistants—despite their "opaque presences" in academic literature (Middleton & Cons, 2014), and "powerless" status (MacFarlane, 2017)—as co-producers of knowledge alongside faculty members. This chapter asks: What is the role of a research assistant in facilitating a community-engaged research project through shared power relations, personal values, and commitments? The authors illustrate the unique positionality of research assistants against the backdrop of a community-engaged project that seeks to improve awareness of teachers on cultural diversity in Hong Kong schools. For the authors, this positionality is marked by its blurred insider-outsider statuses, both as members are employed by an academic institution, while not fully regarded as academic experts. The authors explore how this positionality, through racially grounded experiences, influences the practice and involvement of research assistants, while working alongside faculty members who are members of minoritized communities.

In Chapter Ten, "Injustice in Incentives? Facilitating Equitable Research with People Living with Poverty" Tobin LeBlanc Haley and Laura Pin trouble the academic practice of providing honoraria for research participants who contribute to projects. Providing honoraria to research participants is a well-established practice in academic research. Honoraria serve as a thank you, as a small recognition of the labour of participants (without whom much research would be impossible), and as an incentive to research participation. Yet, for scholars in Canada who do research with people living in poverty, the provisioning of honoraria is a complex and sometimes contested process due to the guidelines around incentives in the Tri-Council Policy Statement (TCPS 2) and university practices related to the administration of research funds. In this chapter, the authors consider the impact of the dual pressures of the TCPS 2 language around incentives and the practices of university financial services on the research process and research relationships through an autoethnographic exploration of the authors' experiences as community-based academic researchers in Ontario, Canada. LeBlanc Haley and Pin contend that there is an opportunity to address these issues as universities and funding agencies work to foreground equity, diversity, and inclusion in their strategic plans. They conclude this chapter with recommendations for change and areas for further exploration.

Amelia Thorpe's contribution in Chapter Eleven, "Queering Pride Facilitation: An Autoethnography of Community Organizing," considers the ways in which a researcher's insider-outsider status provides the potential to both disrupt and reinscribe homonormative and homonationalist discourses. Thorpe's chapter examines how ethics, queer politics, and identity intersect when facilitating research for social change with/in community, raising questions of power, subjectivity, intent, and intervention. Thorpe queries: What strategies might the researcher employ to disrupt discourses of respectability or address injurious statements made in facilitation spaces? How does the ethical facilitator respond to the reaffirmation of homonormative and homonationalist ideologies? In recognizing that community facilitation must acknowledge a multiplicity of intersecting experiences, identities, and politics, how might the researcher theorize social change from various social locations? Thorpe highlights her experiences at the crossroads of leading and listening to community with/in Pride as a politically invested activist and an ethical researcher and considers what it means to queer the act of facilitating research for social change.

Part IV: Art and Ethical Practices in Research Facilitation

The final section of the book explores the specific challenges and opportunities to facilitating arts-informed and participatory visual research. Offering specific strategies and highlighting work in embodied and online contexts before and during the COVID-19 pandemic, these chapters describe the ways in which facilitation strategies in arts-based research are contextual, relational, and require sustained attention.

We open this final section of the book with Sabine Lebel's "Facilitating Queer Art in the Climate Crisis." Lebel describes facilitation strategies that she implemented during a "Queer Environmental Futures" art residency. Lebel contends that facilitation during the residency required flexibility and creativity as facilitators and participants navigated a range of factors including studio schedules, shared languages, communal spaces, meals, and weather. Two critical factors that emerged from this experience were space and process. "Queer Environmental Futures," like most rural residencies, brought participants together in shared working and living spaces, with limited access to the outside world. In art and activism, a focus on process can centre ethical ways of relating; a good process considers feelings, power dynamics, and resources. Lebel makes a case for understanding process and the ways in which queer methods "mak[e] space for what is," a notion particularly apt for thinking through an ethics of queer facilitation (Love et al. quoted in Ghaziani & Brim, 2019, p. 18). Facilitation always involves meeting participants where they are at physically, politically, emotionally, and spiritually. With an art practice, it might also include funding, technical skills, and the point the artist is at in the process of creating a work. She asks: how can ethical facilitation grapple with process and space? What might queer art facilitation look like?

In Chapter Thirteen, "Ethnodramatic Inqueery" Patrick Tomczyk highlights his facilitation of a queer ethnodrama—a community-based approach grounded in arts-based research, queer theory as an augmentation of critical pedagogy, and ethnography and theatre—about the lived experience of 2SLGBTQ+ youth in Alberta high schools. Facilitating this study necessitated navigating heteronormativity and cisnormativity within school spaces. Tomczyk argues that facilitating through ethnodramatic inqueery can be a form of intervention as it demonstrates young people's agency and provides spaces for audience engagement with issues that matter most to queer, trans★, and non-binary youth.

Chapter Fourteen, "Round and Round the Carousel Papers: Facilitating a Visual Interactive Dialogue with Young People" is a collaboration between Catherine Vanner, Yasmeen Shahzadeh, Allison Holloway, Claudia Mitchell, and Jennifer Altenberg. Carousel paper activities involve the rotation of small groups around multiple flip chart papers upon which participants respond to a prompt or question about a social issue. From June 2019 to March 2020, the authors used carousel papers as a participatory visual method of consultation in three workshops where they consulted Canadian adolescents about their experiences learning about gender-based violence (GBV) and their recommendations for how to improve education about GBV. A protocol emerged from an initial workshop with Indigenous girls, in which the authors drew on Indigenous epistemologies and methodologies (Battiste, 2014; Kovach, 2009). The carousel activity supported participants to express themselves flexibly, recognizing many are reluctant to speak in groups (Bay-Cheng et al., 2011). This participatory analysis process enabled the team to deepen and verify their analysis of what was written with the participants. The approach enabled young people who had opted out of audio-recorded focus groups to participate, showing unexpected youth-friendly forms of interactions, including expressions of solidarity through slang and drawings. The chapter raises questions about the ways in which these simultaneously public and private visual carousel papers can facilitate participatory dialogue amongst youth.

In Chapter Fifteen, "Screening Stories: Methodological Considerations for Facilitating Critical Audience Engagement, Tess Kendrick, Katie MacEntee, and Sarah Flicker argue that the products of participatory visual methods projects yield creative materials that have educative potential to catalyze social change. Nevertheless, the impact(s) of mobilizing these products and engaging diverse audiences are understudied. In their collaborative piece, they describe opportunities and challenges that arise when screening cellphilms produced by people who trade sex amongst three difference audiences: at a parent meeting, at a sex shop, and at a youth group. The authors of this chapter consider the dilemmas, tensions, and ethical considerations that were raised during the process of audience engagement in order to feature practical approaches for other participatory visual researchers to consider.

In Chapter Sixteen, Genevieve Cloutier, Alison Shields, Lap-Xuan Nguyen Do, Samira Jamouchi, and Yoriko Gillard offer a reflection on assemblage and performance in their collaborative piece, "'Becoming I/We Together' as Critical Performative Pedagogy: Facilitating Intra-Actions and Metissage from Inhabiting/Living Practice." The performance, as an event, generates an "assemblage" (Deleuze & Guattari, 1980) created by their intra-action act as co-making or an intra-action. As Barad (2014) describes it, the concept of intra-action tells of an event, or a phenomenon, as a relationship that emerges. Together, they reflect on the ways that the performance was facilitated by each entity present in the room: all the participants' bodies and actions, the water, the wool fibres, the pine tree soap, the duration, the gestures, the flux of the movements, the space, the voices, the rhythms, and the echoes. Therefore, the authors consider assemblage as a means to frame the heterogeneity of elements involved in lived and living context that is facilitation and performance art.

In the final chapter, "What We Think We Know For Sure: Concluding Thoughts on Facilitation," Casey Burkholder, Funké Aladejebi, and Josh Schwab-Cartas summarize the contributions of the book, provide major methodological takeaways, and explore the possibilities of future work. In addition, we highlight several lessons for application, taken from the chapter contributions. By featuring key past, present and future issues, and challenges, we hope to help the reader/researcher situate the exemplars in the existing literature, justify their choices, and also consider how one contributes to the larger field of research facilitation.

Why Facilitation Matters

We think that making facilitation a specific area of methodological inquiry is important in research, especially research that is grounded in community and ethical praxis. By foregrounding the incremental decisions that researchers make, and explicitly focusing on tensions that arise in engaging in community research that intersects with institutions like schools, universities, non-profits, and art organizations, we seek to make visible the processes that are anecdotally whispered about, and rarely make their way into academic writing. We seek to highlight failures, discomforts, and modes of repair in research facilitation practices. Rather than suggesting best practices for facilitators, we argue that all facilitation is necessarily grounded in relationships, in structures, and influenced by power relations. We offer this collection to further a conversation about ethical research facilitation, including when facilitation fails. As axiomatic as it may sound, it is worth reiterating that not all research or community projects end in total success, failure of varying degrees is something every researcher or community activist working in a community encounter at some point, but it is often glossed over or simply not mentioned. By including open and candid discussions of missteps, unforeseen circumstances, and failures—this volume seeks to reframe traditional

Western responses to failure as something to be avoided at all cost, not talked about, and even disregarded. Instead, we argue that failure is something that due to a variety of reasons cannot be avoided, but when it arises or if it arises, don't disregard it as such, rather embrace the valuable lessons learned through these setbacks or failures, so as to be able to navigate failures in future projects more skillfully and ethically. We do this work to strengthen understandings about research processes, especially those that seek to make change in communities and society.

References

Bartlett, C., Marshall, M., & Marshall, A. (2012). Two-eyed seeing and other lessons learned within a co-learning journey of bringing together indigenous and mainstream knowledges and ways of knowing. *Journal of Environmental Studies and Sciences, 2*(4), 331–340.

Barad, K. (2014). Diffracting diffraction: Cutting together-apart. *Parallax, 20*(3), 168–187.

Battiste, M. (2014). Decolonizing education: Nourishing the learning spirit. *Alberta Journal of Educational Research, 60*(3), 615–618.

Bay-Cheng, L.Y., Livingston, J.A., & Fava, N.M. (2011). Adolescent girls' assessment and management of sexual risks: Insights from focus group research. *Youth & Society, 43*(3), 1167–1193.

Brown, A., & Danaher, P.A. (2019). CHE principles: Facilitating authentic and dialogical semi-structured interviews in educational research. *International Journal of Research & Method in Education, 42*(1), 76–90.

Burawoy, M. (2003). Revisits: An outline of a theory of reflexive ethnography. *American Sociological Review, 68*(5), 645–679. https://doi.org/10.2307/1519757

Burkholder, C., MacEntee, K., Mandrona, A., & Thorpe, A. (2021). Coproducing digital archives with 2SLGBTQ+ Atlantic Canadian youth amidst the COVID-19 pandemic. *Qualitative Research Journal.* ahead-of-print. https://doi.org/10.1108/QRJ-01-2021-0003

Burkholder, C., & Thorpe, A. (2021). Facilitating gender-affirming participatory visual research in embodied and online spaces. *Visual Studies.* https://www.tandfonline.com/doi/abs/10.1080/1472586X.2021.1982650

Cajete, G. (1993). An enchanted land: Spiritual ecology and a theology of place. *Winds of Change, 8*(2), 50–53.

Deleuze, G., & Guattari, F. (1980). *Capitalisme et schizophrénie. Paris: Les.*

Doucet, A. (2018). Revisiting and remaking the listening guide: An ecological and ontological narrativity approach to analyzing fathering narratives. In A.M. Humble & E. Radina (Eds.), *How qualitative data analysis happens* (pp. 80–96). Routledge.

Ghaziani, A., & Brim, M. (Eds.). (2019). *Imagining queer methods.* NYU Press.

Graham, A., Powell, M.A., & Truscott, J. (2016). Exploring the nexus between participatory methods and ethics in early childhood research. *Australasian Journal of Early Childhood, 41*(1), 82–89.

Groundwater-Smith, S., Mitchell, J., Mockler, N., Ponte, P., & Ronnerman, K. (2012). *Facilitating practitioner research: Developing transformational partnerships.* Routledge.

Guishard, M., & Tuck, E. (2013). Youth resistance research methods and ethical challenges. In E. Tuck & K.Y. Yang (Eds.), *Youth resistance research and theories of change* (pp. 193–206). Routledge.

Haug, F. (1987). *Female sexualization: A collective work of memory.* (Trans. by Erica Carter), Verse.

Kim, D. (2011). Catalysers in the promotion of migrants' rights: Church-based NGOs in South Korea. *Journal of Ethnic and Migration Studies, 37*(10), 1649–1667.

Kovach, M. (2009). Emerging from the margins: Indigenous methodologies. *Research as resistance: Revisiting critical, Indigenous, and anti-oppressive approaches.*

Macfarlane, B. (2017). The ethics of multiple authorship: Power, performativity and the gift economy. *Studies in Higher Education, 42*(7), 1194–1210.

Middleton, T., & Cons, J. (2014). Coming to terms: Reinserting research assistants into ethnography's past and present. *Ethnography, 15*(3), 279–290.

Milne, E. (2012). Saying 'NO!' to participatory video: Unravelling the complexities of (non)participation. In E. Milne, C. Mitchell, & N. deLange (Eds.), *The handbook of participatory video.* AltaMira Press. https://rowman.com/ISBN/9780759121133

Nic Gabhainn, S., & Sixsmith, J. (2006). Children photographing well-being: Facilitating participation in research. *Children & Society, 20*(4), 249–259.

Powell, M.A., Graham, A., Truscott, J., & Vicars, M. (2016). Ethical research involving children: Facilitating reflexive engagement. *Qualitative Research Journal, 16*(2). https://doi.org/10.1108/QRJ-07-2015-0056

Raheim, M., Magnussen, L.H., Sekse, R.J.T., Lunde, Å., Jacobsen, T., & Blystad, A. (2016). Researcher–researched relationship in qualitative research: Shifts in positions and researcher vulnerability. *International Journal of Qualitative Studies on Health and Well-Being, 11*(1), 30996.

Reid, A.M., Brown, J.M., Smith, J.M., Cope, A.C., & Jamieson, S. (2018). Ethical dilemmas and reflexivity in qualitative research. *Perspectives on Medical Education, 7*(2), 69–75.

Simpson, L.B. (2016). Indigenous resurgence and co-resistance. *Critical Ethnic Studies, 2*(2), 19–34.

Stein, S. (2017). Internationalization for an Uncertain Future: Tensions, Paradoxes, and Possibilities. *The Review of Higher Education, 41*(1), 3–32.

Switzer, S. (2020). "People give and take a lot in order to participate in things:" Youth talk back–making a case for non-participation. *Curriculum Inquiry, 50*(2), 168–193.

Switzer, S. (2021). Community engagement in COVID-19: Exploring online and remote pedagogies amongst practitioners: About. *Beyond the Toolkit* [Website]. https://www.beyondthetoolkit.com/about

Tuck, E. (2009). Re-visioning action: Participatory action research and Indigenous theories of change. *The Urban Review, 41*(1), 47–65.

Tuck, E., & Yang, K.W. (2014). Unbecoming claims: Pedagogies of refusal in qualitative research. *Qualitative Inquiry, 20*(6), 811–818.

Urrieta Jr, L. (2015). Learning by observing and pitching in and the connections to native and Indigenous knowledge systems. In M. Correa-Chávez, R. Mejía-Arauz & B. Rogoff (Eds.), *Advances in child development and behavior* (Vol. 49, pp. 357–379). JAI.

Voloder, L. (2013). Secular citizenship and Muslim belonging in Turkey: Migrant perspectives. *Ethnic and Racial Studies, 36*(5), 838–856.

PART I
Troubling Equity within Research Facilitation

1

"IF YOU'RE GOING TO WORK WITH BLACK PEOPLE, YOU HAVE TO THINK ABOUT THESE THINGS!"

A Case Study of Fostering an Ethical Research Process with a Black Canadian Community

Sadie K. Goddard-Durant, Andrea Doucet and Jane-Ann Sieunarine

Introduction

Although there has been some reflection on facilitating socially just research with people of African descent in African countries, the Caribbean, and the United States, only a few scholars have addressed these issues in research with Black Canadians (see Aladejebi, 2016; Lawson, 2002). Building on these works, our chapter reflects on our efforts to facilitate an ethical research process with young Black Caribbean Canadian mothers.[1] We approached these mothers within the context of their geopolitical positioning as members of the Global South,[2] and their daily lived experiences within a society built on racial disadvantage (Aylward, 1999; UNHRC, 2017). We wanted to break away from damage-centred research in North America (Tuck, 2009) by ensuring that our research process did not reproduce, extend, or legitimize anti-Black racism and colonizing practices in our Black Canadian participants' lives or in the research community. We follow the insights of Indigenous, decolonial, anti-racist, and feminist researchers (see Bowers et al., 2016; Code, 2006; Jackson, 2002; Semali et al., 2007; Tuck & Guishard, 2013; Tuck & Yang, 2014), who move away from a narrow conceptualization of ethics as something that is concerned with procedures aimed at protecting individual rights and autonomy, towards a wider framing of relational and reflexive ethics, where partnership, commitment, accountability, epistemic responsibilities, and social justice are emphasized. In this chapter, we reflect on how our anti-racist interpretation of the three core ethical principles outlined in the Tri-Council Policy Statement (TCPS)[3] that guides research with human subjects in Canada (respect for persons, concern for welfare, and justice) translated into research and relationship-building practices for working with a group of young Black Caribbean Canadian mothers.

Background

Scholars have repeatedly raised concerns about the treatment of Black persons in research, ranging from how their daily lives and stories might be misunderstood by researchers, both in the research process and in the scholarly narratives produced about them, to when they *are* included in research (see Corbie-Smith et al., 2004; Hill Collins, 2009; Washington, 2007). Many of the decisions about how to *do* the research, from conceptualization to dissemination, have reinforced anti-Black racist ideologies, scientific racism, Eurocentric concepts and epistemologies, and imbalances in power relationships in scientific inquiry. Such choices about the ontological, axiological, epistemological, and methodological assumptions guiding research projects have both theoretical and empirical implications for academic research with Black persons, and harmful real-world consequences. We begin the chapter with a brief overview of the historical anti-Black racist experiences of Black communities in North America within the research process, including how this has shaped the nature of Black participation in research today. We then highlight current thinking about *how* to conduct a more ethical, meaningful, and beneficial research process with Black communities.

Our research team consisted of a young Black Caribbean Canadian mother of two (Sieunarine), two Black Canadian staff members from an Afrocentric community-based organization working with youth/Black mothers (Kim & Princilia), a Black Caribbean Ph.D. student new to Canada (Goddard-Durant), and a white Canadian professor (Doucet). Over a year-long period, in the process of designing the study, the team engaged in ongoing frank and direct conversations with each other about the experiences, needs, and concerns of all stakeholders involved, including those of the community, community members, the project, the community organization, and the academics (see also: Goddard-Durant, Sieunarine, & Doucet, 2021).

Exploitative and Harmful Histories of Academic Research with Black Communities

Historically, researchers' methodological and epistemological decisions in studies with Black communities in North America have been coercive, deceptive, and physically harmful to participants; they were also used to justify slavery and negate the humanity of Black persons, to reinforce racial segregation, and to buttress the idea of Black persons being inferior to white persons (see Jackson, Howard Caldwell & Sellers, 2012; Savitt, 1982; Washington, 2007). One of the most famous examples of unethical research conditions Black participants were exposed to is the Tuskegee experiments in the United States in 1932. Researchers used coercion and deception to recruit African American men in a 40-year study intended to observe the extent of medical deterioration among men with untreated syphilis, and to explore mass treatment possibilities (Kim & Magner, 2018). Another famous example that has more recently come to light is that of

African American woman Henrietta Lacks. After her death in 1951, researchers harvested her cells without her or her family's informed consent, and repeatedly used her cells to advance research in areas such as in vitro fertilization and cancer (Stump, 2014). These examples in the United States demonstrate the physical and material harm that researchers making methodological decisions grounded in anti-Black racist agendas have inflicted on Black participants and communities.

The ways in which Black persons have been conceptualized in research have also caused and perpetuated what Kirstie Dotson (2012) refers to as "epistemic oppression," which is "primarily characterized by detrimental exclusions from epistemic affairs" and "epistemic exclusion" where all "forms of epistemic injustice ... involve some form of pervasive, harmful epistemic exclusion" (p. 36). Nobles (1978) makes a compelling argument for how researchers' use of interpretive and/or conceptual frameworks grounded in white supremacy, drew conclusions about Black families in the United States have resulted in Black families being monolithically represented as deviant and dysfunctional. Black feminist thinkers have provided similar arguments about the consequences for Black American and Canadian women, whose experiences have often been excluded from studies by white feminists (see Hill Collins, 2009; Kitossa, 2002; Spates, 2012). Both epistemic oppression and exclusion are present in research that has privileged Global North[4] research frameworks to the detriment of the representation of Black persons in research, especially in cases where conceptual frameworks are not designed in partnership *with* Black communities.

Developments in ethical guidelines for research with human subjects, particularly around informed consent, and risk analyses, strive to better protect participants from research facilitation processes that might be physically and psychosocially harmful (see GCPRE, 2019). Nevertheless, Black communities have noted and resisted anti-Black racist, colonial decision-making by researchers. For example, researchers have documented that African Americans are concerned that there is lack of awareness about their lived experiences, and hence, that researchers are ill prepared to study them; that the findings will not benefit the African American community, only white people; that the government stands to gain from research at the expense of African American communities; that research will lead to reinforced stereotypes; and that the personal information they provide will be used against them at a later date (Caldwell et al., 1999; Scharff et al., 2010; Smith et al., 2007). Black persons' refusal (Tuck & Yang, 2014) to participate in research might be considered a way in which they resist experiencing unethical research facilitation and the fallout for them and their communities (Corbie-Smith et al., 2004; Smith et al., 2007).

Recent Thinking/Directions in Ethical Research Practices with Black Communities

Black scholars, guided by their own experiences of anti-Black racism, have also participated in this "refusal" and resistance to engage in research with Black communities. Some Black scholars (as well as non-Black ones) have been theorizing about or conducting research with Black communities using Afrocentric and select decolonial Global North frameworks, epistemologies, and methodologies, which centre daily lived experiences, stories, ways of knowing, and the well-being of Black participants and communities (see Bowers et al., 2016; Corbie-Smith et al., 2004; Davis, Williams, & Akinyela, 2010; Jackson & Howard Caldwell, 2012). These efforts work towards reducing the harmful, racialized, real-world implications of research for Black participants and communities. Semali et al. (2007) critique Global North frameworks and promote partnering with Black communities so that the community determines what research is needed. Jackson (2002) focused on the importance of upholding promises to disseminate research, accessibly, for community members. Through frameworks that centre the experiences and perspectives of Black persons, these scholars have demonstrated how researchers can minimize anti-Black racism in their work with Black communities.

Some researchers argue that the experiences of Black persons should be understood through Black lenses and ways of knowing, including understanding the lived experiences of Black communities through the intersectional understanding of Black people's lives (see Kitossa, 2002; Medina, 2013; Nobles, 1978; Wright, 2015). To this end, some scholars have developed Afrocentric research frameworks based on Molefi Kete Asante's (1987) theory of Afrocentrism. Afrocentric research is grounded in the history, culture, lived experiences, and knowledge of people of African descent; this information is used to formulate research problems throughout the entire research design and implementation process (see Akom, 2011; Davis, Williams, & Akinyela, 2010; Reviere, 2001). African-Canadian feminist frameworks further expand the intersectional focus in empirical studies (see Hampton & Rochat, 2019; Lawson, 2002). For example, Aladejebi (2016) explicitly identifies her methodological decision to document the presence of Black women in Canada's education system "as a way of disrupting the national narrative of Canadian teacher identity and its schooling system as primarily 'white,' middle class and female" (p. 6). By engaging these frameworks, scholars validate Black communities' ways of knowing, and disrupt historical exclusions of anti-Black racism in Black persons' everyday lives, and in so doing, empower Black persons to advocate for changes to structures and policies that are harmful to their lives.

Much of the information available on ethical research facilitation with Black communities is centred on the U.S context. While there is an acknowledgement by the United States of their racist past and present, the experiences of Black persons in Canada, from their enslavement to their contribution to Canadian society, are generally erased from educational curricula and the public's conception of the history of Canada (ACLC, 2015). Until 2015, Statistics Canada was neither collecting, nor making publicly-accessible race-based disaggregated data about Black persons (ACLC, 2015). But Canada was partially developed through anti-Black racism, including the enslavement of Black people (Winks, 2000).

Silence about anti-Black racism in Canada does not equate to its absence—in 2017 Canada was rebuked by the United Nations Human Rights Council for ongoing violations of the civil rights and liberties of Black persons. It is because of this context that our anti-racist approach to facilitating an ethical research process with Black Canadian young mothers was crucial.

In this next section, we briefly describe the relationship the academic members of the research team (Goddard-Durant and Doucet) cultivated with staff members from a Black-led, Black-serving community-based organization, and with a community member (Sieunarine) who enlightened the researchers about the realities of daily life for young Black Caribbean Canadian mothers in an urban area in Ontario. Sieunarine held the researchers accountable to prevent anti-Black racist practices and ideologies into the community-based research process. We discuss how we thought through the implications of ethical practices in our research for the young Black Caribbean Canadian mothers' daily lived experiences. We outline our research process and how we strived to be respectful of and attend to the welfare of the participants. This included our attempts to reflect on our ethico-onto-epistemic[5] research responsibilities (Doucet, 2018a) while navigating the challenges of working within the structural, temporal, and relational injustices that become a part of the research process. In doing so, our research contributes to efforts to honour and protect the humanity of Black communities in the facilitation of the research process.

Brief Overview of the Project

We sought to understand the experiences and needs of young Black Caribbean Canadian mothers aged 16–29, who had their first child by their mid-20s.[6] The study was a part of a wider project funded by the Canadian Social Sciences and Humanities Research Council (SSHRC). We drew on decolonial (e.g., Adams et al., 2015; Atallah, 2017; Martín-Baró, 1994), critical race (e.g., Aylward, 1999; Crenshaw et al., 1996), Afrocentric (e.g., Asante, 1987), Black feminist (e.g., Hill Collins, 2009), and feminist epistemological (e.g., Code, 2006; Doucet, 2018a) thinkers to build our approach. We utilized narrative and photo-elicitation methods for data co-making (see Doucet, 2018b) and an adaptation of the listening guide narrative approach to data analysis (see Doucet & Mauthner, 2008) in combination with constructivist grounded theory (Charmaz, 2014, Goddard-Durant, 2019) and the qualitative software Atlas.ti for both data analysis and the management of interview data, fieldnotes, and research literatures.

Each research participant engaged in two in-depth interviews about her life growing up as a Black Caribbean Canadian girl and her experiences as a young Black mother. During the interviews, the women were invited to provide photographs of their childhood families and the families they had made to guide the discussions about their lived experiences. The women were also offered the opportunity to create visual collages of what they wanted their family lives to look like in the future and what they needed to achieve this. We also invited the women to participate in focus groups to discuss what would be needed for young Black women in similar positions to improve their lives. All participants were compensated in gift cards for their time at the provincial hourly minimum wage rate; 13 Black Caribbean Canadian women participated in the individual interviews, and five participated in the focus group. In the next section, we outline how we facilitated an anti-racist interpretation of guiding ethical frameworks for research in Canada.

Anti-Racist Interpretation of the TCPS II Core Principles

Respecting Participants of Black Communities

Principle 1 of Canada's the Tri-Council Policy Statement: Ethical Conduct for Research with Humans II (TCPS 2) (GCPRE, 2019) is concerned with respect for persons; the researcher ensures that participants are free to make choices about their participation (GCPRE, 2019). This is facilitated by ensuring that the participant is fully informed about what is involved in their participation, and the benefits and risks to themselves, their family, and community. Anti-racist research requires shifting away from only focusing on individual autonomy and moving towards the deeper issues of cultivating trusting partnerships (see Semali et al., 2007; Tuck & Guishard, 2013). Our peer researcher and organizational staff noted that there was a history of distrust between this specific Black Canadian community in which we were working and researchers.

Through our conversations about the distrust of research in this community, we came up with five strategies to build trust with young Black Caribbean Canadian mothers. These strategies reflected the way in which relationship is enacted, according to the Black Caribbean Canadian-identifying members on our team: we are all interconnected, everything happens within relationship, and relationships need to be honoured and nurtured. The first strategy was using the Black Caribbean Canadian-identifying research team members' existing networks to recruit participants so that we could rely on relationships with people who already trusted us and could vouch for our integrity (Blanchet et al., 2017; Smith et al., 2007). Second, we provided specific details about our backgrounds and identities, particularly in relation to the community, and outlined our motivations for doing the research study. Each member of the research team prepared a script with this information (specific to herself) to use when introducing herself to persons expressing an interest in the research. Third, we made the decision to provide compensation to participants before they began the interview (Smith et al., 2007). Fourth, we formulated a flexible plan for how we would address concerns expressed by persons interested in participating, that we might be operating unethically. The final strategy related to validating and honouring the legitimate distrust that this Black community has about research relationships with white academics in Canada. Consequently, we made the decision that the Principal Investigator (PI) (Doucet), a white tenured Full Professor, would not participate in the field work.

Our decision to exclude Doucet only in the fieldwork phase, but not from the entire research process, was guided by three principles. First, we took a pragmatic approach to reflexivity, with the view that a researcher's presence and appearance (in this case their race) might affect research interactions and participants' comfort with sharing their life stories (see Schwartz-Shea & Yanow, 2012). Second, we took a relational approach to reflexivity, recognizing the multilayered relationships and responsibilities involved in research. We view research as an unfolding process that occurs not only between researchers and participants but between researchers, epistemic communities, and wider social worlds; research, as processes and relationships, produces many nonlinear interventions and effects (e.g., Doucet, 2018a). Finally, drawing from Ruth Frankenberg's (1993) "race cognizant" paradigm and her research on race relations and "whiteness studies," we did not pretend that we could remove whiteness from the research process; instead, we held the view that "attending to racial difference becomes an anti-racist strategy" (Hill Collins, 1995, p. 730). Based on these considerations, Doucet participated in research design, some meetings with project staff, and data analysis.

These five strategies were aimed at bringing greater balance to the power disparity with participants. Despite these efforts, we were unprepared for the level of distrust we experienced. We had to repeatedly prove that we respected participants and would facilitate informed consent. In some cases, we were explicitly accused of having a secret agenda to use the information we were collecting to harm young Black mothers. In other cases, participants made choices around their participation that we thought suggested their distrust, such as being evasive about parts of their stories that might be judged as illegal within the Canadian context. Our key takeaway from these unexpected experiences was that negotiating a trusting relationship between the researcher and researched is the backbone of facilitating informed consent and must be active and ongoing if we are to respect the realities that have historically threatened Black Caribbean Canadian participants' autonomous participation in the research process. This process starts with acknowledging the legacy of damage done to Black communities by the academic community in Canada; as a team with university-based researchers, we are part of the history of these harms and participants viewed us this way, regardless of our good intentions.

Attending to the Welfare of Participants from Black Communities

The second principle of the TCPS 2, Concern for Welfare, speaks to the possibility that the research can negatively impact various aspects of the person's life, such as their mental health and their housing, employment, or family life, among others (GCPRE, 2019). We thus strove to learn about structural injustices against Black Canadians that we might perpetuate via our specific research activities. Based on our conversations with the peer researcher (Sieunarine), we learned that for Black mothers in the region, a key site of systemic injustice related to the families' over-involvement with the Children's Aid Society (CAS).[7] Although Black families in this region do not neglect or abuse their children at any higher rate, they are 40% more likely to be investigated compared to white children, and their children are more likely to be taken during these investigations (OACAS, 2016). According to our sources in the community, single Black Caribbean Canadian mothers were often challenged, in the face of racial oppression, to ensure childcare while also modelling parenting practices held up as normative for middle class white parents in the country. These social expectations repeatedly brought them into contact with CAS and, with the Child and Family Service Act's (2001) dismissal of structural barriers, cultural differences, and immigration patterns, the relationship was often more punitive than supportive in terms of helping them meet the system's expectations (Clarke, 2011). One of our community sources indicated that mothers involved with CAS are subjected to unannounced spot visits and mandatory accounting of their time and income as part of investigations about the living circumstances of the child. Although participants in studies are typically in control of who has knowledge of their participation in a study, this right could not always be afforded to participants involved with CAS. CAS could show up during the interview (at the participant's home, via phone, or an online platform) and ask about how the participant was spending their time. CAS could demand that the participant account for their time if we did the interview at the community partner offices, or ask about the source of the compensation. We were concerned that participants might feel obligated to answer honestly for fear of losing their child or harming their case in some way. Moreover, because some of the questions we were asking young mothers could involve their experiences with CAS, disclosing their participation could result in retaliation from an unscrupulous worker who did not appreciate what the participant shared. At the same time, participants' sharing about the reality of their relationship with CAS could benefit the community of young Black mothers by enabling the researchers and the community partner to use that information to advocate for policy reform.

Overall, we were aware that Black mothers have historically needed to find ways to protect their families from institutionalized racism (Dow, 2019; Hill Collins, 2009; Lawson, 2019; Reynolds, 2005) and we did not want to place our participants in this position. Black women's willingness to participate in research about their experiences and needs to benefit other young Black mothers and their children could be framed as an act of political activism (Hill Collins, 2009; Lawson, 2019) and we were compelled to protect these mothers during their participation in our research. We saw it as our responsibility, based on our interpretation of the TCPS 2 principle of "concern for welfare," to minimize potential risks to the young Black Caribbean Canadian mothers in our study. It was our responsibility to alert mothers to the possible risk of CAS' knowledge of their participation so they could make an informed decision about participating. After exploring a few possibilities, we secured the community partner's agreement to provide the women with a cover story they could use with their CAS worker if a risky scenario presented itself. As researchers trained to uphold the Ethics Review Boards' valuing of individual rights and autonomy (Tuck & Guishard, 2013), we can often uncritically presume that people have the right to share or not share information about their participation in a study with whomever they choose. However, in this case, the young Black mothers' right to confidentiality could be in jeopardy because of their involvement with the CAS, and, if they exercised this right, they could potentially risk losing their child. Yet, not disclosing their participation was still a right they were entitled to according to the TCPS 2. Working with the peer researcher from the community was fundamental to us recognizing and addressing this risk of participation for the young Black mothers in this region. Our concern for the participants' welfare was critical to an ethical research process.

Facilitating Justice

The third principle of the TCPS 2, Justice, relates to researchers' obligation to treat persons fairly and equitably, so that participants are not unduly burdened by the risks or excluded from the benefits of research (GCPRE, 2019). Our interpretation of this principle was central to our choice of methodologies. As part of the project, we worked with participants' family photos, with the idea that families were meant to be understood according to their own definitions, and guided by the view that photographs could assist in the telling of family stories and memories (Doucet, 2018b; Kuhn, 2007). We learned four factors that could affect our use of photos with the participants. Because of the immigration patterns of Black Caribbean persons, some family members may have immigrated to Canada while others may remain in the Caribbean or be located elsewhere (Stuart, 1996; Reynolds, 2006). Secondly, overinvolvement with CAS could mean that some family members were absent from the person's life (Clarke, 2011). Thirdly, due to violence (individual and structural), some participants' family members could be dead or incarcerated (Bailey, Hannays-King, Clarke, Lester, & Velasco, 2013). And finally, a dominant feature of Black Caribbean family structures is that they are ones of extended kinship with transnational family and kin relationships (Stuart, 1996; Reynolds, 2006). All these factors meant that it might have been complicated to choose just a few family photos when their family realities were highly complex.

In broader methodological terms, we are highlighting how visual and photographic methods, while increasingly popular in social science research, especially in data collection, may not be well suited for research contexts (see Lowndes & Braedley, 2018). Many participants opted not to provide a picture of their family. We were not clear if this decision was related to their lack of trust in us to protect their identity; or a sense that their family structure might be interrogated; or a concern that images of their families might be used to validate stereotypical representations of them—a practice used to subordinate Black women (Lawson, 2002). Out of respect for their "no" response to furnishing family photos, we did not engage in a discussion about their reasons for this decision. However, we acknowledge that knowing more about their decisions would have been instructive for using visual research with Black Canadian communities in the future. Facilitating justice, in this case, meant being aware that our participants are members of a group that historically, have not had the power to influence how they were researched and presented, nor the power to have the methods used in research about their experiences appropriately account for their daily realities. It was important that we not repeat this pattern if we were to claim that our research process was justice-oriented.

Lessons Learned

Minimizing the likelihood of legitimizing, reproducing, or extending anti-Black racist practices in our research process required that we extend our interpretation of the TCPS 2 ethics requirements. It also required deep reflection about what adhering to these principles might translate to in the context of the daily lives of our participants. In this final section, we briefly provide three takeaways from our facilitation of what we see to be an ethical research process that might be useful for others seeking to conduct research with Black Caribbean Canadian mothers in the context of Canada.

Many of the insights into how anti-Black racism played out in participants' lives and how this could translate into research risks or opportunities were only made possible because of the academics' openness to the community members' perspectives. Our commitment to not reproduce the research-based anti-Black racism that the community has experienced, meant that the academics on the team released some of our ideas about how the research process should go. It also included a willingness to consider that our research training—including taken-for-granted assumptions we had about research processes—might be racist. However, it proved necessary to maintain reflexivity about our practices if we wanted to claim that our research process was ethical.

A third key lesson pertains to centralizing accountability to our participants and the community in our ethical decision-making. We had to answer to the community about how we facilitated the research process with its members. Our commitment to cultivating a transparent relationship between the academics, the peer researcher, and the staff of the community-based organization was a key vehicle for maintaining accountability. Cultivating an intimate working relationship makes it that much harder to ignore the needs participants presented.

Conclusion

Decolonizing research processes with Black Canadians involves reflecting on how to facilitate an ethical process that might be beyond the boundaries of what is required by the TCPS 2 in their interpretation of respect for persons, welfare, and justice. Working with members of one Black Caribbean Canadian community in Canada meant appreciating how young mothers live, with special attention to how anti-Black racism has shaped their lives. Historically, anti-Black racism has played out in some studies, including through the conceptual, theoretical, epistemological, and methodological frameworks researchers have applied, with real-world consequences for Black participants and their communities. Although there is limited documentation of anti-Black racism in research occurring in Canada, our experience suggests that a habit of obscuring how anti-Black racism has historically shaped the lives of Black Canadians is a more probable explanation for this absence than an assumption that injustices did not occur due to a lack of research studies about Black Canadians. Facilitating an ethical research process while attempting to confront and address anti-Black racism in research involves expanding and deepening the TCPS 2's interpretation of what constitutes ethical research facilitation. In Canada, some of this expansion could occur through Black community and research stakeholders reviewing the ethical guidelines for research with Indigenous peoples that have been established by the *Tri-Council Policy Statement on Research Involving the First Nations, Inuit, and Métis people of Canada* and the OCAP principles (Ownership, Control, Access, and Possession) established by First Nations organizations (see FNIGC, 2020). These guidelines stipulate that data and its use should be both guided and owned by communities. We argue that similar guidelines, could be developed, in an asset-informed manner, for working with community members and organizations that serve Black Canadian communities.[8]

Grounding ethical decision making in deep knowledge of the specific Black community, whether from community members or from documented reports[9] about the everyday lives of Black participants, is crucial for understanding their experiences of the research process and what is needed to facilitate an ethical, meaningful, and impactful research process *with* these communities. So, too, is a willingness on the part of academics to consider the possibility that colonizing, anti-Black racist concepts, theories, and ideologies are embedded within their existing research frameworks and practices. Thoughtful attention to what disrupting anti-Black racism in research processes might look like is fundamental for scholars seeking to engage in ethical studies with Black communities in Canada. This reflexive work of conceptualizing and designing ethical research studies can only bode well for efforts to address the historical and ongoing anti-Black racism that has shaped the everyday lives of Black persons in Canada.

Notes

1 Ethical clearance for this study was provided by the Brock University Research Ethics Board.
2 We use the term Global South to refer to people whose ancestors were colonized. These included Indigenous people of South America, North America, New Zealand, Australia, South Asia, and Africa and descendants of Africans who were enslaved and transplanted to places like the Caribbean, the U.S., Canada, and the U.K., referred to as the African diaspora (Chilisa, 2012; Dirlik, 2007).

3 The Tri-Council Policy Statement on Ethical Conduct for Research Involving Humans is a joint policy of Canada's three federal research agencies: The Canadian Institutes for Health Research (CIHR), the Natural Sciences and Engineering Research Council of Canada (NSERC), and the Social Sciences and Humanities Research Council of Canada (SSHRC).
4 The term Global North is used here to refer to the U.S., and European countries like England, Spain, France, and Portugal, which, from the 1600s, through brute force and genocide, established colonies across the globe to develop their home countries into rich industrialized democracies (Chilisa, 2012; Dirlik, 2007).
5 The term "ethico-onto-epistemology" was first developed in the work of feminist physicist-philosopher Karen Barad (2007) to highlight the inseparability of ethics, ontology, and epistemology when engaging in, and being responsible for, our knowledge making practices and production.
6 We arrived at this definition of the age of young motherhood based on data that Black women and girls were meeting mainstream developmental milestones of young adulthood related to education, employment, and financial independence (typically held up as indicative of readiness to parent) behind their peers due to systemic barriers and social disparities (Canadian Centre for Policy Alternatives, 2019).
7 The Children's Aid Society (CAS) is an organization intended to prevent and protect children and youth from abuse and neglect. Learn more about them here https://www.torontocas.ca/vision-mission-and-values
8 We thank Eva Jewell for discussing this point with us.
9 At the time of research design and data collection, there were very few reports about the experiences of Black Canadians. Several have been published in the last two years, perhaps as part of the response to the United Nations Human Rights Council Working Group of Experts on People of African Descent Report in 2017.

References

Adams, G., Dobles, I., Gómez, L.H., Kurtiş, T., & Molina, L.E. (2015). Decolonizing psychological science: Introduction to the special thematic section. *Journal of Social and Political Psychology, 3*(1), 213–238. http://dx.doi.org/10.5964/jspp.v3i1.564

African Canadian Legal Clinic (ACLC). (2015). Civil and political wrongs: The growing gap between international civil and political rights and the African Canadian life. A report on the Canadian government's compliance with the International Covenant on Civil and Political Rights. African Canadian Legal Clinic. https://tbinternet.ohchr.org/Treaties/CCPR/Shared%20Documents/CAN/INT_CCPR_CSS_CAN_20858_E.pdf

Akom, A.A. (2011). Black emancipatory action research: Integrating a theory of structural racialisation into ethnographic and participatory action research methods. *Ethnography and Education, 6*(1), 113–131. https://doi.org/10.1080/17457823.2011.553083

Aladejebi, F.O. (2016). Girl you better apply to teachers' college: The history of Black women educators in Ontario, 1940's-1980s. [Doctoral dissertation, York University].

Asante, M.K. (1987). *The Afrocentric idea*. Temple University Press.

Atallah, D.G. (2017). A community-based qualitative study of intergenerational resilience with Palestinian refugee families facing structural violence and historical trauma. *Transcultural Psychiatry, 54*(3), 357–383. https://doi.org/10.1177%2F1363461517706287

Aylward, C.A. (1999). *Canadian critical race theory: Racism and the law*. Fernwood Publishing.

Bailey, A., Hannays-King, C., Clarke, J., Lester, E., & Velasco, D. (2013). Black mothers' cognitive process of finding meaning and building resilience after loss of a child to gun violence. *British Journal of Social Work, 43*(2), 336–354. https://doi-org.proxy.library.brocku.ca/10.1093/bjsw/bct027

Barad, K. (2007). *Meeting the universe halfway: Quantam physics and the entanglement of matter and meaning.* Duke University Press.

Blanchet, R., Sanou, D., Nana, C.P., Pauzé, E., Batal, M., & Giroux, I. (2017). Strategies and challenges in recruiting Black immigrant mothers for a community-based study on child nutritional health in Ottawa, Canada. *Journal of Immigrant and Minority Health, 19* (2), 367–372.

Bowers, B., Jacobson, N., & Krupp, A. (2016). Can lay community advisors improve the clarity of research participant recruitment materials and increase the likelihood of participation? *Research in Nursing & Health, 40*(1), 63–69. https://doi.org/10.1002/nur.21752

Caldwell, C.F., Jackson, J.S., Tucker, M.B., & Bowman, P.J. (1999). Culturally-competent research methods in African American communities: An update. In R.L. Jones (Ed.), *Advances in African American psychology: Theory, paradigms, methodology, and reviews* (pp. 101–127). Cobb and Henry.

Canadian Centre for Policy Alternatives. (2019). Unfinished Business: A Parallel Report on Canada's Implementation of the Beijing Declaration and Platform for Action, 2019, pp. 29–39. https://www.policyalternatives.ca/sites/default/files/uploads/publications/National%20Office/2019/10/Unfinished%20business.pdf

Charmaz, K. (2014). *Constructing grounded theory* (2nd ed.). Sage Publications.

Chilisa, B. (2012). *Indigenous research methodologies.* Sage Publications.

Clarke, J. (2011). The challenges of child welfare involvement for Afro-Caribbean families in Toronto. *Children and Youth Services Review, 33*(2), 274–283. https://doi.org/10.1016/j.childyouth.2010.09.010

Code, L. (2006). *Ecological thinking: The politics of epistemic location.* Oxford University Press.

Corbie-Smith, G., Moody-Ayers, S., & Thrasher, A.D. (2004). Closing the circle between minority inclusion in research and health disparities. *Archives of Internal Medicine, 164*(13), 1362–1364. https://doi.org/10.1001/archinte.164.13.1362

Crenshaw, K., Gotanda, N., Peller, G., & Thomas, K. (Eds.). (1996). *Critical race theory: The key writings that formed the movement.* New Press.

Davis, S.K., Williams, A.D., & Akinyela, M. (2010). An Afrocentric approach to building cultural relevance in social work research. *Journal of Black Studies, 41*(2), 338–350. https://doi.org/10.1177%2F0021934709343950

Dirlik, A. (2007). Global South: Predicament and promise. *The Global South, 1*(1), 12–23. Retrieved from https://muse.jhu.edu/article/398223/summary

Dotson, K. (2012). A cautionary tale: On limiting epistemic oppression. *Frontiers: A Journal of Women Studies, 33*(1), 24–47. https://doi.org/10.5250/fronjwomestud.33.1.0024

Doucet, A. (2018a). Feminist epistemologies and ethics: Ecological thinking, situated knowledges, epistemic responsibilities. In R. Iphofen, & M. Tolich (Eds.), *The Sage handbook of qualitative research ethics* (pp. 73–88). SAGE Publications Ltd. https://www.doi.org/10.4135/9781526435446

Doucet, A. (2018b). Decolonizing family photographs: Ecological imaginaries and non-representational ethnographies. *Journal of Contemporary Ethnography, 47*(6), 729–757. https://doi.org/10.1177%2F0891241617744859

Doucet, A., & Mauthner, N. (2008). What can be known and how? Narrated subjects and the Listening Guide. *Qualitative Research, 8*(3), 399–409. https://doi.org/10.1177%2F1468794106093636

Dow, D. M. (2019). *Mothering while black*. University of California Press. https://doi.org/10.1525/9780520971776

First Nations Information Governance Center. (2020). A First Nations data governance strategy. https://fnigc.ca/wp-content/uploads/2020/09/FNIGC_FNDGS_report_EN_FINAL.pdf

Frankenberg, R. (1993). *White women, race matters: The social construction of whiteness*. University of Minnesota Press.

Goddard-Durant, S.K. (2019). Resilience in Barbados: Bein' uh work in progress. [Doctoral dissertation, University of Guelph]. The Atrium.

Goddard-Durant, S.K., Sieunarine, J., & Doucet, A. (2021). Decolonizing research with Black communities: Developing equitable and ethical relationships between academic and community stakeholders. *Families, Relationships and Societies, 10*(1), 189–196. https://doi.org/10.1332/204674321X16104823811079

Government of Canada Panel of Research Ethics. (2019, September 23). TCPS 2 (2018) Chapter 1: Ethics Framework. https://ethics.gc.ca/eng/tcps2-eptc2_2018_chapter1-chapitre1.html#b

Hampton, R., & Rochat, D. (2019).To commit and to lead: Black women organizing across communities in Montreal. In T. Kitossa, E. Lawson, & P.S. Howard (Eds.), *African Canadian leadership: Continuity, transition, and transformation* (pp. 149–169). University of Toronto Press.

Hill Collins, P. (1995). Review of the books "White women, race matters: The social construction of whiteness" by R. Frankenberg and "Black popular culture", by G. Dent and M. Wallace. *Signs: Journal of Women in Culture and Society, 20*(3), 728–731.

Hill Collins, P. (2009). *Black feminist thought: Knowledge, consciousness, and the politics of empowerment*. Routledge.

Jackson, F.M. (2002). Considerations for community-based research with African American women. *American Journal of Public Health, 92*(4), 561–564.

Jackson, J.S., Howard Caldwell, C., & Sellers, S.L. (2012). Conceptual and methodological challenges in studies of Black populations. In J.S. Jackson, & C. Howard Caldwell (Eds.), *Researching black communities* (pp. 3–30). University of Michigan Press.

Kim, O.J., & Magner, L.N. (2018). *A history of medicine*. Taylor & Francis Group, LLC.

Kitossa, T. (2002). Criticism, reconstruction and African-centred feminist historiography. In N.N. Wane, K. Deliovsky, & E. Lawson (Eds.), *Back to the drawing board: African-Canadian feminisms* (pp. 85–116). Sumac Press.

Kuhn, A. (2007). Photography and cultural memory: A methodological exploration. *Visual Studies, 22*(3), 283–292. https://doi.org/10.1080/14725860701657175

Lawson, E. (2002). Images in Black: Black women, media and the mythology of the orderly society. In N.N. Wane, K. Deliovsky, & E. Lawson (Eds.), *Back to the drawing board: African-Canadian feminisms* (pp. 199–223). Sumac Press.

Lawson, E. (2019). Mercy for their children: A feminist reading of Black women's maternal activism and leadership practices. In T. Kitossa, E. Lawson, & P.S. Howard (Eds.), *African Canadian leadership: Continuity, transition, and transformation* (pp. 149–169). University of Toronto Press.

Lowndes, R., & Braedley, S. (2018). Snap happy? The problems and promises of photovoice. In P. Armstrong, & R. Lowndes (Eds.), *Creative teamwork: Developing rapid, site-switching ethnography* (pp. 129–142). Oxford University Press.

Martín-Baró, I. (1994). *Writings for a liberation psychology*. Harvard University Press.

Medina, J. (2013). *The epistemology of resistance: Gender and racial oppression, epistemic injustice, and resistant imaginations*. Oxford University Press.

Nobles, W.W. (1978). Toward an empirical and theoretical framework for defining Black families. *Journal of Marriage and Family, 40* (4), 679–688.

Ontario Association of Children's Aid Societies (OACAS). (2016). *One vision one voice: Changing the Ontario child welfare system to better service African Canadians – Practice Framework Part 1: Research Report*. Ontario Association of Children's Aid Societies. https://www.oacas.org/wp-content/uploads/2016/09/One-Vision-One-Voice-Part-1_digital_english.pdf

Reynolds, T. (2005). *Caribbean mothers: Identity and experience in the U.K.* The Tufnell Press.

Reynolds, T. (2006). Caribbean families, social capital and young people's diasporic identities. *Ethnic and Racial Studies, 29*(6), 1087–1103. https://doi.org/10.1080/01419870600960362

Reviere, R. (2001). Toward an Afrocentric research methodology. *Journal of Black Studies, 31*(6), 709–728. https://doi.org/10.1177%2F002193470103100601

Savitt, T.L. (1982). The use of Blacks for medical experimentation and demonstration in the Old South. *The Journal of Southern History, 48*(3), 331–348.

Scharff, D.P., Mathews, K.J., Jackson, P., Hoffsuemmer, J., Martin, E., & Edwards, D. (2010). More than Tuskegee: Understanding mistrust about research participation. *Journal of Health Care for the Poor and Underserved, 21*(3), 879–897. https://dx.doi.org/10.1353%2Fhpu.0.0323

Schwartz-Shea, P., & Yanow, D. (2012). *Interpretive research design: Concepts and processes*. Routledge.

Semali, L.M., Ackerman, R.M., Bradley, S.G., Buzinde, C.N., Jaksch, M.L., Kalavar, J.M., ... & Chinoy, M.R. (2007). Developing excellence in indigenously-informed research: Collaboration between African communities and the academy. *AlterNative: An International Journal of Indigenous Peoples, 3*(2), 8–23. https://doi.org/10.1177%2F117718010700300202

Smith, Y.R., Johnson, A.M., Newman, L.A., Greene, A., Johnson, T.R.B., Rogers, J.L. (2007). Perceptions of clinical research participation among African American women. *Journal of Women's Health, 16*(3), 423–428. https://doi.org/10.1089/jwh.2006.0124

Spates, K. (2012). "The missing link": The exclusion of Black women in psychological research and the implications for Black women's mental health. *SAGE Open, 2*(3), 1–8. https://doi.org/10.1177%2F2158244012455179

Stump, J.L. (2014). Henrietta Lacks and the HeLa cell: Rights of patients and responsibilities of medical researchers. *The History Teacher, 48*(1), 127–180. https://www.jstor.org/stable/43264385

Stuart, S. (1996). Female-headed families: A comparative perspective of the Caribbean and the developed world. *Gender and Development, 4*(2), 28–34. https://doi.org/10.1080/741922017

Tuck, E. (2009). Suspending damage: A letter to communities. *Harvard Educational Review, 79*(3), 409–428. https://doi.org/10.17763/haer.79.3.n0016675661t3n15

Tuck, E., & Guishard, M. (2013). Uncollapsing ethics: Racialized sciencism, settler coloniality and an ethical framework of decolonial participatory action research. In T.M. Kress, C. Malott, & B. Porfilio (Eds.), *Challenging status quo retrenchment: New directions in critical qualitative research* (pp. 3–28). Information Age Publishing, Inc.

Tuck, E., & Yang, K.W. (2014). R-Words: Refusing research. In D. Paris, & M.T. Winn (Eds.), *Humanizing research: Decolonizing qualitative inquiry with youth and communities* (pp. 223–248). SAGE Publications, Inc. https://www.doi.org/10.4135/9781544329611

United Nations Human Rights Council (UNHRC) Working Group of Experts on People of African Descent. (2017). Report of the working group of experts on people of African descent on its mission to Canada. https://digitallibrary.un.org/record/1304262?ln=en#record-files-collapse-header

Washington, H.A. (2007). *Medical apartheid: The dark history of medical experimentation on Black Americans from colonial times to the present.* Doubleday.

Winks, R. (2000). *The blacks in Canada.* McGill-Queen's University Press.

Wright, M.M. (2015). *Physics of blackness: Beyond the middle passage epistemology.* University of Minnesota Press.

2
LESSONS LEARNED, LESSONS SHARED
Reflections on Doing Research in Collaboration with Sex Workers and Sex Worker-led Organizations

Ryan T. Conrad and Emma McKenna

Introduction

The COVID-19 outbreak led to undue financial hardships for sex workers and their associates resulting from stay-at-home measures and the sudden closure of strip clubs, holistic spas, and massage parlours (Lewis, 2020; Rancic, 2020). These lost wages were compounded by increased caregiving responsibilities for children, elders, disabled community members, and those who have contracted COVID-19 (Fox et al., 2020). As early demands for demographic data insisted, workers already living in poverty, and those who are racialized, Indigenous, queer, trans★, or disabled, are particularly vulnerable both to COVID-19 and to its effects (Bryant et al., 2020; Jean-Pierre & Collins, 2020; Ontario Human Rights Commission, 2020; Public Health Ontario, 2020). Already working within grassroots sex worker organizations, we witnessed the economic devastation and institutional alienation faced by the community. We also saw the community's resilience and lateral support as mutual-aid strategies were swiftly rolled out (Butterfly, 2020). To produce data that is useful for both researchers and sex worker organizations, we developed a research study based on one of our respective organizations. Our successful application has enabled us to begin this critical research while facilitating a small redistribution of economic resources to sex workers.[1]

As white, queer, working-class, and middle class activist academics working from an intersectional, anti-oppressive framework, we are keen to use our access to institutional resources to support sex worker-led organizing (Shaver et al., 2011). Our attempts to capture the effects of COVID-19 on sex workers were stymied by a "lack of data" that has contributed to a broader silence in scholarship on sex work (Amnesty International Canada, 2020; Platt et al., 2020; UNAIDS, 2020). Our research contributes to sex work[2] studies in the social sciences and humanities in the Global North examining: sex work and feminism (McKenna,

DOI: 10.4324/9781003199236-4

2021, Forthcoming; Valverde, 2018); sex work and data (Conrad, Forthcoming); the criminalization of sex work (Belak & Bennett, 2016; Bruckert & Parent, 2018; Goodall, 2019; Lowman, 2004); the impact of criminalization on sex workers and their clients (Khan, 2015; Sterling & van der Meulen, 2018); the stigmatization of sex workers (Brock, 2009; Bruckert, 2002; Ferris, 2015; Lowman, 2000); sex work as a labour issue (Durisin et al., 2018; Logan, 2017; Parent et al., 2013; Smith & Mac, 2018); sex work and municipal governance (Anderson et al., 2015; Lam, 2016; Law, 2015; Lewis & Maticka-Tyndale, 2000); and sex worker-led community activism (Ferris & Lebovitch, 2020; Heying, 2018).

We explore how to ethically facilitate this research by reflecting on our engagement with sex worker organizing. While doing collaborative research with sex worker-led organizations and individuals who do sex work, we contribute to scholarship that may benefit academics and community workers (Huysamen & Sanders, 2021; Jeffreys, 2010). These recommendations emerge from our personal histories as activists, and from our partnership with Prostitutes of Ottawa-Gatineau Work, Educate, Resist (POWER). Our collaboration with POWER examines the economic impact of COVID-19 on sex workers, in particular investigating how they negotiated state-sponsored income-replacement schemes, such as the novel Canadian Emergency Response Benefit (CERB), Employment Insurance (EI), as well as pre-existing welfare and disability support programmes.[3]

In this chapter, we highlight the ethical and methodological challenges that underscore academic research with sex workers (Bruckert, 2014; Forgel, 2007; Liamputtong, 2007). To understand the unique ethical questions facing research on the sex industry, we provide a brief summary of the legal context of sex work in Canada. Second, we reflect on mutual-aid projects initiated by sex worker-led organizations that provided $100.00 emergency grants to local sex workers at the beginning of the pandemic. We end by offering suggestions for others interested in doing research with sex work communities. We believe that these suggestions can support research with sex working communities by encouraging researchers to prioritize research outcomes that are useful to sex workers themselves (Maggie's, 2021).

Legal Context of Sex Work

Sex work is currently regulated under the Canadian Criminal Code, reflecting an ongoing history of de-facto criminalization (Durisin et al., 2018). In 2014, the *Protection of Communities and Exploited Persons Act (PCEPA)* (2014) updated the language on sex work and affiliated crimes to expand the reach of the criminal law (Belak & Bennett, 2016). While the act of selling sex is not illegal, communicating for the purpose of selling sex in public is illegal (s. 213 1.1), as is referring a sex worker to a client (s. 286.3). For the first time in Canada, *PCEPA* determined that clients can be criminally charged with purchasing sex (s 286.1), third parties could be charged with advertising a sex worker's services (s. 286.4), and with obtaining a "material benefit" from a sex worker (s 286.2). It is within this legal context that sex workers perform their labour, navigating confusing and contradictory legislation around sex workers' rights to labour protections, workplace health and safety, and employment benefits. Since the onslaught of COVID-19, the precarity and illegitimacy of sex work have once again been urgently highlighted.

Consensual sex work is a legitimate form of labour that has been deemed illegitimate by a confluence of state, legal, and civil actors. We distinguish sex work from human trafficking, and particularly from feminist arguments that conflate the two (Belles, 2015; Bindle, 2017; Bourgeois, 2018). We acknowledge the abuses involved in the involuntary movement of people across locations, worksites, and borders for the purposes of non-consensual labour (Kaye, 2017; Kempadoo, 2005; Maynard, 2015). We remain critical of the discourse of sex trafficking, in particular the privileging of police reporting over that of victims (Lepp, 2017; Zhang, 2009). While all sex workers are vulnerable to criminalization, violence, and stigma, systemic racism and colonialism impact how Black, Indigenous, and racialized sex workers negotiate the sex industry, criminal justice, and attendant resources (Brooks, 2020; Hunt, 2013; Maynard, 2017).

COVID-19, Canadian Emergency Income Support, and Sex Workers

Canada's federal government scrambled to address the massive unemployment engendered by the pandemic lockdown through the creation of the Canadian Emergency Response Benefit (CERB) and the expansion of Employment Insurance (EI) (Government of Canada, 2020). CERB was rolled out as a temporary income relief plan, enabling workers whose income was reduced to under $1,000 to receive up to $2,000 in monthly support (Petit & Tedds, 2020). Individuals who earned less than $5,000 in the previous year were ineligible to apply, which excluded the poorest category of workers from the benefit. While between 9 and 13% of Canadians suffered a major economic hit, approximately 10% of workers in the lowest and highest income levels received CERB (Achou et al., 2020; Zajacova et al., 2020).

Sex worker and civil society organizations ranging from Women's Shelter Canada, the Canadian Labour Congress, and the Canadian Alliance for Sex Work Law Reform circulated a letter calling on the federal government to clarify sex workers' inclusion in CERB and provincial income assistance plans (Canadian Alliance for Sex Work Law Reform, 2020). Specifically, these organizations pointed to the requirement of workers having filed income tax in 2019 (Government of Canada, 2020). As precarious, stigmatized, and criminalized labourers in an informal sector of the economy, filing taxes can pose a problem for sex workers (Benoit et al., 2016; Bruckert & Hannem, 2013). Some sex workers were faced with a cost-benefit analysis between the potential advantages of applying for the CERB and a future reduction in provincial income assistance as a penalty. The "trust but verify later" strategy of CERB has jeopardized access to government income supports (Pettinicchio et al., 2021; Robson, 2020).

The exclusion of some sex workers from CERB prompted grassroots sex worker-led organizations to create mutual aid emergency funds for sex workers. As a member of POWER, Ryan worked with the board to raise and distribute $12,000 directly to sex workers in the capital region. Emma was a board member of Sex Workers Action Project (SWAP) of Hamilton, where the board collectively fund-raised and allocated $4,720.00 to sex workers in the area. In both cases, emergency grants were advertised via social media and local networks of workers and allies. SWAP's mandate for receiving an emergency grant was simply to email a request to the Executive Director, providing an eligible email address for the e-transfer. POWER's case was more complicated, as it involved multiple organizations in the distribution of funds. POWER setup a low-barrier online application form that was advertised on their website and social media to distribute money directly to sex workers while also transferring sizable funds directly to two other sex worker-focused organizations in the city (Willow's Drop-In and Ottawa Independent Companions) so that they could distribute funds directly to service users and members respectively. Both SWAP and POWER fundraised in the same way, receiving non-charitable donations from community members. These local emergency grants were part of global efforts, yet another example of the creativity and determination of the international sex workers' rights movement (Lam, 2020).

Introducing Our Collaborative Research Project

This project is grounded in community-based research with a hidden population in which the research team is positioned as both insiders and outsiders (Benoit et al., 2016). Our positionality reflects much sex work research, where individuals with fluid experience in sex work, sex work organizing, and sex work research share a common asset-informed agenda (Lowthers et al., 2017). We recruited Chris Bruckert—Emma's postdoctoral supervisor and a founding member of POWER. The POWER board spearheaded our search for a Research Assistant (RA), internally recruiting a student who serves on POWER's board. As the only paid employee on the project, the RA is the conduit through which the research team and the POWER board communicate. Our varied positionalities are an asset to this project, providing us individual and collective opportunities for reflection, growth, and solidarity (Fenge et al., 2019).

Following approval by the Research Ethics Office at the University of Ottawa, our research project was launched on June 1, 2021. The research team developed a digital quantitative survey composed of 54 research questions. The objectives of the quantitative study are to understand how diverse sex workers negotiated COVID-19, in particular, their loss of income and whether they were able to access government income support and assistance programmes. Establishing quantitative data on sex workers' access to recent emergency income replacement programmes will address this gap in knowledge (Kelly et al., 1992; Reinharz, 1993). The qualitative aspect of our study includes interviews with key informants involved in disseminating emergency mutual-aid funds from Ottawa-Gatineau sex worker-led organizations. As activist academic Elene Lam has observed, sex worker organizations have been at the forefront of mutual-aid support for sex workers during the first year of the pandemic (Lam, 2020; Spade, 2020). This project joins this vital dialogue on sex workers' financial negotiation of the COVID-19 pandemic in Canada.

Discussion: Ten Questions to Consider When Researching Sex Work/ers

As researchers embedded in various marginalized communities, we know the importance of approaching community-based research with respect, care, and caution (Olshansky & Zender, 2016; Sanders, 2006). There is very little scholarship on how to ethically engage with sex workers (Jeffreys, 2010). Given the legal context of sex work, it is important that researchers are not only advocates of sex workers' rights and dignity in the study design and implementation, but are also aware of the danger their research could pose to sex workers if their information is mishandled (Israel & Hay, 2012; Palys & Lowman, 2014). For these reasons, we have developed a tool for scholars thinking about conducting qualitative research on sex work, or in collaboration with sex workers and sex worker-led organizations (See Table 2.1).

TABLE 2.1 Ten Questions to Consider When Researching Sex Work/ers

1. *What is your relationship to commercial sex industries?*
   Before jumping into a research project ask, why me? What are my relations with people from this community? Am I the right person to do this research? Am I a member of this community? Am I an ally? Am I an outsider? What am I willing to offer this community in return? If you are a current or former sex worker in the academy, how will you manage your evolving relationship to the community? How much will you disclose, to whom, when, and how?

2. *Has the research already been done?*
   Sex workers are an over-researched group who often have to repeat themselves time and time again. Before reaching out to a sex worker or an organization, ensure that your research questions have not already been answered by other scholars by first carrying out a thorough literature review.

3. *Who benefits most from the research?*
   If sex workers do not benefit from the research in clear and tangible ways, a research project involving sex workers should be reassessed. A graded practicum, thesis, scholarly article, book chapter or book should not be the sole outcome of the project.

4. *Do you really need to bother sex workers to do useful research?*
   Consider consulting the work sex workers and sex work organizations have already done. Social media is a useful public platform for hearing from sex workers in their own words. If you don't follow any sex workers, start there, and before asking any questions, listen to what they are already saying! Furthermore, instead of turning the gaze on sex workers, why not focus your research towards critically examining the police, politicians, and moralists who terrorize sex workers and undermine their safety?

(Continued)

TABLE 2.1 (Continued)

5. *What role do sex workers have in shaping the research project?*
   Is your research accountable to sex workers in the planning, implementation, data collection, data analysis, and outcomes? While not all research includes sex workers at every stage of research, you should consider what kind of relationship you will have to sex workers throughout your whole research process.

6. *How are you compensating sex workers for their time?*
   If your research project includes speaking with or surveying sex workers and/or staff at a sex worker-led organization, how will you compensate them for their time? Endeavour to write a research budget that acknowledges the time staff will contribute to your project, and ensure that honorariums for research participation are commensurate with the amount of work you're asking of sex workers. Avoid gift cards and raffles and simply pay people for their time.

7. *How will you protect your research participants?*
   Sex workers are made vulnerable by a web of laws designed explicitly to control their lives. While most formal scholarly research requires Ethic Review Board approval, working with members of this community often require higher levels of care regarding the safety and well-being of participants.

8. *Who owns the research outputs?*
   Publications, whether scholarly or community-based, are often the primary outputs of research. Whose names will be on these publications? Who will receive credit? Who will appear in the acknowledgements? Will you share your results with the participants, before, during, or after publication? How will you respond to criticism?

9. *How generalizable will your findings be?*
   Researchers must reflect on the specificity of their research and how generalizable the findings are. Sex workers are a diverse group of people with various backgrounds and life experiences. Be sure not to make large claims about the nature of sex work beyond the scope of your study. Women or men, cis or trans*, working poor or middle class, street-based or indoor, independent or working for a third party, citizen or migrant, Indigenous and racialized or white—there are so many axes of difference that limit how much we can generalize. It's best to remain specific about the part(s) of the sex working community you've been working with.

10. *How will your research be mobilized beyond academia?*
    An article in a scholarly publication behind a pay wall that hardly anyone will read is not particularly helpful to sex workers or sex worker-led organizations. If a scholarly publication is necessary output, how might you mobilize the research findings in other ways as well? An educational tool-kit for your class, workplace, or community group? A community-based report co-authored with a sex worker organization? A press event? What about donating any proceeds from your publication to a sex worker-led organization?

These ten questions have structured our own research process with POWER, and we offer our responses to them as a model for other researchers. To be of utmost use to sex worker, activist, and academic communities, a shareable list of questions follows our reflections below.

What Is Your Relationship to Commercial Sex Industries?

Our project comes directly out of our connections to sex worker-led organizations (SWAP and POWER). We are both postdoctoral researchers with expertise in sexuality and sex work, and vocal advocates for the decriminalization of sex work. One of us has over a decade of experience as a part-time sex worker while the other has been in close proximity to underground economies, but not as a sex worker. Emma joined SWAP Hamilton in July 2019, and served as an elected board member from September 2019 to June 2020. Ryan was instrumental in helping relaunch POWER in 2019, and he volunteers with MAX Ottawa and sits on their Male Sex Workers Outreach Project Advisory Board.

Has the Research Already Been Done?

Sex work scholarship should be useful to the community. Since the core focus of our project relates to the COVID-19 pandemic, our research is urgent. The collaborative report generated from our project will be the first mixed methods study in Canada to examine sex worker mutual aid strategies during this crisis (Butterfly et al., 2020; Lam, 2020; Spade, 2020). While it is important to note that COVID-19 is a health crisis, our project does not primarily examine research on sex workers' health (e.g., Hoefinger et al., 2020; Lazarus et al., 2012).

Who Benefits Most from the Research?

Research on the sex industry should be of benefit to sex workers themselves. Our primary goal is to provide usable data for sex workers and their organizations, which will lend statistical evidence to anecdotal reporting on the difficulty of accessing state support and filing income taxes. While this is critical given COVID-19 and Canada's emergency relief funding (e.g., CERB), this study will provide longitudinal evidence that existing policy—e.g., EI, social assistance, and disability programmes—discriminate against sex workers. We seek to share our findings with the communities most affected by the research through a public report written in collaboration with POWER. This report will support future activism around sex workers' full inclusion in civil society, including social benefit programmes geared towards precarious and gig workers. It will be written in accessible language, without jargon, will be bilingual (English and French), and contain visualizations of our data. The report will be an open-access document hosted on POWER's website and shared by our partner organization via listserve and social media.

Do You Really Need to Bother Sex Workers to Do Useful Research?

While our research project was undergoing rigorous ethics review, a student journalist contacted POWER with an online survey on sex workers and COVID-19. The survey did not contain a consent form, it had no guarantee of confidentiality, and the questions were invasive. Our research team and the broader activist community swiftly responded, and the survey was taken down. Responding to such inquiries is an exhausting task for sex worker organizations.

Yet, establishing data on diverse sex workers' access to the CERB, EI, disability, and welfare in the context of the COVID-19 pandemic is urgent. Sex workers have the lived experience to explain the barriers they encounter when approaching state support. Their personal reflections on navigating the CERB, EI, disability, and welfare are critical to making these systems more accessible to sex workers. Sex workers can best assess how the Canadian state uses the threat of stigma, criminalization, or violence in bureaucratic processes. We have developed a low barrier, bilingual, short, remunerated online survey for 200 sex workers in the Ottawa-Gatineau area. We will also engage in one-on-one key informant interviews with the handful of activists in the capital region who distributed POWER's emergency funds. Our goal is to gather data in the least invasive way possible; critically, both members of POWER and sex workers are involved in every stage of this research, including the drafting of our research questions and questionnaire.

What Role Do Sex Workers Have in Shaping the Research Project?

Participants must have a stake in the outcomes of the research process (Bloom & Sawin, 2009). Members of our research team have experience doing sex work. Others have been involved in the sex worker rights movement for years, have experienced poverty, and have navigated judicial and state support systems. Beyond the research team, the structuring of this research project allows for regular and ongoing feedback with POWER's board.

How Are You Compensating Sex Workers for Their Time?

Trying to figure out how to get money into the hands of sex workers during the pandemic considering their exclusion from EI and the CERB sparked this research project. We see our research project as a small resource redistribution mechanism with over 65% of our total budget going towards paying sex workers directly for their time. Participants taking the questionnaire were not required to answer any questions beyond an eligibility question and providing consent. To receive an honorarium, they were directed to a secondary survey in which to input an email address. Our interview participants will also receive their honorarium in advance and may cancel, pause, or stop the interview at any time. We insist that direct payments are a better compensation for marginalized people contributing their time to our research. Much of our remaining budget is used to pay our Research Assistants—one of whom ensures our questionnaire and reports are bilingual. Our remaining funds support the publication costs of the bilingual report. The budget also ensures that any publication outputs, digital launch events, or workshops that come out of the research are paid for by the research grant and require no additional financial inputs from POWER. And finally, the researchers did not receive financial compensation for their work.

How Will You Protect Your Research Participants' Privacy?

Research participants' privacy is key to this project (Wiles et al., 2008). Naming someone as a sex worker without their consent can have deleterious effects on their lives, and may affect their employment, tenancy, childcare or custody arrangements, and access to health care. For these reasons, our questionnaire will not collect any identifying information. Participants' email addresses (collected for the purpose of providing honoraria) are kept separate from the rest of the survey data online and destroyed upon the closure of the survey. For the qualitative interviews, we cannot guarantee anonymity. We do our best to protect our participants' privacy, but given the small research sample, there is always a risk of exposure. Emma and Ryan have sole access to the names of the key informant interviews, which are coded using gender-neutral pseudonyms. No identifying or demographic information will be requested from the interviewees, and we will not name the organizations participants volunteer with as a further step of confidentiality.

The online questionnaire seeks demographic information like age, race, gender identity, disability, and citizenship/migration status, to provide a more sophisticated and disaggregated analysis of our data. We follow an intersectional feminist approach that establishes these axes of difference as key variables in an individual's experiences and perceptions (May, 2015). We understand that collecting this type of data may inadvertently expose sex workers from more marginal groups to scrutiny, and we will exercise caution when performing data analysis along these axes of difference. Our research report will work to dispel stereotypes about sex workers while drawing attention to the intersectional oppressions sex workers navigate.

Who Owns the Research Outputs?

We are clear that academic outputs have limited value to sex working communities, and understand the inaccessibility posed by paywalls required to engage with academic texts. Our community-based report of our findings seeks to engage sex workers and sex worker advocates. The research team will draft the report, solicit input from both POWER's board and our key informant interviewees, and release a final report based on that feedback. The bilingual report will join a digital collection of POWER's previous publications and its Research Repository.

How Generalizable Will Your Findings Be?

Generalizability has been a central preoccupation throughout our research design process. Due to social distancing, curfews, stay-at-home orders, and various levels of lockdown, we require all our research participants to have access to the internet and online banking to be remunerated for their time. We are aware that our research findings will be limited to indoor workers as well as people with a legal status that allows for them to open a Canadian bank account (citizens, permanent residents, international students, and some temporary foreign workers). This means our data set will not likely include many responses from migrant workers and sex workers who are working from street-based economies. This is a limitation of our study.

We also know that street-based sex workers, who are estimated to make up 5–20% of the sex working community, are over-represented in both the media and Canadian scholarship on sex workers (Government of Canada, 2006). We believe co-factors like poverty, being chronically unhoused, substance use disorders, and a lack of compassionate and comprehensive mental health care services for many street-based sex workers take precedence over concerns about tax law and the minutia of EI regulations. In short, indoor-based sex workers will have more to gain from the results of the collaborative report than street-based workers who have their own specific needs.

How Will Your Research Be Mobilized beyond Academia?

The community report will be written in non-academic language and will include graphics to help illustrate key findings. We will also print and mail out 50 reports to key stakeholders across the country. Upon the release of the community report in Fall 2021, our research team will collaborate with POWER's board to organize a press event to share our key findings. We anticipate other events instigated by the findings in our community report, for instance, a tax and accounting workshop explicitly geared towards independent sex workers. Our report may also include consultations between public policy makers and sex worker activists. We are working on these documents with an eye towards leveraging future actions that support sex workers' dignity, integrity, and rights to work free from surveillance, violence, and criminalization.

Conclusion

During the COVID-19 pandemic, a lack of government financial aid for sex workers once again shed light on the marginalization of sex workers from social rights. Yet, the pandemic also revealed the strength, resilience, and compassion of sex worker communities, who rallied together to support those hit by pandemic restrictions. State-sanctioned violence and criminalization of sex workers combined with sensational representations in the media and news cycle has contributed to a near-constant gaze on the sex industry. We believe that it is an ethical imperative for researchers, students, and advocates, interested in sex work to ground their work in a commitment to social change. This includes developing research agendas that reflect the needs of sex workers and including sex workers in the research design. In turn, if sex workers are not the primary beneficiaries of new knowledge about sex work, then the research is not community-based. We have demonstrated how as activist academics we have sought to be liaisons between funding institutions, the academy, and sex workers with the primary purpose to share resources whilst developing data to support urgent policy change. When the next pandemic hits, sex workers must not be forgotten. We hope this chapter will guide future allies, advocates, and academics engaged in the struggle for sex workers' rights.

Notes

1 Our funding was granted by the federally funded Social Science and Humanities Research Council (SSHRC) of Canada. Funding is competitive and available to researchers from graduate school onwards.
2 We use the term "sex work" to delimit the labour performed in the sex industry, including, but not limited to, escorting, erotic masseuse, stripping, camming, and pornographic acting and modelling. Our use of sex work follows the politicization of the term between 1979-80 by sex worker activist Carol Leigh, insisting on sex work not as sexual exploitation, but as sexual labour (Mac & Smith, 2018; Grant, 2014; Leigh, 1998).
3 The Canadian Emergency Response Benefit was announced on March 15, 2020, and closed on December 2, 2020. It provided up to $2,000 every 4 weeks for up to 4 months to individual's whose incomes were impacted by COVID-19.

References

Achou, B., Boisclair, D., D'Astous, P., Fonseca, R., Franca, G., & Michaud, P.-C. (2020). Snapshot of households that received the Canada Emergency Response Benefit and paths for further investigation. *Cirano: Allier savoir et decision.* https://cirano.qc.ca/files/publications/2020PE-30.pdf

Amnesty International Canada. (2020, June 4). *Canada must protect the rights of sex workers during COVID-19 by ensuring access to emergency income supports.* https://www.amnesty.ca/news/canada-must-protect-rights-sex-workers-during-covid-19-ensuring-access-emergency-income

Anderson, S., Jia, J.X., Liu, V., Chattier, J., Krüsi, A., Allan, S., Maher, L., & Shannon, K. (2015). Violence prevention and municipal licensing of indoor sex work venues in the Greater Vancouver Area: Narratives of migrant sex workers, managers and business owners. *Culture, Health & Sexuality, 17*(7), 825–841. https://doi.org/10.1080/13691058.2015.1008046

Belak, B., & Bennett, D. (2016). *Evaluating Canada's sex work laws: The case for repeal.* Pivot Legal Society. https://d3n8a8pro7vhmx.cloudfront.net/pivotlegal/pages/1960/attachments/original/1480910826/PIVOT_Sex_workers_Report_FINAL_hires_ONLINE.pdf?1480910826

Belles, N. (2015). *In our backyard: Human trafficking in America and what we can do to stop it.* Baker Books.

Benoit, C., Smith, M., Magnus, S., Ouellet, N., Atchison, C., Casey, L., Phillips, R., Reimer, B., Reist, D., & Shaver, F.M. (2016). Lack of confidence in police creates a "blue ceiling" for sex workers' safety. *Canadian Public Policy, 42*(4), 456–468.

Bindle, J. (2017). *The pimping of prostitution: Abolishing the sex work myth*. Palgrave MacMillan.

Bloom, L.R., & Sawin, P. (2009). Ethical responsibility in feminist research: Challenging ourselves to do activist research with women in poverty. *International Journal of Qualitative Studies in Education, 22*(3), 333–351.

Bourgeois, R. (2018). Race, space, and prostitution: The making of settler colonial Canada. *Canadian Journal of Women and the Law/Revue Femmes et Droit, 30*(3), 371–397. https://doi.org/10.3138/cjwl.30.3.002

Brock, D. (2009). *Making work, making trouble: Prostitution as a social problem*. University of Toronto Press.

Brooks, S. (2020). Innocent white victims and fallen black girls: Race, sex work, and the limits of anti-sex trafficking laws. *Signs: A Journal of Feminist Philosophy* (Supplement: Feminist Frictions: Sex Work). http://signsjournal.org/feminist-frictions-innocent-white-victims-and-fallen-black-girls/

Bruckert, C. (2002). *Taking it off, putting it on: Women in the strip trade*. Women's Press.

Bruckert, C. (2014). Activist academic whore: Negotiating the fractured otherness abyss. In J.M. Kilty, S.C. Fabian, & M. Felicez-Luna (Eds.), *Demarginalizing voices: Commitment, emotion, and action in qualitative research* (pp. 306–325). UBC Press.

Bruckert, C., & Hannem, S. (2013). Rethinking the prostitution debates: Transcending structural stigma in systemic responses to sex work. *Canadian Journal of Law & Society, 28*(1), 43–63.

Bruckert, C., & Parent, C. (2018). *Getting past the pimp': Management in the sex industry*. University of Toronto Press.

Bryant, T., Aquanno, S., & Raphael, D. (2020). Unequal impact of COVID-19: Emergency neoliberalism and welfare policy in Canada. *Critical Studies: An International and Interdisciplinary Journal, 15*(1), 22–39.

Butterfly (Asian and Migrant Sex Workers Support Network). (2020, May). *How are Asian and migrant workers in spas, holistic centers, massage parlours, and the sex industry affected by the COVID-19 pandemic?* POWER (Prostitutes of Ottawa-Gatineau Work, Educate, Resist). https://www.powerottawa.ca/wp-content/uploads/2020/06/Butterfly-COVID-19-Final-Report_2020_6-pdf.pdf

Canadian Alliance for Sex Work Law Reform. (2020, May 22). *Letter to Minister Maryam Monsef: Emergency income supports for sex workers urgently needed*. https://documents.clcctc.ca/whr/WAC/JointLtr-Monsef-SW-IncomeSupports.pdf

Conrad, R. (Forthcoming). Generated vulnerability: Male sex workers, third-party platforms, and data security. In P. Keilty (Ed.), *Queer data* (n.p.). University of Washington Press.

Durisin, E.M., van der Meulen, E., & Bruckert, C. (Eds.). (2018). *Red light labour: Sex work, regulation, agency, and resistance*. UBC Press.

Fenge, L.A., Oakley, L., Taylor, B., & Beer, S. (2019). The impact of sensitive research on the researcher: Preparedness and positionality. *International Journal of Qualitative Methods, 18*, 1–8. https://1609406919893161.

Ferris, S. (2015). *Street sex work and Canadian cities: Resisting a dangerous order*. University of Alberta Press.

Ferris, S., & Lebovitch, A. (2020). *Sex work activism in Canada: Speaking out, standing up*. ARP Books.

Forgel, C. (2007). Ethical issues in field-based criminological research in Canada. *International Journal of Criminal Justice Sciences, 2*(2), 109–118.

Fox, E., Higgins, H., & Kerry, E. (2020, September 3). *Caregiver needs during COVID-19*. Canadian Science Policy Centre. https://sciencepolicy.ca/posts/caregiver-needs-during-covid-19/

Goodall, Z. (2019). United by the problem, divided by the solution: How the issue of Indigenous women was represented at the deliberations on Canada's Bill C-36. *Canadian Journal of Women and the Law/Revue Femmes et Droit, 31*(2), 232–265.

Government of Canada. (2006, December). *The challenge of change: A study of Canada's criminal laws prostitution laws*. Report of the Subcommittee on Solicitation Laws & Report of the Standing Committee on Justice and Human Rights. House of Commons.

Government of Canada. (2020, March). *COVID-19 benefits and services*. https://www.canada.ca/en/services/benefits/covid19-emergency-benefits.html

Grant, M.G. (2014). *Playing the whore: The work of sex work*. Verso.

Heying, M. (2018). Prostitutes' movements: The fight for workers rights. *Journal of Social History and the History of Social Movements, 9*, 5–12.

Hoefinger, H., Musto, J., Macioti, P.G., Fehrenbacher, A.E., Mai, N., Bennachie, C., & Giametta, C. (2020). Community-based responses to negative health impacts of sexual humanitarian anti-trafficking policies and the criminalization of sex work and migration in the US. *Social Sciences, 9*(1), n.p. https://doi.org/10.3390/socsci9010001

Hunt, S. (2013). Decolonizing sex work: Developing an intersectional Indigenous approach. In E. van der Meulen, E.M. Durisin, & V. Love (Eds.), *Selling sex: Experience, advocacy, and research on sex work in Canada* (pp. 82–100). UBC Press.

Huysamen, M., & Sanders, T. (2021). Institutional ethics challenges to sex work researchers: Committees, communities, and collaboration. *Sociological Research Online*. https://doi.org/10.1177/13607804211002847

Israel, M., & Hay, I. (2012). Research ethics in criminology. In D. Gadd, S. Karstedt, & S.F. Messner (Eds.), *The SAGE handbook of criminological research* (pp. 500–515). SAGE Publications Ltd. http://dx.doi.org/10.4135/9781446268285.n33

Jean-Pierre, J., & Collins, C. (2020, November 12). *COVID-19 effect on Black communities in Quebec*. The Royal Society of Canada. https://rsc-src.ca/en/covid-19/impact-covid-19-in-racialized-communities/covid-19-effect-black-communities-in-quebec

Jeffreys, E. (2010). Sex worker driven research: Best practice ethics. *Dialogue*. http://citeseerx.ist.psu.edu/viewdoc/download?doi=10.1.1.737.5897&rep=rep1&type=pdf

Khan, U. (2015). 'Johns' in the spotlight: Anti-prostitution efforts and the surveillance of clients. *Canadian Journal of Law and Society, 30*(1), 9–30.

Kaye, J. (2017). *Responding to human trafficking: Dispossession, colonial violence, and resistance among Indigenous and racialized women*. University of Toronto Press.

Kelly, L., Regan, L., & Burton, S. (1992). Defending the indefensible? Quantitative methods and feminist research. In H. Hinds, A. Phoenix, & J. Stacey (Eds.), *Working out: New directions for Women's Studies* (pp. 149–160). RoutledgeFalmer.

Kempadoo, K. (Ed.). (2005). *Trafficking and prostitution reconsidered: New perspectives on migrations, sex work, and human rights*. Paradigm Publishers.

Lam, E. (2016). Inspection, policing, and racism: How municipal by-laws endanger the lives of Chinese sex workers in Toronto. *Canadian Review of Social Policy/Revue Canadienne de politique sociale, 75*, 87–112.

Lam, E. (2020). Pandemic sex workers' resilience: COVID-19 crisis met by rapid responses by sex worker communities. *International Social Work, 6.3*(6), 777–781.

Law, T. (2015). Licensed or licentious? Examining regulatory discussions of stripping in Ontario. *Canadian Journal of Law & Society, 30*(1), 31–50.

Lazarus, L., Deering, K.N., Nabess, R., Gibson, K., Tyndall, M.W., & Shannon, K. (2012). Occupational stigma as a primary barrier to health care for street-based sex workers in Canada. *Culture, Health & Sexuality, 14*(2), 139–150.

Leigh, C. (1998). Inventing sex work. In J. Nagle (Ed.), *Whores and other feminists* (pp. 225–231). Routledge

Lepp, A. (2017). Collateral damage: Anti-trafficking campaigns, border security, and sex workers' rights struggles in Canada. In P. Gentile, G.W. Kinsman, & P.L. Rankin (Eds.), *We still demand! Redefining resistance in sex and gender struggles* (pp. 222–249). UBC Press.

Lewis, J. (2020). Sex workers are criminalized and left without government support during the coronavirus pandemic. *The Conversation.* https://theconversation.com/sex-workers-are-criminalized-and-left-without-government-support-during-the-coronavirus-pandemic-141746

Lewis, J., & Maticka-Tyndale, E. (2000). Licensing sex work: Public policy and women's lives. *Canadian Public Policy, 26,* 437–449. https://doi.org/10.2307/3552610

Liamputtong, P. (2007). *Researching the vulnerable.* Sage Press.

Logan, T.D. (2017). *Economics, sexuality, and male sex work.* Cambridge University Press.

Lowman, J. (2004). Reconvening the federal committee on prostitution law reform. *CMAJ: Canadian Medical Association Journal/journal de l'association medicale canadiene, 171,* 147–148.

Lowman, J. (2000). Violence and the outlaw status of (street) prostitution in Canada. *Violence Against Women, 6*(9), 987–1011.

Lowthers, M., Sabat, M., Durisin, E.M., & Kempadoo, K. (2017). A sex work research symposium: Examining positionality in documenting sex work and sex workers' rights. *Social Sciences, 6*(2), 39–45. https://doi.org/10.3390/socsci6020039

Mac, J., & Smith, M. (2018) *Revolting Prostitutes: The fight for sex workers rights.* Verso.

Maggie's. (2021). *A note for researchers, academics, artists, and reporters.* https://www.maggiesto.org/research

May, V.M. (2015). *Pursuing intersectionality: Unsettling dominant imaginaries.* Routledge.

Maynard, R. (2015). Fighting wrongs with wrongs: How Canadian anti-trafficking crusades have failed sex workers, migrants, and Indigenous communities. *Atlantis, 37*(2), 40–56.

Maynard, R. (2017). *Policing black lives: State violence in Canada from slavery to the present.* Fernwood Publishing.

McKenna, E. (Forthcoming). An assumption of shared fear: Feminism, sex work, and the sex wars in 1980's Kinesis. In C. Gidney, L. Campbell, & M. Dawson (Eds.), *Activism and affect: Second-wave feminism and the history of emotions* (n.p.). UBC Press.

McKenna, E. (2021). The white-painters of Cabbagetown: Neighborhood policing and sex worker resistance in Toronto, 1986–1987. *Sexualities.* https://doi.org/10.1177/13634607211028500

Olshansky, E.F., & Zender, R. (2016). The use of community-based participatory research to understand and work with vulnerable populations. In M. de Chesnay & B. Anderson (Eds.), *Caring for the vulnerable: Perspectives in nursing theory, practice, and research* (pp. 243–252). Jones & Bartlett Learning.

Ontario Human Rights Commission. (2020, April 30). *OHRC statement: Demographic data necessary to fight COVID-19.* http://www.ohrc.on.ca/en/news_centre/ohrc-statement-demographic-data-necessary-fight-covid-19

Palys, T., & Lowman, J. (2014). *Protecting research confidentiality: What happens when law and ethics collide.* Lorimer & Company.

Parent, C., Bruckert, C., Corriveau, P., Mensah, M.N., & Toupin, L. (2013). *Sex work: Rethinking the job, respecting the workers.* UBC Press.

Platt, L., Elmes, J., Stevenson, L., Holt, V., Rolles, S., & Stuart, R. (2020, May 15). Sex workers must not be forgotten in the COVID-19 response. *The Lancet.* https://www.thelancet.com/journals/lancet/article/PIIS0140-6736(20)31033-3/fulltext

Petit, G., & Tedds, L.M. (2020). The effect of differences in the treatment of the Canada Emergency Response Benefit across provincial and territorial income assistance programs. *Canadian Public Policy, 46*(Supplement 1), S29–S43. https://doi.org/10.3138/cpp.2020-054

Pettinicchio, D., Maroto, M., & Lukk, M. (2021). Perceptions of Canadian federal policy responses to COVID-19 among people with disabilities and chronic health conditions. *Canadian Public Policy* (Forthcoming). https://doi.org/10.3138/cpp.2021-012

Public Health Ontario. (2020, May 14). *Enhanced epidemiological summary: COVID-19 in Ontario: A focus on diversity.* https://www.publichealthontario.ca/-/media/documents/ncov/epi/2020/06/covid-19-epi-diversity.pdf?la=en

Rancic, M. (2020, May 8). *Can sex workers count on government support during COVID-19?* TVO. https://www.tvo.org/article/can-sex-workers-count-on-government-support-during-covid-19

Reinharz, S. (1993). Neglected voices and excessive demands in feminist research. *Qualitative Sociology, 16*(1), 69–76.

Robson, J. (2020). Radical incrementalism and trust in the system: Income security in Canada in the time of COVID-19. *Canadian Public Policy 46*(Supplement 1), S1–S18. https://doi.org/10.3138/cpp.2020-080

Sanders, T. (2006). Sexing up the subject: Methodological nuances in researching the female sex industry. *Sexualities, 9*(4), 449–468. https://doi.org/10.1177/1363460706068044

Shaver, F., Lewis, J., & Maticka-Tyndale, E. (2011). Rising to the challenge: Addressing the concerns of people working in the sex industry. *Canadian Review of Sociology/Revue Canadienne de Sociologie, 48*, 47–65. https://doi.org/10.1111/j.1755-618X.2011.01249.x

Smith, M., & Mac, J. (2018). *Revolting prostitutes: The fight for sex workers' rights.* Verso.

Spade, D. (2020). Solidarity not charity: Mutual aid for mobilization and survival. *Social Text, 38*(1), 131–151.

Sterling, A., & van der Meulen, E. (2018). 'We are not criminals': Sex work clients in Canada and the constitution of risk knowledge. *Canadian Journal of Law and Society/La Revue Canadienne Droit et Société, 33*(3), 291–308.

UNAIDS. (2020, April 8). *Sex workers must not be left behind in the response to COVID-19.* www.unaids.org/en/resources/presscentre/pressreleaseandstatementarchive/2020/april/20200408_sex-workers-covid-19

Valverde, M. (2018). Canadian feminism and sex work law: A cautionary tale. In E.M. Durisin, E. van der Meulen, & C. Bruckert (Eds.), *Red light labour: Sex work, regulation, agency, and resistance* (pp. 247–255). UBC Press.

Wiles, R., Crow, G., Health, S., & Charles, V. (2008). The management of confidentiality and anonymity in social research. *International Journal of Social Research Methodology, 11*(5), 417–428.

Zajacova, A., Jehn, A., Stackhouse, M., Choi, K., Denice, P., Haan, M., & Ramos, H. (2020). Mental health and economic concerns from March to May during the COVID-19 pandemic in Canada. *SocArXiv Papers,* 1–26. https://10.31235/osf.io/76me2

Zhang, S.X. (2009). Beyond the 'Natasha' story: A review and critique of current research on sex trafficking. *Global Crime 10*(3), 178–195. https://doi.org/10.1080/17440570903079899

Legislation

Bill C-36, Protection of Communities and Exploited Persons Act (S.C. 2014, c. 25)

3
RESEARCHER DON'T TEACH ME NONSENSE

Engaging African Decolonial Practices in a Critical Mathematics Education Project

Oyemolade Osibodu

> *So, it's not just like a research as research but it actually has a personal impact on me personally.*
> *– Mendrika*

> *Like, I want to thank you Molade for teaching us, for showing us that research can be done, it can be done in whatever way you choose… Like at least me who wants to go to the public sector and you kind of have to do some type of research…I want to actually involve people in what they are being researched about and I don't want to only treat people like subjects… I know there's a lot of work to do still, but yeah, I just wanted to point that out that the method is not, I've never seen this before. I've done one research project … but it was very individualized.*
> *– Sanyu*

I open this chapter with words from Mendrika and Sanyu, two of the African youth I collaborated with on a project centred on understanding how Sub-Saharan African (SSA) youth conceptualize critical mathematics education. As a Black Nigerian critical mathematics scholar, I wanted to conduct research in a manner that was affirming to the SSA youth I partnered with. This led me to create and develop the Fela Anikulapo-Kuti Music (FAM) methodology (Osibodu, 2020). Though I unpack FAM later, briefly, it is a methodology rooted in a commitment to co-learning with research collaborators, disrupting the status quo, and seeking joy in the research process. Weaving FAM with the Ghanaian philosophy Sankofa (reaching to the past to look to the present and future) and the South African humanist philosophy Ubuntu (uplifting and centring the collective) disrupted the colonial legacy of research[1] (Chilisa, 2011; Paris, 2019; Smith, 1999; Tuck, 2009; Tuck & Yang, 2014) and fostered ethical, collaborative facilitation. I reflect on two key learnings that reinforced my stance towards ethical facilitation to show my journey along this path.

DOI: 10.4324/9781003199236-5

During my graduate studies, I was introduced to scholars who challenged "damage-centered" research and advocated for "desire-based" or "Strength-based" framings of marginalized communities (Paris & Winn, 2014; Thurber et al., 2020; Tuck, 2009; Tuck & Yang, 2014; Wandera, 2019). These scholars push beyond normative Western[2] views of research that prioritize extracting data from participants and communities and move toward one that views participants as collaborators and knowledge producers.

My methods are also informed by the work of Valerie Kinloch whose approach to co-creation sits at the heart of FAM. In a project that examined youth's experiences with gentrification, race, and literacy, a participant, Phil, challenged her to share her thoughts on gentrification in Harlem, to which she responded, "you don't know what I think?" (Kinloch & San Pedro, 2014, p. 37). Phil responded, "I know what you think about it, but I'd like to hear you say it. Put words to it" (p. 37). This conversation is indicative of Phil's attempt to break down the power differential between researcher and participant—disrupting who asks and who answers questions.

These experiences led me to develop and implement decolonizing methodologies (Chilisa, 2011; Smith, 1999; Tuck & Yang, 2012) that shift focus away from Western approaches to value voices beyond mainstream academia (Patel, 2015). Decolonizing methodologies draw from decoloniality as a relational approach to engaging research that centres the worldviews of the colonized Other (Chilisa, 2011; Patel, 2015; Smith, 1999; Wilson, 2008). In other words, decolonizing methodologies foreground and elevate multiple knowledges, including African Indigenous knowledges (AIK) (i.e., Dei, 2012). Chilisa (2011) states, "decolonization is thus a process of conducting research in such a way that the worldviews of those who have suffered a long history of oppression and marginalization are given space to communicate from their frames of reference" (p. 14). A decolonizing approach to research provides the space for participants to heal, transform, and determine meaning from within their respective contexts and communities (Smith, 1999).

In listening to Fela Anikulapo Kuti's (1986) song "Teacher, Don't Teach Me Nonsense" (TDTMN), I was struck by the song's parallels to decolonizing research. Specifically, Fela frames the west as the "teacher" and SSA countries as the "student," wherein there exists an uneven and imbalanced relationship (Fagbayibo, 2019). Some research approaches replicate this unequal and predatory relationship, which I disrupt in this study through the FAM methodology (Osibodu, 2020). FAM enabled me to develop a relational three-pronged definition of what ethical facilitation means for me as a researcher working with SSA youth. I suggest that mutual learning (i.e., co-learning) in research processes disrupts Western research and allows participants and researchers to experience joy in the work. In this chapter, I draw on excerpts from a previous study (Osibodu, 2020) while reflecting on the tensions that arose during the process. I begin by explaining FAM, Ubuntu, and Sankofa through a discussion on how they helped me stay rooted in my commitment towards ethical facilitation.

Fela Anikulapo-Kuti Music Methodology

Fela Anikulapo-Kuti was an activist who used music as a tool for social change in Nigeria and throughout the African diaspora (Fagbayibo, 2019; Hari, 2014). Fela spoke against the Nigerian government's corruption while broadly upholding the message of pan-Africanism. As Fagbayibo (2019) has explored, Fela was inspired by Black revolutionaries in Africa and its diaspora including Sandra Smith, James Baldwin, Kwame Nkrumah, and Steve Biko. Although Fela's work has been categorized as anti-feminist; for the purposes of this research, I emphasize his focus on pan-Africanism to create a more inclusive understanding of the power within research facilitation (one that also includes the knowledge and expertise of Black African women such as Fela's activist mother, Funmilayo Ransome-Kuti).

Anikulapo-Kuti's (1986) TDTMN speaks to a desire for teachers to be explicit in sharing their evolving understandings of issues of (in)justice in their communities with students. As a result, TDTMN speaks to the value of co-learning with students and disrupting oppressive hierarchies. Using critical discourse analysis (Rogers, 2011), I analyzed TDTMN by asking how Fela's music disrupts power relationships and Western ideals, while inviting researchers to stop sharing *nonsense*[3] knowledge (e.g., the assumption that any ideas that are not British or Western are inferior). Fela challenges us to turn away from the white man's gaze and instead value and uphold AIK (Dei, 2012; Wandera, 2019)—in this case, African decolonial practices. Fela once stated he uses his music as a weapon to create change and TDTMN, like other Black music, incites "collaborative rebellion" (McKittrick, 2021, p. 167). When transposed into research contexts, the tenets of FAM become co-learning, disruption, and making space for joy, even when discussing tough social issues. Colloquially, I called our weekly sessions and WhatsApp group "FAM," as it also gestures to family.

Bridging FAM with Sankofa and Ubuntu

FAM is undergirded by the South African philosophy of Ubuntu and the Ghanaian philosophy of Sankofa. Ubuntu is a humanist perspective rooted in African thought that empowers us to shift from *I* to *we*. Archbishop Desmond Tutu (1999) has further explained, "It is not, 'I think therefore I am.' It says rather: 'I am human because I belong. I participate, I share'" (p. 31). Ubuntu is "borne out of the philosophy that community strength comes of community support, and that dignity and identity are achieved through mutualism, empathy, generosity and community commitment" (Swanson, 2007, p. 55). Ubuntu was central to my study as we were constantly reminded that each of us were valued, and this manifested in the ways we took turns facilitating the study (see Vignette 2). Ubuntu ensured we recognized the connections between the political, cultural, social, and environmental in the study (Swanson, 2007). Additionally, through Ubuntu, we recognized our understanding was dependent on the support we received from each other.

Sankofa comes from the Twi people of Ghana and roughly translates to going back to retrieve what was lost (Dei, 2012; Temple, 2010; Watson & Knight-Manuel, 2017). Invoking Sankofa in FAM enabled us to examine what was *lost* in our prior mathematics learning as we prepared to study the social issues at the heart of this study. Sankofa thus allowed us to *go back* to our various African contexts in considering, questioning, critiquing, and seeking truths. Given this, Sankofa is an act of decolonization that makes possible the disruption of false narratives, which helped us begin a journey of healing "without thinking of ourselves as damaged" (Tuck, 2009, p. 415). Sankofa was instrumental to the facilitation process because we centred the voices of our elders and ancestors in the work we were doing as a collective.

The Research Context

To ground my practice in conducting ethical facilitation, I draw on my study (Osibodu, 2020) situated within the Critical Mathematics Education (CME) landscape. CME scholars begin from the premise that mathematics is not a neutral subject—that it is a political enterprise (Martin, Gholson, & Leonard, 2010; Osibodu, 2021). CME uses mathematics to challenge social injustices in communities (Bullock, 2018; Gutstein, 2016; Kokka, 2018). While it has typically been conducted within school contexts in the United States by weaving mathematics with community knowledge (Gutstein, 2016; Osibodu, 2021), research in CME with SSA youth has begun to take shape (Osibodu & Cosby, 2018; Osibodu, 2020). Recognizing that CME is not a concept that originated from an African context, I sought to interrogate to what extent it applies to an African context, understanding that "concepts come with their own cultural and philosophical baggage" (Oyewùmí, 1997, p. xi). I wanted to understand how the youth used mathematics to understand social issues related to the African continent.

I knew I wanted to work with a diverse group of young Africans. In 2019, I worked in partnership with SSA youth[4] who self-identified as four young women (Mendrika,[5] Manyoni, Njo, and Sanyu) and one young man (Soro). The youth came from The Gambia, Zimbabwe, Madagascar, Uganda, and Cote d'Ivoire. As previous CME work has been done in formal schools (e.g., Brantlinger, 2013; Brelias, 2015; Gutstein, 2016; Raygoza, 2016) and resulted in conflict between social justice goals and mathematics goals, I chose to eliminate this barrier by conducting the study beyond a formal mathematics classroom. Though we were physically located in the mid-Western U.S., our work was centred almost entirely on Sub-Saharan Africa. I did not focus on the impact of Afro-diasporic belonging, as each of the youth still identified with their SSA countries and had temporarily relocated to the U.S. for their studies.

CME research largely has not documented the power dynamics between researchers (often teacher-researchers) and student-participants (Osibodu, 2021). In designing my study, I was clear in my commitment to decolonizing approaches to research and did not design the study with the assumption that mathematics was the only way to understand a social issue. I wanted to co-create a space that envisioned CME in an African context based on their experiences.

Prior to the official start of the study, I met with the five collaborators—a term I am intentional in using as opposed to participants—because I wanted them to have active roles in building the study *with* me. At our meeting, I shared the concepts of FAM, Sankofa, and Ubuntu along with my rationale, the project's timeline and asked for their feedback. Mendrika immediately noted the proposed deadline of two months for data generation might not be sufficient and suggested we plan for four months. We incorporated this change as a step towards relational, ethical facilitation. The youth suggested we meet once more to schedule the research prior to our official start. I highlight these examples to demonstrate how we co-facilitated the study before the research began.

Through ethical facilitation as co-learning, we were able to imagine CME in the Sub-Saharan African context as a construct to connect to AIK. Importantly, the youth collaborators conceived another important aspect of CME as emphasizing cognitive justice to redress the loss of AIK (Abdi, 2002; Dei, 2012; Ndlovu-Gatsheni, 2015, 2018; Shizha, 2013; Wane, 2009). In the next section, I discuss my positionality in this work.

Bringing My Whole Self into This Research

We bring our whole selves into our projects and cannot separate the "researcher" self from the other facets of our identities (Wane, 2008). As a Black, Nigerian, and African woman, these identities served as a bridge into the research and were reflected in the epistemologies and methodologies embedded in this work. My previous experience using the Cambridge Assessment International Examination (CAIE) curriculum to teach mathematics at the pan-African institution African Leadership Academy (ALA) in Johannesburg, South Africa also informed my inquiry. Using CAIE seemed counter to ALA's mission of *developing the future generation of African leaders*, leading me to wonder about the role of mathematics in effecting positive change in African communities.

ALA seeks to create a generation of transformative young African leaders, yet ALA used the CAIE, which is a Western, colonial curriculum (Osibodu, under review). I often wondered where mathematics fit in engendering this mission. I saw students having thought-provoking discussions about how to positively impact Africa in their African studies and entrepreneurial leadership courses and wished I could do the same in my mathematics classes, but I did not know how to do so. This led me back to the U.S., where I studied mathematics (along with other knowledges) to understand social issues and consider ways to seek justice in society.

In mathematics education, I was enthralled by CME (Osibodu, 2021)—exploring (in)justice using mathematics to make sense of structural inequities.

Yet, much of the work I read seemed to take place in the U.S. and Europe. I began to wonder:

> What did CME look like with African students? Did teachers share their journeys in coming to learn about and take a stand for justice with students? Could people use mathematics to make sense of their realities and lives? What other lenses and knowledges might be brought into the classroom, particularly those lenses and knowledges that are often under-appreciated or unrecognized in academic contexts?

These questions drove me to facilitate a project focused on mathematics and social justice. As a Nigerian scholar deeply invested in a socially-just world with emphasis on Black Africans, I was uninterested in drawing on methods that reaffirmed white supremacy. I committed to desire-based methods (Tuck, 2009) and unshackled myself from colonial lenses as much as I could through the process of learning with the SSA youth collaborators. My goal was to understand their views on (in)justice and see whether they thought mathematics had a role to play in the quest for freedom. Taking up this lens meant decentralizing mathematics—a radical move given my doctorate in mathematics education. Instead, I realized that, in decolonizing approaches to research, it was imperative to elevate the voices of the colonized Other (Chilisa, 2011).

Ethical Facilitation in Action

In this section, I share three short vignettes to illustrate how I wove ethical facilitation throughout the research process. I envisioned ethical facilitation as a practice wherein mutual learning or co-learning occurs, there is an intentionality in disrupting traditional research roles and emphasis on creating room for joy in the process.

Vignette 1: Facilitation as Co-learning

MANYONI: *Uhm, but like you know, how we['re] getting into such deep conversation over just pictures? What if we actually instead of having something written or whatever, have a series of videos where we talk about these issues? Because I feel like we started talking and we were getting really into it. So, if we had more time and you pick on other issues, we could talk about some really, really, really deep social issues. So, I think a video, like you know how you take like you record this. We have a series of those. Like, it doesn't have to be like 'oh, today we're talking about this,' you could just, you know, the way you just threw in that question, like pick a picture to come to next week [and] throw another question and we [are] allowed to just get into it and just get deep about it.*

In this vignette, I highlight how my modeling of facilitation as shared mutual learning prompted one of the youth collaborators, Manyoni, to propose a specific format for the next phase of our research. Manyoni saw value in how each member of the research team was seen as an expert. Manyoni asserted that sharing this responsibility of facilitation, wherein each person discussed their individual stories, allowed us to delve deeper into a variety of social issues.

Drawing on FAM and Ubuntu, I was committed to the goal of ethical facilitation as co-learning and wanted to do research *with* my collaborators. I was transparent in sharing the theoretical and methodological approaches driving this work because I wanted collaborators to be part of the research as much as possible (See also: Kinloch & San Pedro, 2014). I wanted collaborators to hear my reflections *during* the work instead of saving them for publications they might never read. Because Sankofa was a core component of this work, the first phase of our time together was spent reflecting on previous experiences.

In our first session, I asked collaborators to find an image that represents what Africa means to each of them. We all uploaded our images on a shared Google document and discussed why we picked them. In some instances, we added stories to pictures. I propose that the first component of ethical facilitation is recognizing facilitation as a form of co-learning. Accordingly, the themes that emerged from this activity included the role of women in African society, elder knowledge, the impact of Western colonization in Africa, the role of community in African society, African ingenuity and creativity, and pan-Africanism. This activity allowed us to listen deeply and build relationships based on the ethos of Ubuntu. It also set the tone for our collaboration because each member of the collective added to the fabric of our storying. These themes guided much of the work we took up in the space. For instance, because the role of elder knowledge resonated with everyone in the group, it became a touchstone throughout the project as we engaged elders in our communities in the participatory action research we embarked on at a later stage. The centring of community in this way was represented with a picture of a Baobab tree[6] and this theme of trees and herbs became core to our findings. Manyoni's vignette resonated with and highlighted value in the co-learning-in-the-moment we had established with our initial activity. This vignette thus shows the affordances of researcher transparency in negotiating power in a CME project.

Vignette 2: Facilitation as Disruption

MOLADE: *Maybe a good way to go about this is to discuss what is it that we want to...*
SANYU: *Disrupt*
NJO: *Does anyone remember an experience with the public health department in their country?*
SANYU: *To me, is like what I'm trying to disrupt is the idea that Western medicine is God. You know what I mean? To use local, homemade things that actually have never failed to work. I've never had someone say, 'oh they gave me this and it didn't work,' or 'I felt worse,' and make it public. So like, it's an African medicine, to make African medicine public.*

Co-learning in FAM is, in itself, an act of disruption, as it positioned me and the youth collaborators as equal contributors to the project. In TDTMN, Fela evoked themes of disruption throughout his song. This pushed me to stress disruption by rejecting reliance on "Oyinbo people," the Nigerian pidgin for white people, which he states explicitly in TDTMN. The song rejects reliance on colonizers using the Nigerian governmental system. In his view, democracy—which he termed "demo-crazy"—is a Western construct from Oyinbo people and therefore should not be seen as a model for Nigerian (and other African) countries.

I was transparent in my explorations with the youth of the different African frameworks I wanted to honor in our work together. Before unpacking the second vignette, it is important to explain what led to this conversation. After engaging Sankofa, we went on to outline several social issues to explore together. We discussed each issue and narrowed the list down to public health. In the first line of the vignette, I was about to ask the group what we specifically intended to disrupt, but before I could, Sanyu immediately said "disrupt." Further, another collaborator, Njo, took charge of the conversation by asking if anyone had any experiences with public health in their communities. After a spirited conversation, Sanyu returns, specifying that, through our research, she hoped to disrupt the notion that traditional medicines are subpar and undervalued.

The second component of ethical facilitation is disrupting the roles in academic research. Facilitation as disruption puts greater emphasis on the epistemologies, theories, and methodologies that arise from one's own communities and those that unearth the narratives we have all been told over time. Returning to TDTMN, I assert that Fela rejected whiteness in a later part of the song, singing, "the white man is teaching us, but they live in Europe. The white men have taught us many things, but I refuse to copy the ways of the white man, so we don't think that the white man has advanced beyond us" (Anikulapo-Kuti, 1986). Fela can be seen as corroborating Lorde's (1984) claim that "the master's tools will never dismantle the master's house" (p. 111). Disruption in facilitation helped me reframe how I asked my research questions. I wanted to learn how they used mathematics and to explore what other knowledge bases they drew on. This approach to facilitation enabled me to identify the multiple ways youth were drawing on the AIK systems as I highlight in the third vignette.

Vignette 3: Facilitation Leading to Joy

NJO: *So, I think it was all [a] planned matter of sort of. Extracting that part of us without us knowing what was going on. From kindergarten, you start knowing there's a subject called mathematics but I'm just realizing this! Like, in your own life, like from childhood till the time you start going to school, you've already been learning math in home.*

Like, if students were introduced to maths using those things telling them like, 'yea, you're actually doing this, you're actually doing all this,' I think that would have boost the desire for people to know this maths they are doing in school and that might even increase their own maths that they already know.

> So that's just a realization I'm getting because I never liked maths in school but I never knew that I already knews maths in my own way!"

While catching Sanyu up on a session she had missed, she suddenly stated, "there's a saying that, wherever you see a right-angle, a white man has been there." Sanyu continued, "So like houses, the way we used to build our houses, well I wasn't there, but it's said they used to be circular, round. But as soon as the British came, they became right-angled." We wondered about her comment but quickly moved on to brainstorming social issues we might want to examine. After the session, I could not stop thinking about her comment because Sanyu was unintentionally in conversation with CME scholars who contest the neutrality of mathematics and instead work to reveal its Eurocentricity (e.g., Martin, Gholson, & Leonard, 2010). Patel (2015) stresses that, "pausing is useful, even necessary, particularly in these modern times in which colonial projects have shaped ... deadlines, all competing for our attention" (p. 1).

Catalyzed by Sanyu's comment, I wrote on the FAM WhatsApp group, asking everyone to bring an artifact from their home countries to our next session. I made this decision because of Sanyu's comment that associated the right-angle, a mathematical term and concept, with white people. Building again from my ethos as a co-learner with the team, I wanted to unpack AIK and highlight the embedded mathematics that exists in our communities. This move pivoted the initial goals of the study and process became a space for healing and transformation (Chilisa, 2011; Smith, 1999). Much of what we engaged with in this vignette can be categorized as ethnomathematics, or the mathematics practiced by identifiable cultural groups (D'Ambrosio, 1985). Ethnomathematics is similar to research focused on Indigenous ways of knowing as a means for de-Europeanizing and decolonizing mathematics (e.g., Lipka et al., 2005; Meaney et al., 2013; Nicol et al., 2020), but with notable exceptions. In particular, mathematics research on Indigenous ways of knowing is often conducted by members of the communities, whereas ethnomathematics research has often been conducted by Europeans with the goal of "uncovering" mathematics in non-Western societies.

There have been critiques of ethnomathematics in theory and in practice including how it has objectified the Other (Pais, 2011; Wolfmeyer, 2017) and the difficulty in applying it to school mathematics (Vithal & Skovsmose, 1997). Like Paris (2019), I wondered what ethnomathematics might offer "beyond the white gaze" (p. 218). Eliminating the white gaze (TheAncestorsGift, 2012) in our inquiry enabled us to find an immense amount of joy as we recognized the depth of knowledge in our communities. Dei (2012) asserted that "African scholarship, research and knowledge production must help us to recover and reclaim ourselves, our knowledges and our voices" (p. 105) because "Indigenous cultural knowledge is about searching for wholeness and completeness" (p. 112). Thus, this activity depended on African Indigenous ways of knowing that to us had only been apparent in school mathematics.

The third aspect of ethical facilitation involves making space for joy to exist. We rarely consider the role of joy in the research itself. Yet, joy shows up when facilitation practices encourage research collaborators to be their full selves. As Njo spoke the words featured in this vignette, she was beaming with joy. I see Black joy as radical—highlighting the possibilities of living freely beyond the confines of white supremacy. Because I listened to Sanyu's right-angle comment, I was able to support the youth collaborators in an activity that foregrounded African ways of knowing. In the third vignette, Njo showed how these practices enabled her to exude this moment of joyful realization in the rich mathematical practices of her community.

Lessons Learned in Ethical Facilitation

Ethics as a Continuous Process

Often in research, there is an assumption that obtaining ethics approval from the relevant bodies is a static process. In considering ethical facilitation, especially in work built around social justice, it was imperative for me to check in with my collaborators to obtain continuous consent. I was purposeful in revisiting consent throughout the study because I recognized that a decolonizing approach to research means consent is not requested once but is ongoing as situations evolve. It was essential for me to connect with the collaborators on their comfort levels throughout the facilitation process. This meant that, when I noticed how tired they were from the semester, we paused our official plans for the session and just chatted about life. At our last FAM session, Mendrika thanked everyone for our "wonderful group," while Sanyu shared that this work had shown her a different way research could be done. Sanyu stated, "I feel like looking back propelled us forward…everything we have done so far has come from looking back." Sanyu's reflection fully embodied the significance of the Adinkra symbol for Sankofa shown in Figure 3.1 below.

This would not have been possible had I not stayed committed to mutual learning, disrupting traditional roles within the research, and centring joy in the process.

Comfort with Discomfort

Methodological fluidity recognizes movement and curiosity as essential to making space for surprising findings in research (Koro-Ljungberg, 2012; McKittrick, 2021). To foster new conclusions in research, I committed to elevating the youth's voices in zigzag routes rather than linear ones. Methodological fluidity privileges vulnerability in the discomfort of this zigzag process. I chose to share these discomforts when I felt unsure whether there would be a sense of cohesion between engaging Sankofa and the exploration of the social issues. Nevertheless, I trusted the African frameworks guiding this work and believed the connections would

FIGURE 3.1 Adinkra symbol for Sankofa.

become evident as we went along. I was trying to learn to live in the discomfort this generated, and asked the collaborators to join me in this journey even as they experienced their own apprehensions regarding the direction of our project. Because we stayed committed to trusting one another, our collective meaning-making moved CME towards a more collaborative, relational process that created space for us to apply CME to our SSA context.

Conclusion

Almost a year after starting our work together, we met as a group to check in with one another and I shared updates about the writing of our research. Njo shared that, because of our research, she had organized a clinic day in her community over the 2019 summer break. She noted that she had asked the village leaders why they were now open to manufactured medicines and was surprised to hear their answer. The village leaders shared that, due to climate change and the loss of trees, they no longer had access to the traditional herbs they were accustomed to. Furthermore, there was a loss of AIK around the types of traditional medicines for different ailments due to a lack of documentation. It was powerful to see that the ideas we discussed still resonated long after our formal collaboration ended.

Using the three vignettes, I have shown how collaborative ethical facilitation is a method of valuing co-learning, disrupting the Western approach to research, and finding space for joy to emerge in the process. In considering the role of decolonizing methodologies in ethical facilitation, I am grateful the youth and I were able to unpack some of the harms done in mathematics, recognize our shared commitment to the African continent, and consider how to highlight Africa's strengths within and beyond mathematics. Our dedication to learning together was crucial, as it allowed new understandings to emerge. The shift towards African Indigenous ways of knowing was not planned but opened new possibilities that ultimately anchored the work. Specifically, I rejected the "researcher-as-colonizer" paradigm and shifted toward a "researcher-as-collaborator" paradigm, which led the youth to take up the work as *ours*. Despite this shift, I still recognize the inherent power hierarchies and tensions that are difficult to fully flatten (Osibodu et al., under review). Engaging ethical facilitation with decolonial African practices allowed for a reframing of CME that was applicable to the SSA context. Through ethical facilitation, I did not *teach nonsense* but instead, through our collective voices, we were able to imagine new possibilities together.

Acknowledgments

I thank the five youth collaborators for their time and commitment to learning together in this research. I thank Kate Firestone for suggestions on improving the clarity of the writing. Finally, I thank Christopher Dubbs, Natalia Balyasnikova, Erika Bullock, and the editors for their thoughtful feedback and insights on earlier drafts of this chapter.

Notes

1 Colonial research embodies what Tuck (2009) has described as *damage-centered* research in that it functions to erase and reduce participants using a framework based in whiteness.
2 I am using the lowercase form of western because it is my goal to decenter western framings and instead uphold Other ways of knowing.
3 See also Chimamanda Ngozi Adichie's TED talk "The danger of a single story," Burna Boy's song "Monsters you made," and Binyavanga Wainaina's "How to write about Africa."
4 I refer to co-researchers as "youth" and not "students" because positioning them as students implies I am their teacher—a dichotomy I did my best to disrupt. Moreover, the African Union (2006) defines youth as those ranging from 15–35 and all five co-researchers fit the classification of youth in the African context.
5 All names are pseudonyms
6 The Baobab tree is commonly referred to as the tree of life given the range of resources it provides to communities, and due to its longevity. Moreover, this magnificent tree is the national tree of Madagascar, Mendrika's home country. For more on the role of trees in African communities, read Motswana poet Kenneth Maswabi's (2016) poem.

References

Abdi, A.A. (2002). *Culture, education, and development in South Africa: Historical and contemporary perspectives.* Bergin & Garvey.

Anikulapo-Kuti, F. (1986). Teacher don't teach me nonsense [Song]. *On teacher don't teach me nonsense* [Album]. Mercury.

African Union (AU). (2006). *African youth charter.* United Nations. https://www.un.org/en/africa/osaa/pdf/au/african_youth_charter_2006.pdf

Brantlinger, A. (2013). Between politics and equations: Teaching critical mathematics in a remedial secondary classroom. *American Educational Research Journal, 50*(5), 1050–1080.

Brelias, A. (2015). Mathematics for what? High school students reflect on mathematics as a tool for social inquiry. *Democra, 23*(4), 1–11.

Bullock, E.C. (2018). Intersectional analysis in critical mathematics education research: A response to figure hiding. *Review of Research in Education, 42*(1), 122–145. https://doi.org/10.3102%2F0091732X18759039

Chilisa, B. (2011). *Indigenous research methodologies.* Sage Publications.

D'Ambrosio, U. (1985). Ethnomathematics and its place in the history and pedagogy of Mathematics. *For the Learning of Mathematics, 5,* 44–48.

Dei, G.S. (2012). Indigenous anti-colonial knowledge as 'heritage knowledge' for promoting Black/African education in diasporic contexts. *Decolonization: Indigeneity, Education & Society, 1*(1), 102–119.

Fagbayibo, B. (2019). Critical pedagogy of international legal education in Africa: An exploration of Fela Anikulapo-Kuti's music. In R. Adeola, M. Nyarko, A. Okeowo, & F. Viljoen (Eds.), *The art of human rights: Commingling art, human rights and the law in Africa* (pp. 7–22). Springer. https://doi.org/10.1007/978-3-030-30102-6_2

Gutstein, E. (2016). "Our issues, our people—Math as our weapon": Critical mathematics in a Chicago neighborhood high school. *Journal for Research in Mathematics Education, 47*(5), 454–504. https://doi.org/10.5951/jresematheduc.47.5.0454

Hari, S.I. (2014). The evolution of social protest in Nigeria: The role of social media in the "#OccupyNigeria" protest. *International Journal of Humanities and Social Science Invention, 3*(9), 33–39.

Kinloch, V., & San Pedro, T. (2014). The space between listening and storying: Foundations for projects in humanization. In D. Paris & M. Winn (Eds.), *Humanizing research: Decolonizing qualitative inquiry with youth and communities* (pp. 21–42). SAGE.

Kokka, K. (2018). Healing-informed social justice mathematics: Promoting students' sociopolitical consciousness and well-being in mathematics class. *Urban Education, 54*(9), 1179–1209. https://doi.org/10.1177%2F0042085918806947

Koro-Ljungberg, M. (2012). Methodology is movement is methodology. In S.R. Steinberg & G.S. Cannella (Eds.), *Critical qualitative research reader* (pp. 82–90). Peter Lang.

Lipka, J., Hogan, M.P., Webster, J.P., Yanez, E., Adams, B., Clark, S., & Lacy, D. (2005). Math in a cultural context: Two case studies of a successful culturally based math project. *Anthropology & Education Quarterly,* 367–385. https://doi.org/10.1525/aeq.2005.36.4.367

Lorde, A. (1984). *Sister outsider: Essays and speeches.* Crossing Press.

Martin, D.B., Gholson, M.L., & Leonard, J. (2010). Mathematics as gatekeeper: Power and privilege in the production of knowledge. *Journal of Urban Mathematics Education, 3*(2), 12–24.

Maswabi, K. (2016). *The big African tree.* Retrieved June 16, 2021, from https://www.poemhunter.com/poem/the-big-african-tree/

McKittrick, K. (2021). *Dear science and other stories.* Duke University Press.

Meaney, T., Trinick, T., & Fairhall, U. (2013). One size does not fit all: Achieving equity in Māori mathematics classrooms. *Journal for Research in Mathematics Education, 44*(1), 235–263.
Ndlovu-Gatsheni, S.J. (2015). Decoloniality as the future of Africa. *History Compass, 13*(10), 485–496. https://doi.org/10.1111/hic3.12264
Ndlovu-Gatsheni, S.J. (2018). The dynamics of epistemological decolonisation in the 21st century: Towards epistemic freedom. *Strategic Review for Southern Africa, 40*(1), 16–45.
Nicol, C., Gerofsky, S., Nolan, K., Francis, K., & Fritzlan, A. (2020). Teacher professional learning with/in place: Storying the work of decolonizing mathematics education from within a colonial structure. *Canadian Journal of Science, Mathematics and Technology Education, 20*, 190–204. https://doi.org/10.1007/s42330-020-00080-z
Osibodu, O. (2020). *Embodying ubuntu, invoking sankofa, and disrupting with Fela: A co-exploration of social issues and critical mathematics education with Sub-Saharan African youth* (Publication No. 27962619) [Doctoral dissertation, Michigan State University]. ProQuest Dissertations Publishing.
Osibodu, O. (2021). Necessitating teacher learning in teaching mathematics for social justice to counter anti-Black racism. *For the Learning of Mathematics, 41*(1), 18–20.
Osibodu, O., & Cosby, M.D. (2018). Shades of blackness: Rehumanizing mathematics education through an understanding of Sub-Saharan African immigrants. In R. Gutierrez & I. Goffney (Eds.), *Annual perspectives in mathematics education 2018: Rehumanizing mathematics for black, indigenous, and latinx students* (pp. 39–49). National Council of Teachers of Mathematics.
Osibodu, O. (under review). Artifacts of coloniality: Analyzing the Cambridge assessment international examination in Nigeria and sub-Saharan Africa.
Osibodu, O., Byun, S., Hand, V., & LópezLeiva, C. (under review). A participatory turn in mathematics education: Tensions and possibilities.
Oyewùmí, O. (1997). *The invention of women: Making an African sense of western gender discourses.* University of Minnesota Press.
Pais, A. (2011). Criticisms and contradictions of ethnomathematics. *Educational Studies in Mathematics, 76*, 209–230.
Paris, D. (2019). Naming beyond the white settler colonial gaze in educational research. *International Journal of Qualitative Studies in Education, 32*(3), 217–224. https://doi.org/10.1080/09518398.2019.1576943
Paris, D., & Winn, M.T. (2014). *Humanizing research: Decolonizing qualitative inquiry with youth and communities.* Sage.
Patel, L. (2015). *Decolonizing educational research: From ownership to answerability.* Routledge.
Raygoza, M.C. (2016). Striving toward transformational resistance: Youth participatory action research in the mathematics classroom. *Journal of Urban Mathematics Education, 9*(2), 122–152.
Rogers, R. (2011). *An introduction to critical discourse analysis in education.* Routledge.
Shizha, E. (2013). Reclaiming our Indigenous voices: The problem with postcolonial sub-Saharan African school curriculum. *Journal of Indigenous Social Development, 2*(1), 1–18.
Smith, L.T. (1999). *Decolonizing methodologies: Research and Indigenous people.* Zed Books.
Swanson, D.M. (2007). Ubuntu: An African contribution to (re)search for/with a 'humble togetherness'. *Journal of Contemporary Issues in Education, 2*(2), 53–67.
Temple, C.N. (2010). The emergence of Sankofa practice in the United States: A modern history. *Journal of Black Studies, 41*(1), 127–150. https://doi.org/10.1177%2F0021934709332464

TheAncestorsGift. (2012, June 20). *Toni Morrison refuses to privilege White people in her novels!* [Video]. YouTube. https://www.youtube.com/watch?v=F4vIGvKpT1c

Thurber, K.A., Thandrayen, J., Banks, E., Doery, K., Sedgwick, M., & Lovett, R. (2020). Strengths-based approaches for quantitative data analysis: A case study using the Australian longitudinal study of Indigenous children. *SSM-Population Health, 12,* 1–12. https://doi.org/10.1016/j.ssmph.2020.100637

Tuck, E. (2009). Suspending damage: A letter to communities. *Harvard Educational Review, 79*(3), 409–428. https://doi.org/10.17763/haer.79.3.n0016675661t3n15

Tuck, E., & Yang, K.W. (2012). Decolonization is not a metaphor. *Decolonization: Indigeneity, Education and Society, 1,* 1–40.

Tuck, E., & Yang, K.W. (2014). R-words: Refusing research. In D. Paris & M.T. Winn (Eds.), *Humanizing research: Decolonizing qualitative inquiry for youth and communities* (pp. 223–247). Sage.

Tutu, D. (1999). *No future without forgiveness.* Doubleday.

Vithal, R., & Skovsmose, O. (1997). The end of innocence: A critique of 'ethnomathematics'. *Educational Studies in Mathematics, 34,* 131–158.

Wandera, D.B. (2019). Resisting epistemic blackout: Illustrating Afrocentric methodology in a Kenyan classroom. *Reading Research Quarterly, 55*(4), 1–20. https://doi.org/10.1002/rrq.283

Wane, N.N. (2008). Mapping the field of indigenous knowledges in anti-colonial discourse: A transformative journey in education. *Race Ethnicity and Education, 11*(2), 183–197. https://doi.org/10.1080/13613320600807667

Wane, N.N. (2009). Indigenous education and cultural resistance: A decolonizing project. *Curriculum Inquiry, 39*(1), 159–178. https://doi.org/10.1111/j.1467-873X.2008.01443.x

Watson, V.W., & Knight-Manuel, M.G. (2017). Challenging popularized narratives of immigrant youth from West Africa: Examining social processes of navigating identities and engaging civically. *Review of Research in Education, 41*(1), 279–310. https://doi.org/10.3102%2F0091732X16689047

Wilson, S. (2008). *Research is ceremony: Indigenous research methods.* Fernwood.

Wolfmeyer, M. (2017). *Mathematics education: A critical introduction.* Routledge.

4
DECOLONIZING FROM THE ROOTS

A Community-Led Approach to Critical Qualitative Health Research

Tenzin Butsang

Introduction

I once believed the relationship between ontology, epistemology, and methodology to be like that of a nesting doll: ontology dictating epistemology, epistemology informing methodology, and methodology subsequently determining method. However, in preparing to undertake Indigenous health research, I found myself struggling to articulate a paradigmatic positioning congruent with the work I intend to do and the community I intend to work with. In troubling the ontological, epistemological, and methodological grounds of my proposed doctoral work, I was confronted with issues of identity, ethics, and paradigmatic positioning in the context of Indigenous health research. Considering the implications of theory in practice for community-led work that seeks to further the cause of systemic change for social justice while negotiating the bounds of the neoliberal academic institution presents several tensions in both the conceptualization and facilitation of this work. As such, this chapter reflects a personal, ongoing process of disentanglement, both from positivist notions of reality and the colonial academic project. First, I situate myself in the context of my substantive area of interest, which examines notions of race, gender, parenthood, and criminal justice. Grounded by this critical self-location, I then describe the relationships and theoretical framework which inform my ongoing and evolving doctoral work. I conclude with a discussion of ethics and practice, both in relation to my specific project and in the broader process of decolonization.

Locating the Self

In the critical social sciences, reflexivity is well-established as a method of refuting positivist notions of objectivity (Eakin et al., 1996; Finlay, 2002). Eakin et

DOI: 10.4324/9781003199236-6

al. (1996) acknowledge an important function of reflexivity as allowing researchers to recognize different conceptualizations of "reality." By taking a reflexive approach, researchers gain a tool for the analysis of subjective and intersubjective influences on their work, position themselves to be more attuned to existing power dynamics, and open themselves up to different worldviews (Finlay, 2002). In her book *Indigenous Methodologies*, Nêhiyaw and Saulteaux scholar Margaret Kovach (2009) identifies reflexivity as a necessary practice for upholding epistemological congruence within Indigenous research. She describes reflexivity as a situating of the self for the fundamental purpose of revealing the knowledge systems which inform a researcher's approach and motivations (Kovach, 2009). In this way, Kovach elaborates, reflexivity affirms holistic epistemologies of self-knowledge, while always in relation to another. Canada's history of exploitative research involving Indigenous peoples further amplifies the importance of confronting these motivations when conducting Indigenous health research. According to Absolon and Willett (2005), locating oneself in Indigenous inquiry "ensures that individual realities are not misrepresented as generalizable collectives" (p. 123). In essence, the authors observe that reflexivity qualifies knowledge as the product of one's own place of experience, while also recognizing other truths (Absolon & Willett, 2005). Considering these conceptualizations of reflexivity, both situated in Indigenous inquiry and in the broader sphere of critical social science, I am aware that undertaking a reflexive stance is not limited to a singular instance but is instead a cyclical process one will return to over the course of time.

Throughout this chapter, I cite the writing of Linda Tuhiwai Smith, Eve Tuck, Shawn Wilson, and Margaret Kovach, all of whom have informed my evolving understanding of what it means to do Indigenous health research. Their insights raise several questions which force me to reflexively consider the methodological, ontological, and epistemological grounds of my work and how they inform the facilitation of this project. As a Tibetan woman born and raised in the settler state of Canada to refugee parents, my interest in examining systemic oppression and state violence developed long before my entry into the academy. I have witnessed the many ways colonial violence shapes and threatens the lives of Tibetan people inside Tibet, as well as the lives of Indigenous people on the dispossessed lands I currently call home. Research has given me the opportunity to address the ways in which settler colonialism and state violence affect the lives of families and communities.

While working as a tutor in a youth prison, I developed an interest in the multigenerational cycle of incarceration and wondered at the social contexts that contributed to these cycles. From the staff at the prison, I would hear brief, unaffected stories of the abuse and trauma that some of the youth had experienced, but the most common of these stories were those of difficult parental relationships, often involving parental incarceration. While the prison primarily held boys, when girls were present, they were all Indigenous, a disproportionate representation which exists in both the youth and adult prison systems (Zinger, 2020).

Despite comprising less than 5 per cent of the general population, 42 per cent of women incarcerated in federal institutions identify as First Nations, Métis, or Inuit (Zinger, 2020). Some of the young women had children of their own, and I considered what their incarceration meant for their children and families. As I began my graduate studies and deepened my awareness of the colonial legacies contributing to the overincarceration of Indigenous people in Canada, I realized that through research, I could engage in work that was not just about, but rather *relevant* to girls and women in the prison system. Although both Indigenous men and women are incarcerated at disproportionately high rates (Singh et al., 2019), Indigenous women face a distinct set of challenges once they are released from prison. More than half of Indigenous women experiencing incarceration identify as single mothers of multiple children (National Inquiry into Missing and Murdered Indigenous Women and Girls, 2019), extending the scope of the impact of incarceration across generations. The dissolution of parental rights as a result of incarceration is directly associated with the overrepresentation of Indigenous children in the foster care system (Navia et al., 2018), perpetuating a cycle of family separation and displacement. As a legatee of the invasion of Turtle Island, I use this opportunity to elucidate the ways in which settler colonialism and state violence affect Indigenous life and livelihood.

Building Relations

Shortly after moving across the country to complete a Master of Public Health degree in Indigenous Health at the University of Toronto, I began volunteering at Elizabeth Fry Toronto (EFT), a member of the Canadian Association of Elizabeth Fry Societies, an abolitionist organization which serves and advocates for women and gender diverse individuals in contact with the criminal justice system. In supporting the work of the counsellors at EFT and assisting in the facilitation of a court diversion program for women charged in domestic violence situations, I recognized common threads of experience among the women in these programs and the youth at the detention facility. Many of the women identified as mothers and spoke frequently about the impact of their experience with the criminal justice system on their children and their relationships with their children. A few of the women in these groups were Indigenous and described the discrimination and racism they experienced in interactions with both criminal justice and child welfare systems. They also noted the lack of culturally specific programming for parents in these situations. In considering this, and later in discussions with my supervisor Dr. Angela Mashford-Pringle, I brought forward the idea of developing a research project which would centre the knowledge of Indigenous mothers, mother-figures, and Two-Spirit[1] parents with experiences of incarceration to inform the development of supportive programs and services for these individuals as they transition out of prison and into the community. While agreeing on the importance of such a project, Angela suggested that we first bring this idea to two urban Indigenous organizations whose work aligned with this area, might be interested in the project, and most importantly, would tell us if this work could be of any use to their organization or the community.

Despite being the most populated city in the country, Toronto is small and familiar in many respects, most evident through the ties that many of the Indigenous organizations in the city have to one another and to the members of the urban Indigenous community. Through my supervisor's existing relationships, I met with staff from the Native Women's Resource Centre of Toronto (NWRCT), a non-profit organization which provides resources, skills development, cultural ceremonies and teachings, and capacity-building programs for Indigenous women and their children. Our meeting began with an offering of tobacco, introductions, which involved sharing a bit about myself and my intentions, and then discussing the half-formed idea with the staff and community members and listening to their feedback on whether a project like this was wanted. I also met with Aboriginal Legal Services Toronto (ALST), an organization which provides legal aid services and operates legal-related programs for Indigenous people in Toronto. Despite witnessing firsthand, the intersecting crises of incarceration and family displacement that disproportionately impact this community and having an acute knowledge of the impacts that these issues have, staff at both organizations expressed difficulties with securing the resources necessary to respond to the needs of their communities. They discussed the challenges they encountered with potential funders who hesitated over the lack of academic research and literature documenting the issues the organization was raising, acting as perpetuators of a hegemony of knowledge which values "scholarship" over community knowledge. Bringing these issues to the forefront for funding bodies by leveraging the perceived credibility of a recognized academic institution and centring community knowledge were the practically grounded goals which informed our formal partnership with both these organizations and the initial skeleton of this project. These goals also represented the tightrope walk of a collaborative community project, which attempts to negotiate the expectations of hegemonic, paternalistic institutions who decide which resources are distributed where and to whom, with anti-colonial research and the needs of the community.

With our goals aligned and new relationships formed, the project began to move at a quickened pace. We began to work out the specifics of how the project would be carried out, from how potential participants could be reached, how the conversations were to occur (we decided on having both an individual, one-on-one interview, and a Sharing Circle), to what kind of questions would be asked and who would be asking them. In subsequent meetings with the partners, we identified areas that the organizations were interested in learning more about from their clients and the community, contributing to an iterative process which helped us develop the first version of questions to be asked. Engaging with the principles of community-led research and upon the advice of our partners, a community member joined the team as a research assistant to contribute to the conducting of interviews and Circles, and for the analysis and creation of final project materials. Our partners suggested the idea of using the Medicine Wheel, a conceptual framework of healing and Indigenous knowledge comprised of physical, emotional, spiritual, and mental components (Dapice, 2006), to guide the analysis of the collected stories from participants. In subverting Western notions of qualitative analysis, we aim to achieve a closer understanding of the experiences, needs, and possibilities of the community with which we engage.

Decolonization as Praxis

Writer and activist bell hooks states, "Theory is not inherently healing, liberatory, or revolutionary. It fulfills this function only when we ask that it do so and direct our theorizing towards this end" (1991, p. 2). While I struggle with the notion of conducting "liberatory" or "emancipatory" work as a settler researcher (an issue I will discuss later in this chapter), hooks describes an intent or an activation of theory, that guides my work. She argues that engaging in theorizing simply by knowing and naming a theory does not bring it into being (hooks, 1991). hooks elaborates:

> Indeed, the privileged act of naming often affords those in power access to modes of communication that enable them to project an interpretation, a definition, a description of their work, actions, etc. that may not be accurate, that may obscure what is really taking place.
>
> *(1991, p. 3)*

As a doctoral student, this project also constitutes the basis of my thesis, which comes with its own set of expectations and guidelines. In deciding upon a theoretical framework to inform the development of the project, Indigenous feminisms grounded my goals to lessen the gap between theory and practice that so often creates an intellectual class hierarchy and perpetuates class elitism.

Rooted in Indigenous ontologies and epistemologies, Indigenous feminisms offer critical approaches to conceptualizing power, relationships, and survival. Although a nascent field of scholarly inquiry, Indigenous feminisms have existed in a multitude of forms as part of Indigenous women's long history of resisting colonial and patriarchal oppression through activism and intellectual thought (Hokowhitu et al., 2020). Indigenous feminisms constitute knowledges across time and geographies, from the epistemologies of the South to the settler colonial nation-states of the West and beyond. Reflecting the relational worldview foundational to Indigenous ways of knowing, they have been theorized as a "project of kinship" (Anderson, 2020, p. 37), a perspective that Yazzie and Baldy (2018) building upon defining Indigenous feminisms for its decolonizing possibilities as "radical relationality" (p. 2). Acknowledging its evolving and contextual definitional state, Anderson (2020) defines Indigenous feminisms "as a process of revisioning in the service of Indigenous futurities" (p. 41). As an analytical strategy, Nickel and Fehr (2020) writes that Indigenous feminisms "reflect and capture the multiple ways in which gender and race, and therefore the systems of power related to these (sexism, racism, and colonialism) shape Indigenous peoples' lives" (p. 3). Through multiple definitions, we can come to understand Indigenous feminisms as a multi-sited project committed to Indigenous life and self-determination while simultaneously illuminating the realities of decolonial struggle.

In "Decolonization is not a Metaphor," Eve Tuck (Unangax̂) and K. Wayne Yang contest the increasing usage of "decolonization" as an empty signifier, arguing that to simply be critically conscious of issues related to social justice (e.g., racism, sexism, xenophobia) falls short of a true decolonizing project. Tuck and Yang explain,

> [T]he pursuit of critical consciousness, the pursuit of social justice through a critical enlightenment, can also be settler moves to innocence diversions, distractions, which relieve the settler of feelings of guilt or responsibility, and conceal the need to give up land or power or privilege.
>
> *(2012, p. 21)*

Instead, the authors contend that a critical consciousness which fails to rectify issues of land, or power, or privilege is a form of "settler harm reduction," the goal of which is to reduce the harm that settler colonialism has had on Indigenous people (Tuck & Yang, 2012). This settler harm reduction, Tuck and Yang argue, is not an inherent act of decolonization. In my doctoral work, I use Indigenous feminisms and Tuck and Yang's claims of what decolonization both can be, and what it is not, as complementary informants to my project's theoretical framework.

Cree scholar Shawn Wilson (2008) describes relationality as the foundation of an Indigenous research paradigm. Wilson argues that there is no single definite reality, and that in both an Indigenous ontology and epistemology, reality *is* relationships or a "process of relationships" (2008, p. 73). He goes on to emphasize that Indigenous ontology goes beyond individual knowledge, and instead reflects a more complex concept of relational knowledge (Wilson, 2008). This relational ontology and epistemology align with my interest in describing parent–child relationships, but also in uncovering the relationships one has with social constructs such as parenthood, criminal justice, and gender, all within the context of settler colonialism. In conversation with Eve Tuck, Michi Saagiig Nishnaabeg writer and activist Leanne Betasamosake Simpson (2016) states that building a radical Indigenous resurgent movement means building relationships with communities already doing work in the context of their "movement-constellations of co-resistance" (p. 33) to address issues of heteropatriarchy, white supremacy, capitalism, and anti-Blackness. Simpson further articulates how the dispossession of Indigenous people from the land, and all its consequences, must be considered within the broader constellation of settler colonialism (Simpson, 2016). Although Simpson is not explicitly referring to theory in her writing, in considering the holistic and relational epistemology of an Indigenous research paradigm to inform my theoretical approach, I found a congruency in uniting ideas for the purpose of describing an Indigenous feminist framework.

My conceptualization of this framework is not one that stands in opposition to intersectionality, postcolonial feminism, or other critical theories, rather it examines many of the perspectives these theories consider, while remaining grounded in Indigenous alternatives and Indigenous intelligence. This grounding is not possible without collaboration and co-theorizing between me and the community members and organizations who are situated in this work in their everyday lives. The process of co-theorizing, much like many components of community-led research, is fluid. It emerges from seemingly mundane conversations which happen in passing, and in the more intentional, hours-long dialogue that can only be recalled and digested through multiple plays of a recording. Drawing from this epistemological and ontological foundation, our research asks the following questions: (1) How are conceptualizations of Indigenous motherhood informed by Canada's settler colonial and carceral project; (2) What forms of subjugation and subversion exist in the lives of formerly incarcerated Indigenous mothers, mother-figures, and Two-Spirit parents; and (3) how do these experiences influence their mothering and wellbeing?

In an interview with Margaret Kovach, Cree scholar Cam Willett posits that one's epistemology in research cannot be extricated from one's way of approaching general life (Kovach, 2009). Undertaking an Indigenous research paradigm, therefore, challenges the assumption that people can select methodologies solely in relation to research curiosity, without a reflection of the self. The explication of this reflexive presence, which Indigenous scholars such as Absolon and Willett (2005), Smith (1999) and Kovach (2009) view as a form of resistance against colonial modes of scholarship, has been instrumental in shaping my methodological approach. While there is no definitive set of guidelines or methodology associated with Indigenous feminisms, Indigenous theorists have long relied on storytelling methodologies as a means to draw insights and possibilities to Indigenous experiences and reclaim narratives which have historically been "re-interpreted, re-presented, and re-told" (Archibald et al., 2019, p. xi) by dominant perspectives. Guided by the work of writers and scholars such as Thomas King and Margaret Kovach, this project uses an Indigenous storytelling methodology to generate a close examination of colonial power in the lives of parents with experiences of incarceration—as told by them. Of course, the telling of these stories is not void of the researcher's presence, an issue which is not only apparent in the facilitation of Circles or interviews, but in the sharing of these stories once they are told. Abandoning the positivist notion of an "objective" researcher, facilitating conversations on difficult topics with a relative stranger, has required not only a listening ear but a willingness to share in commonalities or differences, while also being mindful to create space for silence. Bringing these issues to the attention of the public, a critical component of generating momentum for social change also requires translating these stories in a way that will capture and retain their interest. In discussing this with our partners and some of our early participants, we considered using an audio-based medium to share the experiences of participants who wanted their voices and stories to be shared with the public, ultimately arriving at the creation of a podcast series. Podcasting preserves the context of stories by honouring them in a format conducive to Indigenous methods of oral storytelling and is an emerging decolonizing method in Indigenous research (Day et al., 2017). Each podcast will feature a single participant, with only their voice to be heard during the episode to create a space that is wholly dedicated to the individual telling their story. The content and creative direction of each episode will be determined by the participant, with technical support from the research team. The podcasts will be edited by the research team or the participants depending on their comfortability with audio editing software, with direction and feedback from the participants, who will hold final cut approval for their episode.

The Ethics of Decolonization

Reciprocity, or mutual benefit, is a central tenet of Indigenous research methodologies (Smith, 1999). Like critical theory, the axiology of Indigenous decolonial frameworks is rooted in the belief that research is not assumed to be ethical if it does not help to improve the reality of the research participants (Wilson, 2008). Informed by this spirit of reciprocity, Dene scholar Glen Sean Coulthard's notion of grounded normativity offers an ethical framework for Indigenous health research and this project. Defined in Coulthard's book *Red Skin, White Masks* as, "the modalities of Indigenous land-connected practices and longstanding experiential knowledge that inform and structure our ethical engagements with the world and our relationships with human and nonhuman others over time" (2014, p. 13), our project is informed by a grounded normativity of reciprocal relations and obligations to community. From assisting with year-end statistics and reports to acting as sous-chef in the kitchen for the daily lunch support program, conducting client intake interviews, or writing grant applications, reciprocity has taken on many different forms throughout this project, and will continue to evolve as we approach different phases of the research cycle.

Research involving Indigenous people often neglects to recognize the nuances of Indigeneity which exist across Turtle Island (specifically "Canada") and around the world. As this project involves urban Indigenous people in Toronto, Ontario, Canada, it is important to note that these participants will have varying relationships to Indigenous identities. To assume that everyone who chooses to participate is connected with an Indigenous culture is to misrepresent these individuals and underestimate the effects of colonization. In further articulating my chosen theoretical framework, it is necessary to acknowledge some of the history within which this work is situated. Generalizing the experiences of Indigenous people, or pan-Indigenizing, obscures the realities of the varying relationships diverse communities have with the land and each other. Resistance to the "feminist" label among Indigenous communities is rooted in a refusal of the whiteness of mainstream ("whitestream") feminism, which historically marginalized the experiences of Indigenous women (Arvin et al., 2013). In this regard, my application of "Indigenous" feminisms do not seek to encompass or explain all the different worldviews present across the various Nations, peoples, communities, and cultures involved, rather it serves as a foundation for decolonial work in the settler colonial context. I recognize however, that as a settler researcher, this "theoretical disclaimer" is one that cannot be issued without continuous, critical revisitation. Here, reflexivity provides one strategy necessary to hold the researcher accountable to these claims and to mitigate misrepresentation throughout the research process. As a community-led project, direction from Indigenous organizations and community members continues to ensure that this project does not reify harm or marginalize identities.

Guillemin and Gillam (2004) contend that while reflexivity does not have an explicitly ethical purpose, adopting a reflexive practice brings necessary scrutiny to the ultimate purpose of the research, alerting the researcher to ethical dimensions in their research practice. This is particularly salient when considering what Tuck (2009) defines as a "paradox of damage." In an open letter to Indigenous communities, researchers, and educators, Tuck (2009) describes the historical framing of Indigenous people within a victim/perpetrator binary through research primarily conducted by outsiders who often invoke a damage-centred narrative for their own benefit. The paradox emerges from what Tuck acknowledges as the need to explicate something to refute it, which at the same time perpetuates a pathologizing of individuals and communities. This research is not devoid of stories of pain or loss, nor do I intend for these stories to constitute the entirety or focal point of this project. By focusing my inquiry through a lens of resistance and resilience, I hope to counteract damage-centred narratives with a critical exploration of what Tuck aptly describes as "the complexity, contradiction, and self-determination of lived lives" (2009, p. 416).

In her influential work, *Decolonizing Methodologies*, Maori scholar Linda Tuhiwai Smith (1999) reminds us that, "espousing an emancipatory model of research has not of itself freed researchers from exercising intellectual arrogance or employing evangelical and paternalistic practises" (p. 180). My Tibetan identity does not preclude my settler identity. In doing Indigenous health research, I am confronted with the irony of seeking to do "emancipatory" work with communities that have been and continue to be oppressed by many forms of structural violence—violence from which I have benefitted and, to a lesser extent, been subjected to, through the rules and regulations which dictate the doing of this work. As a student in a neoliberal institution which has historically marginalized Indigenous knowledges, in a discipline which has committed immeasurable harm against Indigenous peoples in the name of public health, I often struggle to understand how the benefits of research for communities outweigh the harms. At the same time, I am cognizant of how public visibility and advocacy through research has the power to contribute to meaningful social change, from increased funding for mutual aid projects to community organizing and solidarity building, with the ultimate aim of dismantling the oppressive structures and systems that continue to exist unabated in this country. Questioning my own involvement in this work and the motivations that first led and continue to keep me here has become a common occurrence. At first a source of anxiety, this constant questioning has now become a necessary touchpoint that forces me to regularly consider why I engage with communities, whether this engagement supports anti-colonial, abolitionist, and feminist futures, or whether, no matter my intention, my work has been co-opted by the colonial academic project. Beginning by asking community partners whether this project addresses a need and is worthy of undertaking, involving them in the design of questions asked of participants, and collaborating with them to synthesize and disseminate the findings, are several ways in which I attempt to combat any forms of heteropaternalism that may exist throughout this work.

In practice, ethical positioning is rendered in several ways. Adapting this practice became a necessity because of the COVID-19 pandemic, which moved our research and partnership interactions from the community to the virtual space. Aside from changes to the administrative aspects of the research process, the pandemic limited our ability to attend community events, volunteering with partner organizations, and build relationships with community members and potential participants. All interviews held to date have been conducted online or by phone. As a facilitator, the process has at times felt detached and unfinished, with anonymous phone conversations that often end earlier than expected for any number of reasons, not the least of which involves living through an unprecedented global pandemic. Engendering a sense of trust and connection with someone you have never met before can present a challenge under normal circumstances, and so these issues are amplified in the virtual space. As we continue our project in a constantly evolving public health situation, we have taken each conversation as an opportunity to refine our virtual facilitation approach.

Ethics also includes adhering to the protocols set forth by the community and partners, particularly when in a Sharing Circle. This also means ensuring that participants can engage in ceremony, have access to medicines, and that all participants, as well as Healers, Elders, or Knowledge Keepers present in the Circle and assisting with its facilitation, are compensated for their time and knowledge. When in-person research returns, our partnerships will allow us to offer participants access to Healers and Knowledge Keepers at any point throughout the interview or Sharing Circle. Participants are also provided with a transcript of what they shared and can withdraw or supplement their story at any point prior to the publication of the final materials. Decolonization in Indigenous health research ethics can also take the form of self-determination in data governance. OCAP→ principles were established in 1998 as a response to the historical and ongoing exploitation of First Nations communities by researchers. It supports the aim of First Nations data sovereignty, asserting First Nations' right to own, control, have access to, and possess study data (First Nations Information Governance Centre, 2019). Ownership refers to the relationship of a First Nation community to its cultural knowledge, data, or information, including their rights to intellectual property. Control extends to all aspects of information management, from collection of data to the use, disclosure, and ultimate destruction of data. The principle of Access refers to the right of First Nation communities to manage and make decisions regarding access to their collective information, while Possession refers to the physical state or location of data. (First Nations Information Governance Centre, 2019). By transferring data into First Nation stewardship and developing knowledge practices and relationships that abide by its principles, OCAP→ is a tool that can be used to facilitate ethical practice and data repatriation. Through data-sharing agreements, OCAP→ holds researchers accountable to First Nations and affirms First Nations' autonomy in decisions regarding who can access their collective information. While my doctoral project is not being conducted with a specific First Nations community, it involves the urban Indigenous population in Toronto and as such, my partnerships with two urban Indigenous organizations, ALST and NWRCT, will be central to data governance in this project. These partners will act as data stewards, with all data and findings to be handled in accordance with OCAP→ and data-sharing agreements.

In describing the ethical and practical considerations of my doctoral work so far, I return to the notion of decolonization, and the meaning it holds in relation to this project. Taking up Tuck and Yang's definition of decolonization as the "repatriation of Indigenous land and life" (2012, p. 1), my project fails. In this first year of my doctoral studies, I have gone back and forth (perhaps more back than forth) on whether a settler can actually "decolonize" research. I know for certain that any research that is conducted, should it be necessary to conduct at all, must be driven by the needs and interests of the Indigenous communities involved. However, even as a community-based researcher, I receive more tangible benefit from this project as an individual—through awards, a doctoral degree, publications—than the participants and communities I engage in this work. As a student, it is helpful to have supervisors who also grapple with these imbalances and set an example as grant holders to allocate funds for community partners, hire peer researchers, and prioritize support for community initiatives. Despite these efforts, it is difficult to reconcile the academic project as anything but inherently extractive and exploitative, particularly of Indigenous communities both historically and now in the "Truth and Reconciliation" era.[2] This is a process which demands that I take a critical look at my complicity in the domestication of decolonization, first through language and second through practice. For me, at this point in my learning, decolonizing research is not merely a project of ethics; it is one of theory, methodology, and method, woven together with the threads of resistance and resurgence. A decolonizing project is accountable to the community, and it is this community that sanctions the integrity and credibility of a story, of *their* story. In building relationships with community and attending to stories as knowledge, a decolonizing researcher is better positioned to recognize the nuance and complexity of experience. It is with these lessons in mind that I undertake this work.

Notes

1 Two-Spirit is a translation of the Anishinaabemowin term niizh manidoowag and refers to an individual who identifies as having both a masculine and feminine spirit. It is also used by some Indigenous people to describe their gender, sexual, or spiritual identity.
2 In 2007, the Government of Canada established the Truth and Reconciliation Commission as part of a settlement with former students, families, and communities impacted by the residential school system. From the 1880s to 1996 when the last residential school closed, Indigenous children were forcibly removed from their families and subjected to abuse, scientific experiments, and cultural genocide at the hands of the Government of Canada and Christian churches. The Commission's final report, released in 2015, outlines 94 "Calls to Action" aimed across the public sectors, including post-secondary institutions and research funding bodies.

References

Absolon, K., & Willett, C. (2005). Putting ourselves forward: Location in aboriginal research. In L. Brown, & S. Strega (Eds.), *Research as resistance: Critical, indigenous and anti-oppressive approaches* (pp. 97–126). Canadian Scholars' Press.

Anderson, K. (2020). Multi-generational indigenous feminisms: From F word to what IFs. In B. Hokowhitu, Andersen, C., Larkin, S., Moreton-Robinson, A., & Tuhiwai-Smith, L. (Ed.), *Routledge handbook of critical indigenous studies* (pp. 37–51). Taylor and Francis.

Archibald, J., Lee-Morgan, J.B.J., & Santolo, J.D. (Eds.). (2019). *Decolonizing research: Indigenous storywork as methodology*. Zed Books.

Arvin, M., Tuck, E., & Morrill, A. (2013). Decolonizing feminism: Challenging connections between settler colonialism and heteropatriarchy. *Feminist formations*, 25(1), 8–34. https://doi.org/10.1353/ff.2013.0006

Coulthard, G.S. (2014). *Red skin, white masks: Rejecting the colonial politics of recognition*. University of Minnesota Press. https://doi.org/10.5749/j.ctt9qh3cv

Dapice, A.N. (2006, July). The medicine wheel. *The Journal of Transcultural Nursing*, 17(3), 251–260. https://doi.org/10.1177/1043659606288383

Day, L., Cunsolo, A., Castleden, H., Martin, D., Hart, C., Anaviapik-Soucie, T., Russell, G., Paul, C., Dewey, C., & Harper, S.L. (2017). The expanding digital media landscape of qualitative and decolonizing research: Examining collaborative podcasting as a research method. *Media Tropes*, 7(1), 203–228.

Eakin, J., Robertson, A., Poland, B., Coburn, D., & Edwards, R. (1996). Towards a critical social science perspective on health promotion research. *Health Promotion International*, 11(2), 157–165.

Finlay, L. (2002). "Outing" the researcher: The provenance, process, and practice of reflexivity. *Qualitative Health Research*, 12(4), 531–545. https://doi.org/10.1177/104973202129120052

First Nations Information Governance Centre. (2019). *The first nations principles of OCAP®*. Retrieved March 28 from https://fnigc.ca/ocapr.html

Guillemin, M., & Gillam, L. (2004). Ethics, reflexivity, and "ethically important moments" in research. *Qualitative Inquiry*, 10(2), 261–280.

Hokowhitu, B., Andersen, C., Larkin, S., Moreton-Robinson, A., & Tuhiwai-Smith, L. (2020). *Routledge handbook of critical indigenous studies*. Taylor and Francis. https://doi.org/10.4324/9780429440229

hooks, b. (1991). Theory as Liberatory Practice. *Yale Journal of Law and Feminism*, *4*(1), 1–12.

Kovach, M. (2009). *Indigenous methodologies: Characteristics, conversations, and context*. University of Toronto Press.

National Inquiry into Missing and Murdered Indigenous Women and Girls. (2019). *Reclaiming power and place: The final report of the national inquiry into missing and murdered indigenous women and girls*. https://www.mmiwg-ffada.ca/final-report/

Navia, D., Henderson, R.I., & Charger, L.F. (2018, June). Uncovering colonial legacies: Voices of indigenous youth on child welfare (dis)placements. *Anthropology & Education Quarterly*, *49*(2), 146–164. https://doi.org/10.1111/aeq.12245

Nickel, S.A., & Fehr, A. (2020). *In good relation: History, gender, and kinship in indigenous feminisms*. University of Manitoba Press.

Simpson, L.B. (2016). Indigenous resurgence and co-resistance. *Critical Ethnic Studies*, *2*(2), 19–34. https://doi.org/10.5749/jcritethnstud.2.2.0019

Singh, D., Prowse, S., & Anderson, M. (2019, May 6). Overincarceration of indigenous people: A health crisis. *CMAJ*, *191*(18), E487–E488. https://doi.org/10.1503/cmaj.181437

Smith, L.T. (1999). *Decolonizing methodologies: Research and indigenous peoples* (2nd ed.). Zed Books.

Tuck, E. (2009). Suspending damage: A letter to communities. *Harvard Educational Review*, *79*(3), 409–428. https://doi.org/10.17763/haer.79.3.n0016675661t3n15

Tuck, E., & Yang, K.W. (2012). Decolonization is not a metaphor. *Decolonization: Indigeneity, Education & Society*, *1*(1), 1–40.

Wilson, S. (2008). *Research is ceremony: Indigenous research methods*. Fernwood Publishing.

Yazzie, M.K., & Baldy, C.R. (2018). Introduction: Indigenous peoples and the politics of water. *Decolonization: Indigeneity, Education & Society*, *7*(1), 1–18.

Zinger, I. (2020). *Indigenous people in federal custody surpasses 30%: Correctional investigator issues statement and challenge*. https://www.oci-bec.gc.ca/cnt/comm/press/press20200121-eng.aspx

5
A REFLEXIVE ACCOUNT OF PERFORMING FACILITATION IN PARTICIPATORY VISUAL RESEARCH FOR SOCIAL CHANGE

Katie MacEntee, Jennifer Thompson, Milka Nyariro and Claudia Mitchell

Introduction

Facilitation is a generative site of inquiry and critical learning. In this chapter, we present a new way to study *pedagogies of facilitation* for participatory visual research for social change. To demonstrate this method, we consider our facilitation practices through what we are calling "autoethnographic performances of facilitation" that each author originally presented at the American Educational Research Association (AERA) conference in 2019. We tell the story of our autoethnographic performances and what led us to this approach. We describe how we take up Michael Burawoy's (2014) reflexive revisiting to position our work. We present four individual performances: 1) Jen's "Textures of trust"; 2) Milka's "Participate or facilitate?"; 3) Claudia's "In the bag"; and 4) Katie's "Cellphilm method." We then each reflect on moments of discomfort as well as moments of opportunity around our performances and facilitation practices. We conclude by recommending areas of pedagogical focus to consider when learning how to facilitate participatory visual methods for transformative social change.

Situating Ourselves

Our reflexive experiment emerges from almost a decade of working together through the Participatory Cultures Lab, a Canadian Foundation Innovation-funded unit at McGill University focusing on research, training, and community-based interventions. As co-authors, we identify diversely and with complexity. At the time of writing our reflexive pieces, Claudia (white settler Canadian) was the former doctoral supervisor to Jen and Katie (white settler Canadians) and the current doctoral supervisor for Milka (Black Kenyan newcomer to Canada). Claudia has committed decades to building relationships with communities and

DOI: 10.4324/9781003199236-7

organizations that work together on research as an intervention. Jen and Katie were postdoctoral fellows working to establish their own communities of practice and Milka was in the final stages of her PhD and considering what next steps to take to pursue research at an institution in Canada.

We seized this writing project on facilitation because it was not that different from the work that we typically facilitate in participatory visual workshops. These workshops integrate "methods that actively engage participants in creating and analyzing visual media (e.g., photography, video, or drawings) as part of the research process" (MacEntee & Flicker, 2019, p. 352) such as photovoice (taking photographs and sometimes pairing them with short descriptive captions (Liebenberg, 2018)) or cellphilms (making videos using cellphones or tablets (MacEntee et al., 2016)). Participants might produce photographs or a short cellphilm, and the rest of the workshop takes on a reflexive mode to consider how, why and for whom the media is for. These facilitated reflections could range from a type of SHOWeD (Shaffer, 1983)—a set of questions to guide an analysis process—or a deep version of "working with a single photograph" (Moletsane & Mitchell, 2007), to the idea of speaking back through cellphilm production (Mitchell et al., 2017). Typically, our work focuses on gender, which anchors our facilitation practices with groups of young women, educators, and health practitioners in Southern contexts to address social change in their communities, organizations, and lives.

Framing Facilitation

Facilitation sits at the intersection of methodology and pedagogy, influencing both the research process and findings. Facilitators play an active role in orchestrating the sequence and timing of participant engagement and assessing how methodologies are working or not working. They make strategic and spontaneous decisions that re-shape the research process, including how workshop spaces are set up, and deciding when to pause and when to keep things moving. Shifts in process can be motivated by reading the room and may influence decisions to focus on one topic over another, or choosing to adapt a prompt or method to increase participant engagement. Research facilitation is an embodied, relational, and contextual practice that must be continually examined with an appreciation for the local research setting, intersecting social identities, and the global system of knowledge production. We reflect on this understanding of facilitation specifically as it relates to participatory visual research.

We draw on facilitation theory emerging from social justice educators (Landreman, 2013), with attention to feminist questions about subjectivity and intersectionality. Franco and Nielsen (2018) questioned the neutrality of facilitators in group workshop settings that are designed to help groups engage in productive discussions that challenge assumptions and develop new perspectives. Switzer (2019) emphasized how facilitators influence the means of participant visual production and the participants' visual products. She demonstrated the role of researcher reflexivity in engaging with this influence and highlighted the pedagogical nature of working with communities to create visual media that opens up space for critical engagement. Building on Switzer's work, we are interested in strategies that facilitators can use to reflect on their practices as a way of working towards more socially just facilitation.

Reflexivity of Discomfort

Our reflection on our facilitation practices considers methodologies that forefront discomfort in social justice research and teaching. Pillow's (2003) *reflexivity of discomfort* focuses on the messy complexities of engaged qualitative research that advance methodological understandings. Boler's (1999) *pedagogy of discomfort* addresses the role of emotion in anti-racist and anti-sexist teaching, and specifically how discomfort might be necessary for producing change. For both Boler and Pillow, discomfort marks internal shifts in understanding. MacEntee and Mandrona (2015) took up pedagogy of discomfort to engage with challenging interactions between teachers and students when screening cellphilms about sexual health education. They relate moments of discomfort with hopeful instances of critical engagement with the socio-cultural influences on sexual practices. By identifying the emotional comfort zones that constitute familiar ways of seeing, facilitators can learn to inhabit ambiguous positions to witness and act on their ethical responsibility for change. In this chapter, we apply a reflexivity of discomfort to bring together the concomitant intentions of research and teaching that we see encompassed in participatory visual facilitation processes.

Method

Our reflections on facilitating visual methodology workshops follows a two-stage method: I) our initial autoethnographic performances at AERA; and II) returning to our performances to produce a reflexive account.

Method 1: Autoethnographic Performance

Autoethnography involves systematic inquiry into researchers' individual experiences with the intention of making sense of wider social or cultural experiences (Ellis et al., 2011). The self-study work of Cole and McIntyre (2001) is particularly relevant to our own facilitation practices. Performance also has many benefits within academic settings (Cole & McIntyre, 2001; Mitchell, 2004). The use of performance as an arts-based research method includes a range of possibilities (Saldaña, 2018), including Goldstein's (2013, 2019) work on "performing transcripts" as an approach to bringing research findings alive, and Belliveau and Lea's (2016) research-based theatre using drama as both an analytic process and knowledge translation tool. Two that stand out for us relate to containment (brief, tightly scripted) and audience (meanings to be conveyed, the notion of affect, and performance space).

Performing facilitation at AERA came out of the challenge of figuring out how we could present our individual reflections about facilitation in participatory visual research interventions across a range of settings in both the Global North and South in a short (10 mins) timeframe of the conference presentation format. Our two-minute performances involved working with a single image and textual prompt that offered a doorway into deeper considerations of participatory visual research facilitation. By performing autoethnography at a conference, we engaged in the act of inquiry *in situ*.

Method II: Reflexive Revisiting

To engage reflexively with our performances, we work with Burawoy's (2014) interpretive revisit. Burawoy reinterpreted his earlier work on Zambian copper mining by considering the racial dynamics and the transnational, global economic influences on the national industry that he did not include in the earlier ethnographic analysis. The result was a more nuanced and critical reading of racial and neocolonial forces. He proposed four approaches to the interpretive revisit: (1) refutation of the original study based on the reaction of participants, (2) historical change since the original study, (3) reformulation based on comparative studies, and (4) theoretical reconstruction. The revisit extends knowledge contributions: from observer to participant, observations over time and space, from micro to macro analyses, and extend theory. He explained, the revisit serves "as an auto-critique as well as an assessment of 40 years of postcoloniality" (p. 963). We take up Burawoy's interpretive revisits to explore our autoethnographic performances of facilitation practices in PVM workshops. We explore our participation in the facilitation process (extension of observer to participant) and how our accounts of facilitation at AREA missed a critical lens of analysis (extension of observation of time and space and from micro to macro analyses). The re-interpretation of our initial accounts leads us to sketch a pedagogy of facilitation (extension of theory).

Our interpretive revisits differ from Burawoy's (2014) in some substantial ways. Where Burawoy considered the extended case method to understand mining in the Copperbelt, we are visual methodologists who use photo-elicitation (Mitchell et al., 2017) as an entry point to study our facilitation practices. We are also a group of authors writing collaboratively. Thus, where Burawoy situates his findings within his 40 years of experience as a sociologist, we reflect on 5–25 years of PVM facilitation experience. Our findings focus on facilitation practice, where our positionalities and learning experiences are at the centre of our analyses. We consider *how* we learn to be critical and reflexive facilitators.

This is not the first time that an AERA conference venue has been a field site. MacEntee (2016) published a reflexive account of a roundtable on cellphilms addressing sexual violence. However, this was our first collective foray into a systematic revisiting of the process. Thus, we developed the following prompts to guide our inquire:

- Create a slide of your image and script.
- Upon re-reading your performance script and remembering, what does it mean to facilitate critically or for social change?
- Identify moments of tension and discomfort, or moments of opportunity for transformation and learning.

Building on Mitchell et al.'s (2020) questions about "what's missing?" or "whose stories are not represented?" our questions pushed us to explore how we facilitate and what we could do better. We considered: how might we bring more emphasis on social justice into our facilitation practice? To make sense of our individual pieces as a collection, we followed what Akesson et al. (2014) refer to as "stepping back" (p. 75), which involved a collective process over several months by email, Zoom, and re-writing our individual pieces to dive more deeply into the meaning of our reflections and how they might influence actionable conclusions.

Four Autoethnographic Performances and Reflections

In this section, we each present a brief self-positioning statement, our autoethnographic performance, and our individual reflection on our performance. We encourage readers to also consult the images and scripts from our performances (Figures 5.1–5.4) to making sense of our reflections.

Jen: Textures of Trust

My facilitation practice emerged through my early work with children with disabilities in Montreal. My graduate and postdoctoral research has focused on facilitating and conducting training about participatory visual methodologies, often in collaboration with local organizations. I have worked with women and youth across community-based and institutional settings in Cameroon, Ethiopia, Kenya, Mozambique, Myanmar, Sierra Leone, Canada, and the UK to address issues related to gender, water, education, and COVID-19. The salience of different aspects of my positioning—as able-bodied, as a white cis-gendered woman, as a university researcher, and as an Anglophone who also speaks some French and Pidgin/Krio (*lingua francas* in Cameroon/Sierra Leone)—tend to shift in different contexts.

Reflections on Trust and Trustworthiness

Before our performance, I remember my usual apprehensiveness about public speaking, amplified by our attempts to transgress the familiarity of a talk with a performance. The piece I had prepared aimed to construct a spacious narrative

A Reflexive Account of Performing Facilitation **81**

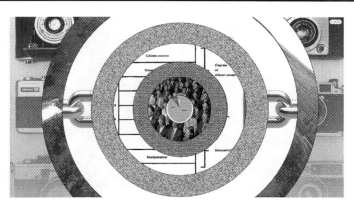

Jen: Textures of Trust

To facilitate – to ease, assist or make possible - from the French, *facile* or Latin *facilis* meaning easy. But facilitation is anything but easy.

My image takes up textures of trust. *What does she mean?* At first, I tried to focus or zero in on three concentric rings: 1) for trust in myself as a facilitator; 2) for trust with participants as we engage together; and 3) for the trust that makes co-facilitation in teams.

Trust your gut, they say. Trust the process. *But what does that mean?* Do the participants trust me? Do I trust me? That I can bring people along carefully, with intention, with integrity? There is that tension between being present in the texture of how a moment wants or needs to evolve – this listening to the silence and noise in the room - while at the same time responding to and acting on the moment by orchestrating the very next moment. Trust that the process, the steps, my intentions will need to change, creatively and pragmatically. *Do we have enough time to reflect before the break?*

Rarely do I facilitate alone. As Claudia says, 'we all see different things.' With friends and colleagues, we read and trust each other through our histories, through how we communicate. There are countless emails about strategy. *What [should] we do?* There are micro-glances, whispers and notes scribbled on napkins as we restructure the shape of the day on-the-go. *What is happening now?* And there are hours and hours of reflection together at the end of the day, over tea or beer or in the back of taxis. *What just happened?*

Our positionalities, assumptions, and ways of seeing and doing—alone and together—are simultaneously exposed and fundamental to making facilitation work. Stepping back, it can't be three rings. Trust emerges, overlaps, and sometimes dissolves. Trust is built inward and outward across textures, between the lines, between the circles, and between the relations that make up facilitation. *I [want] to reflect on this with you.*

FIGURE 5.1 Jen's AERA image and performance script.

open to interpretive possibilities. I wanted to break from more conventional linear presentations where I offer a concrete message and conclusion, and to play with performance in a poetic and abstract way so that the audience might interpret meaning in relation to their own work and facilitation practice. I intentionally left out information like who I work with, where I have worked, and what topics I work on because I wanted to avoid telling a closed story tied to a particular location.

In my performance, I focused on trust within the immediate, interpersonal dynamics that I have encountered in workshop spaces: my trust in the process

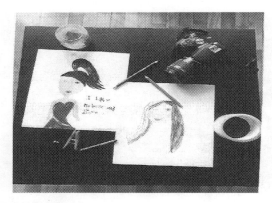

Milka: To Facilitate and Participate?

The single image above represented my deeper understanding of facilitating photovoice workshops to address sexual and gender-based violence with marginalised girls and young women in different contexts. A routine part of the preparation for the workshops includes, gathering the material that will be needed in the workshop and having a step-by-step guide to facilitate the workshop and effectively lead participants through conceptualizing the problem at hand and reflecting on ways in which these problems could be addressed through arts-based participatory and visual methodologies. Usually, I begin my workshops by gathering all the material that will used for the workshop. Subsequently:

> I create rapport with the participants.
>
> I introduce the topic to the participants.
>
> I introduce the prompt to the participants.
>
> Often, they repeat the prompt aloud as they try to reflect on it.
>
> At this point they look at me, look at each other, and everyone looks around as if trying to find something.

The prompt gets thrown back and forth, between me and the participants and among the participants themselves. This is always the critical moment of my facilitation when I ask myself whether my role is to facilitate, participate, or both.

Understanding that, although the principle of facilitation is that I should remain neutral, my facilitation will influence the outcome of the workshop, I interrogate my boundaries and check my powers in the process of facilitation. As a facilitator working with disenfranchised groups, I acknowledge that I embody power by factors such as my level of education and age – depending on the context where I am facilitating.

FIGURE 5.2 Milka's AERA image and performance script.

and myself, participants' trust in me, and trust among facilitation teams, ultimately circling around the trustworthiness of the knowledge claims we produce together. These are layered relationships. The trustworthiness of my facilitation practice relies on what I say and do within workshop spaces overlaid by my actions and reciprocities that I perform outside these spaces. These include the exchanges that take place while planning or debriefing in meetings or over email, in how I allocate research funds, and in how I acknowledge and work across intersectional differences.

Claudia: In the Bag

I know that this bag is a bit shapeless and undefined. I think it might be a type of muslin. I am pretty sure it is made in Ethiopia where I am often conducting, I mean facilitating, workshops on addressing sexual violence in agricultural colleges and universities.

It's definitely a bag and not a toolkit or a tickle trunk or a treasure chest. Not a bag of tricks though. No, just a bag. Not a hand bag but a bag for a hand to reach into.

Well, you can reach in but not necessarily get to the bottom. You have to grope around a bit and maybe what you think is there actually isn't. At least not today. You forgot to put it in.

But then even if you can't find what you are looking for, it still is sort of there, isn't it? Or something like it. Not a condom or a sanitary pad or a cellphone or whatever else you usually put into a bag for a workshop, but maybe a flyer or a pamphlet on safe sex.

Does it totally matter right now? Just put your bag down and figuratively, at least, ask everyone to look into theirs. Isn't that why you are here? Isn't that why they came to the workshop?

It's not that you are unprepared. It's that no one has expressed something exactly like that before…

But that's the point. It's never in the bag, as in 'in-the-bag.'

FIGURE 5.3 Claudia's AERA image and performance script.

Revisiting my performance, I see the missing information about the context of my work as putting my embodied positionality "between the lines." This obscures the structural aspects of research facilitation—who does research with whom—and the ways that race and colonialism shape my positionality within North-South relations. Boler (1999) identified the need to address emotions like anger, fear of change, and guilt among both students and instructors in social justice pedagogies. These potentially uncomfortable emotions can be present when doing anti-racist and decolonizing facilitation, and how they are addressed (named, given space, or ignored) have implications for trust. If trust is important for participants and researchers to believe in the process together, what is the role of transparency in naming the specific injustices like racism, colonization, and patriarchy within this work? Does this approach need to be made explicit at the start or can it emerge, through facilitated discussion? And how does this work,

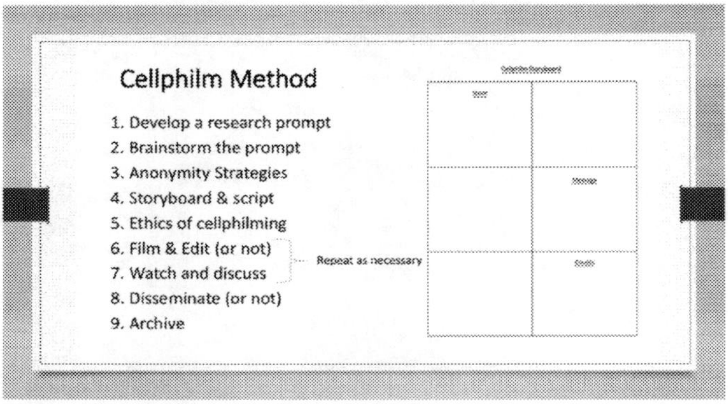

Cellphilm Method

1. Develop a research prompt
2. Brainstorm the prompt
3. Anonymity Strategies
4. Storyboard & script
5. Ethics of cellphilming
6. Film & Edit (or not)
7. Watch and discuss
8. Disseminate (or not)
9. Archive

Repeat as necessary

Katie: Cellphilm Method Steps

Here is a slide that I use in cellphilm workshops to address gender-based violence. Cellphilms are short videos *made by research participants* using a cellphone or another mobile device. The slide presents cellphilm method in nine defined steps. The steps are clean and concise. It suggests a process that moves smoothly. They are deceiving in this simplicity. The facilitator is made invisible in the black text on white background. But it's the facilitators job to identify the complexities that exist 'between the lines.'

Groups work collaboratively around circular tables. I stand back from the tables to let the groups work. When I am working with a team of facilitators, sometimes we stand back together. Or we stand away from each other, to seem more approachable and to survey the room. I try to position my face to say: 'We are available for support.'

I watch participants 'work the steps.'

Are people talking? Who is holding the pen and writing down ideas? Are people leaning in and engaged?

I should have a gulp of water.

How quickly are people moving through the steps? Who is sitting back from their groups – Is this a sign of disengagement or discomfort?

I move around the room - stalking, silent, listening, gaging the group dynamics.

I am trying not to disturb, to be invisible. But I'm not invisible. Eyes follow me as I move past their table. I am an interruption. I am in the way. I am not here to say you are doing it right or wrong.

I need to keep moving. Markers scratch paper. People genuflect towards each other in discussion. Some groups are loud, applauding their ideas. Others are quiet and secretive.

I circle the room and watch as the different groups begin to find their pace. Like in a race, a group charges ahead with firm ideas of what they want. I adjust my pace to the groups. There is a group who just want to get up and jump in, figure out the details as they come. With those who are definitive about their cellphilm method, I ask to hear about their decision process – did everyone get a say or is there one person who has taken control? How does everyone feel about the decision-making process? Other groups take more time. I slow down, sit for a bit with a group unsure about how to bring their different ideas together. They are planners, thinking about every detail before they get started.

The participatory researcher in me encourages the group to come together and find their own way, to trust *their* expertise and the process.

FIGURE 5.4 Katie's AERA Image and Performance Script.

transnationally and cross-culturally? Many facilitators that I know seem to work intuitively, relying on sense or feeling (within themselves or through reading the room) to guide the group. Yet intuition also seems risky. I am left confronting the idea of comfort with discomfort and how to integrate this within my facilitation pedagogy and practice.

Milka: To Facilitate and Participate? Interrogating the Limits to Facilitation in Arts-based Participatory Visual Workshops

I am a Black international student from Kenya considering co-facilitation in Canada. My doctoral research worked with young mothers in Korogocho slums in Nairobi. For this, I was the lead researcher and co-facilitated photovoice workshops alongside my project assistants who had prior experience in this context. However, I have more experience co-facilitating with experienced facilitators in arts-based workshops that explored issues of gender-based violence in and around school in Canada. As a doctoral student and an emerging black female scholar of facilitation from the Global South, co-facilitating with more experienced facilitators at the Participatory Cultures Lab—like Claudia, Jen, and Katie—has been very beneficial to me.

Reflection

My image of facilitation included a drawing, a roll of duct tape, pegs, a tin of pins, colouring pencils, and a camera on a small table. I assembled and photographed these materials in one frame to signify the multifaceted dimensions of facilitation. Upon revisiting my script, I question the possibility of being a neutral facilitator.

I re-lived moments in my facilitation when my positionality might have influenced workshop processes. For example, I co-facilitated a participatory visual workshop with undergraduate and graduate scholars from Sub-Saharan Africa at McGill University to reflect on their experiences navigating gender norms as international students. Although I co-facilitated this workshop with Dr. Catherine Vanner (see Chapter 14 in this volume), I embodied a similar position as participants, moving between working and studying in Canada and Sub-Saharan Africa. Many participants were interested in knowing my own experiences of navigating the gender norms between the two contexts. Catherine and I (as co-facilitators) decided to participate in the drawing workshop to show what gender norms looked like in our own communities and how we navigate these experiences in different contexts.

At AERA, my performance was uncomfortable as I was not sure how my positionality influenced the workshop processes. I felt what Pillow (2003) refers to as "uncomfortable reflexive practices." Knowing that practising reflexivity as a facilitator helps to interrogate power relations to make the workshop participant-centred does not make reflexivity any easier.

As I develop my facilitation practices within a transnational context (at home and in Canada), I continue to reflect on the ways to minimize power hierarchies in facilitating PVM workshops. The performance offered me the opportunity to step out of the normative, structured, and procedural step-by-step academic normalcy of presentation into a fluid realm with less formality. I found freedom to explore "between the lines" in facilitating arts-based participatory workshops. Through performance, I felt more comfortable to speak about the complexities that can arise when doing facilitation. My experience of facilitation has been inspired by the discomfort and opportunities working with the participants in different contexts. Acknowledging that I embody privilege because of my age and social status and my education, I normally turn to participating and collaborating with participants. Having co-facilitated workshops with groups that I closely relate to and identify with worked to create trust between myself and participants, and to minimize the power that I hold as a facilitator.

Claudia: In the Bag

I locate my performance piece on facilitation in what I would describe as an "on-the-ground" career of close to 25 years of working in the global context of youth, education, and equity. This has meant collaborating with numerous governments and international NGOs, and at the same time, supporting new researchers in both the Global North and the Global South. So much of this work is about facilitating workshops. Race, geography, sexuality, and ableism intersect. Often, I am the only white person in the room or one of only a couple of people over the age of twenty.

Reflecting on "in the Bag"

I have a double reading about the bag performance: there is the script above, and a programme notes piece that I wrote immediately after I produced the script. I sent both pieces of writing to my co-authors before our conference presentation. I was not that comfortable about presenting my two-minute script without some explanation.

> The bag is full of objects from my hotel room – maybe a boarding pass, a key, a cellphone, or a pen. But then I will add in a potato or a condom or whatever I can ask for at the front desk of the hotel or in the kitchen. Once I asked for a condom and promised to bring it back. So there is something quite concrete about what's in the bag. The materiality of the contents is key. But the real reason why I thought of the bag for talking about facilitation isn't really about these objects and things that I put in and plan to use. No, it is really more about thinking of the idea of the bag as both 'the container' but also something that expands or gets transformed.
>
> *(Program Notes, April 2019)*

But why the discomfort all these months later? Perhaps one of the most obvious concerns for me now is the idea of the white woman from the Global North "performing" the bag of objects in Ethiopia, Mozambique, and South Africa. I have photographs of me standing in the middle of a circle, surrounded by 15–20 or more workshop participants. It is not just that I am at the centre of the circle. I am the one who is dispensing the objects. And while many of the objects, as I point out in the script, are local—a condom, a potato, or a pen—now I cringe to admit that there could be a boarding pass (mine), camera, or credit card. To complete the cringe factor of this scene, I gather up all the objects at the end of the activity and return them to my bag.

While I ponder the idea of whether all facilitation is somehow a colonizing act, I also wonder how a level of consciousness related to power can become part of the pedagogy of training (see also Garcia et al., forthcoming.). While I try to avoid the "silver lining" discourse of COVID-19, I can't help but reflect on how the restrictions on international travel can transform relationships with colleagues in the Global South and with my co-facilitators. Much of my work that would have been about face-to-face facilitation has now become facilitation through online platforms with partners who are themselves preparing to facilitate arts-based workshops. How can a theory of the bag be helpful?

Katie: Cellphilm Method Steps

My experience facilitating participatory visual methodology workshops (in person and virtually) includes using cellphilm method, photovoice, digital storytelling, drawing, and collage, in Canada, Austria, South Africa, Ethiopia, India, Mozambique, and Sierra Leone. The workshops aim to build local responses for addressing HIV and AIDS, gender-based violence, ableism, as well as girls' and young women's and students with disabilities' access to education. Often the media produced during these workshops are shared locally to select audiences or more publicly to stimulate discussion and social change.

Performance Reflections

At the conference, I stepped out from behind the podium and moved through the audience as I read my script. I contrasted my image that compresses cellphilm method into nine steps with my multiple steps around the room. I felt the audience shift uncomfortably in their seats as I stepped past them. I was uncomfortable too! I struggled to infiltrate the aisles, almost tripping over one woman's suitcase. When I talked about how I try to position myself to seem more approachable, I stood still and tried to enact this expression in the performance. Re-reading my script, I remember the sense of embodiment that I wanted to perform using both my steps and my words to question the step-by-step method that I usually promote in my facilitation practice. My intent was to trouble the procedural and seemingly concrete, numbered steps depicted in my image. However, facilitation means always shifting and adapting these steps to meet the needs of the group. I wanted the audience to viscerally connect with the dynamic facilitation pace.

The COVID-19 pandemic has made me stay home. I have supported political activism, including Black Lives Matter and Wet'suwet'en Nation's sovereignty movement. I celebrated demands for de-funding systems to promote the construction of anti-racist knowledge systems. These movements have made me reconsider facilitation. In my presentation, I stated that I was "trying not to disturb, to be invisible." But the very act of the performance demands a sense of visibility and claiming space. Who I am—a white, upper-middle class, female academic—provides me with contested authority, especially when working on unceded territories.

A central tenet of facilitation is to work *with* people. When facilitation is done well, there is a coming together to create something new. Connections are built over time—one step at a time —by sharing ideas, listening, and exploring. Recognizing *everyone* in the workshop helps bridge differences. It is the *collaborative* creative construction that forms the basis of participatory visual activities. The steps in my image present a structure, a series of targets that groups (or individuals) may achieve in producing a cellphilm. It is the joint commitment to create something together that contributes insight and promotes change. In the workshop space, I see this collaborative construction contributing to bridging differences and building solidarity.

Reflecting on my discomfort has pushed me to embrace the embodied nature of facilitation. Revisiting my script has led me to situate my performance and facilitation as rooted in my privileged position. My discomfort challenges me to transform as a facilitator. My future work will require starting more explicit conversations with communities to discuss how our work will strive to be explicitly transformative. I need to ask: What is my role here? What is the role of others? How do I embody facilitation in a way that I can be proud of?

Towards a Pedagogy of Transformative Facilitation

As a key feature of our reflexive account, we tasked ourselves with the goal of exploring what it means to do transformative facilitation. Our development of autoethnographic performances of facilitation was motivated by wanting to critically examine how we learned to facilitate through doing and through collaborating with others. Considering our discomfort in relation to the themes of this edited volume, this includes thinking about how we can assert our commitments to social change by learning to facilitate in ways that are anti-racist and decolonizing. These commitments include actively pushing back and disrupting "everyday racism" (Essed, 1991) with the intention of dismantling intersecting micro and macro systems of racial oppression (Aquino, 2020) including those in which we benefit from (e.g., universities). We were further motivated by Connell's (2014) critique of the dominance of the Global North in knowledge production systems.

Recognizing ourselves as established and emerging researchers in Canada, we query our privileges as intellectual workers through our facilitation processes.

So, *how* are we engaging in facilitation to break these systems of oppression—built on stolen land, cultural genocide, and the labour of enslaved peoples? Our individual reflections offer specific responses to this question. We explore the subjective, embodied, and emotional facilitator, the facilitator who makes errors in judgement but who also seizes the moment. We highlight the risks and opportunities of working intuitively and the importance of relationship building, transparency, and community-based work towards social change. We suggest how travel restrictions related to the COVID-19 pandemic that limit the mobility of Northern researchers, and the shift to consultations online may start to disrupt North-South knowledge hierarchies. Yet, these strategies are also imperfect given inequities in access to online spaces and technologies, as well as to research funding and support.

Following Boler's (1999) *pedagogy of discomfort*, we name our reflections as evidence of the productive capacity of challenging what Zembylas (2015) described as normative and hegemonic beliefs. But discomfort, alone, is not enough to suggest progress towards transformative facilitation. A more general application of our work focuses on our process: a first collaborative leap into documenting our continued engagement in developing a *pedagogy of facilitation*. The first component of a pedagogy of facilitation recognizes that facilitators should be actively and discomfortingly reflexive. This interest in reflexivity and discomfort is commonplace amongst qualitative and feminist researchers (e.g. Pillow, 2003; Ward & Wylie, 2014). Here, we focus specifically on its application to facilitation of participatory visual methods that aim to both produce images and to support participants to engage in reflexivity, and ultimately to inspire dialogue and social change. We underscore the need for facilitators to continually question and challenge the (in)visibility of our embodied, emotional, and relational positionings within our practice. This aspect of a pedagogy of facilitation supports Switzer's (2019) assertion that facilitators are active participants (and certainly not objective) in the creative production process alongside workshop participants. Reflexivity needs to be an iterative and recursive process to explore how facilitation is challenging and fraught as well as a source of joy and connection. Working *together* to present this reflexive account was essential in pushing ourselves towards larger ethical, methodological, and epistemological questions about pedagogies of facilitation in working with participatory visual methodologies.

Second, a pedagogy of facilitation emphasizes the importance of engaging critically with *how* facilitators maintain and disrupt overarching systems of racist and colonizing oppressions. As a group of authors who lean on each other when preparing to facilitate in new settings, we identify international work as potentially colonizing in its very nature. Claudia, Jen, and Katie reflect primarily on their work in the Global South, which is predicated on their capacity as white settlers with Canadian passports to travel relatively unhindered globally and access competitive research funds. These funds are influenced by Canada's vested interest in gender-orientated global development projects. Milka is a Black international doctoral student unsure if she will be able to remain in Canada after her degree. Some of our discomfort comes from naming the inequities within our group, itself. By observing how race and nationality are important, we do not mean to essentialize these interpretations as the only significant identities in facilitation. Our different professional trajectories also shape the types of questions and positioning that we might engage in. Milka considers bias as a doctoral student of participatory visual methods in Canada and Kenya. Jen and Katie's focus on relationships might reflect their positions as postdoctoral fellows seeking both maintain international connections, and broaden their research programmes in Canada with uncertain hopes of securing tenure-track positions. Claudia, who has spent years developing and nurturing her relationships by working internationally, considers how her physical presence may or may not be necessary in continuing her work in Canada and abroad. We are each embedded within, both benefiting from and limited by, the potentially colonizing nature of development work and the multi-faceted geo-political context of North/South relations.

Together, these two components of a pedagogy of facilitation—that participatory visual facilitators engage critically with reflexivities of discomfort, and with *how* they maintain and disrupt intersecting systems of oppression such as patriarchy, racism, and colonialism—highlight *why* we facilitate visual processes. PVMs are intended to build sustainability within research processes. We strive to facilitate in ways that recognize, support, and work towards community-based action and social change. We also strive to build relationships and existing strengths within our collaborating communities and organizations that include teachers, youth, and young women, so that they can adopt and adapt visual methodologies to achieve their objectives. As we reflect on our performances and images, we suggest that revisiting autoethnographic performances of facilitation, individually and collectively, can be a generative strategy in working towards a transformative pedagogy of facilitation.

References

Akesson, B., D'Amico, M., Denov, M., Khan, F., Linds, W., & Mitchell, C. (2014). 'Stepping back' as researchers: Addressing ethics in arts-based approaches to working with war-affected children in school and community settings. *Education Research for Social Change, 3*(1): 75–89. ersc.nmmu.ac.za/articles/Vol_3_no_1_Akesson_pp_75-88_April_2014.pdf

Aquino, K. (2020). Anti-racism and everyday life. In J. Solomos (Ed.), *Routledge international handbook of contemporary racism* (pp. 216–229). Routledge.

Belliveau, G., & Lea, G.W. (Eds.). (2016). *Research-based theatre: An artistic methodology.* Intellect.

Boler, M. (1999). *Feeling power: Emotions and education.* Routledge.

Burawoy, M. (2014). The colour of class revisited: Four decades of postcolonialism in Zambia. *Journal of Southern African Studies, 40*(5): 961–979. https://doi.org/10.1080/03057070.2014.946213

Cole, A.L., & McIntyre, M. (2001). Dance me to an understanding of teaching: A performative text. *Journal of Curriculum Theorizing, 17*(2): 43–60.

Connell, R. (2014). Using southern theory: Decolonizing social thought in theory, research and application. *Planning Theory, 13*(2), 210–223.

Ellis, C., Adams, T.E., & Bochner, A.P. (2011). Autoethnography: An overview. *Historical Social Research, 36*(4): 273–290. https://doi.org/10.12759/hsr.36.2011.4.273-290

Essed, P. (1991). *Understanding everyday racism: An interdisciplinary theory* (Vol. 2). Sage.

Franco, L.A., & Nielsen, M.F. (2018). Examining group facilitation in situ: The use of formulations in facilitation practice. *Group Decision and Negotiation, 27*(5): 735–756. https://doi.org/10.1007/s10726-018-9577-7

Garcia, C.K., Mitchell, C., & Ezcurra, M. (forthcoming). Not just any toolkit! What's facilitation got to do with it? In S. Shariff & C. Dietzel (Eds.), *IMPACTS: Reclaiming the role of universities to address sexual violence through multi-sector partnerships in law, arts and social media*. University of Toronto Press.

Goldstein, T. (2013). *Zero tolerance and other plays: Disrupting xenophobia, racism and homophobia in school*. Sense.

Goldstein, T. (2019). The bridge: The political possibilities of intergenerational verbatim theater. *Qualitative Inquiry, 26*(7): 833–839. https://doi.org/10.1177/1077800419843947

Landreman, L. (Ed.). (2013). *The art of effective facilitation: Reflections from social justice educators*. Stylus.

Liebenberg, L. (2018). Thinking critically about photovoice: Achieving empowerment and social change. *International Journal of Qualitative Methods, 17*(1): 1–9. https://doi.org/10.1177/1609406918757631

MacEntee, K. (2016). Facing responses to cellphilm screenings of African girlhood in academic presentations. In K. MacEntee, C. Burkholder, & J. Schwab-Cartas (Eds.), *What's a cellphilm? Integrating mobile phone technology into participatory visual research and activism* (pp. 137–152). Sense.

MacEntee, K., Burkholder, C., & Schwab-Cartas, J. (2016). What's a cellphilm? An introduction. In K. MacEntee, C. Burkholder, & J. Schwab-Cartas (Eds.), *What's a cellphilm? Integrating mobile technology into visual research and activism* (pp. 1–18). Sense.

MacEntee, K., & Flicker, S. (2019). Doing it: Participatory visual methodologies and youth sexuality research. In S. Lamb & J. Gilbert (Eds.), *The Cambridge handbook of sexual development: Childhood and adolescence* (pp. 352–372). Cambridge University Press.

MacEntee, K. & Mandrona, A. (2015). From discomfort to collaboration: Teachers screening cellphilms in a rural South African school. *Perspectives in Education, 33*(4), 42–56. https://journals.ufs.ac.za/index.php/pie/article/view/1929

Mitchell, C. (2004). Was it something I wore? In S. Weber & C. Mitchell (Eds.), *Not just any dress: Narratives of memory, body and identity* (pp. 83–88). Peter Lang Associates.

Mitchell, C., de Lange, N. & Moletsane, R. (2017). *Participatory visual methodologies: Social change, community and policy*. SAGE.

Mitchell, C., Moletsane, R., MacEntee, K., & de Lange, N. (2020). Participatory Visual Methodologies in Self-Study for Social Justice Teaching. In J. Kitchen, A. Berry, S. M. Bullock, A. R. Crowe, M. Taylor, H. Guðjónsdóttir, & L. Thomas (Eds.), *International handbook of self-study of teaching and teacher education practices* (pp. 683–712). Springer.

Moletsane, R., & Mitchell, C. (2007). On working with a single photograph. In N. de Lange, C. Mitchell, & J. Stuart (Eds.), *Putting people in the picture: Visual methodologies for social change* (pp. 131–140). Sense.

Pillow, W. (2003). Confession, catharsis, or cure? Rethinking the uses of reflexivity as methodological power in qualitative research. *International Journal of Qualitative Studies in Education, 16*(2): 175–196. https://doi.org/10.1080/0951839032000060635

Saldaña, J. (2018). Ethnodrama and ethnotheatre. In N.K. Denzin & Y.S. Lincoln (Eds.), *The SAGE handbook of qualitative research* (Vol. 5, pp. 377–394). Sage.

Shaffer, R. (1983). *Visual methodologies: An introduction to researching with visual materials.* Sage.

Switzer, S. (2019). Working with photo installation and metaphor: Re-visioning photovoice research. *International Journal of Qualitative Methods, 18*, 1–14. https://doi.org/10.1177/1609406919872395

Ward, E., & Wylie, G. (2014). 'Reflexivities of discomfort': Researching the sex trade and sex trafficking in Ireland. *European Journal of Women's Studies, 21*(3), 251–263. https://doi.org/10.1177/1350506813518759

Zembylas, M. (2015). 'Pedagogy of discomfort' and its ethical implications: The tensions of ethical violence in social justice education. *Ethics and Education, 10*(2), 163–174. https://doi.org/10.1080/17449642.2015.1039274

PART II
Facilitating in the Digital Realm

6

"NAH YOU'RE MY SISTERS FOR REAL!"

Utilizing Instagram and Mobile Phones to Facilitate Feminist Conversations with Asian Migrant Women in Aotearoa

Helen Yeung

Introduction

I am Hong Kong-Chinese / a woman of colour / a migrant daughter / "Asian" / colonized / feminist / tauiwi of colour / oriental persuasion / exotic / Chinese / not the right kind of Chinese / Cantonese / in diaspora / lonely / submissive / outspoken / quiet / perfectionist / privileged / a writer / self-taught artist / zinester / potter / illustrator / white-washed / anxious / outspoken / too opinionated / strong / resilient / soft / an activist / community organiser / facilitator / a scholar / an activist-scholar / caring / a protector / lonely / a bit of everything / sometimes nothing.

In November 2020, I set a timer for 3 minutes and wrote down a list of identity markers I have been associated with as an Asian migrant woman in Aotearoa (New Zealand). Earlier in the year, I began facilitating *Asian Feminist Project Aotearoa:* a community-based research project on Instagram with a group of six Asian migrant women. This was one of the first prompts I provided for participants in a set of 20 prompts. I begin with this prompt to introduce my positionality, and as an exhaustive list of identifiers: a diasporic feminist, a self-taught artist, facilitator, community organiser, zinester, a daughter of migrants, and an activist-scholar. These identities signal resistance to the colonial structures and institutions which attempt to categorize myself and those around me. I began with this exercise as a rejection of identification through exclusive categories, which has the potential to reconfigure identity in open-ended, transformative ways. Although I entered this research aware that my positionality as a researcher entailed a degree of privilege and power, I struggled as a woman of colour researcher to embrace the colonizing practices within academia, including the ways in which I was *Othered* institutionally as a gendered-racialized subject. Problematically, most of the research in migration studies are Eurocentric, and marginalize Asian migrant

DOI: 10.4324/9781003199236-9

women to roles of victims, oppressed, and lacking autonomy. Following the footsteps of feminist of colour scholars, I employ critical praxis to challenge the binaries which seek to define us as racialized peoples (Ahmed, 2017; Olufemi, 2020; hooks, 2000; Walia, 2013), and acknowledge the multiple subjectivities of the researcher, subject, and communities, beyond dichotomies of community/academia, activism/scholarship, and subject/researcher (Téllez, 2005).

This project encapsulates my resistance to being the "compliant, peacekeeping, accommodating, silent, grateful and hardworking Asian migrant woman" (Quah, 2020, p. 213). As the project progressed, I found it difficult to separate my overlapping identities with the complex, multi-layered, and hyphenated identities articulated by my research participants. Like many minorities, queer, and women of colour scholars, I was striving to mentor a safe space for participants while navigating institutional dangers where we are often discredited for writing about ourselves and face difficulties in being validating for our lived experiences (Cloud, 2020). I was intertwined in what Caldera et al. (2020) described as a sister–friend bond with my participants, with the goal of "creating an environment of emotional, physical, and political safety and well-being" (p. 72). I title this chapter, "Nah You're My Sisters for Real!" in homage to a heart-warming message Gwen—a participant—sent to the project group chat on Instagram:

> In a display of unintended shared authority, participants became researchers themselves with questions of their own... We talked about our intimate relationship struggles, our mothers, and more. I, too, became vulnerable, and this vulnerability was part of what made us sister-friends. We became so close, in fact, that it became difficult to separate my identity as a researcher from my identity as their sister-friend. I embodied them both, sometimes simultaneously.
>
> *(Caldera et al., 2020, pp. 70–71)*

The idea for the project sparked when I read Sara Ahmed's *Living a Feminist Life*. Questioning what makes feminism "feminist," Ahmed asserted that feminism requires an ongoing commitment to challenge everyday sexism, including those manifesting in academia. How can we practice feminism within these spaces? Ahmed suggests, "A feminist project is to find ways in which women can exist in relation to women; how women can be in relation to each other. It is a project because we are not there yet" (Ahmed, 2017, p. 14). This quote influenced my decision to name the project *Asian Feminist Project Aotearoa*, because with the rise of online activism, we are often met with the white supremacist imperialist myths of linear activist progression. This myth pressures us to be infallible and "no longer making mistakes once [we] are politically conscious, radical, or involved enough" (Brown, 2018, p. 21). To create genuine social change, we require innovative methods built on co-creation and spaces which facilitate collaboration while recognizing our vulnerabilities and shared experiences of trauma (Ahmed, 2017). I introduced a facilitation process carried out through a set of interactive prompts on Instagram to aid Asian migrant women in facilitating feminist conversations via their mobile phones.[1] I bring together a theoretical framework informed by my lived experiences, fourth-wave feminism and DIY self-publishing. I analyse how the creation of visual, audio and video, and text content for participant's personal Instagram accounts aided in creating feminist dialogues, self-learning, and consciousness-raising on intersectionality and resisting patriarchal gender norms.

Feminism and (Re)Situating Asian Migrant Women

I begin by situating Asian migrant women, and myself, my sister-friends, and those in my communities within the wider context of globalized hegemonic structures. In the discussion of intersectionality as a critical method, Davis (2014) stressed the importance of the politics of location—including social identities such as gender, class, ethnicity, and sexuality—as it enables "the production of feminist knowledge which is accountable, reflexive and admittedly partial" (Davis, 2014, p. 22). I interweave my experiences throughout this chapter, including my migration story. Through these gendered-racialised narratives, I was able to bond with participants, facilitating an environment in which they were comfortable to tell their stories (Caldera et al., 2020).

In 1996, I migrated from Hong Kong to Tāmaki Makaurau (Auckland), Aotearoa with my parents before my first birthday. Like many Asian migrant families who left their countries in the nineties, our journey was impacted by border imperialism, resulting from "the violence of colonial displacements, capital circulations, labor stratifications in the global economy, and structural hierarchies of race, class, gender, ability, and citizenship status" (Walia, 2013, p. 25). I write this chapter with a commitment to an intersectional praxis, bolstered by fourth-wave feminism where digital platforms have enabled a shift in feminist protest culture, and new ways to unpack intersectional forms of oppression (Baer, 2016; Bayne, 2018; Looft, 2017).

I write this chapter in an indefinite period of heartbreak for Hong Kong. I long to see my grandmother, to be surrounded by the familiar sounds of the dense cityscape—my other home. "Home" is not a specific location, but a range of places, people, objects, and spaces which instigate a sense of familiarity, community, and nostalgia. I use the term diaspora[2] to describe the lived experiences of Asian migrant women, to discuss the impact brought on by migration to a foreign land, including "new meanings, identities, and alignments of power and articulations of identities and culture" (Zalipour, 2018, p. 5). I refer to myself interchangeably with the identifiers of Hong Kong-Chinese and as an Asian migrant woman[3] to highlight the racial politics and Sinophobia specific to Aotearoa, a settler colonial nation-state which continues to operate through white supremacy and the dispossession of Māori people. The term "Asian migrant women" is not meant to homogenize, but rather, a political tactic of strategic essentialism whereby the use of a shared identity aids in creating unity within the opposition against gendered-racialized oppression (Spivak, 1988). It is vital to note that the term women in this project refers to cis and trans* women, and non-binary people who are comfortable with in a space that centres the lived experiences of women.

Aotearoa relies on colonial myths to justify "illegitimately dispossessing Māori and usurping our power, often brutally and violently, forcing [them] into poverty, deprivation, marginalisation and powerlessness" (Mutu, 2019, p. 1). As such, Aotearoa is governed by a racialized nation-building project which legitimises Pākehā (white people) as the norm (Mutu, 2019; Rata & Al-Asaad, 2019; Spoonley, 2017). White settler colonialism perpetuates a racialized hierarchy which rejects Māori cultural identities and practices, and excludes settlers from Asia (Spoonley, 2017).

When represented in mainstream discourses, Asian women are often reproduced as the marginalized *Other*, through Colonial, Orientalist, and Eurocentric narratives as "exotic, tradition-bound, ahistorical, subordinate subjects" (Yee, 2016, p. 7). This acts as a reflection of the gendered-racialized experiences of Asian migrant women as "twice marginalised" due to wider structures of "transnational inequality, racial hierarchy, marginalisation and exclusion" (Kim, 2011, pp. 88–89).

I grew up in a traditional Chinese setting where patriarchy affected the women around me—myself, my mother, grandmother, sisters, cousins, aunties alike. Although I am unable to place a finger at the instant I became politicized, as a girl, "I felt the oppressive way the world was organised with my body and through interpersonal relations long before I could articulate what those feelings meant" (Olufemi, 2020, pp. 1–2). I recall feeling anger, frustration, injustice, powerlessness, and isolation, which lead me to community organizing and feminist activism, sharing my experiences with migrant women and girls to generate collective social action. I found solace and collective healing in feminist organizing as it became a space "to redeem and liberate myself from all the injustices, categories, and assumptions laid on me" (Walia, 2013, p. 169).

In the ideation process of my research project, I reflected on the research projects I had participated in, and recalled the anxieties I felt after an interview, the rawness I felt discussing trauma with an "insider" researcher of colour while they checked if the microphone was recording. I was reminded of Tuck and Yang (2014) who said, "The stories that are considered most compelling, considered most authentic in social science research are stories of pain and humiliation" (p. 812). Such analytic practices continue to perpetuate settler colonial, heteropatriarchal, and white supremacist codes of knowledge production, whereby the academy fetishsizes, commodifies, and exposes stories of pain and oppression for marginalized peoples (Tuck & Yang, 2014).

I did not want my study participants to experience discomfort during the research. Caldera et al. (2020) pointed out, when women of colour researchers conduct research, they can become both the colonizer and the colonized, "a dilemma requiring close examination of positionality, privilege, and power" (Caldera et al., 2020, p. 64). Drawing from feminist works surrounding Black domestic violence survivors as well as the work of midwives, Davis and Craven (2011) argued feminist ethnographers must reassert feminist activist values at the core of theory, method, and practice.

Considering the COVID-19 Pandemic, I felt an urgency to incorporate methodological innovations beyond merely researching women's stories. Contextually, this was vital for my research participants, as COVID-19 spread across borders, it simultaneously brought on a spate of racist attacks towards East and South Asian peoples. Sinophobia served as a reminder of the colonial histories behind Asian bodies, as the violence was racialized and gendered, with Asian migrant women bearing the brunt of attacks in various white settler colonial societies. In Tāmaki Makaurau, accounts of sexism and racism surfaced from Asian migrant women in the news, on Twitter and Instagram. My mother was harassed at the supermarket by a white man clamouring for her to "go back to China" while bystanders remained silent. In addition, while Aotearoa was considered safe and COVID-free, changes to social distancing and working from home largely increased issues of domestic and family violence, unpaid care work, and wage disparities for women (Roy, 2020). This was particularly pertinent to Māori, Pasifika, migrant, and refugee women who face gender inequity, and lack representation in public decision-making, policy, and scholarly publications to begin with (Sumihira, 2020).

With COVID-19 radically shifting societal structures, I grasped the opportunity for reimagining and embracing multimodality to facilitate feminist change in my research. Through forms of sisterhood, Sumihira (2020) suggests that women of colour can connect to make sense of their oppression and speak back to their erasure from public discourse. The COVID-19 pandemic made digital the default. Social media was reinforced as a platform for information sharing, activism, and social learning (Hantrais et al., 2020). The proliferation of digital activism shifted the ways in which community-building and radical forms of care occurred in the relationships I had with my participants. With prior experiences as a researcher and community organizer involved in fourth-wave feminism and digital activism, I was determined to bring some of these strategies to my own communities through accessible practices. Central to this being the idea of generating or capturing feminist conversations in aspects of art, writing, and storytelling through the mobile phone while performing daily tasks. I wanted to share stories of hope, agency, love, thoughts, and frustrations, where Asian migrant women could be (re)constructed through our complexities.

Zines and DIY Self-Publishing

The research facilitation process was heavily influenced by my position as a zinester, and the experiences I have co-authoring and co-producing zines—DIY print productions—with marginalized communities. Piepmeier (2009) noted, feminist zines have a longstanding history of acting to provide a space for women of colour to navigate intersectional subjectivities, hyphenated identities and subvert stereotypical notions as the *Other*. Zines have been a significant medium "for personal expression, as an outlet for creativity, out of isolation, as a supportive space and network tool in search of like-minded friends and community, and as a form of cultural resistance and political critique" (Zobl, 2009, p. 5). I was introduced to zines through the microblogging platform Tumblr. Living in a suburban white neighbourhood, the digital sphere exposed me to Riot Grrrl, punk and underground feminist zines from the depths of my bedroom. While I was instantly captivated by the voices of anarcho-feminists, particularly on the covers of Mimi Thi Nguyen's zine *Slant*, where I first saw depictions of Asian women as rebellious and defiant. I later became a feminist organizer, and part of Mellow Yellow, a zine run by Asian feminists in Aotearoa to challenge dominant white feminisms, colonization, and all forms of social injustice. In 2017, I founded Migrant Zine Collective, an activist-based zine collective aiming to open a space for migrants of colour to unapologetically tell their stories.

I continue to implement the lessons I learn from workshop facilitation as praxis, especially the need to balance critical theory with practice. I consciously incorporated the do-it-yourself (DIY) ethos of zine publishing which allowed myself and others to fill blank pages unapologetically with whatever rage, sadness, grief, or injustices had been overwhelming our thoughts. This included the emotions surrounding migration, and unpacking the trauma, including racism, misogyny, and intergenerational wounds. While feminist research methods are centred on shifting the status quo, there is a need to move further from the academy to focus on generating non-hierarchical, community-driven spaces where participants can navigate the plurality of feminist expressions. Licona (2012) explained how zines allow for the creation of third-space sites for diasporic subjects to navigate existing binaries, "where traditional knowledges circulate and sometimes collide with newer knowledges to produce innovative and informed practices" (p. 2). This sense of knowledge production is significant to archival work of the untold stories of migrant women of colour. Drawing a link between archival work and migration, Appadurai (2003) argued that the making of archives is a significant memory practice for migrants in documenting "one's own life and family world in the old place, and official memory about the nation one has left have to be recombined in a new location" (p. 14). Digital archives, with the potential of sharing photos, sounds, and text to multiple users at a time, can gradually create a deliberate site for the construction of "intentional communities" beyond the state (Appadurai, 2003, p. 17).

Migrating my feminist self-publishing framework to Instagram felt intuitive. Participants regularly consumed (and sometimes produced) memes, hashtags, infographics, and viral videos. As Bayne (2018) argues, women's narratives archived through ephemera such as zines, pamphlets and newspapers have moved into digital spaces, such as storytelling via hashtag activism. I wanted to ensure the preservation of acts of subversion, self-representation, and storytelling as found in DIY publishing, and relay these approaches into a digital space. My research design was guided by the desire to produce a space where participants did not wait for permission to write or speak. Participants were not bound by rigid forms of communication, and created in formats including audio, video, photos, imagery, and voice clips. Participants were encouraged to use existing materials to tell their stories and engaged with cultural material to play with and remake dominant constructions of race, ethnicity and gender—including repurposing stereotypical imagery of the "silent Asian woman" to reveal hidden power structures meant to be addressed and altered (Piepmeier, 2009). I sought to resist pervasive neoliberal white feminist narratives which situate the experiences of women of colour through the desires of middle class white women. While acknowledging that digital technologies come with limitations, feminist self-publishing creates macro-level change, and is a powerful tool of resistance for migrant women of colour who also enact material changes in offline spaces.

Fourth-wave Feminism, Mobile Phones, and Instagram

While weary of the controversies surrounding fourth-wave feminism, it is a useful starting point to capture the participatory engagement I aimed to facilitate through Instagram. The #MeToo movement piqued my interest in digital activism, feminism and advocacy. Rather than fixating on a particular platform, or format, digital activism is defined by a sense of community building, and the creation of new cultural and political practices (Kaun & Uldam, 2018). In the context of feminism, Baer (2016) argued that digital platforms have shifted feminist action to translocal and transnational articulations in neoliberal societies. Fourth-wave feminism has brought resistance into the online sphere, utilizing digital technologies to create new modes of dissemination for information, participation, and engagement across cultural and national borders (Looft, 2017).

Hashtag feminism has brought on an "interplay of individual stories and collective modalities enabled by digital platforms" (Baer, 2016, p. 18). Looft (2017) examined the #Girlgaze project on Twitter and Instagram from 2016, which showcased the work of women photographers around the globe. She explained that social media platforms have become increasingly synonymous with wider political engagement, and in mobilizing support for issues such as reproductive rights and sexual violence prevention. Hashtags and social media platforms have provided marginalized groups with accessible technologies to collectivize and resist, this includes content creation from selfies, artwork, event fliers, and photos of everyday acts of activism (Bayne, 2018). For myself and my participants, digital technologies have become a space to resist, connect, and seek support while we tackled the realities of surviving in a white supremacist, heterosexist, and patriarchal setting. Social media platforms have played an active role in empowering the voices of women of colour, queer women, working-class women, and transgender women (Kaba et al. qtd. in Looft, p. 895). However, I also recognize the limitations of social media as a space governed by surveillance capitalism, whereby the content and data of participants are accessible to multinational corporations often without explicit consent.

For migrant women of colour, the online world can highlight important concerns like bodily autonomy, legal issues or their invisibility in mainstream public brought on by narratives of victimization (brownfemipower, 2018). Instead of waiting for promises of inclusion and diversity, "We must also create our own feminist media that centers not only our needs, but also the ways in which our community members can organize around those needs" (brownfemipower, 2018, p. 130). In my activism, I use social media platforms to raise awareness on forced marriage, domestic and family violence, racism, and xenophobia to migrant women and allies. Beyond forms of policy outreach, networking, and publicly calling out injustices, Caldeira et al. (2018) emphasize how social media platforms like Instagram have generated forms of "everyday activism" which are framed around women's personal stories, interests, and experiences and how these are political, even if not specifically constructed as such (p. 24). The user-friendly interfaces on Instagram "are integrated into smartphones and are already widely used in everyday life, have simplified and democratised the means for visual creation, editing, and distribution" (Caldeira et al., 2018, p. 24). I have found the visual and curatorial aspect of Instagram to be extremely useful as it offers—"accessible, informal and convenient spaces" for women of colour to create new social truths and resist reductionist constructions as the gender-racialized *Other* (Islam, 2019, p. 219).

From Prompts to Feminist Conversations

Combining these theoretical and methodological frameworks, I designed a set of 20 written prompts for participants. Besides actively centring Asian migrant women's lived experiences, I turned to cooperative modes of data gathering in the facilitation process to ensure "an open, inclusive, accessible, creative and dynamic process between people, activities and ideas" (Poonacha, 2004, p. 397). I actively listened to requests from participants to form a group chat on Instagram to engage with each other during the project. Although unexpected, the group chat dramatically shifted the course of the facilitation process, in particular non-hierarchical forms of knowledge sharing, interconnectedness, and solidarity within the group. For each prompt, participants were given an activity or instruction to carry out and post on their personal Instagram account. I emphasized that prompts were open to interpretation, and participants should only share to the extent they felt comfortable in their online communities. I recommended participants utilize a range of basic mobile phone applications and Instagram editing functions to create their posts. Participants were given a loose timeframe of four to five weeks to complete the prompts at their own pace. I was surprised to find that participants spent much longer on each prompt than the recommended 30 minutes as they enjoyed the creative aspect of the tasks and found the activities thought-provoking. To better understand the process of creation, participants were asked to document any thoughts or experiences through online journal entries.

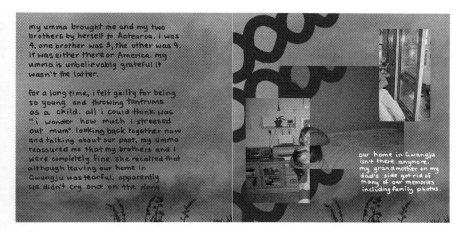

FIGURE 6.1 Min-Young's content from Asian Feminist Project Aotearoa (2020).

In the first week, the prompts asked participants to rethink identity and its intersections. These included retelling participants' migration stories, reclaiming their ethnic or cultural names, and redefining ways to think of home. Participants' migration stories included collaging family photos, significant locations, and documenting the decision to migrate along with overlooked aspects of the journey (See Figure 6.1). The thought process behind the prompts was intuitive, where I embraced lived experience as a way of knowing and recalled each small step to which I became politicized (Caldera et al., 2020). Olufemi (2020) explains,

> Some of us are politicised by the trauma of our own experiences, by wars waged in our names, by our parents and lovers, by the internet. It's useful to share the ways we become politicised if only because it helps politicise others
>
> *(p. 1)*

I encouraged participants to collage old photographs and ephemera as this was how I first deconstructed my own migration story, through a cut and paste community zine which centred my story along with ones from migrant youth in Tāmaki Makaurau. I shared that although storytelling is something we do daily, it is political in nature, an expression of identity, and impacted by the structural limitations we encounter in our everyday lives. For many participants, this was the first time they had actively asked their family about their experiences. As Nahyeon recounted in her journal entry, this was the first time she had spoken to her mother about their migration journey because of the nature of their relationship:

> "I'm doing this for a friend's research project" was all she needed to not stop talking. She spoke of her connections to Korea and never felt like NZ was home after 25 years. She'd never expressed such deep uncertainty before to

me. We had a conversation that spanned her regrets, her fears, the language barrier, her lack of planning, her sacrifice, all in the twenty minutes she was cooking fish on a pan.

Women's life histories, cultural knowledge, and memories are often a precise methodological tool in which stories can create discourse to act in opposition to dominant narratives (Téllez, 2005). The identity marker activity centred intersectionality as a starting point for participants to challenge an essential notion of self as unified and whole, and the contradicting, hyphenated identities which accompany the diasporic experience. Participants described the thought process behind the activity as introspective, powerful, and liberating yet aptly capturing the essence of living between two worlds.

In the second week, I attempted to encourage conversation around gender and migration through the prompts. This included having participants interview their mothers on their dreams and aspirations, rethinking the familial kitchen as a gendered space, archiving recipes, documenting objects in the private sphere, and describing women in their family using their mother tongue. The prompts were intentional and built on a theoretical approach that values women's ideas and daily experiences as well as the mode of articulation this takes place in (Poonacha, 2004). The activity of interviewing participants' mothers was inspired by a handwritten account of my mother's migration memories from one of my zines. In the prompt, I asked participants to listen and reflect on Indian-American singer and songwriter Raveena's song "Mama" which was dedicated to her mother and grandmother, and the sacrifices they made during their migration journey to the United States in the 1980s. I integrated elements of popular music into multiple prompts as self-representation on Instagram is often embedded in popular culture, where one re-appropriates mainstream conventions to construct an image of themselves (Caldeira et al., 2018). In revisiting the lives of the women closest to them, I wanted participants to rethink why these voices are often silenced and rendered powerless under shared experiences of systemic oppression. I recall crying at the outcome of a lot of these prompts, the all too familiar situation of pain, grief, and lost dreams of migrant mothers captured in the content created (Figure 6.2).

In the third week, I encouraged participants to reflect on feminist themes and their own positionality in Aotearoa. This included generating new forms of feminist knowledge, discovering feminist histories from home, and reflecting on gendered-racialized stereotypes and representations surrounding Asian women. I focused on the production of knowledge as a feminist praxis, asking participants to create a typographic artwork of a quote from a feminist, friend, family member, or mentor. Following Ahmed (2017), "Citation is how we acknowledge our debt to those who came before; those who helped us find our way when the way was obscured because we deviated from the paths we were told to follow" (pp. 15–16). The responses to this prompt ranged from women of colour politicians, film directors to treasured friends and art mentors. Pauline's creation stood out as she decided to post a photo of a cake with the words, "Don't settle for the

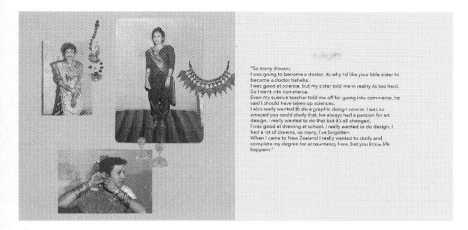

FIGURE 6.2 Shivani's content from Asian Feminist Project Aotearoa (2020).

FIGURE 6.3 Pauline's content from Asian Feminist Project Aotearoa (2020).

crumbs" as the icing (Figure 6.3). She reflects in her journal that a wise woman of colour once gave her this advice as a reminder to stand up for herself during a past relationship. Pauline realized, "There's a lot in the past that was toxic, but I put up with—memories I may not realise I've been repressing. I am however grateful for the women I've gotten close to since participating in this research." I chose to display the photo posted on Pauline's Instagram as it serves as a reminder that a simple snapshot can also be value-laden in social science research, "painful, but also wise, full of desire and dissent" (Tuck & Yang, 2014, p. 812).

I aimed to inspire participants to disrupt prevalent stereotypical representations of Asian women and unpack the emotions behind these prevailing power inequalities (Poonacha, 2004). Quah (2020) explored how instances of rage, shock, fear, grief, despondence, unbelonging, and other painful emotions for Asian migrant women could be transformed into emotional fuel for survival and "feminist superpowers" (p. 211). For this process to be impactful, we must start with the everyday ways that participants deconstruct their realities through accessible forms of storytelling. I wanted participants to generate self-representations that spoke back to the exotification and fetishization of Asian women's bodies, including a longstanding imperialist history of being represented as apolitical, subservient, passive, submissive, and hypersexualized. I again utilized popular music, this time British-Japanese singer Rina Sawayama's song "STFU," a response on the microaggressions faced by Asian women in white settings. In attempts to retrace the DIY ethos behind zines, I asked participants to create a digital collage or artwork to reflect their emotions. I did not anticipate the range of interpretations participants had to the prompts that week, which included remixing other popular media, selfies, illustration, and memes (See Figure 6.4). Gwen and Anjuli's selfies acted as visual forms of self-representation, cultural resistance, and intersectional feminism exercised at their own curatorial agency (Caldeira et al., 2018). In her journal entry, Anjuli explained the intent of her selfie as an act of reclaiming cultural appropriation, "As I have grown up I have decided to #reclaimthebindi [...] When I wear a bindi (and my therefore my culture so clearly) with my usual 'western' clothing I feel so pretty, liberated and proud."

FIGURE 6.4 Gwen (left) and Anjuli's (right) content from Asian Feminist Project Aotearoa (2020).

Next, I invited participants to reimagine forms of self-care and radical love for women in their communities, along with what feminist media futures could look like, and how their identity markers have changed since the project began. While taking COVID-19 and the implications on mental health and wellbeing into account, I wanted to end the project with a reflection on hope. The prompt on radical love asked participants to consider practicing love not only as care for themselves and their communities, but as an act of survival, political resistance, and cultivating resilience beyond the status quo. Anjuli discussed the timeliness of this activity in relation to self-preservation as women of colour in a post-COVID world. She posted collaged photos of different textures, and shared,

> I then began to focus on the small things that brought me joy over the last few years which have been extremely tough for me. The theme organically started to centre around two basic things: nature and food. Air and sustenance.

As hooks (2000) explains,

> feminist theory and practice are predicated on self-love, self-acceptance, and self-actualisation. As a woman of colour researcher, I often find myself prone to burnout in the battle to build critical and activist spaces in White institutional settings. Participants' responses, which ranged from making art and cooking delicious foods, served as a reminder that survival can sometimes be as simple as having "the capacity to produce ideas and to be heard. It is inherent in bodies of knowledge produced by the oppressed. It is love".

(Cloud, 2020, p. 374)

With the facilitation process coming to an end, I asked participants to showcase what feminist media would look like to them, particularly with how new media technologies have influenced the accessibility of knowledge production and distribution. Reading through participants' journal responses, I was touched to find the positive feedback participants had given the project. While Min-Young commented that we need more projects to shift depictions of people of colour from diversity quota checkboxes to agents of change. Pauline said that the project is what she envisioned for feminist media,

> While we're nearing the end of the prompts, there's nothing I would love more than to continue amplifying marginalised voices and empowering Asian women to share their stories with these pure souls. I may be projecting here but how do picnics and podcasts sound?

The image she posted included her favourite interactions in our group chat (Figure 6.5).

108 Helen Yeung

FIGURE 6.5 Pauline's content from Asian Feminist Project Aotearoa (2020).

In the months that followed, participants began collaborating on each other's podcasts, artworks, making zines with myself, and supporting each other at events. As a researcher in Communication Studies, I find myself reminded of how I got here in the first place, for the sake of creating resources, platforms, and strategies for my communities to feel valued, to heal, and generate social change.

Conclusion

I began this project with the goal of facilitating feminist conversations with Asian migrant women on Instagram, and found forms of tenderness, care, and feminist solidarity in new and unimaginable ways. I thank my sister-friends, co-researchers, and fellow Asian migrant women: Nahyeon, Min-Young, Anjuli, Gwen, Pauline, and Shivani for their trust, enriching knowledge, endless support, and for reminding me that we have each other in our battles for survival. While being digitally together, yet physically apart, participants and myself co-created a support system and digital space for Asian migrant women and women of colour who shared similar struggles. We continue to follow each other on Instagram, share each other's posts on Instagram's Stories function or leave supportive comments on each Instagram post. These interactions have become an act of visibility and togetherness. Our posts remain public, whether temporarily or until Instagram is no longer a popularized platform, as a form of collective memory and archival of Asian migrant women's stories—amidst the COVID-19 Pandemic. In order to shift beyond academia's fixation and commodification of the pain, trauma, and oppression of marginalized peoples, I urge researchers to consider alternative facilitation methods which place participants in the position to generate their own narratives for their own purposes. As Ahmed (2017) said, "Don't let her speak on her own. Back her up; speak with her. Stand by her; stand with her. From these public moments of solidarity so much is brought into existence" (p. 260). These everyday interactions capture dissent, break silences, and become the building blocks for feminist futures that decentre whiteness.

Notes

1 The entire project was carried out digitally across the course of two lockdowns due to COVID-19 in Aotearoa.
2 The term diaspora loosely describes "individuals and groups who involuntarily or voluntarily have left their country of origin, including their children and succeeding generations who reside in the new place" (Zalipour, 2019, p. 5).
3 I also identify as tauiwi of colour (a non-Māori person of colour), to acknowledge that the land I reside on is one built on forms of imperial violence and dispossession of Māori land.

References

Ahmed, S. (2017). *Living a feminist life*. Duke University Press.
Appadurai, A. (2003). Archive and aspiration. In J. Brouwer, & A. Mulder (Eds.), *Information is alive* (pp. 14–25). V2_ publishing. https://v2.nl/publishing/information-is-alive
Baer, H. (2016). Redoing feminism: Digital activism, body politics, and neoliberalism. *Feminist Media Studies*, 16(1), 17–34. https://doi.org/10.1080/14680777.2015.1093070
Bayne, C.N. (2018). #nolitetebastardescarborundorum: Self-publishing, hashtag activism, and feminist resistance. *Communication, Culture and Critique*, 11(1), 201–205. https://doi.org/10.1093/ccc/tcx016
Brooks, A. (2007). Feminist standpoint epistemology: Building knowledge and empowerment through women's lived experience. In S.N. Hesse-Biber, & P.L. Leavy (Eds.), *Feminist research practice: A primer* (pp. 53–82). SAGE. https://dx.doi.org/10.4135/9781412984270
Brownfemipower. (2018). Immigration at the front: Challenging the "every woman" myth in online media. In J. Hoffmann, & D. Yudacufski (Eds.), *Feminisms in motion: Voices for justice, liberation, and transformation* (pp. 187–198). AK Press.
Brown, L.X. (2018). Rebel - Don't be palatable: Resisting co-optation and fighting for the world we want. In A. Wong (Ed.), *Resistance and hope: Essays by disabled people* (pp. 15–32). Disability Visibility Project.

Caldeira, S.P., De Ridder, S., & Van Bauwel, S. (2018). Exploring the politics of gender representation on Instagram: Self-representations of femininity. *DiGeSt. Journal of Diversity and Gender Studies, 5*(1), 23. https://doi.org/10.11116/digest.5.1.2

Caldera, A., Rizvi, S., Calderon-Berumen, F., & Lugo, M. (2020). When researching the "Other" intersects with the self: Women of color intimate research. *Departures in Critical Qualitative Research, 9*(1), 63–88. https://doi.org/10.1525/dcqr.2020.9.1.63

Cloud, D.L. (2020). The spiral of survival. *Communication and Critical/Cultural Studies, 17*(4), 369–377. https://doi.org/10.1080/14791420.2020.1829658

Davis, D., & Craven, C. (2011). Revisiting feminist ethnography: Methods and activism at the intersection of neoliberal policy. *Feminist Formations, 23*(2), 190–208. https://doi.org/10.1353/ff.2011.0018

Davis, K. (2014). Intersectionality as critical methodology. In N. Lykke (Ed.), *Writing academic texts differently: Intersectional feminist methodologies and the playful art of writing* (pp. 17–29). Routledge.

Hantrais, L., Allin, P., Kritikos, M., Sogomonjan, M., Anand, P.B., Livingstone, S., Williams, M., & Innes, M. (2020). COVID-19 pandemic and the digital revolution. *Contemporary Social Science: Journal of the Academy of Social Sciences*, 1–15. https://doi.org/10.1080/21582041.2020.1833234

Hooks, B. (2000). *Feminism is for everybody: Passionate politics.* Pluto Press.

Islam, I. (2019). Redefining #YourAverageMuslim woman: Muslim female digital activism on social media. *Journal of Arab & Muslim Media Research, 12*(2), 213–233. https://doi.org/10.1386/jammr_00004_1

Kaun, A., & Uldam, J. (2018). Digital activism: After the hype. *New Media & Society, 20*(6), 2099–2106. https://doi.org/10.1177/1461444817731924

Kim, Y. (2011). *Transnational migration, Media and identity of Asian women: Diasporic daughters.* Routledge.

Leavy, P., & Harris, A. (2019). *Contemporary feminist research from theory to practice.* The Guilford Press.

Licona, A.C. (2012). *Zines in third space: Radical cooperation and borderlands rhetoric.* SUNY Press.

Looft, R. (2017). #girlgaze: Photography, fourth wave feminism, and social media advocacy. *Continuum: Journal of Media and Cultural Studies, 31*(6), 892–902. https://doi.org/10.1080/10304312.2017.1370539

Mutu, M. (2019). 'To honour the treaty, we must first settle colonisation' (Moana Jackson 2015): The long road from colonial devastation to balance, peace and harmony. *Journal of the Royal Society of New Zealand, 49*(sup1), 4–18. https://doi.org/10.1080/03036758.2019.1669670

Quah, S.E. (2020). Navigating emotions at the site of racism: Feminist rage, queer pessimism and fire dragon feminism. *Australian Feminist Studies, 35*(105), 203–216. https://doi.org/10.1080/08164649.2020.1830703

Olufemi, L. (2020). *Feminism, interrupted: Disrupting power.* Pluto Press.

Piepmeier, A. (2009). *Girl zines: Making media, doing feminism.* NYU Press.

Poonacha, V. (2004). Recovering women's histories: An enquiry into methodological questions and challenges. *Indian Journal of Gender Studies, 11*(3), 389–404. https://doi.org/10.1177/097152150401100306

Rata, A., & Al-Asaad, F. (2019). Whakawhanaungatanga as a Māori Approach to Indigenous–settler of colour relationship building. *New Zealand Population Review, 45*, 211–233. https://population.org.nz/app/uploads/2019/12/NZPR-Vol-45_Rata-and-Al-Asaad.pdf

Roy, E.A. (2020) New Zealand domestic violence services to get $200m as lockdown takes toll. *The Guardian.* https://theguardian.com/world/2020/may/11/new-zealand-domestic-violence-services-to-get-200m-as-lockdown-takes-toll

Spivak, G.C. (1988). Can the subaltern speak? In G. Nelson, & L. Grossberg (Eds.), *Marxism and the interpretation of culture* (pp. 271–313). University of Illinois Press.

Spoonley, P. (2017). The Asianisation of Aotearoa: Immigration impacts. In A. Bell, V. Elizabeth, T. McIntosh, & M. Wynyard (Eds.), *A land of milk and honey?: Making sense of Aotearoa New Zealand* (pp. 77–83). Auckland University Press.

Sumihira, A. (2020). Intersectionality and sisterhood in the time of COVID-19. *Aotearoa New Zealand Social Work, 32*(2), 49–54. https://doi.org/10.11157/anzswj-vol32iss2id743

Téllez, M. (2005). Doing research at the borderlands: Notes from a Chicana feminist ethnographer. *Chicana/Latina Studies, 4*(2), 46–70. http://www.jstor.org/stable/23014465

Tuck, E., & Yang, K.W. (2014). Unbecoming claims: Pedagogies of refusal in qualitative research. *Qualitative Inquiry, 20*(6), 811–818. https://doi.org/10.1177/1077800414530265

Walia, H. (2013). *Undoing border imperialism.* AK Press.

Yee, G. (2016). Speaking as a settler Chinese woman in Aotearoa New Zealand: An "utterly charming picture of oriental womanhood". *Hecate, 42*(1), 7–30.

Zalipour, A. (2018). Introduction: Migration and diaspora histories and screen representation in New Zealand. In A. Zalipor (Ed.), *Migrant and diasporic film and filmmaking in New Zealand* (pp. 1–31). Springer.

Zobl, E. (2009). Cultural production, transnational networking, and critical reflection in feminist zines. *Signs: Journal of Women in Culture and Society, 35*(1), 1–12. https://doi.org/10.1086/599256

7
FACILITATION AS LISTENING IN THREE COMMUNITY-BASED MEDIA PROJECTS

Chloë Brushwood Rose, Bronwen Low and Paula M. Salvio

Introduction

Despite the explosion of interest in participatory media as a tool for individual and community education and development across the globe, there has been a lack of research on its processes, including comparative studies of various programmes. In response, we conducted a three-year comparative exploration of three participatory media projects, one in New York, one in Toronto, and one in Montreal.[1] Once we began to interpret our observations, interviews and reflections, we realized that we needed to incorporate the act of listening into our study of storytelling. Listening was central to the storytelling practices used in each of these community spaces—the listening of project facilitators to participants, of participants to each other, and of the participants to themselves as they engaged in multi-modal storytelling practices that gave an expressive form to histories that were half-spoken or relegated to the margins of history. Although the projects were structured in different ways, all were committed to documenting the stories of people who are socially, economically, and physically marginalized by systemic racism, poverty, forced migration, and the impacts of globalization, all were deploying participatory narrative and arts-based methods in an inner-city setting, and all three sites had an explicit commitment to enhancing community engagement and public dialogue around issues disproportionately affecting project participants. In each of the projects we discuss here, an emphasis on listening was key to our social justice aims. We suggest that one of the most significant potential effects of listening is the creation of the "commons," a mediating space between the private and public realms, which challenges politics that are predicated on their opposition (Low et al., 2017, p. 116).

The Toronto digital storytelling project is part of a leadership programme for women who are newcomers to Canada, through which they produce multimedia

DOI: 10.4324/9781003199236-10

first-person narratives about the complexities of migration, loss, and survival, and of relating to the people and places that constitute the new communities in which they live and work. The New York site is a participatory video project for civic engagement, and supports young people conducting and videotaping urban investigations of social issues that affect them, such as the lack of healthy food available in local bodegas. The Montreal project formed in relation to a larger oral history project entitled "Life Stories of Montrealers Displaced by War, Genocide, and other Human Rights Violations." It featured audio and multimedia stories tied to specific places in the city created by youth with refugee experience, which were then presented on a narrated bus tour and in schools. Our research methodology varied across the three sites, including participant-observation of the media production process in the Toronto project, but not in the New York and Montreal ones. However, all three case-studies included in-depth interviews with participants and facilitators after the projects were completed, examination of organizational documents, including details of curriculum and pedagogy, and close analysis of media products created through the programmes. We did not facilitate any of these projects, and so our insights into the facilitation process are based on our observations of the expert facilitators in all three sites, which we discuss in more detail below.

We had not anticipated this turn to listening. Our first set of research questions centered on the experience of the narrating "I." The community and participatory media field emphasizes the individual and social benefits of storytelling, so first-person perspectives tend to dominate, particularly in the form of accounts from those more often spoken about in the public sphere. The fluorescence of participatory media projects, all dedicated to story creation and dissemination, is directly tied to the belief that storytelling is a significant resource, requiring preservation and cultivation. This emphasis on storytelling has meant that the dominant metaphor in the field has long been *voice* (Campbell & Burnaby, 2001). However, we discovered that participants and facilitators spent much more time listening than speaking, and this listening, which we describe as *intersubjective*, was central to the pedagogies and politics of these multimedia projects (Low et al., 2017). In this chapter, we revisit our study paying special attention to the particular listening strategies adopted by the various project facilitators: listening as invitation and reverie, playful listening informed by curiosity, and aesthetic listening attuned to form and craft. We see intersubjective listening as integral to ethical facilitation practices, supporting the media makers to negotiate difficult conversations about gender inequality, racial injustices, and socio-economic disparities, and illuminating both the singularity and relationality of each person's story.

Our concept of intersubjective listening builds on theories of dialogic listening, which understand listening as a relational project. Intersubjectivity deepens notions of relation by positing the interdependence of teller and listener, understanding listening as a form of collaboration, a mediation of self and other. McCall (2011) suggests that whenever we install a sharp opposition between listener and speaker, we overlook "the forms of intersubjectivity that the told-to narrative produces" (p. 9). Both the listener and the speaker participate in acts of meaning making: their roles are interdependent, and the meaning produced requires both participants. The notion of mediation invokes a kind of experience that exceeds dialogue between two singular participants, and instead suggests that speaker and listener together form a kind of intersubjective agency for the making of meaning about themselves and the world.

In the mode of listening as inter-subjective, no one is innocent or free from the implications of a mutually affecting relationship (Butler, 2005; Cavarrero, 2000). Cavarrero (2000) describes an experience of narrative reciprocity, in which telling and listening are mutually constitutive roles. Butler (2005) writes about the ways in which the opacity of the subject to themselves sustains an ethical obligation to the other, to be in relation to the other, to listen to the other. Butler suggests that it is only in relation to the other that the subject may begin to know themselves. This opacity in need of another resonates with Gordon's (2008) assertion of the singularity of the subject as comprising a complex personhood, in need of interpretation, rather than a narrow identity. The dynamics of intersubjectivity pose an ethical obligation on the part of the listener to develop the capacity to welcome the complex singularity of the others to whom we listen and the willingness to explore how the others we encounter interact with function as objects in our internal worlds.

These ethical and productive modes of intersubjective listening are difficult to actualize and may be experienced fleetingly in practice. And yet, when deep and mutual listening occurs between facilitator and participant, it can be transformative in unanticipated ways. While the achievement of such listening may be somewhat unpredictable, our research on community-based media pedagogies suggests that good-enough facilitation—a concept that borrows from Winnicott's (1971) notion of the "good-enough mother" (p. 10)—involves the kind of listening that invites people and their stories more fully into the world. In each of the sections below, we illustrate our theory of intersubjective listening through examples of facilitation in the three community-based media projects we studied.

Toronto: Listening as Intersubjective Invitation and Reverie

Listening is the larger part of the complex dialogue in which community-based storytelling occurs. Listening to others, who have in turn listened to us, functions as a form of community-building and self-building, where the listening helps us to metabolize our experience and articulate the story we tell others. Bion (1962) describes this kind of listening as a form of service to the other, an active engagement with the other that might be contrasted with the passivity of hearing. This kind of listening, which Bion calls "reverie," is an active receptivity that augments the experience of being heard by also lending the one being listened to a psychic space in which to take the risk of exploring their own stories. In the Toronto digital storytelling workshops for newcomer women, we noticed how the facilitator's listening offered an invitation to tell the untold story, unanticipated by the storyteller and yet welcomed by the facilitator. This kind of invitation is made possible only through the kind of reverie Bion describes, in which the facilitator sets aside the demands of the workshop (the asked for story) and invites the storyteller to explore links between thoughts, memories, and symbols in the development of an unasked for and as yet untold story.

The facilitators of the Toronto-based digital storytelling project were both experienced, having conducted numerous workshops over a span of many years. Based on their experience and reputation in the community, they were asked by the community-based agency providing a leadership training programme for newcomer women to develop and offer a digital storytelling workshop. The facilitators elaborated the traditional approach to the digital storytelling process to incorporate a stronger emphasis on place-based and multi-modal storytelling, and added workshop experiences for participants that included, drawing maps to represent one's perceptions of and relations to community, a silent neighbourhood walk, and discussion of and experimentation with photographic techniques. The collaborative group experience typical of digital storytelling workshops was heightened by the extended nature of the workshop in this leadership programme, which also impacted Chloë's experience as a researcher who attended all of the digital storytelling workshop sessions, listened to, read, and watched the participants' stories evolve, and at times offered support or feedback with technical and creative issues. Chloë had a pre-existing relationship, as a collaborator and researcher, with the two community-based facilitators who ran the workshops, and her presence in the space of the workshop as a witness, her familiarity with the facilitators, and her informal interactions with participants during the more social features of the programme (including potlucks and screenings), all contributed to a sense that she was a member of the workshop community, as well as an outsider. Chloë was a witness and researcher rather than a participating storyteller, and she had prior experience with the workshop practices and technologies being introduced. While ongoing data collection and findings were discussed with the facilitators, they were not formally involved in the data analysis.

The digital storytelling facilitators in Toronto actively invited conversation on significant social issues. At the same time, they also described the telling of stories as personally transformative and emphasized the emotional significance of the digital storytelling workshop as central to its method. The facilitators demonstrated an implicit awareness of the workshop's value as both social and emotional that mirrored their regard for participants as complex subjects (Gordon, 2008). Their attention to the emotional lives of the workshop participants was motivated both by a refusal to reduce participants to the identity categories of immigrant, woman, mother, and so on, and by a commitment to the aesthetic of the story itself, which they invited participants to take the risk to explore. In an interview with Chloë, one facilitator, Jane,[2] described these risks in her storytelling work with participants:

> the complexity of immigrant experiences is that you don't just immigrate and have to find a job. You immigrate and have to find a job and at the same time you lose your mom, and... it gives that, like, reality of life having this

really big shape to it. So, the dangers are… that someone goes to a story that they're in too deeply, and that they haven't found their way out of. And so then it's too hard for them to process. Or… that they shut it down, and so then they tell a very shallow story, and they can't, they can't go beyond that.

Jane was alert to the emotional complexities faced by participants and to their potential risks. Participants were grappling with immense social challenges and unfamiliar social worlds while also facing, in many cases, both ordinary and extraordinary emotional challenges that accompany life changes. Jane observed that the difficulties of immigration for the women in her workshop not only required a great deal of adjustment to new social contexts—"you have to find a job"—but also involved the emotional work, evident in their personal stories, of forging new identities and communities while contending with both quotidian and exceptional losses and desires.

During the workshop, the facilitators offered the participants a particular storytelling prompt: "tell a story about a place in your community." This prompt was consistent with the facilitators' development of a place-based focus for the workshop to align it with the community development aims of the overall programme. And yet, the facilitators' sense of the complex lives lived by the participants in their communities, and "the complexities of immigrant experience" as articulated by Jane, seemed to work against any strict adherence to a particular agenda around what kinds of stories might get told in response to their prompt. Indeed, very few participants ended up making digital stories that could be seen as explicitly responding to this place-based prompt. And as participant stories emerged, the facilitators seemed quite willing to give up any idea they might have had about the kinds of stories the prompt should elicit.

When a participant named Aarifa first spoke in the story circle, she began by telling a story about her struggles with the way she is perceived by other people in her neighbourhood, as a woman who wears a hijab. Aarifa described experiencing what felt like suspicion from other community members as she walked around distributing a needs-assessment survey she had developed as part of her community leadership training. When she went to a church on Sunday morning to distribute the survey there, she described "the way people were looking at me like I've come to hurt them or do something wrong." While Aarifa insisted that she didn't want to make wearing hijab the central issue in her story, she shared that she had only started wearing hijab three years earlier, when her mother first got sick, and she became more connected to her religion.

Perhaps to respond more precisely to the place-based prompt offered by the facilitators and to divert attention away from wearing hijab as the central issue in her story, Aarifa ended her storytelling in the circle by describing a storefront community centre in her neighbourhood that had been a great resource and source of support for her. She contrasted the suspicion she experienced from strangers with the kind of inclusion she felt at the storefront, where she was active on several committees. Following the story circle, Aarifa further developed this focus in her story, talking with the facilitators and beginning to write a script about finding support and beginning to feel at home in her community. However, the next day, when the facilitator invited Aarifa to share what she was feeling, she told the facilitator that she would instead like to write a story about her mother, who had recently passed away. She described the story she ended up writing this way:

> That was not my first story… all of a sudden, my tears just start coming. [The facilitator] was talking to me, and I said, 'I felt like I want to write about my mom.' And she said, 'I can see that story coming up all the time…' [I said], 'I don't want to write this one. I just want to write about my mom.' [She said], 'just go ahead.'

There is repetition in Aarifa's recollection of this moment, of the movement from the first story to the second, which suggests a kind of testing of the facilitator and her tolerance for such a story. In the interview, there was some ambiguity around the phrase "that was not my first story" and what it might refer to. She may have been conveying that the digital story Chloë had asked her about was not the first story she had in mind to tell. However, there is also a suggestion that telling the story of her mother's death "first" to the facilitator, and experiencing the facilitator's ability to receive it, enabled Aarifa to make the digital story she wanted—telling the "first story" allowed for her development of this capacity. In the interview, she repeated the desire "to write about my mom" twice, each time noting the facilitator's encouraging response. In each case, the facilitator assured her that she would listen to the story Aarifa wanted to tell and that the structure of the digital story could "contain" Aarifa and her story.

When she revealed her desire to tell the story of her mother's death, the facilitator told Aarifa, "when a story needs to be told, it comes up; it's a way for you to honour [your mother] and process it." Jane described Aarifa's need to change her story and to work through the unexpected feelings that came up as shaping "her notion of community work." Jane went on to describe how Aarifa,

> came back later and was like, 'I just lost my mom about a year ago, and actually, that's the thing that, um … is so hard for me to get through,' that even her notion of community work is shaped by that, right? Like, that she needed space to just… to process that, or heal from it, or just voice it.

The facilitator clearly saw Aarifa's ability to pay attention to her emotional life as linked to the ability to live and work well within social and community contexts. Indeed, for Jane, telling the story about her mother signaled a way for Aarifa to claim greater agency and to resist the narrative predominantly made available to newcomers, that "things were hard and now they're better."

The facilitator's way of listening and its implicit invitation to tell the story that needs to be told, even when it is not the story that was expected, holds space for the participant's becoming and offers the reverie that Bion describes—a receptivity to the other that supports them in the process of making sense of an emotional experience. When met by the listening facilitator, storytelling becomes a mode of self-making, and a method for creating the stories that are least expected and most untold, either because they are socially or culturally marginalized, or because they represent a new dimension of emotional experience that required a good-enough listener to be articulated.

New York: Listening and the Play of Curiosity

In our New York case study, we were struck by the way that facilitators, or teaching artists, employed a way of listening to participants and their environments that privileged play and curiosity, rather than expertise. The Center for Urban Pedagogy (CUP) is a New York City based non-profit community-based participatory media center that uses what they describe as "the power of art and design to increase meaningful civic engagement" (http://welcometocup.org). CUP teaching artists, who serve as facilitators, collaborate with designers, educators, advocates, students, and community leaders to create curricula that demystifies complex policy and planning issues, asking questions such as what could police accountability look like? Who owns the internet? Where does our garbage go? The signature of CUP's approach to inquiry is the urban investigation—a project-based curriculum that engages high school students in exploring fundamental questions about how the city works. Facilitators of urban investigations conceptualize inquiry as a process that involves rigorous field work beyond the borders of conventional classrooms and produces multimedia teaching materials that are shared with neighbourhood organizations.

Jonathan Bogarin, the facilitator of *Bodega Down Bronx*, brought expertise as a filmmaker, teacher, and visual artist. CUP facilitators share Bogarin's artistry—they all have backgrounds in designing multimedia curricula—and all facilitators work with students on designing products for community members with the aim of encouraging civic participation. Bogarin, now an award-winning documentary film director places strong value on what he described in his interview as "active listening," an approach that resonates with the concept of reverie explored in the Toronto-based digital storytelling project. He is drawn to the ordinary stories of everyday people and embedded in ordinary objects. Drawing on his years of experience creating videos and digital strategies for some of the world's top museums and arts organizations, Bogarin positions himself as an artist intent on listening for half-spoken images that capture the emotional lives of the communities he works with. Like all CUP teaching artists, Bogarin focused on building participants' interviewing skills, placing a strong emphasis on using videography and photography as media through which to listen to the voices of the community.

As a researcher, Paula began to work with CUP to learn about their approach to using design to increase meaningful civic engagement. Paula, whose research incorporates aesthetics into the study of curriculum theory and public pedagogy, was positioned as a student of CUP who was both an outsider and an insider. She was an insider to the philosophical principles characterizing CUP's civic commitments, but was an outsider to the organization as well as to the making of *Bodega Down Bronx*. Paula's contact with participants was as a researcher interested in their work on the project, and she interviewed the Director of CUP, Valerie Mogilevich, as well as the teaching artists and students who participated in *Bodega Down Bronx* after the urban investigation was complete.

According to Paula's interviews with students who participated in *Bodega Down Bronx*, they experienced the urban investigation as "authentically meaningful." This authenticity emerged in what CUP co-founder and facilitator, Rosten Woo, described as a potential space—another concept drawn from Winnicott (1971)—where participants play at observation and research and work toward maintaining a level of receptivity to the situations under investigation. These potential spaces—which bring students into the city and face-to-face with public officials and neighbourhood residents—are sites where participants work on amplifying their rhetorical and aesthetic repertoires so they can more confidently engage in the public sphere as active citizens. In order to facilitate the creation of these potential spaces for urban investigation, we were struck by the way in which facilitators modelled and encouraged a form of listening that privileged curiosity and experimentation.

Here, we frame CUP's model of the urban investigation as a form of playfully listening to the city with the aim of making politics legible and transparent. By drawing students into the public realm, CUP works to cultivate a particular form of listening that engenders interest rather than expertise. Facilitators share their own curiosity about the issues under investigation rather than transmitting information or teaching students. In contrast to instrumental approaches to teaching and facilitation where objectives and learning outcomes are excessively controlled in advance, the urban investigation calls for playfulness and collective participation. Several participants described their experience of this; for example, Nayelly recalled, "we had so much fun during the investigation, *Bodega Down Bronx*, and, there was no failing." Kimberly noted that the most educational part of the project was learning to interview people, manage a camera, develop interview questions, record and, in Margaret's words, "gaining a lot of knowledge so we can spread it." The capacity for receptivity is contingent upon both the teaching artists and students engaging in a form of attentiveness that involves what Georgis (2013) describes as the paradox of "ethical listening": "it attends to being affected but is neither disengaged nor wanting to master what it sees and hears" (p. 18). The play of ethical listening works against the demand for expertise.

In fact, during one of Paula's interviews with the CUP Director, Mogilevich underscored a valuable attribute for teaching artists who serve as facilitators: a lack of expertise. It was striking to us that Mogilevich drew an inverse relationship between curiosity and expertise—as if expertise itself might devour curiosity. CUP requires a particular kind of attentiveness that Bogarin demonstrated while facilitating the urban investigation, *Bodega Down Bronx*, an investigation into the food sold in neighbourhood grocery stores in the Bronx. Teaching artist Bogarin had no background in food pathways or nutrition. His questions began with an interest in the geographical layout of bodegas in the Bronx. What is their common geography? What do they say about immigrant economies and immigration patterns in the city? And, do they contribute to the nutrition-related illnesses so prevalent in poor and working-class urban neighbourhoods? What would be lost if bodegas were to disappear?

During interviews with students about the difference between their work on *Bodega Down Bronx* and their experiences in high school classrooms, they emphasized how much they valued their work with their teaching artist. Unlike teachers at school, student participants emphasized that the teaching artists were not experts; rather, Elizabeth described them as "more on my level because they were passionate." Nayelly described the teachers as "different, not like normal teachers. They talked to us, they listened to us and were really passionate about teaching – they tried to figure stuff out with us." Passion and curiosity opened spaces for authenticity, and play, and in the case of making *Bodega Down Bronx*, engaged youth in authentic expression in the social and political fields. Cities are not fully transparent. The city is a question for the imagination spun out of myriad cultures and histories. For facilitators at CUP, the enigmatic city is an aesthetic text that presents an endless fund of questions that inspire us to listen. The urban investigation, as performed by CUP participants, invited youth to address serious questions germane to their lives without succumbing to the standard press for certainty, mastery or easy answers. This invitation calls for a playful approach to facilitation—among students, teaching artists, community partners, and residents of the city—who, in the case of *Bodega Down Bronx*, collectively engaged in the challenges posed by food pathways in the city.

As it was practised among CUP teaching artists, playing is implicitly a way of listening, and as Winnicott (1971) reminds us, play is contingent upon reciprocity among the players. Playing stops when someone gets dogmatic, or when the facilitator imposes an interpretation rather than treating the investigation as an open, collaborative concern. While Winnicott emphasized the child's sense of self, he recognized that compromises must be made. While all communication with others is contingent upon degrees of compliance, the challenge is to navigate the delicate tension called for by a playful reciprocity. It is out of this potential space, Winnicott claimed, that a creative reaching out can take place. The form of psychic freedom valued by Winnicott and practised by CUP facilitators flourishes in the company of teaching artists who value this reciprocity over their own expertise, and who listen with a heightened sense of interest in and curiosity about creating narratives that represent self and society, *with* rather than *for* their students.

Montreal: Aesthetic Listening and Making Stories Public

There is a tendency when listening to a story that is different from one's own to either reject it as incomprehensible, or to assimilate it into one's own stories.

However, both the rejecting and incorporative responses disavow the uniqueness of the other. While intersubjective listening emphasizes the deep, mutually affecting engagement of listener and speaker, it also attends to the ethics of that relation. Ethical listening is self-aware and engaged but does not seek mastery over what it hears.

The Going Places media making process consisted of a series of story creating and telling experiences for youth with refugee experience, and the stories took two forms: digital stories related to identity, home, and place shared on the project's website (https://mappingmemories.ca), and audio versions played by the participants to an audience on a bus touring Montreal to destinations relevant to the narratives. The group later decided to create a high-school tour in which three participants would screen and answer questions about their digital stories to high-school students in the Montreal region. The Montreal Going Places project facilitators were very experienced in participatory media and pedagogies. Liz Miller is a Communications professor at Concordia and a well-established community media and documentary filmmaker. She worked closely with Michele Luchs, an English Language Arts teacher and media specialist who had written the media competencies in the provincial curriculum and led many workshops for teachers and students related to digital media learning. Bronwen was connected to the Going Places project as co-director of the Education working group in the larger Life Stories of Montrealers project; she played the role of researcher rather than facilitator of the Going Places project, interviewing facilitators and participants and attending related public events (including a book launch, conference presentations, and an exhibition, as well as the bus tour) and social gatherings.

Working closely with the Canadian Council for Refugees, and informed by Liz's experience with documentary making with vulnerable populations, the facilitators were very aware of the risk that people might not listen well to the participants' stories. As a result, in order to protect the youth from incorporative, rejecting, or other potentially damaging responses from audiences, the facilitators introduced the concept of the public versus private story to participants early in the workshop process. Participants were going to be telling their stories to a wide and unknown audience, and the themes of identity, home, and place could potentially elicit very difficult material from people with refugee experience. These deliberations about what and how to share were particularly important since the digital stories were to be uploaded online. As with all decisions about dissemination, the youth retained the right to change their mind about sharing their stories at any point; Liz and Michelle remained informed about this ongoing consent through the close ties developed among the project members and extended long after the project's end.

This project posed a question: How might we work to prevent the youth participants from feeling exposed or having their experiences sensationalized? Describing this distinction in a book about the process, the facilitators noted that:

> private stories originated from a personal memory or lived experience. ... Some details regarding private stories would remain in their journals,

while other details would be shaped to share with the larger public. With private stories, we emphasized that it was important to consider if any personal details might make a participant feel vulnerable later. It was especially important to be sensitive to any details that might compromise a participant's safety or asylum application. Public stories, on the other hand, were focused on collective memories, public events, or places important to a larger community.

(Miller et al., 2011, pp. 59–60)

They add that with this distinction, they wanted to open various options for participants to share their experiences, and to make clear that "ultimately, they were in charge of what story they would tell and how much they would share" (p. 60). The concept of the public story marks a distance between the storyteller and their story. Rather than embodying their personhood, which is then made vulnerable in the sharing of the story, the story that is shaped to share becomes an aesthetic object which has work to do in the world, what we have elsewhere referred to as a "crafted object" (Brushwood Rose and Low, 2014, p. 30).

In an interview, the instructor who facilitated writing workshops for the participants in the Montreal bus tour project revealed that she viewed her role primarily as a literary listener. She described how, "When the person is explaining what he or she wants to write, I pick up structures, I pick up forms or metaphors that are already in what they want to say." The facilitator listened for word-choice, image, and embedded genre patterns, offering her insights about their significance back to the teller. For instance, one of the participants in the workshop wanted to tell the story of his arrival at the airport in Montreal, alone at seventeen, claiming refugee status from Zimbabwe. The facilitator noticed that there was a spatial quality to his account, in that he seemed to focus on his experience of the spaces and places he moved through on this journey. Noticing this, she "asked more and more questions, [in a way that was] kind of Socratic" so that the spatial qualities that she heard in his story generated the descriptions that were the foundation of his media project.

This strategy seemed particularly valuable in the case of very difficult stories shared during the workshops. In the facilitator's discussion with another participant who, at four, witnessed the murder of her family members during the genocide of the Tutsis in Rwanda, she heard uncertainty about what part of her story to tell, but also that she had "a form in mind." She described how this young woman "perceived her story as a fairytale … which was a very appropriate and telling form for her, because her story is about childhood, so it was a moving and poignant theme for her to want to tell it that way".

This engagement through close and careful listening is attentive to the shape of the story and attentive to its aesthetic qualities, asking us to think in terms of formal structures and how these reflect and possibly direct experience. Aesthetic listening from the facilitators supports the agency of the storytellers in making formal choices about the kind of story they want to tell. The participants are artists crafting experience into public stories to be shared with others. This experience provides raw material but does not overdetermine how the storytellers give it meaning, nor are its meanings fixed—we might perceive our story differently at another moment.

The participants all told of being very pleased with their public stories. The participant from Rwanda described the value of the experience of crafting a story for public sharing. She appreciated having been helped to think about what was necessary to include and what was not to create a public story that could help people "change," and that could be passed on to "people that come from me, my children." She described her eventual relationship to her Going Places story as one of "love." When Liz contacted her after the project's end about a new opportunity to share her story, she responded "you don't have to ask me permission to use my story because it is now a public story" (Miller et al., 2011, p. 69). This public story can exist in the world without doing harm to the teller.

This strong attachment to the story told in public also characterized the feelings of another participant, the daughter of a Palestinian who sought refuge in Montreal. She said, "there was a time when my story was who I am ... now that I see it, I find it is so beautiful, how wonderful that it can be used so no suffering can be duplicated. A contribution, rather than, I'm the victim". This way of thinking about and telling her family's story also seemed to involve a shift away from "this is what happened, [to] what do I really make of it, how do I work with it"—a move to interpretation and public purpose.

Part of preparing the participants to take their stories public included training in speaking to the media, such as strategies for how to deal with questions you might not want to answer, such as giving a collective rather than individual response (e.g., "the refugee experience impacts all of us in different ways" (Miller et al., 2011, p. 66)) or declining to answer a question. The facilitators helped to frame and politicize the narratives in relation to an overarching message about the importance of immigration rights, which were under debate due to the introduction of new federal legislation in Canada at the time. In this way, they built a political dimension to their intersubjective agency forged through shared listening, anticipating the demands and misconceptions of a listening audience. This aesthetic listening is attuned to the politics of representation and works to craft a story which both advocates for and humanizes the nameless refugees assumed in the policy debates.

Conclusion: Facilitator as Good-Enough Listener

Embedded in a dynamic interplay among people, intersubjective listening opens thinking up to difficult emotional meanings, to new ways of seeing the world, and to the possibility of ethical engagement with others. The intersubjective listening of the facilitators we observed did not simply set up the conditions for dialogue between people, but enacted a more profound exchange in which each participant was altered due to the experience of listening with others. We argue that this sense of mutuality is a central paradox in the work of facilitation and the project of listening—the sense of self and other are held in dialectical tension. Intersubjective listening is an ethical relation that poses the interdependence of storyteller and listener, self and other. As such, the experience of intersubjective listening is not so much a practice that can be taught as a relation and a commitment that must be chosen. The facilitators in the community-based media projects we studied all demonstrate a commitment to the work of listening in this way and offered conditions that made it possible for participants to make their own similar choices.

And yet, because intersubjective listening is the kind of interdependent, responsive, active, and ethical engagement we describe, it would be impossible to achieve it all the time. The subject has many possible defences against the vulnerability and change that this kind of intersubjectivity can pose. Given these ordinary and very human limitations, just as Winnicott (1971) proposed the idea of the "good-enough mother" (p. 10) in order to offset the dangers of idealization and to value the ordinary good mother who works hard to parent well, we conclude by proposing the notion of the good-enough listener as something to strive for. This refocuses our attention on how and why the ordinary subject might engage in the extraordinary work of listening deeply to another. The good-enough listener is one who is aware of their personal investments when listening, their associations, frustrations, and anxieties, and their limitations. As well, rather than controlling for tensions in the listening relationship, the good-enough listener recognizes the generative possibilities that are made possible within the site of differences and conflicts. Rather than teaching the practice of good-enough listening to interested community media facilitators, we believe that the best we can offer are certain facilitating conditions, which include practice, reassurance, and direction. Being reflexive is learned in degrees, over time, and in relationship with others. It is never fully mastered; the capacity for reflexivity emerges as a listener cultivates a stronger capacity to hold conflicting emotions and ideas and sustain engagement with contradictory theories.

In each of our case studies, we observed the ways that a good-enough listener can enable participants to take emotional risks—to confront political oppression, to tell traumatic histories, and to risk the vulnerability of sharing a story of personal experience. Sara Ahmed (2010) writes about the ways that listening to these kinds of stories calls on us to question the promise of happiness and to bear witness to our own complicity in the erasure and marginalization of stories that remain untold. When listening is not good-enough, emotional difficulty, conflict, and struggle can emerge in the relations of the community-based project itself, for example, when participants push back against the frames offered them or resist the emotional culture of the group (Brushwood Rose, 2019). And yet, attending to the emotional complexities and limits of listening also reveals some of its greater possibilities: while difficult emotions, including conflict and resistance, might first appear to denote the absence of listening, they may actually suggest vital methods for listening differently, actively, or "at an angle" (Thompson, 2010). This kind of listening "holds not wholeness but angles, not a nameable identity but movement. Broken listening is not meant to dispel contradiction, eliminate confusion, and impose clarity" (Thompson, 2010, p. 7). Intersubjective listening does not belong to one person but is forged between self and other, as an active engagement with each other.

The facilitators of the community-based media projects we studied demonstrated this kind of reflexivity, challenging taken-for-granted understandings, values and normalizing beliefs about the social complexities that shape lives, commitments, and desires. They attended to their own associations and attachments, and those potentially held by listening others, throughout the process. They modelled an intersubjective listening that is not only sensitive to what is stated, but is sensitive to what is left unsaid. This approach to listening is critical for cultivating new stories and new modes of relating that are not wedded to an understanding of language as a transparent medium, but rather welcome the emotional risk-taking, curiosity and experimentation, and expression of aesthetic complexity that can enrich practices of storytelling.

We believe that community-based media projects are important sites for learning how to be good-enough listeners. In an era of high stakes testing and accountability measures, practices of listening have either been reduced to demands to sit still and listen to the teacher, or replaced with bureaucratic measures that understand listening as a behavioural objective to be taught and mastered. To our minds, there is a serious need to create spaces where the cultural heritages that are carried by narratives, particularly those narratives that are vulnerable to being forgotten by history, can be collectively composed within listening relationships. The community-based media pedagogies and storytelling projects discussed in this chapter use narratives to redeem us from alienation, the grip of stereotypes, and the press of national narratives that strip away the specificity of one's experience. They highlight the individual's ethical and relational obligations to attend to others, creating new forms of relationality and reinvigorating public space and action in the process. The community-based projects we studied in Montreal, New York, and Toronto understand public pedagogy as activist, experimental, and demonstrative (see also: Biesta, 2014). The work aims to create actual social alternatives—as demonstrated by the urban investigations in the case of *Bodega Down Bronx*, where CUP works to secure and sustain healthy food pathways in the city. The projects in both Montreal and Toronto use storytelling to invent new ways of understanding traumatic histories and new ways of being in light of these understandings. In each case, storytelling is practised as properties of collectives, as non-tangible resources for the common (Godard, 2013).

Notes

1 The project was funded by a Social Sciences and Humanities Research Council Standard Research Grant (2009–2012) entitled *Community-based media pedagogy and production in a globalized world: Documenting transnational and transitional subjects, self-representations, and spaces.* (Principal investigator Bronwen Low, Co-investigators Chloë Brushwood Rose and Paula M. Salvio).
2 All names used are pseudonyms to protect the identity of participants.

References

Ahmed, S. (2010). *The promise of happiness*. Duke University Press.
Biesta, G. (2014). Making pedagogy public: For the public, of the public, or in the interest of publicness? In J. Burdick, J.A. Sandlin, & M.P. O'Malley (Eds.), *Problematizing public pedagogy* (pp. 15–26). Routledge Press.
Bion, W. (1962). *Learning from experience*. Karnac Books.
Brushwood Rose, C. (2019). Resistance as method: Unhappiness, group feeling, and the limits of participation in a digital storytelling workshop. *International Journal of Qualitative Studies in Education, 32*(7), 857–871.
Brushwood Rose, C., & Low, B. (2014). Exploring the 'craftedness' of multimedia narratives: From creation to interpretation. *Visual Studies, 29*(1), 30–39.
Butler, J. (2005). *Giving an account of oneself*. Fordham University Press.
Campbell, P., & Burnaby, B. (2001). *Participatory practices in adult education*. Lawrence Erlbaum Associates.
Cavarrero, A. (2000). *Relating narratives: Storytelling and selfhood* (P.A. Kottman, Trans.). Routledge.
Georgis, D. (2013). *The better story: Queer affects from the Middle East*. SUNY Press.
Godard, A. (2013, December 13). *The cultural commons lies hidden in plain sight: How we can be midwives to a huge shift in creativity, connection and citizenship*. On the Commons. http://onthecommons.org/magazine/cultural-commons-lies-hidden-plain-sight
Gordon, A.F. (2008). *Ghostly matters: Haunting and the sociological imagination*. (2nd ed.). University of Minnesota Press.
Low, B., Brushwood Rose, C., & Salvio, P. (2017). *Community-based media pedagogies: Relational practices of listening in the commons*. Routledge.
McCall, S. (2011). *First person plural: Aboriginal storytelling and the ethics of collaborative authorship*. UBC Press.
Miller, L., Luchs, M., & Dyer Jalea, G. (2011). *Mapping memories: Participatory media, place-based stories, and refugee youth*. Mapping Memories: Experiences of Refugee Youth. http://mappingmemories.ca/book.html
Thompson, A. (2010). Listening at an angle. In G. Biesta (Ed.), *Philosophy of education 2010* (pp. 1–10). Philosophy of Education Society.
Winnicott, D.W. (1971). *Playing and reality*. Routledge.

8
THEORIZING NON-PARTICIPATION IN A MAIL-BASED PARTICIPATORY VISUAL RESEARCH PROJECT WITH 2SLGBTQ+ YOUTH IN ATLANTIC CANADA

Brody Weaver, Amelia Thorpe, April Mandrona, Katie MacEntee, Casey Burkholder and Pride/Swell

Introduction

Non-participation in face-to-face research has been theorized in multiple ways (Brushwood Rose, 2019; Hayward et al., 2004; Milne, 2012; Switzer, 2020). However, current events have brought great shifts in our understanding of participation and what constitutes engagement in distance-based and virtual research (Switzer et al., 2021). Specifically, we wonder: what does non-participation look like in this specific place and time—during the COVID-19 pandemic? How might facilitators work with participants as they engage (and disengage) in multiple ways in participatory visual research projects conducted at a physical distance? We also ask: in what ways are we providing opportunities for people to participate and making space for them to disengage? What does non-participation look like in distanced and digital-based research with 2SLGBTQ+ youth here and now? How might we adjust our work as facilitators to make space for multiple forms of participation and non-participation in research projects over time?

We write together as members of Pride/Swell, a distanced, mail-based art and activism project with 2SLGBTQ+ youth in Atlantic Canada. Between July 2020 and July 2021, 50 2SLGBTQ+ youth from across Atlantic Canada received monthly packages in the mail containing: 1) art supplies; and 2) a prompt. Through art making and collaborative archiving (Burkholder et al., 2021), we shared experiences creating queer-focused community around identities and space during COVID-19. In this chapter, we focus on what non-participation has looked like in this project. In what follows, we highlight our project intentions, our aims as facilitators, and discuss the specific ways in which we have identified non-participation and facilitated through these instances. We highlight the negotiation of participation which has been complicated by our virtual engagement with participants.

Pride/Swell: Conceptualizing Participatory Art-Making and Archiving

We come to this project as collaborators engaged in art, research, and activism with youth, and in the writing of this article members of Pride/Swell[ii]. Our project seeks to support 2SLGBTQ+ youth (aged 13–25) from Atlantic Canada to create a digital exhibition—housed on a dedicated website as well as Instagram, Facebook and Twitter—of youth-produced collages, zines, face masks, dolls, dioramas, postcards, screen-printed bags, shrinkable plastic jewellery, and cellphilms among other art practices. We have developed these participatory and public facing digital archives to catalyse dialogue about 2SLGBTQ+ youth's participation in their communities. Pride/Swell conceptualizes participation as encompassing both the art-making and archiving components of the project.

In developing 2SLGBTQ+ youth-led approaches to exhibition and archiving in Atlantic Canada, Pride/Swell has direct implications for Atlantic educators, policymakers, and youth, as well as researchers who engage in participatory visual research methods. Although teachers work directly with 2SLGBTQ+ youth, there is an absence of school-based initiatives and curriculum in the region (beyond Gender-Sexuality Associations [GSAs]) that directly take up the unique challenges and experiences of these students. Similarly, current policy in areas of sexual health, civic and cultural participation, and artistic literacy require the direct input of 2SLGBTQ+ communities to be responsive and inclusive. Pride/Swell encourages conversations about how participatory approaches may be extended to archiving and exhibition, and how participants might have more say in the ways in which research projects are shared, exhibited, screened, and archived (Burkholder et al., 2021). Thus, participatory archiving and exhibition practices intervene into structures that are normally unavailable for youth, by centring collectivity and fostering solidarity across identities. Pride/Swell also mobilizes place-based pedagogies, facilitates future university-youth collaborations, and forms unique educational knowledge networks.

Pride/Swell is inspired by the community exhibition and archiving practices of activist artists, academics, and community organizations, such as the Native Youth Sexual Health Network's Sexy Health Carnival (2014-present), *Walking with our Sisters* memorial (2012-present), the New Brunswick Queer Heritage Initiative (2016-present), Imprint Youth (2016-present), and Claudia Mitchell's 2018 *Circles within Circles* project. Pride/Swell engages 2SLGBTQ+ youth to produce art and teach us—the research team as well as policymakers, communities, and school-based stakeholders across Atlantic Canada—about the social and community issues that matter most to them. Pride/Swell's methods draw on feminist participatory visual research practices (Gubrium & DiFulvio, 2011; Gustafson, 2000), and engage 2SLGBTQ+ youth in creating a digital exhibition of their media to share across geographical contexts. In bringing 2SLGBTQ+ youth to the knowledge mobilization process, we seek to highlight the ways that the intersectional experiences, histories, and activist practices of queer, trans*, and non-binary youth can be included in larger discourses in Atlantic Canada about civic and political participation.

In developing the participatory digital archive with 2SLGBTQ+ youth, we learn how they understand and speak back (hooks, 1989; Mitchell, de Lange, & Moletsane, 2017) to dominant historical narratives through exhibition and archiving practices. We draw on the scholarship and activism of Syrus Marcus Ware (2017), as we argue for a radical queering of archiving practices—which he calls "counter archiving"—to resist homonationalism, and the overreliance on white archives and artifacts in existing queer archives, and to foster memory-keeping communities outside of institutional lines. Lee (2017) conceptualizes the production of queer archives as an act of both action and resistance, through the creation of "spaces through which meaning is made in order to demonstrate the converging and diverging relationships that records and records creators have with dominant and normativizing metanarratives" (p. 9). They illustrate the crucial importance of participatory approaches to queer archiving to actively counter the hierarchies of power frequently reproduced within archiving, in line with Ware's (2017) conception of counter archiving (Lee, 2021). We seek to uncover the ways in which non-participation can similarly be positioned as a mode of action and resistance and how we, as facilitators, can create and hold space for myriad forms of engagement.

By centring ephemeral art production in the creation of these archives, we tap into a rich history of alternative archival practices and methodologies that have been developed by and flourished within queer and trans* communities. Visual production and the affective excess it necessitates allows us to make use of a queer archival tradition which, after Ann Cvetkovich (2011), stands at the crossroads of critiques of archival spaces and passion for the radical potential of counter archives. Through the development of the participatory and queer digital archives, we believe that 2SLGBTQ+ youth will have increased opportunities to make connections with other 2SLGBTQ+ youth and adult leaders—with the support of presenters who are queer artists living and working in Atlantic Canada—in relation to their archiving, political, and resistance activities.

Positionality

We come to the project as people with commitments to queer organizing and participatory visual research in Atlantic Canada and elsewhere. Brody is a young, white, settler, nonbinary-transfemme artist, student, and researcher. As a Pride/Swell team member and student organizer, they are committed to youth-led intervention through art and action research, and believe in the transformational nature of collective art production and self-representation. They are interested in queer/trans* community-based archiving practices and projects, and recently collaborated on an intergenerational public installation that critically presented queer archival material from Atlantic Canada at community-specific locations in K'jipuktuk (Halifax, Nova Scotia).

Amelia is a white, cis, queer, and neurodiverse PhD candidate whose involvement in queer activism began nearly two decades ago in junior high and spans three provinces. Amelia works with a local Pride organization on Wolastoqiyik territory and recently developed a nonprofit to facilitate connection and capacity building among 2SLGBTQ+ activists and community organizers within the colonially named province of New Brunswick. Her research focuses on education, advocacy, and community building within gender and sexual minority communities.

April is an Assistant Professor and the Director of Art Education at NSCAD University in Mi'kma'ki, on the sovereign ancestral and unceded territory of the Mi'kmaq Nation. She is white, straight, and of settler background. Her community-based art education research looks at issues of rurality and spatial justice, young people's visual culture, ethical practice, and creative approaches to research participation and policy change.

Katie is a white, cisgender woman who does not define her sexuality. She has extensive experience working with participatory visual methodologies for research on sexual and reproductive health rights and education access and inclusion in different contexts internationally. She is currently a postdoctoral fellow working in Tkaronto, the traditional territories of the Mississaugas of the Credit, Anishinaabe, Chippewa, Haudenosaunee, and Wendat peoples.

Casey is a bisexual, white, cis femme, and an Associate Professor whose work responds to racist, transphobic, and homophobic schooling structures with youth and teachers through arts-based approaches. She is interested in co-creating, co-disseminating, and co-archiving these works as a mode of speaking back and engaging in solidarity building in response to systemic oppressions.

Participatory Visual Research with Queer Youth

Critical perspectives on participation and non-participation are emerging from youth-centred participatory visual research (Switzer, 2020), but important questions about non-participation in exhibition, archiving, and dissemination in community spaces are still underexplored. There are few studies and academic articles that detail and recommend best practices for participatory research with queer and trans* communities. In psychology, feminist participatory action research (PAR) practitioners Anneliese Singh, Kate Richmond, and Theodore Burnes recommended best practices towards ethical PAR research-design with transgender communities (2013). They note, participatory frameworks are fundamental for countering what Vivian Namaste (2009) has described as the cis-centric nature of knowledge that is produced about rather than created by transgender (and queer) people. Of relevance to participatory visual research, they recommend dissemination strategies that are entwined with the social ecologies and communities of queer and trans* people, which might include arts-based outputs, peaceful demonstration, email and social media networks, or formal conversations with powerholders (2013, pp. 101–102). Without explicitly disseminating research with and for queer and trans* communities, participants' ways of knowing and representation are minimized.

In the Canadian context, social work scholar Kenta Asakura et al. (2020) used participatory visual research with trans* and non-binary youth to develop strategies for trans* self-representation and intervention. Researchers worked with five youth for more than a year. Mentorship and guidance were provided by the researchers and local trans* artist Cara Tierney. They found that arts-based methods used within a PAR framework provided space for the youth to develop counter-narratives, promote self- reflection and expression, and develop community spaces for witnessing and world-making. Reflecting on the use of arts-based methods in this context, the co-authors note that arts-based methods are "valuable when doing research with trans* youth and other marginalized youth populations, especially when the purpose is to de-center conventional (e.g., cisnormative, heteronormative) knowledge and put a spotlight on the perspective of those who have been historically and presently marginalized" (p. 1073). This arts-based research both provides encouraging accounts of visual research with queer and trans* youth, and extends Asakura's earlier qualitative research into the resilience of queer and trans* youth communities (2016; 2017).

In line with MacEntee and Flicker (2018), we assert that the use of participatory visual methodologies with youth in the context of sexuality research functions to destabilize hierarchical research relationships and create space for new and creative modes of self-expression. Leung and Flanagan (2019) contend that visual methods such as photovoice provide valuable opportunities for self-expression, where marginalized "youths are rendered experts in their own lives and are offered a platform to share with the public" (p. 502). Further, we note the value of visual methods in engaging and empowering youth, highlighting the importance of listening to their voices and experiences (D'Amico et al., 2016; Leung & Flanagan, 2019; MacEntee & Flicker, 2018). Casey Burkholder (2020) has explored participatory visual research methodologies in her work with queer, trans*, and non-binary youth in Atlantic Canada to "learn about the existing and desired supports and barriers for queer, trans*, and non-binary youth in schools, society, and social studies through art making and qualitative interviewing" (p. 134). Through this work and in a similar vein the use of PAR with transgender communities as described by Singh, Richmond, and Burnes (2013), Burkholder describes how she works collaboratively with youth co-researchers to identify community-based spaces for the dissemination of context specific outputs—from zines to cellphilms—within the youth's schools and communities. In contrast to these foci, and our previous work (Burkholder & Thorpe, 2019; Burkholder, MacEntee, Mandrona, & Thorpe, 2021), this article focuses primarily on what was not said or expressed throughout this project. In particular, we ask ourselves what does non-participation look like with 2SLGBTQ+ youth in order to highlight our specific facilitation strategies and a rethinking of what participatory visual research might do during the COVID-19 pandemic.

Theorizing Non-Participation within and beyond Participatory Visual Research

Considering non-participation in participatory visual research illuminates the nature of the researcher and participant relationship. Bonny Norton (2001) observes, "Non-participation in some communities is inevitable because our experiences include coming into contact with communities to which we do not belong, in Wenger's graphic words, 'catching, as we peek into foreign chambers, glimpses of other realities and meanings'" (1998, p. 165). This kind of non-participation differs from research practices within communities to which we *do* belong. In the latter case, his distinction between *peripherality* and *marginality* is a useful one. By "peripherality," he refers to the fact that some degree of non-participation can be an enabling factor of participation, while "marginality" is a form of non-participation that prevents full participation" (p. 161). People can actively choose to not participate or be actively prevented from participating as a result of their experience on the margins. It is important to address the difference between these two situations so as not to confuse oppression and silencing with participants' use of non-participation as a site of resistance. Communities are described as "underrepresented" or "hard to reach" without teasing apart what this means socially and politically.

Theron et al. (2011) discuss the potential of participants feeling self-conscious about their artistic outputs within visual research projects, noting the importance of creating space to continually renegotiate boundaries of privacy and modes of sharing participants' work. As explored by Furman et al., "arts-informed methods can feel awkward to participate in" despite the widespread assumption that creative modes of engagement are more accessible (2019, p. 9). Their assertion of the value of challenging art-making as a "professional, exclusive, and elitist space," by engaging in social, political, and community-based art practices reflects our commitment to DIY creation and self-expression as a mode of speaking back to archival practices and spaces that are similarly exclusive (2019, p. 9). However, this is not to say that in community-based arts practice there is no discomfort in participating in both the creation and exhibition of works, particularly those of a personal nature.

EJ Milne's (2012) critical reflection on the mass non-participation of two housing estates communities in a participatory video project theorizes non-participation as a form of resistance and refusal, acting as an assertion of agency more than marginalization. As Milne notes, "non-participation was, for them, a means of protection, a way of overcoming powerlessness and perhaps most importantly, an opportunity to subvert funders' agendas and objectification by external audiences" (p. 258). Milne's reflection reminds us that resisting the appropriation of a community's image and self-perception transcends close, trusting, and long-term relationships between community researchers and participating communities. Often, the outcome driven onus of research, even community-based research, requires a tangible product or material deliverable. In Milne's study, communities and soon-to-be-participants were well aware of the afterlife of research outputs, and feared that the films produced in the context of participatory video would "be appropriated for the funder's own ends and acclaim, and they did not trust them not to edit them or screen them without their permission" (p. 265). Through this act of non-participation, we can appreciate why long-term consent is fundamental to participatory visual research that produces enduring and digitally networked outputs, whether this be films, the development of participatory archives (see Burkholder et al., 2021) or other forms of visual action and research.

Milne's analysis of non-participation as an exercise of community solidarity and agency is in line with Indigenous theories of refusal that have long resisted the disempowering and dispossessive nature of research as an extension of Indigenous movements for political and intellectual sovereignty (Simpson, 2007; Tuck, 2009; Tuck & Yang, 2014a, 2014b). Feminist PAR researchers Alison Bain and William Payne (2016) have described "de-participation" within the process of co-creating academic articles with participants and collaborators in participatory visual research, noting how the demanding and context specific requirements of an academic capitalist cultural economy render the full participation of all involved parties difficult to fully achieve. Bain and Payne describe how de-participation functioned through the very processes of academic editing and refereeing, wherein testimonials that critiqued a white queer elder were subsequently recommended for removal for the article to be published. This involved excluding the writing of a collaborator, a complete rewriting of their article, and the loss of active participation of several other collaborators due to the demanding timeline of academic publishing. Bain and Payne call for an increased awareness of these micro instances of negotiation and power "if knowledge is really to be co-produced and valued for its situatedness" (p. 8). This situation is an example of non-participation, wherein participation is demanded and/or forfeited to produce academic knowledge. The co-authors do not weigh in on whether this redaction of participation was an active resistance to editorial distortion, but one can begin to imagine how instances such as these have erased critical perspectives from academic literature.

In Sarah Switzer's (2020) work on facilitating through non-participation in face-to-face participatory visual research, she speaks to how the concept of participation must be considered critically, noting: "[t]he logic of participation has implications when thinking about Black and Indigenous youth, disabled youth, and/or queer and trans* youth living in poverty who already have their lives surveilled by the state (Cruz, 2013; Kwon, 2013)" (p. 171). She cites that the structural oppressions that limit the participation of minoritized youth while valorizing productivity and capacity-building, can be mirrored in community-based research projects.

As such, it is necessary to consider how participation is not always viewed as beneficial or desirable for minoritized youth, nor "an option that they feel 'free' to choose" (p. 172). In Switzer's (2020) work, non-participation is presented as a mode of navigating the complex nature of engaging in research, where actively choosing to not participate in a specific activity or removing oneself from the project is an agentic and autonomous action of negotiating tension and setting boundaries. She notes that while the assertion that one is choosing to "opt out" is at times direct, "[o]ther times, they function as everyday forms of resistance masked behind indirect claims (Cruz, 2011; Kelley, 2014; Scott, 1990)" as to their departure, which provides the individual an opportunity to remove themselves without articulating this active choice (p. 172). In our work, this ambiguous negotiation of participation is further complicated by our virtual engagement with participants within a distance-based participatory visual project.

Pride/Swell

Through 12 different art practices and prompts (detailed below), we explore and share instances of non-participation while engaging in distance-based participatory visual research with 2SLGBTQ+ young people in Atlantic Canada. These projects are a means of making community and connections across the digital realm, while also sharing young people's ways of knowing through art production amidst the COVID-19 pandemic. Each month, participants receive a package in the mail of art supplies focusing on a specific prompt and art practice. We began in August 2020 with collage making in response to the prompt, "finding community amidst COVID-19." Next, in September, we created zines using the prompt, "I am _____ and _____ and ___" as we sought to explore the intersectional realities of participants' experiences and identities, including but not limited to race, Indigeneity, gender, ability, sexuality, age, class, rurality, and urbanity. We sought to disrupt homogenous depictions of 2SLGBTQ+ youth, and instead highlight commonalities as well as differences. In October 2020, we embroidered and sewed face masks that took up the prompt, "keeping safe, but never silent" as a way of looking at mask wearing as community care and its use in protest movements. In November 2020, we created dioramas that explored the prompt, "queering environmental futures," drawing on the art and activism of Dr. Sabine Lebel (see Chapter 12 this volume). Next, we created dolls that took up the prompt, "embodying future selves." In January 2021, we experimented with printmaking and postcard production in response to the prompt, "what do you want to say? Who do you want to say it to? Who isn't listening?" In February 2021, we made stickers out of vinyl that took up the prompt, "queering and subverting visual narratives." Next, we practiced screen printing on canvas bags in response to the prompt, "relationships to home in a time of social isolation." In April 2021, we made jewellery and keychains out of shrinkable plastic in response to the prompt, "transformations." In May 2021, we created cellphilms (cellphone + film production + prompt) that explored the prompt, "transforming the frame," followed by DIY pride floats in June that responded to the prompt, "A parade. A march. A protest." Our final art practice was to create terrariums that take up the prompt, "Self-care as community care; community care as self-care." We wanted to end the year's projects by thinking through how we might continue to nurture and tend to the bonds we have built this past year through art and activism and getting to know one another at a distance. While we have produced art alongside many participants, we have also facilitated through non-participation in the project.

Non-Participation in the Project

Non-participation in our distanced project has occurred in a number of ways. We sought to recruit 55 participants, and registered 50. In the first six months, five people withdrew. Of the 50 participants who receive art packages each month, the same 5–10 participants submitted their pieces to be shared on the digital archive. We have noticed participation increasing and waning at different points, and we highlight several areas here: 1) on Zoom, 2) in sharing the art produced in public digital spaces; 3) in responding to each other's art piece in the digital archives; 4) withdrawing from the project; and 5) in calling for folks from outside the project to respond to our works through art production.

On Zoom

We have been holding monthly meetings to reflect on the previous month's art practice, products, and explain what will happen next. Each meeting usually features a queer guest speaker who presents on their art production and career. Participation in the Zoom calls has diminished over time. Our early Zoom meet ups (August–November, 2020) featured four to five members of the research team, and 5–10 participants from the project. In December, only three members of the research team came on the call, and no participants, so we cancelled the meeting. From January to July 2021, we have had three to five members of the research team at all of the Zoom calls, and one to three participants. We record the Zoom calls and share the audio recordings with all Pride/Swell members via email to support people who are unable or unwilling to attend.

Whereas in-person acts of non-participation and refusal (that aren't complete omission) can be registered verbally, there are fewer indicators of group dynamics and emotions over video-conferencing platforms. As Switzer (2020) notes, non-participation can be recognized through instances of micro-refusal: "Nah, no thanks. I think I'll pass. I'm gonna' go for a smoke. I have to leave early" (p. 172). While not all forms of non-participation can or should be visible to facilitators, in the context of video-conferencing, such small-scale interjections and refusals are more difficult to notice, engage with, and facilitate.

In addition to the lack of embodied and non-verbal communication that would regularly act as markers of energy levels, group dynamics, and emotional responses, video conferencing is notoriously demanding. While participants were made aware that they were more than welcome to join our digital hang-outs with their cameras and mics turned off, the ubiquity of the sentiment of "Zoom fatigue" is enough to understand why participation in this context is challenging. As a chronically-ill scholar with ADHD and cognitive dysfunction, Amelia (Author 2) has engaged in active non-participation on virtual platforms since the beginning of the pandemic by turning her camera off when necessary. The availability of audio recordings for participants who are not present at these hang-outs is a valuable mode of facilitating accessibility and maintaining a sense of engagement that does not require consistent or, active participation.

Through Art Production

The sharing of Pride/Swell art has also waned over time. At the beginning of the project, participants made collages, and as of June, 2021, 38 were shared. For our final art practice, terrariums, six participants shared their pieces. We observed that simpler techniques, such as collage, zine-making, and drawing images on shrinking plastic were more readily taken up by participants in contrast to more involved processes such as sewing and diorama-building. However, we also note that participants continue to send in art pieces over time and out of order. We are encouraged by this participant-centred queering of the project! Only 12 of the 50 participants have never shared their productions with the research team. We are also heartened by the notion that participants are receiving art supplies in the mail, especially those participants who live in rural, or remote communities. Sharing artworks with the research team is not required and does not necessarily imply that the materials are not being used or engaged. The materials and prompt-based packages are not time sensitive and can be visited and revisited. We think what is more important is to share resources with these participants, and share our thinking about how we might make sense of this space and time through art production and forging digital solidarities.

Speaking to a research project centred on the practice of drawing, Tidwell and Manke (2009) note the importance of the researcher(s) engagement with artistic production alongside participants, to both experience and reflect on the ways in which the prompt and action of creating art can be interpreted and embodied. Similarly, to observations regarding participants' discomfort in sharing their creations Tidwell and Manke (2009) cite the hesitancy of researchers, especially those who do not consider themselves to be artistic, to share their artistic products. Among the co-authors, some were more hesitant to share their work than others. While Casey was regularly the first to complete and share her artworks, Amelia experienced some anxiety regarding her creative outputs, rooted specifically in the social or political messaging within each artwork, from deciding on which political issue or topic to engage with to questioning whether her artworks and ideas conveyed enough of a "statement." Brody created artworks as a component of their work in the project, and shared them in DIY production videos for the participants. April and Katie shared a few pieces during the year. Participants may experience a similar anxiety surrounding this act of sharing one's artistic products, particularly for those who do not identify as artists, this may have also contributed to non-participation within this project.

In the Digital Archives

While other participants might be producing art, we can only speak to the pieces that have been shared with us. We have seen participants interact on Instagram and Facebook with one another's pieces. We also note that the archiving function on our website has been used on all of the participant-produced art works. However, we do not yet understand to what extent audiences are viewing the various archives. The visibility and perceived permanence of sharing artistic products on the Internet through digital platforms may have further contributed to non-participation. The research team sought to assuage these concerns through continual processes of consent and regular check-ins along with a commitment to ongoing monitoring of digital archives across platforms. Participants were made aware throughout the project that they retained ownership of their work, and they could request their images be removed from the online archives at any time during and beyond the project. We wonder, but we are unsure, if people are hesitant to share because the archives are online. We offer participants to share their work just with Casey—which one participant has taken up a few times during the year. But we wonder: do any participants create pieces and share them "off line" or out of our view? Does this impact participation?

Central tenets regarding consent and collective archiving practices cannot fully anticipate the actions of the public, including saving or resharing images of participant artworks unbeknownst to the research team (Sandals, 2016). For participants who, like co-researcher Amelia, may question the quality, messaging, or content of their artworks, this hypervisibility and the inability to fully control the permanence of the work may have impacted non-participation, prompting some participants to create artworks that were not shared with the research team. The digital publication (i.e., posting on social media) of submissions could foster non-participation due to hypervisibility and the perceived permanence of the Internet. We suggest that facilitating on-going consent is imperative in queer-focused digital archives, rather than the established institutional practice where ownership is signed over at the time of donation.

We—the research team—have begun thinking about next steps with participants. Recently, we sent out a survey to participants to see what folks might be interested in doing with the collected works in the future. Everyone who replied (nine participants) is interested in putting together a book for the general public that includes our thinking, writing, and making. Some participants are interested in co-writing academic articles. Most participants want the research team to check in periodically (yearly) to ensure that they still want their art pieces included in the online archives. And, we are also going to work with libraries, galleries, schools, and so on, to bring the art pieces to new audiences through a travelling exhibition.

Calling for Participation in Response to Our Artworks

On the Pride/Swell website, we call for participants to create art in response to our work. We write,

> We are interested in knowing what you think about our project! We encourage folks (2SLGBTQ+ and ally youth, students, adults, teachers, artists, anyone) to make art in response to our works. Share your creations with us & we will feature your pieces that respond to our work here.

Here is another site of—as yet—non-participation. So far, while we have received comments on our social media pages, we have not yet had anyone external to the project create work and share it with us. While we seek to disseminate our artworks broadly, we acknowledge that so far, we have had limited participation from our audience members. Although we actively invite folks to do this work, we are not providing extra supplies or prompts to people—though we do share our DIY videos and instructions for each art practice and prompt.

Discussion and Concluding Thoughts

Theron et al. (2011) connect the willingness to participate in visual expressions of participatory visual research with participant autonomy. In Pride/Swell, we have tracked participation, which tells us in absentia, where non-participation is occurring. Although we do not always know the reason for this non-participation. Other than being "busy," participants did not share their reasons for (non)participation. How do practitioners negotiate this? Mitchell et al. (2011) suggest that the visual products generated during research projects can function as a "mode of inquiry, a mode of representation, a mode of dissemination, and a mode of transformation" (p. 22). As such, it is important to acknowledge the ways in which creation can impact both the participant and their audience. In Pride/Swell, the exploration of personal narratives of 2SLGBTQ+ youth experiences ranging from erasure and oppression to self-expression and unbridled emotions, stands to have a significant effect on the participants, which may have influenced non-participation through hesitance in engaging with overly personal topics or taking on the mental and emotional labour associated with these modes of inquiry, representation, dissemination, and transformation (Mitchell et al., 2011). We continue to wonder: what does it mean to produce an archive? why is participatory archiving important? and what non-participation in a participatory archiving project might tell us about the "burden" of archiving falling on those who are already marginalized? Some of our findings would suggest that it is the ease of the art practice that impacts (non) participation. While this may be the case, we do not think that we should only do "easy" art with 2SLGBTQ+ youth. We suggest that providing time, resources, DIY videos, and opportunities to build art practices is useful, even if participants are less willing to share their pieces with researchers. This awareness, in addition to the recognition that 2SLGBTQ+ individuals have long been denied affirming, intersectional representation within dominant historical narratives (Namaste, 2000; Rosenthal, 2017) and Western media (Kohnen, 2015; Russo, 1987) can be considered a potential factor in theorizing non-participation on Zoom, in art production, in the digital archives, and in continuing to engage with the project.

References

Asakura, K. (2016). It takes a village: Applying a social ecological framework of resilience in working with LGBTQ youth. *Families in Society*, *97*(1), 15–22.

Asakura, K. (2017). Paving pathways through the pain: A grounded theory of resilience among lesbian, gay, bisexual, trans, and queer youth. *Journal of Research on Adolescence*, 27(3), 521–536.

Asakura, K., Lundy, J., Black, D., & Tierney, C. (2020). Art as a transformative practice: A participatory action research project with trans* youth. *Qualitative Social Work*, 19(5–6), 1061–1077. https://doi.org/10.1177/1473325019881226

Bain, A.L., & Payne, W.J. (2016). Queer de-participation: Reframing the co-production of scholarly knowledge. *Qualitative Research*, 16(3), 330–340. https://doi.org/10.1177/1468794115619002

Brushwood Rose, C. (2019). Resistance as method: Unhappiness, group feeling, and the limits of participation in a digital storytelling workshop. *International Journal of Qualitative Studies in Education*, 32(7), 857–871.

Burkholder, C. (2020). Exploring participatory visual research methodologies with queer, trans, and non-binary youth in a research for social change framework. *Antistasis*, 10(1), 130–142. https://journals.lib.unb.ca/index.php/antistasis/article/view/30376/1882526417

Burkholder, C., MacEntee, K., Mandrona, A., & Thorpe, A. (2021). Coproducing digital archives with 2SLGBTQ+ Atlantic Canadian youth amidst the COVID-19 pandemic. *Qualitative Research Journal*. ahead-of-print, 1–18. https://doi.org/10.1108/QRJ-01-2021-0003

Burkholder, C., & Thorpe, A. (2019). Cellphilm production as posthuman research method to explore injustice with queer youth in New Brunswick, Canada. *Reconceptualizing Educational Research Methodology*, 10(2–3), 292–309.

Cruz, C. (2013). LGBTQ street youth doing resistance in infrapolitical worlds. In E. Tuck & K.W. Yang (Eds.), *Youth resistance research and theories of change* (pp. 209–217). Routledge.

Cvetkovich, A. (2011). The queer art of the counterarchive. In D. Frantz & M. Locks (Eds.), *Cruising the archive: Queer art and culture in Los Angeles, 1945–1980* (pp. 32–35). ONE National Gay and Lesbian Archives.

D'Amico, M., Denov, M., Khan, F., Linds, W., & Akesson, B. (2016). Research as intervention? Exploring the health and well-being of children and youth facing global adversity through participatory visual methods. *Global Public Health*, 11(5–6), 528–545. https://doi.org/10.1080/17441692.2016.1165719

Furman, E., Singh, A.K., Wilson, C., D'Alessandro, F., & Miller, Z. (2019). "A space where people get it": A methodological reflection of arts-informed community-based participatory research with nonbinary youth. *International Journal of Qualitative Methods*, 18, 1609406919858530. https://doi.org/10.1177/1609406919858530

Gubrium, A.C., & Difulvio, G.T. (2011). Girls in the world: Digital storytelling as a feminist public health approach. *Girlhood Studies*, 4(2), 28–46.

Gustafson, D.L. (2000). Best-laid plans: Examining contra- dictions between intent and outcome in a feminist, collaborative research project, *Qualitative Health Research*, 10, 717–733. https://doi.org/10.1111/j.1440-1800.2007.00365.x

Hayward, C., Simpson, L., & Wood, L. (2004). Still left out in the cold: Problematising participatory research and development. *Sociologia Ruralis*, 44(1), 95–108.

hooks, b. (1989). *Talking back: Thinking feminist, thinking black* (Vol. 10). South End Press.

Kelley, D.G. (2014). Resistance as revelatory. In E. Tuck & K.W. Yang (Eds.), *Youth resistance research and theories of change* (pp. 82–96). Routledge.

Kohnen, M. (2015). *Queer representation, visibility, and race in American film and television: Screening the closet*. Routledge.

Kwon, S.A. (2013). *Uncivil Youth*. Duke University Press.
Lee, J.A. (2017). A queer/ed archival methodology: Archival bodies as nomadic subjects. *Journal of Critical Library and Information Studies*, 1(2): 1–27. https://doi.org/10.24242/jclis.v1i2.26
Lee, J.A. (2021). *Producing the archival body*. Routledge.
Leung, E., & Flanagan, T. (2019). Let's do this together: An integration of photovoice and mobile interviewing in empowering and listening to LGBTQ+ youths in context. *International Journal of Adolescence and Youth*, 24(4), 497–510. https://doi.org/10.1080/02673843.2018.1554499
MacEntee, K., & Flicker, S. (2018). Doing it: Participatory visual methodologies and youth sexuality research. In J. Gilbert, & S. Lamb (Eds.), *The Cambridge handbook of sexual development: Childhood and adolescence*(pp. 352–372). Cambridge University Press. https://doi.org/10.1017/9781108116121.019
Milne, E.J. (2012). Saying 'NO!' to participatory video: Unravelling the complexities of (non)participation. In E.J. Milne, C. Mitchell, & N. de Lange (Eds.), *Handbook of participatory video* (pp. 257–268). Rowman and Littlefield.
Mitchell, C., De Lange, N., & Moletsane, R. (2017). *Participatory visual methodologies: Social change, community and policy*. Sage.
Mitchell, C., Theron, L., Stuart, J., Smith, A., & Campbell, Z. (2011). Drawings as research method. In L. Theron, C. Mitchell, A. Smith, & J. Stuart (Eds.), *Picturing research: Drawing as visual methodology* (pp. 19–36). Sense Publishers.
Norton, B. (2001). Non-participation, imagined communities and the language classroom. *Learner Contributions to Language Learning: New Directions in Research*, 6(2), 159–171.
Namaste, V.K. (2000). *Invisible lives: The erasure of transsexual and transgendered people*. University of Chicago Press.
Namaste, V. (2009). Undoing theory: The "transgender question" and the epistemic violence of Anglo-American feminist theory. *Hypatia*, 24(3), 11–32. http://www.jstor.org/stable/20618162
Russo, V. (1987). *The celluloid closet: Homosexuality in the movies*. Harper & Row.
Rosenthal, G. (2017). Make Roanoke queer again: Community history and urban change in a Southern city. *The Public Historian*, 39(1), 35–60.
Sandals, L. (2016). When a private trans archive becomes public art. *Canadian Art*. https://canadianart.ca/features/when-a-private-trans-archive-becomes-public-art/
Scott, J.C. (1990). *Domination and the arts of resistance: Hidden transcripts*. Yale University Press. https://doi.org/10.1086/ahr/99.1.195
Simpson, A. (2007). On ethnographic refusal: Indigeneity, 'voice' and colonial citizenship. *Junctures*, 9, 67–80. https://junctures.org/index.php/junctures/article/view/66/60
Singh, A.A., Richmond, K., & Burnes, T.R. (2013). Feminist participatory action research with transgender communities: Fostering the practice of ethical and empowering research designs. *International Journal of Transgenderism*, 14(3), 93–104.
Switzer, S. (2020). "People give and take a lot in order to participate in things:" Youth talk back – making a case for non-participation, *Curriculum Inquiry*, 50(2), 168–193, https://doi.org/10.1080/03626784.2020.1766341
Switzer, S., Gaztambide-Fernández, R., Alarcón, A., Raza, N. et al. (2021). Community engagement in Covid-19. [website]. https://www.beyondthetoolkit.com
Theron, L., Stuart, J., & Mitchell, C. (2011). A positive, African ethical approach to collecting and interpreting drawings: Some considerations. In L. Theron, C. Mitchell, A. Smith, & J. Stuart (Eds.), *Picturing research: Drawing as visual methodology* (pp. 49–62). Sense Publishers.

Tidwell, D., & Manke, M.P. (2009). Making meaning of practice through visual metaphor. In *Research methods for the self-study of practice* (pp. 135–153). Springer, Dordrecht.

Tuck, E. (2009). Suspending damage: A letter to communities. *Harvard Educational Review*, 79(3), 409–428. https://doi.org/10.17763/haer.79.3.n0016675661t3n15

Tuck, E., & Yang, K.W. (2014a). R-words: Refusing research. In *Humanizing research: Decolonizing qualitative inquiry with youth and communities* (pp. 223–248). SAGE Publications. http://dx.doi.org/10.4135/9781544329611

Tuck, E., & Yang, K.W. (2014b). Unbecoming claims: Pedagogies of refusal in qualitative research. *Qualitative Inquiry*, 20(6), 811–818. https://doi.org/10.1177/1077800414530265

Ware, S.M. (2017). All power to all people? Black LGBTTI2QQ activism, remembrance, and archiving in Toronto. *TQS: Transgender Studies Quarterly*, 4(2), 170–180. https://doi.org/10.1215/23289252-3814961

Wenger, E. (1998). Communities of practice: Learning as a social system. *Systems Thinker*, 9(5), 2–3.

PART III
Ethics and Facilitation in Research Processes

9
RESEARCH ASSISTANTS AS KNOWLEDGE CO-PRODUCERS

Reflections Beyond Fieldwork

Nicole M.Y. Tang and Jan Gube

Research assistants play an indispensable role in research facilitation. Yet, their "powerless" status (Macfarlane, 2017, p. 1196) and "opaque presences" (Middleton & Cons, 2014, p. 282) in academic literature undermine their contribution to scholarship. This chapter draws on an introspective account in an ongoing community-engaged project to explore the roles, contributions, and competence of a research assistant in research facilitation. This account arises from our Hong Kong experience, in which conversations on racial equity and diversity are not the norm (Gube & Burkholder, 2019). We ask: in what ways do research assistants have a bearing on research ethics and knowledge production, through shared power relations, personal values, and commitments?

We discuss the role of research assistants as knowledge co-producer in three sections. The first section opens with a discussion on an ethical grey space in research facilitation, which is overlooked by established research ethics guidelines. Next, we examine the nature of research facilitation by illustrating the positionality of research assistants within research processes. In the third section, we probe the role of research assistants in ethical research practices to highlight how they facilitate knowledge production in scholarly work. We conclude by making a case for the intellectual and moral competence of research assistants beyond execution of fieldwork, and their roles as active contributors to the conversations on racial equity in Hong Kong.

Ethical Grey Areas in Research Facilitation: The Problems with Research Ethics

Whilst research ethics frameworks are set to protect the interest of participants and researchers, institutional guidelines are often not comprehensive in accounting for the contextual considerations in research facilitation (Guillemin

DOI: 10.4324/9781003199236-13

& Gillam, 2004; Nguyen, 2016; Zhang, 2017). In what follows, we reflect on our experience facilitating a research project concerning cultural diversity in Hong Kong's education landscape and explore dilemmas that raise questions regarding researchers' ethical responsibilities. We argue that research ethics guidelines overlook instances of ethically meaningful decisions that are embedded in everyday research practices.

In Hong Kong, the lack of a central organization overseeing research ethics means research ethics reviews are left to individual institutions (Israel, 2014). At The Education University of Hong Kong, the Human Research Ethics Committee (2016) in its *Guidelines on Ethics in Research* gives a detailed account of ethical principles, focusing on participants' right to full disclosure, informed consent, minimized harm, and confidentiality. However, Zhang (2017) problematized the use of a universal code of ethics across all disciplines of inquiry. He noted that ethics reviews were originally designed to regulate medical and scientific studies and questioned whether they can accurately address the realities of social science research (See also: Israel & Hay, 2006). This may be rectified by subjecting research of different disciplines to different review standards. For example, the University of Hong Kong has three different review bodies to cater to different types of research: The Human Research Ethics Committee for Non-Clinical Faculties, The Institutional Review Board of the University of Hong Kong/Hospital Authority Hong Kong West Cluster, and The Committee on the Use of Live Animals in Teaching and Research (Zhang, 2017). Zhang also argued that a universal code of ethics often fails to be geographically and contextually sensitive. For example, demanding research participants to sign consent forms when conducting research in politically charged areas or emotionally sensitive situations may be insensitive and inappropriate.

Likewise, the emphasis on the full disclosure of information fuels discussions on the ethics of covert research (Nguyen, 2016). Covert research—which broadly refers to research conducted without participants' full knowledge—is not limited to those involving active deception. Covert research includes unannounced observations, disguised intentions, and misrepresentations of research. Undertaking covert research involves the use of deception, which could undermine research ethics and integrity. As we reflect on our experience in facilitating our research project, we discover dilemmas that put into question our ethical responsibility as researchers. We ask: to what extent do strategic considerations in facilitation processes constitute covert research?

Ethical Dilemmas and Blurred Covert-Overt Boundaries

Our discussion's point of departure is that conveying diversity-related knowledge to ethnic majority populations in Hong Kong requires careful deliberation. For example, how might ethnically Chinese teachers—who may have grown up with very little contact with non-Chinese individuals—make sense of the systemic inequities that diverse learners face? In a broad sense, our project sets out to address this question. The project is concerned with topics of cultural inclusion and diversity in Hong Kong's education landscape, with a focus on teacher education. The broader goal of the project is to enhance teachers' capacity to work with culturally diverse classrooms. Some of its key initiatives involve:

- developing an informal learning program and relevant resources for teacher educators to advance pedagogies that prepare pre-service teachers for catering to learning and cultural diversity (Equal Opportunities Commission, 2019);
- providing a focused global citizenship knowledge base through experiential learning for pre-service teachers in anticipation of learning contexts in which "life experiences of non-Chinese speaking students are different from that of Chinese speaking students" (Oxfam Hong Kong et al., 2020); and
- guiding pre-service teachers to reflect and draw on this knowledge base to create supportive and inclusive learning environments for all learners.

In the project's context, equity and inclusion mean enabling school teachers to appreciate learners' cultural diversity—such as their backgrounds, lives, values, and practices they bring to the classrooms—and to develop a stronger capacity to remove the obstacles that come the way of these learners (beyond language barriers in Cantonese/Chinese for multilingual students).

Cultural diversity education is relatively new in Hong Kong, compared to many Western, immigrant-receiving societies. The policy treatment towards culturally diverse pupils has tended to centre on remediating their Chinese language proficiency; as a mode of facilitating their integration to Hong Kong's wider society (Education Bureau, 2014). Hong Kong's policy priority on preparing teachers to teach in ethnically diverse classrooms is not as evident (Burkholder, 2013), compared to other societies with a more explicit mention of conflict resolution skills as part of teacher training in policy agenda, such as those observed in Europe (Barajas et al., 2018). This policy focus of Hong Kong suggests that its teacher training provisions still have a long way to go in terms of addressing the learning needs of culturally diverse pupils in equitable terms (Kennedy, 2011), in which teachers are not always cognizant of the systemic inequities that students face. This cultural backdrop draws attention to the fact that Hong Kong's diverse schooling landscape must be interrogated, especially if concepts related to equity and inclusion are to be applied meaningfully in policy and practice. All of these have implications for the way we disclose and disseminate our project's information to stakeholders.

Disclosure of Information

In the initial stages of the project, we designed a launch event for promoting our project to members of the university, schools, and non-government organizations. Nicole was responsible for liaison and outreach, which included the promotion of events, answering phone enquiries, and communicating with participants. In an enquiry phone conversation, she was greeted by a teacher who seemed intrigued by our initiative. "What exactly is this project about?" He asked, "for whom is this project designed?" As Nicole prepared for an answer, she realized that these questions demanded more than a descriptive response on the project's goals and structure. They required her subjective interpretation on the nature of the research project, assumptions on the interest and priorities of her interlocutor, and knowledge on the shared relations between stakeholders of the diversity and inclusion discourse. Some questions surfaced in Nicole's mind: as a member of the majority ethnic group, should she be employing terminologies such as "minoritized groups" and "ethnic minorities," or is it more appropriate for her to characterize the project in more general terms such as "inclusion" and "diversity"? Would the implications of her vocabularies differ when she spoke to an ethnically Chinese person from when she spoke to a non-Chinese individual?

As trivial as these considerations may seem, ethical dilemmas in communication and disclosure of information can be explicit in research facilitation. As the goal of our project is to promote inclusivity and cultural awareness in education, it involves exploring the shortcomings of current practices. Understanding that Hong Kong's mainstream education landscape lacks a common understanding on diversity issues (Kennedy, 2012), we must consider how to present the nature of the project in the most effective way. Being aware that some of our event participants may be education practitioners who may not have received formal teacher training in or have exposure to culturally diverse learning settings (Yeung, 2012), we often deliberate how we are to present diversity issues appropriately. Strategically, that means striking a delicate balance in representing the nature of the project and its anti-racist undertones, without making the practitioners feel alienated or intimidated.

In framing the project as such, we understand that when conversing with practitioners who are less familiar with the cultural inclusion discourse, it may be more comprehensible if we use terms such as "ethnic minority students" and "non-Chinese speaking"—the official terminologies endorsed by government documents. Conversely, working with an audience from diverse ethnic backgrounds, we are aware that these terms are not always preferred. For example, Holmes (2020) argued that the term "non-Chinese speaking" is harmful to minoritized communities, which speaks to the category conundrum associated with the labelling practices on culturally diverse individuals (Halse, 2019). Thus, for the sake of effective communication, our use of terminologies is dependent upon the cultural groups we are speaking to. As we will illustrate below, researchers must constantly navigate decisions on describing research details strategically. Presenting the research in more comprehensible ways in accordance with its audience, is both motivated by a need to build rapport, as well as for effective facilitation. So, what are the ethical demands behind this deliberation process that supports the tactful and strategic interactions with project participants?

Negotiation on Language Choice

The complex decision-making process goes beyond *what* is said about the research but also *how* it is said. Working alongside faculty members, NGO representatives, education practitioners, and pre-service teachers, Nicole at times meets with people from multicultural backgrounds. The choice of language in these situations opens a wide-ranging set of ethical implications. In Hong Kong, there exists an assumption that Cantonese is almost exclusively spoken by the ethnically Chinese population (Ku, 2006), while people of other ethnic backgrounds, including Southeast Asians and South Asians, are largely assumed to be unfamiliar with the local language and more fluent in English. The assumption on language proficiency based on ethnic profiling is problematic as it reinforces a stereotype that a Hong Konger ought to be ethically Chinese and Cantonese-speaking. By extension, this stereotype carries assumptions about cultural membership (Brubaker et al., 2004), which casts people of multicultural backgrounds as outsiders from the local community and downplays their identity as Hong Kongers. Recognizing the critical social and political implications of the situation, Nicole asked herself, what are the different assumptions she conveys through her judgement on the preferred language of her counterpart? Choosing to speak in English—one of the official languages of Hong Kong which could be understood by most—may appear to be favourable. However, defaulting to English may reinforce the assumption that a non-Chinese person is not considered a "local" Hong Konger and hence not expected to be fluent in the local language. Similarly, if it is deemed more inclusive to speak Cantonese, should it turn out that the person is not fluent, Nicole might other her interlocutor by insisting to use Cantonese. There is no simple solution, as either option opens room for interpretations that go against the values of inclusivity and cultural sensitivity that Nicole's work seeks to promote.

The Ethics of Covert Elements in Research

Grey Spaces in Research Ethics

The dilemmas illustrated above are examples of how a researcher's deliberation process may pose ethical considerations. The ethical implication presented by this possibility is significant, as it puts into question the researcher's commitment to full disclosure to research participants. To what extent are researchers justified in leveraging these considerations privately? Are researchers morally obliged to reveal their assumption and negotiation on ethnic labels that go into making these decisions?

Research ethics guidelines often present a view that covert research is broadly considered to be deceitful, misleading, and generally, unethical. Meanwhile, overt research is classified as low-risk, inoffensive, and preferable. However, this dichotomized categorization overlooks the realities of research facilitation because it dismisses the possibility that covert elements could be present in ethical research (Nguyen, 2016). Nguyen (2016) argues not only for the possibility, but also a necessity, for both overt and covert elements to coexist without jeopardizing the ethical status of the research by marking a "grey space" (p. 57) between the two poles of covert and overt research. This ethical grey space refers to the possibility and necessity of covert processes within overt research. The use of covert elements in research facilitation—such as strategic communication and language choice—constitutes this space. This interlacing of covert elements with overt research creates a space where covert–overt boundaries are blurred, which challenges the traditional understanding and connotations of overt and covert research. Research ethics tends to overlook these nuanced yet pervasive examples that invite ethical consideration even in overt research. This is because by neatly distinguishing between research methodologies that involves active deceptions and harm from those that do not, it overlooks possible ethical considerations in "low risk" research. By placing a focus on research design and methodologies, it ignores the possibility for banal decision-making processes to have significant impact on research ethics.

The "Everyday" Quality of Ethically Important Decisions

The examples above also show that even the most commonplace deliberation processes may be laden with ethical implications. Guillemin and Gillam (2004) argued that "ethically important moments" (p. 265)—which refers to the "difficult, often subtle, and usually unpredictable situations that arise in the practice of doing research" (p. 262)—are part of the everyday realities of research facilitation. These ethical decisions are embedded in the doing of research. They present a tension between the ethical responsibilities to research participants and one's professional demands as a researcher (Guillemin & Gillam, 2004). They may be as nuanced as strategic disclosure and concealment of information, framing and characterization, and language choice—considerations that researchers must repeatedly and continuously navigate at every stage of the project (Nguyen, 2016).

Dismissing these considerations as unethical would result in two problems. First, subjecting the complex decision-making processes of researchers during research facilitation to the same treatment as covert research practices would set an unattainable standard for full disclosure. How do researchers fully disclose their assumptions, deliberation process and ethical concerns at every stage of the research? Second, if all undisclosed strategic decisions are to be labelled as covert research practices, it would render overt research impossible. This is because strategic decisions can be located even within what would be considered overt and low-risk research. Instead, these strategies, considerations, and decisions should be seen as covert elements within overt research. When we acknowledge that even the most ordinary practices in research facilitation call for deliberation, it attests to the possibility—and necessity—of covert elements within overt research. Since the use of covert elements is a necessary one, their presence in research facilitation should not put the ethical status of the research into jeopardy simply in virtue of their "covert" statuses.

The Role of Research Assistants: From Positionality to Research Ethics

As research ethics guidelines and review procedures tend to overlook ethical considerations that arise during research facilitation, ethical practices cannot be ensured entirely *a priori* from regulating research design and methodology. Most ethical research practices rest upon the decision-making process in the *doing* of research. For this reason, those at the frontline make a significant impact on research ethics. In this section, we focus on the role of research assistants in facilitating ethical research practices. Through an introspective account on the researcher's positionality, we will explore how it underscores ethical dilemmas and discuss how research assistants enable unique forms of contributions in knowledge production.

The Invisibility of Research Assistants

Discussions on research assistants in qualitative research usually focus on their invisibility and lack of recognition in research. Some have noted the silence and even erasure of research assistants' presence and contributions in academic literature (Middleton & Cons, 2014; Middleton & Pradhan, 2014). Sanjek (1993) went as far as describing the invisibility of research assistants with references to its colonial past as "hidden colonialism" (p. 13), by noting examples of exploitation and power differentials between anthropologists from the West and their local assistants. Yet, the absence of research assistants in academic discussion may reflect deeper problems with regards to their power relations with project leaders. For instance, research assistants problematize institutional and academic norms which privilege individual competence, autonomy, and single authorship (Middleton & Cons, 2014). This results in the silence on the contributions of research assistants, and their invisibility in academic literature, especially if left undiscussed among the project team. These critiques on the inequitable treatment of research assistants underline questions about their contributions and competence.

Scholars have characterized the role of research assistants as field agents, people who facilitate relationship-building with local communities, forge insider gateways, and bridge social, cultural, and language barriers (Holmberg, 2014; Middleton & Pradhan, 2014; Stevens, 2001). However, relatively little has been said regarding the broader role of research assistants beyond the execution of fieldwork and their implications. What is the role of a research assistant in the production of knowledge, with regards to sharing power relations with research leaders? What are their impacts on research ethics? In what follows, we write from our respective stances to underscore our individual encounters in running the project. The first author, Nicole, will describe how her understanding of the role has evolved throughout her own journey as a research assistant; the second author, Jan, will discuss his positioning as an academic to provide a context for Nicole's work.

Beyond Fieldwork and Furthering Other's Grand Design

In an introspective account of an ethnographer–assistant partnership, Middleton and Pradhan (2014) candidly depicted their early relationship as one that initially consisted of "the expectations of a dutiful research assistant hired to do the grunt work of ethnography and little more" (p. 361). Bearing assumptions on both sides, the duo mapped onto each other their expectations of what the partnership would entail. At the early stages of her work as a research assistant, Nicole adopted an understanding of the role as one that afforded her little room beyond the execution of fieldwork. As much as she harboured genuine interest in the work, she understood that the project was designed without her involvement. To put it plainly, the research project was essentially the work of *others* which Nicole gladly became involved with. For the most part, Nicole was "furthering someone else's grand design" (Sawyer, 2017, para. 9). Nicole had little expectations for her contributions as a research assistant to steer or challenge the research's direction, and she did not expect her intellectual capacities to come to the forefront during the facilitation process.

The dynamics underlying work relationships with aspiring researchers is not to be taken for granted. These relationships enable research projects to take place. Fruitful relationships are therefore critical to the completion of research endeavours. As a faculty member, Jan enjoys the privilege of having received the training for conducting and publishing scholarly work. Working with junior members in a team thus underscores the power relations between faculty members and those who engage in a supportive role. Traditionally, this power relation foregrounds an association between those who possess expert knowledge and those who do not but engages in such knowledge domain to acquire expertise. Such is the case between Nicole and Jan. However, Jan sees this collaboration with Nicole not just in terms of a mentor–mentee relationship, but also as a way to gain new insights into the field. This is because the nature of the project requires us to work closely with minoritized communities in Hong Kong, including the organizations and schools that cater to them. This work demands that as a project team we possess the knowledge of both the minoritized community and local schools that are not always exposed to ethnic diversity. For the research facilitation to work effectively, Jan has to actively adopt a more egalitarian work relationship to see Nicole as a partner in the "grand design" of the project, and not as one who would do all the "grunt work."

The other facet of our work relationship is that Jan is a Filipino-Hong Konger and Nicole is ethnically Chinese. In a sense, Jan has access to a cultural capital that affords him an "insider" understanding of Filipino communities in Hong Kong (Burkholder & Gube, 2018). Positionality wise, this understanding allows

Jan to be more cognizant of the experience of being an ethnic minority person, the general feeling of being different from the Chinese population and struggles to fit in the wider society of Hong Kong. Experiences like these made it easier for Jan to grasp concepts frequently discussed in diversity studies, such as racial microaggressions, Othering, exclusion, and so forth. Logistically, Jan's insider status can also be helpful in establishing a common language (e.g., shared concerns on equity issues in education) with organizations that support minoritized groups. As such, Jan's conversations with the leaders of these organizations often remark that we share the same mission.

The understandings of cultural nuances Jan developed as an insider is however not infallible. There may be norms that need to be observed, such as how the discourse on cultural diversity might be taken up by local Chinese teachers. Nicole's perspectives, as Jan sees it, could complement his as they facilitate the understanding of the local Chinese community on the value of equity and inclusion. Kennedy (2011) argued that the local education system and advocates for minoritized communities have different conceptions of equality. For instance, officials tend to value fairness over equitable provisions. That means, curriculum and assessment provisions tended to be about sufficiency—in that minoritized students receive adequate Chinese language support and training would remediate the schooling barriers they face. Yet, advocates felt strongly about the need to address systemic inequities, such as the low representation of minoritized children in kindergartens (Equal Opportunities Commission, 2019). We cite this example because engaging in diversity work is norm-disrupting. In the context of our project, our hope is that educators could appreciate the values of equity and inclusion in Hong Kong classrooms.

Though, as discussed above, this appreciation does not come by easily. For our project to be fruitful, it is crucial to acknowledge that diversity work is not straightforward in contexts where diversity is not the norm, such as Hong Kong. Phrased differently, the success of a research project does not simply depend on its scholarly substance, such as how robust the theories and research design are, but also on how it is communicated to those participating in it through strategic research facilitation. Meanwhile, the extent to which these cultural nuances can be presented and discussed often depend on the methodological orientation of publication outlets and the paradigmatic stances of researchers. These are questions we are yet to answer, but in terms of our own research practice, it is not uncommon between us to end our research meetings with extended conversations about what examples would help local Chinese communities better understand cultural diversity, equity, and inclusion, at times with scribbles and notes on Jan's whiteboard in English and Chinese. Many of these exchanges involve working out how local teachers might (not) understand these diversity concepts. For example, despite the frequent circulation of racial equity advocacies on various social media outlets internationally (e.g., Black Lives Matter), we often deliberate how to connect and translate these experiences in education settings like Hong Kong. Hong Kong is a context where few Black people are represented, where

Chinese language proficiency concerns occupy much of the attention of frontline teachers, and where teachers do not receive robust training to teach in ethnically or racially diverse classrooms.

Blurred Insider-Outsider Statuses

Despite the benefits of the "insider" status afforded to faculty members as academic experts, their presence may sometimes create social and epistemological barriers due to an elitist distance. When working with research participants, especially those from minoritized or disadvantaged communities, the presence of an impersonal, impartial, note-taking scholar may be deemed intrusive. They may be viewed as sociological inquirers rather than understanding, sympathizing allies (Vaidya, 2010). Middleton and Cons (2014) suggest that research assistants could bridge the elitist distance between academic scholars and research participants. Although the power difference between researchers and participants cannot be entirely eradicated, through softening the image of an official inquisitor and diminishing the hierarchical relationship between interviewers and interviewees, research assistants may facilitate rapport building with participants (Vaidya, 2010).

Beyond these bridging roles, Nicole wonders: is there room for her to make contributions to knowledge production and research facilitation in ways unique to her values, experience, and commitment? As she inspected her own positionality within the research project, she discovered that her role as a research assistant, her ethnic identity, and her experience, weaved a complex picture of her ambiguous positionality marked by a blurred insider-outsider boundary. Nicole started to explore how it has contributed to shaping her perspective, values, and commitment to the research project. Not only did her positionality influence the unfolding of ethical dilemmas, it also enabled unique contributions to knowledge production.

Middleton and Cons (2014) argued that research assistants "unsettle rigid understandings of insider/outsider knowledge" (p. 286) by blurring the insider and outsider boundaries in knowledge production. Nicole's status within the academic arena was the first that came to mind. The university categorizes staff positions under four tracks: "Academic/Teaching," "Professional/Administration/Execution," "Research Support," and "Clerical/Support." There is a clear categorical distinction between academic staff and research support staff. Markedly, research support staff members are not regarded as academic experts in the same way a faculty member would be. The designation of research assistants as "research support staff" reflects the emphasis on support and facilitation, which are often prioritized over any intellectual and creative prowess such a role may call for. At the same time, as a member of staff at an institution traditionally focused on teacher education in Hong Kong, Nicole has often been met with assumptions on her job duties being related to teaching and academic work. Her affiliation with a university seems to have afforded her an unduly level of respect and authority by association, presumably due to the assumptions in intellectual abilities and statuses commonly associated with academic scholars. Nicole have been addressed as a teacher or mistaken to be a PhD candidate, even though neither is accurate to the nature of her work. These juxtaposing views paint a conflicting picture of what her role as research assistant entails: she is ambivalently both an insider and an outsider of the academic arena.

The blurred insider-outsider statuses of Nicole's role are also reflected by her ethnic identity. Working on a research project on topics of cultural diversity, being ethnically Chinese—a member of the dominant ethnic group in Hong Kong—positioned Nicole as an outsider. Aware of her positioning, Nicole questions whether her ethnicity may have implications for the work. Might she overlook issues that may not be as visible to members outside of the community she works with? Would her language and behaviour reflect unintended assumptions? These considerations pose challenges that could translate into questions on her professional competence. As Nicole questions the validity and credibility of her contributions, she grew increasingly uncertain whether she should have a say on issues of a domain she seemed to be trespassing in or have little personal experience with.

Yet, these reflections also prompted discoveries on parallels between the experience of the community Nicole works with and her own. During her university years as a student in the United Kingdom, Nicole's identity as a Hong Konger rendered her a minority in a predominantly white British student group. She often found herself in situations where she was the only Asian student present. Intrigued by the inverse of her experience, she became more aware of the nuanced experience of being "othered." Nicole started thinking about how her behaviour may be interpreted as conformation to or rejections of various ethnic or racial stereotypes, and how best to navigate them. She started paying more attention to the power relations that stem from the racial difference between people around her and how they shaped her thoughts and behaviour. Nicole wondered if these experiences were like what minoritized groups might be experiencing without acknowledgement from the majority of the population.

Nicole's experience in the UK illuminated her understanding of diversity and inclusion. It prompted her to negotiate her ethnic identity through racialized experience, and explore how they have influenced her role as a research assistant of a project on cultural diversity. Nicole had new perspectives on looking at the experience of minoritized groups in Hong Kong. This kind of connection is not simply an emotional response of sympathy in feeling for the marginalized groups who experience inequitable treatments, but an experiential knowledge informed by her first-hand experience of the problem itself.

Thapan (1998) commented on the importance of reflexivity in the relationship between researcher and research participants. This reflexivity can serve to reject the prevalent self-other distinction between participants and researchers (Vaidya, 2010). It is easy, sometimes even intuitive, to see research participants as parties whose experiences are to be observed and analyzed. It is also true that researchers are in a privileged position due to their expertise or responsibility in initiating and facilitating the research, regardless of whether they are faculty members or research assistants. However, Nicole's reflections enabled her to establish a connection with the community she worked with, and reject such dichotomies which her outsider status as a member of the majority ethnic group seems to encourage. The parallels in their experiences served as an anchor point in an internalized critique on the credibility and validity of Nicole's perspectives, and opened new spaces for forging stronger commitment to the values of equity and inclusion.

On Positionality and Research Ethics

Positionality influences our understanding of diversity issues and perspectives in navigating ethical grey spaces. Herein lies a dilemma concerning whether to use terminologies, such as "ethnic minorities" or "non-Chinese speaking person," and how the considerations may differ depending on the audience group. The problem rests upon the need to prevent unintentionally inflicting an "othering" sentiment by using these terminologies. However, Nicole's awareness of the "othering" effect these terms carry is highlighted by the parallels between her experience in the UK and the communities she works with. The ethical implications are dependent on her positionality, which influences her perspectives, assumptions, and relations with both the research and its participants. Research ethics guidelines cannot provide a universal solution because the ethical implications of research cannot be determined without paying heed to the positionalities of its researchers. Self-understanding and reflexivity are required to understand how the ethical dilemmas are created, perceived, interpreted, and addressed.

Research Assistants beyond Fieldwork: Impact on Research Ethics and Contributions in Knowledge Co-production

How does positionality impact a research assistant's contributions in knowledge production? In this section, we will argue for the significant impact research assistants bear towards research ethics, and how such impact showcases the moral and intellectual capacities of research assistants. Beyond the execution of fieldwork, there is potential within research facilitation for realizing a research assistant's moral and intellectual capacities, and room for making rich and unique contributions to knowledge co-production.

Moral and Intellectual Capacities of Research Assistants

We have previously established how ethical decisions can be embedded in ordinary practices of research facilitation. What are their implications on research assistants' contributions? Their involvement in and contribution towards ethical research practices illuminates the moral capacity of research assistants in two ways. First, research assistants—who are often tasked with the presentation of research initiatives and communication with participants—are responsible for negotiating decisions laden with ethical implications at the forefront of facilitation work. Guillemin and Gillam (2004) wrote:

> It is within the dimension of "ethics in practice" that the researcher's ethical competence comes to the fore. By this we mean the researcher's willingness to acknowledge the ethical dimension of research practice, his or her ability to actually recognize this ethical dimension when it comes into play, and his or her ability to think through ethical issues and respond appropriately.
> (p. 269)

As a result, research assistants are often caught in a web of tacit ethical dilemmas which constantly challenge their professional and ethical responsibilities as researchers. Second, the ethical dilemmas that unfold during research facilitation are co-created and shaped by research assistants' unique positionality. This positionality attests to the moral capacity of research assistants in challenging existing understanding of research ethics, locating ethical grey spaces in research facilitation, and revealing the uncharted terrains of institutionalized research ethics frameworks.

The contributions of research assistants, however, do not eliminate the conflicts and ambiguity imposed by one's positionality. Nicole's positionality as an "outsider" in fieldwork positioned her to facilitate the crossing of epistemological and cultural barriers. That is, by not being an academic expert, she can grasp how a non-academic audience may respond to the research project's outreach initiatives, and devise strategies that appeal to their interests. By not being a member of minoritized communities, Nicole brings perspective on how issues related to cultural diversity may be perceived by the majority ethnic group, and identifies gaps in understanding that need to be addressed. Nicole came to understand how the dualities and blurred insider-outsider boundaries of her positionality may be an asset in crafting new spaces for unique intellectual contributions.

Conclusion

This chapter aimed to establish the role of research assistants as knowledge co-producers by making a case for the moral and intellectual capacities of research assistants. The introspective account illustrated how our positionality can shape researchers' perspectives, values, and commitments. Our discussion broadened the understanding of research ethics by examining strategic decision-making in research facilitation. Situated at a grey space within the spectrum of covert and overt research, are ethical dilemmas that research assistants—who are at the forefront of research facilitation—must constantly navigate. Not only does it attest to the moral capacity of research assistants in facilitating ethical research practices, but it also makes room for their unique contributions in knowledge co-production by locating spaces where their intellectual capacities may be recognized.

Research assistants' positionality also influences connections with the communities they work with. A research field is not something external to the entity of the researcher, and the "subjects" of the research are not entities to establish rapport with, whose language and culture is to be learnt from (Vaidya, 2010). Rather, it is co-constituted by researchers through reflective and active engagement with one's positionality. Middleton and Pradhan (2014) noted how the production of knowledge often begins with fieldworkers. The same can be argued for the facilitation of other qualitative research, where the negotiation of methods and strategies used—determined through the moral and intellectual capacity of fieldworkers—define the research and constitute the field in question. In this sense, research assistantship is not a mere *role* to be fulfilled but constitutes a research space in which *individuals* engage in a host of ethical decisions and actively contribute to the co-production of knowledge.

Acknowledgements

The authors acknowledge the support of the Faculty of Education and Human Development, The Education University of Hong Kong for the project *Inclusion and Equity for Hong Kong's Diverse Classrooms*, which provided the basis of the discussion of this chapter. The views expressed are those of the authors.

References

Barajas, M., Frossard, F., & Marocco, D. (2018). *ACCORD - Attain cultural integration through conflict resolution skill development: Pedagogical framework, competency model and user requirements*. http://accord-project.eu/wp-content/uploads/2018/05/ACCORD_D3.2_Report_on_pedagogical_framework_competency_model.pdf

Brubaker, R., Loveman, M., & Stamatov, P. (2004). Ethnicity as cognition. *Theory and Society, 33*(1), 31–64.

Burkholder, C. (2013). "Just the school make[s] us non-Chinese": Contrasting the discourses of Hong Kong's Education Bureau with the lived experiences of its non-Chinese speaking secondary school population. *Educational Research for Social Change, 2*(2), 43–58.

Burkholder, C., & Gube, J. (2018). Exploring racial identities through participatory visual and ethnographic methods: (Re)presenting the identities of ethnic minority youth in Hong Kong. *Visual Studies, 33*(3), 219–230. https://doi.org/10.1080/1472586X.2018.1527187

Education Bureau. (2014). *Enhanced Chinese learning and teaching for non-Chinese speaking students*. Government of the HKSAR. https://www.edb.gov.hk/attachment/en/student-parents/ncs-students/new/CM_2014%2006%2005_E.pdf

Equal Opportunities Commission. (2019). *Closing the gap: Report of the working group on education for ethnic minorities*. https://www.eoc.org.hk/s/ClosingtheGap/Closing_the_Gap_Report.pdf

Gube, J., & Burkholder, C. (2019). Unresolved tensions in Hong Kong's racialized discourse: Rethinking differences in educating about ethnic minorities. In J. Gube, & F. Gao (Eds.), *Education, ethnicity and equity in the multilingual Asian context* (pp. 105–121). Springer.

Guillemin, M., & Gillam, L. (2004). Ethics, reflexivity, and "ethically important moments" in research. *Qualitative Inquiry, 10*(2), 261–280.

Halse, C. (2019). Challenges for interethnic relations, language and educational equity in Asia. In J. Gube, & F. Gao (Eds.), *Education, ethnicity and equity in the multilingual Asian context* (pp. 275–284). Springer.

Holmberg, D. (2014). Ethnographic agency, field assistants and the rise of cultural activism in Nepal. *Ethnography, 15*(3), 311–330.

Holmes, M. (2020, December 13). *Why the 'Non-Chinese Speaking' tag is doing real harm to Hong Kong's non-Chinese pupils*. Hong Kong Free Press. https://hongkongfp.com/2020/12/13/the-ncs-tag-is-doing-real-harm-to-hong-kongs-non-chinese-pupils/

Human Research Ethics Committee. (2016). *Guidelines on ethics in research*. https://www.eduhk.hk/human_hrec/view.php?secid=2550

Israel, M., & Hay, I. (2006). *Research ethics for social scientists: Between ethical conduct and regulatory compliance*. SAGE Publications.

Israel, M. (2014). *Research ethics and integrity for social scientists: Beyond regulatory compliance*. SAGE Publications.

Kennedy, K.J. (2011). The "long march" toward multiculturalism in Hong Kong: Supporting ethnic minority students in a Confucian state. In J. Phillion, M.T. Hue, & Y. Wang (Eds.), *Minority students in East Asia: Government policies, school practices and teacher responses* (pp. 155–173). Routledge.

Kennedy, K.J. (2012, August 25). Where's Hong Kong's diversity pledge? *South China Morning Post*. https://www.scmp.com/comment/insight-opinion/article/1022612/wheres-hong-kongs-diversity-pledge

Ku, H.B. (2006). Body, dress and cultural exclusion: Experiences of Pakistani women in 'global' Hong Kong. *Asian Ethnicity, 7*(3), 285–302. https://doi.org/10.1080/14631360600926980

Macfarlane, B. (2017). The ethics of multiple authorship: Power, performativity and the gift economy. *Studies in Higher Education, 42*(7), 1194–1210.

Middleton, T., & Cons, J. (2014). Coming to terms: Reinserting research assistants into ethnography's past and present. *Ethnography, 15*(3), 279–290.

Middleton, T., & Pradhan, E. (2014). Dynamic duo: On partnership and the possibilities of postcolonial ethnography. *Ethnography, 15*(3), 355–374.

Nguyen, N. (2016). The covert researcher: The ethics of a school ethnography. In N. Nguyen (Ed.), *A curriculum of fear: Homeland security in U.S. public schools* (pp. 45–72). University of Minnesota Press.

Oxfam Hong Kong, Loh, K.Y.E., & Hung, O.Y. (2020). *A study on the challenges faced by mainstream schools in educating ethnic minorities in Hong Kong*. https://www.eoc.org.hk/eoc/upload/ResearchReport/researchreport_20200115_e.pdf

Sanjek, R. (1993). Anthropology's hidden colonialism: Assistants and their ethnographer. *Anthropology Today, 9*(2), 13–18. https://doi.org/10.2307/2783170S

Sawyer, D. (2017, March 20). Not just a foot soldier – A researcher on someone else's project. *Patter*. https://patthomson.net/2017/03/20/not-just-a-foot-soldier-a-researcher-on-someone-elses-project/

Stevens, S. (2001). Fieldwork as commitment. *Geographical Review, 91*(1/2), 66–73. https://doi.org/10.2307/3250806

Thapan, M. (Ed.). (1998). *Anthropological journeys: Reflections on fieldwork*. Orient Longman.
Vaidya, S. (2010). Researcher as insider: Opportunities and challenges. *Indian Anthropologist, 40*(2), 25–36.
Yeung, S.S.Y. (2012). Curriculum policy and priorities in an era of change. In S.S.Y. Yeung, J.T.S. Lam, A.W.L. Leung, & Y.C. Lo (Eds.), *Curriculum change and innovation* (pp. 59–91). Hong Kong University Press.
Zhang, J.J. (2017). Research ethics and ethical research: Some observations from the Global South. *Journal of Geography in Higher Education, 41*(1), 147–154.

10
INJUSTICE IN INCENTIVES?

Facilitating Equitable Research with People Living with Poverty

Tobin LeBlanc Haley and Laura Pin

Introduction

Providing incentives to research participants, once called research subjects, is a well-established practice in academia. In addition to fostering interest in participation, incentives, sometimes also called honoraria,[1] can serve as a thank you, and as a recognition of the time and knowledge participants contribute to research. After all, without research participants, much scholarship would be impossible. Yet, for academics in Canada who do research with people experiencing poverty, the provisioning of incentives is a complex and sometimes contested process due to guidelines in the current Tri-Council[2] Policy Statement (TCPS 2) (Tri-Council Policy Statement 2, 2018) and, especially, university practices related to the administration of research funds, which often involves requests for personal information of participants as part of an effort to abide by the rules set out by the Canada Revenue Agency (CRA). First released in 1998, what is now known as the TCPS 2 (2018) is an evolving document that sets out principles for ethical research projects involving humans in Canada. To be eligible for research funding from the Tri-Council and to maintain existing funding, institutions and associated researchers must demonstrate compliance with these principles.

The TCPS 2 states that incentives "should not be so large or attractive as to encourage reckless disregard of risks" and that "researchers and REBs should be sensitive to issues such as the economic circumstances of those in the pool of participants" (2018, p. 29). Every researcher who offers incentives must justify their use and amount to their research ethics board (REB). This implies that researchers doing work with participants experiencing poverty should provide lower incentives than those working with people who are economically secure. The purpose of this statement on incentives was established, presumably, to guard against the use of large incentives to compel people living with poverty to participate in

DOI: 10.4324/9781003199236-14

high-risk research, such as medical trials, thereby asking them to bear the burden of research unjustly. High levels of scrutiny of all parts of the project, including incentives, are used when a project is high risk and involves groups who experience vulnerabilities, and rightly so. Yet this section of the TCPS 2, while seeking to guard against coercion, also runs the risk of undermining community-engaged research that seeks to foreground lived experience. Scholars who work with marginalized communities, which are often overresearched, highlight the important role that incentives can play in facilitating the inclusion of people with lived experience (PWLE), lessening the burdens of participation (such as time away from work or other necessary activities), and disrupting, in a small way, the hierarchies between researchers and participants (Cheff, 2018; Thompson, 1996). There is an uncomfortable tension between guidelines around incentives in the TCPS 2 (2018) and the feedback from stakeholders from structurally marginalized communities and scholars working in these communities.

Administrative practices related to the provisioning of incentives at Canadian universities vary widely. We have worked with five REBs, all of whom work to ensure researchers follow the guidelines laid out in the TCPS 2 (2018). Each institution has had differing approaches to the administration of incentives, as it relates to the collection of personal information and the guidelines around the tax treatment of incentives. In this paper, we have chosen not to name the individual institutions that we have worked with/for. Some universities require that researchers provide the names, signatures, and sometimes even social insurance numbers of participants receiving incentives to guard against unfavourable financial audits, requirements that constitute a clear violation of confidentiality. As a result of these practices, there are pressures on researchers to provide low or no incentives and/or to hand over confidential information to the universities when incentives are used.

Incentives, as a result, have become a site of collision between institutionalized risk management processes geared towards research ethics, and those geared towards financial audits. The result is difficult for researchers who, as part of their practice, take seriously what community members and community-engaged researchers have said about the role of incentives in breaking down barriers to participation and challenging hierarchies. In this chapter, we reflect on these tensions as critical scholars who do community-engaged research with people experiencing socio-economic poverty in Ontario, Canada. We offer our own reflections on the impact of these dual pressures for researchers who must, without exception, work within the bounds of TCPS 2 (2018), as well as our recommendations for change. Critiques that the TCPS 2, and earlier iterations, ignore the realities of community-engaged research are well established (Guta et al., 2013). Yet the specific pressures to provide lower or no incentives to people experiencing poverty merit closer examination.

For research with people experiencing poverty to be respectful and ethical, both TCPS 2 and institutional guidelines concerning incentives must be attentive to the numerous forms of state surveillance experienced by people living with poverty (Maki, 2011; Monahan, 2017), existing conditions of economic deprivation, and the urgent need for the situated knowledges of poverty to be included in research (Feige & Choubak, 2019). These pressures are an issue of intersectional social justice, as poverty in Canada is disproportionately experienced by Black and Indigenous people, People of Colour, lone female parents, transgender* people, and people with disabilities (Block et al., 2019; Gazso & Waldron, 2009; Morris et al., 2018). We contend that there is an obligation on the part of the Tri-Council and universities to address some of these tensions as they work to foreground community-engaged research as a tool for equity, diversity, and inclusion in their strategic plans.

This chapter proceeds as follows. First, we position ourselves, briefly explain the scope of our work, and explain why incentives are an important part of our research practice. Second, we provide a brief history of the TCPS 2 (2018) and situate ourselves in the academic literature on research ethics in the social sciences and humanities. Next, we discuss the inconsistent application of the incentives and associated personal information collection guidelines put forward by Canadian universities and analyse the different institutional anxieties underpinning these policies. Then, we offer our own reflections within the context of our community-engaged work and end with recommendations for change.

A key theme in this chapter is facilitation, how incentives can *facilitate* the participation of people living with poverty in research processes. Surviving the conditions of poverty takes considerable time and skill, and participation in research should not detract from these efforts, which may place an undue burden on participants. Incentives help guard against such harms. As researchers who work with people who live with poverty, we are hopeful that academic institutions are not only recognizing the importance of their inclusion in research processes but are taking steps to change institutional practices to truly facilitate their equitable participation. The aim of this chapter is to provide insights and recommendations that will support and deepen expressed commitments to social justice in knowledge production.

Positioning Ourselves

We are two white-settler, cisgender women in heterosexual relationships. We are also both mothers. Laura is an Assistant Professor of Political Science at Wilfrid Laurier University and a first-generation university student from a working-class family. Tobin comes from a middle class family, is Mad[3]-identified and an Assistant Professor of Sociology at the University of New Brunswick. Since 2017, we have been doing research on housing, homelessness, and poverty in Ontario, Canada, and we strive to build research projects that are community-engaged and in service of social justice. In our work together, we attend to issues of homelessness and near homelessness on the rural–urban fringe (RUF), places where housing struggles are often invisible, manifesting in doubling-up, living in dilapidated housing, living in isolated motels, and tenting in wooded areas.

We came to this work quite accidentally, through a request from a non-profit organization Tobin had worked with in the past to support the implementation of an emergency funds program for people experiencing housing precarity in Southwestern Ontario (Haley et al., 2019). Through this work, we have built long-lasting relationships with people in the community, many of whom requested that more research be done on homelessness and precarious housing on the RUF. We have responded to this request.

Central to this research practice is ensuring that the knowledge, expertise, and time of participants are respected, and that the research process is not dehumanizing or exploitative. In addition to seeking community feedback on findings before disseminating knowledge and involving participants (in a paid capacity) in project governance, we provide all participants with an incentive. There is, even in the most community-minded, collaborative, and useful research projects, an extractive relationship in academic work. After all, as Assistant Professors, we are being paid to do this work and are building our portfolios through these engagements. There is an institutionalized power imbalance between us, as researchers, and community members experiencing homelessness and precarious housing. Despite the goal of creating meaningful relationships of mutual respect and putting out research that is useful and supported by the community, we are always the most privileged people in the room, with academic training and jobs at large post-secondary institutions. Moreover, these power imbalances are enforced through institutional rules around who can apply for and receive REB approval, hold Tri-Council and other grants, and carry out research with the support of the academic institution.

We have found that providing moderate incentives, ranging from $35–$100 per research session, depending on the burden of time and effort placed on participants, sends a clear message that the contributions and expertise of the participants are valuable. This practice also creates conditions under which participants experiencing poverty can take the time to participate in research and is in keeping with the guidelines put forward in the *Principles for Conducting Research in the Jane and Finch Community*, which urges researchers to "establish a sustainable way to compensate community members equitably for their contributions" (Jane and Finch Community Research Partnership, 2020, p. 14). Similar insights are provided by Thompson (1996), who argues that incentives for participants experiencing poverty create conditions under which they are able to take the time away from other necessary activities to participate in research, and in *Research 101: A Manifesto For Ethical Research in the Downtown Eastside*, which draws attention to the importance of paying peer-researchers because "hustling for survival takes time, and if you take our time and don't pay us we might need to hustle in ways that put us at more risk" (Boilevin et al., 2019, p. 18). Cheff's (2018) research on compensation practices among researchers in the Greater Toronto Area demonstrates that this provisioning of incentives is about much more than a token of thanks or enticing someone to engage in the project. It is about addressing the material barriers that often deny people living with poverty the opportunity to be included in research processes. This is a practice that is very much in keeping with the core principles of the TCPS 2, in particular the principle of justice which requires fair and equitable treatment of all people. Equity, according to the TCPS 2, requires that "benefits and burdens of research participation [be distributed] in such a way that no segment of the population is unduly burdened by the harms of research or denied the benefits of the knowledge generated from it" (emphasis added) (TCPS 2, 2018, p. 8).

History of the TCPS and a Literature Review

As a result of the direct relationship between Tri-Council funding and TCPS 2 (2018) compliance, universities require that all research activities involving humans be approved via their REBs. The REBs, required by the TCPS 2, review and approve research projects involving humans (Ells & Gutfreund, 2006; O'Neil, 2011). No researcher may proceed with data collection activities without ethics review. The role of TCPS 2 in Canada is not unique: institutionalized research ethics are now the international standard.[4]

There is a large body of international literature that examines the ever-changing rules and conventions involved in ethics review, their implications, and the personal experiences of researchers with ethics boards (See: Gorman, 2011; Haggerty, 2004; Hedgecoe, 2016; James, 2020; Jones, In Press; Monaghan et al., 2013). It is essential that we position ourselves within the broader conversation about research ethics as there is a tendency to downplay the need for mechanisms of accountability in social science and humanities research (see Guta et al., 2013; Hedgecoe, 2016)—a point on which we disagree, despite our concerns about the tensions related to incentives.

Central to the body of literature that takes up the issue of institutionalized ethics is the concept of "ethics creep." According to Haggerty (2004), ethics creep is both the expansion of the "regulatory structure" of the "ethics bureaucracy" and the simultaneous "intensification of regulation practices... that fall within its official ambit" (p. 394). For Haggerty, the development of the TCPS 2 and the associated ethics review is underpinned by an institutionalized distrust of researchers. Offering a more contextualized examination of changes to ethics in recent years, Guta et al. (2013) and James (2020) provide Foucauldian analyses of contemporary codified ethics in post-secondary institutions, highlighting the ways in which REBs are now sites of neoliberal governmentality. Pushing back against Haggarty's framing of ethics creep, Guta et al. (2013) examine how Canadian university REB staff are simultaneously experiencing an intensification of labour demands, cuts to resources, deskilling (characterized by a focus on checking off requirements rather than rich conversations with researchers) and a pervading sense of risk management as their primary role. James (2020) notes similar trends in the UK, exploring how ethics review has been reduced to rules and protocols and how neoliberal institutional preoccupations with risk management are being downloaded to individual researchers via the ever-present threat of audits and other disciplinary mechanisms.

The concept of risk management is central to understanding the tensions that we have encountered in our research. Our experiences in providing incentives, echo the concerns of Guta et al. (2013) and James (2020) and highlight the impact of audit culture on research design and relationships. When administering research funds in the form of incentives, we have experienced demands to mitigate, for the university, the risk of punitive sanctions by the CRA. The pressures to mitigate these risks for the institution are downloaded to researchers through REBs, where researchers often do the work of educating reviewers about guidelines around incentives that come from the community, and through university financial services departments. To guard against the possibility of a negative audit, financial services departments sometimes require researchers to collect personal information, such as names, addresses, and SINs, from participants in exchange for incentives. These disciplinary practices create barriers to reciprocal research relationships. These disciplinary practices disincentivize incentives.

This does not mean, however, that there need not be limits on researchers or tools to promote accountability. Academic research within and outside of Canada is replete with stories of epistemic, emotional, and physical violence against participants, steeped in and reproductive of the racialized operation of colonial capitalism (Boilevin et al., 2019, p. 3). Notable examples in Canada include the experimentation on Indigenous children in residential schools (Mosby, 2013) and in-patient psychiatric patients (Simmons, 1990). The TCPS 2 (2018) and its predecessors were a response to harmful, high-profile research practices in Canada (O'Neil, 2011). This history is well known and is rehearsed every year in research methods courses across the country as faculty impress upon emerging scholars the "perils and possibilities" of research (p. 180).

Such harms are not purely historical. Tuck and Yang (2014) have written about the problems associated with the contemporary academic industrial complex that encourages the collection of pain narratives and stories of humiliation from the overstudied "Other" for the purposes of commodification (p. 233). This damage-centred work, often positioned as decolonizing, and, we would add, community-engaged, is regularly approved by REBs. Taking seriously these critiques, we reject claims by scholars such as Dingwall (2008) that ethics review could be a form of censorship or undermining of academic freedom (Guta et al., 2013), while also recognizing that what exists provides insufficient protection against many harms, such as confidential but voyeuristic displays of the effects of structural vulnerabilities. We are excited by the development of ethical guidelines and review bodies located in the community, such as the DTES Manifesto, the Jane Finch Community Research Partnership and Mi'kmaw Ethics Watch.

Additionally, we want to ensure our critique of rules governing incentives do not perpetuate false equivalences between the expanding bureaucracy of institutionalized ethics and development of ethics guidelines by overresearched communities (see, for e.g., Haggerty, 2004). Collapsing such distinctions devalues the hard work of Indigenous nations and community organizations to hold researchers accountable for, and to guard against, the harms done via research, and undermines the ways these groups are supporting researchers in creating reciprocal, useful, and respectful projects.

Inconsistent Application of Incentives Rules

Incentives include anything offered to participants, monetary or otherwise, in exchange for participation in research.[5] In their overview of best practices in including PWLE in research, Feige and Choubak (2019) highlight the importance of incentives, stating "It is considered the 'gold standard' to financially compensate PWLE for their work in alignment with professional compensation for similar work" (p. 25). Providing incentives recognizes the value of participants' contributions as central to the research process. It addresses an imbalance where participants are the only parties not being compensated for their contributions to research. Equally important as providing incentives is the ability to maintain confidentiality, yet universities often require that researchers collect, and even hand over, the personal information of participants in exchange for incentives.

As part of the research for this paper, we sought out guidelines governing the payment of incentives to research participants at 24 accredited and publicly funded English-language or bilingual universities across Canada. These included three from British Columbia, ten from Ontario, two from each of the prairie provinces and Quebec, and one from each of the Atlantic provinces. Of these 24 institutions, 19 had the guidelines published on their websites, although many of the finer details around incentive provisioning required a log-in to access. This research helped improve our understanding of how universities addressed the tax treatment of incentives and what kinds of personal information collection we could expect to be required to undertake. What we found from the limited amount of information available is that there is no consistent approach across these universities. For example, the University of Regina allows cash payments for incentives and other honoraria lower than $75 with only a signature from the recipient being required as documentation. However, anything above $75 must be processed through the human resources department in order to generate a T4 (University of Regina, n.d., 2019). A T4 requires considerable personal information, including a SIN number. At the University of British Columbia, T4s are only issued for payments of more than $500 and, presumably, the associated personal information is not collected otherwise (University of British Columbia, n.d.). The threshold for collecting social insurance numbers and addresses to issue a T4 is $250 at Queen's University (Queen's University, n.d.). There is, quite simply, no consistency across universities.

The TCPS 2 (2018) does acknowledge the issues of confidentiality that arise in relation to the collection of personal information for the purpose of paying an incentive. Under "interpretations" it is recommended that researchers submit a coded list of incentive recipients to the university and keep the code key,

> e.g., a sealed envelope containing participant initials or signatures, and dates and amounts of incentive distribution [that] can be made available upon request to third-party auditors… this offers a degree of privacy protection for participants while providing an acceptable audit trail for the use of funds
> *(TCPS 2, para. 1, n.d.).*

While preferable to handing over the identities of participants to the university, the collection of such information can have an impact on research relationships with people living with poverty, such as income assistance recipients, who experience state surveillance over every dollar they earn and spend. More research on this subject is required.

Invested in better understanding what the CRA required universities to do in relation to the payment of incentives, we requested the support of the University of New Brunswick Faculty of Law's Tax Clinic, led by Dr. Vokhid Urinov. An improved understanding of the CRA pressures on universities equips us to better situate the position of financial services and, by extension the requirements of REBs, and to work with REBs and financial services to develop and implement research governance that facilitates the inclusion of economically marginalized participants. The tax law students provided legal research to support and enrich our analysis, not legal advice. Therefore, what follows is not legal advice.

According to the Tax Clinic's research, an incentive falls under the rules for "ex gratia" payments made for services in a volunteer capacity or in a capacity where fees for service are not typically required. The CRA requires the party paying an incentive to issue a T4A, which requires the disclosure of sensitive personal data, such as an address and SIN. Failure to do so can lead to tax audits and financial penalties administered by the CRA. However, in cases where the total payment to an individual by a single payer is less than CAD $500 per calendar year, the CRA has an administrative policy that does not require a T4A slip to be issued. The UNB Law Tax Clinic brief continues (para 5), "as the total payment to each individual is less than CAD $500, the University does not have to issue T4A slips and therefore is not required to ask for the participants' SIN for the purposes of tax reporting."[6] In the case of total honoraria from a single institution totaling less than $500, individual participants are obliged to report any research honoraria payments as income during their annual tax submission.

In the case of incentive payments from a single university totaling less than CAD $500 per calendar year, there is no legal requirement for university research or financial services to request the address or SIN number of research participants. In cases of incentives of $500 or more, to do so is required, and if an institution is found to be noncompliant with this requirement, there are significant consequences, including financial penalties imposed by the CRA. As we discuss further below, a desire among universities to shift the risk of possible non-compliance away from the institution has resulted in a conservative application of tax regulations, where researchers are sometimes required to disclose the SIN numbers and other personal information of research participants to university administrative services in relation to honoraria of as little as $76,[7] far below the $500 threshold. We suggest that this presents a risk to participant confidentiality that is unequally felt, with people experiencing poverty and Indigenous, Black, undocumented, and racialized participants more likely to experience the detrimental impacts of these policies.

The uneven topography of rules governing incentives and the collection of personal information is juxtaposed with an increasing demand among post-secondary institutions for research that is, or can be framed as, community-engaged (Hayne Beatty, 2018). These demands are echoed in governmental and non-governmental organizations outside of the post-secondary arena that highlight the importance of including lived experience in decision-making, knowledge production, and government. For example, the National Housing Strategy (NHS) states that "all programs in the National Housing Strategy will be based on best evidence and ongoing input from people with lived experience of housing need" (Government of Canada, 2017, p. 4).

There is also growing demand for community-engaged research that takes up issues facing groups that have been both historically excluded from spaces of higher education and subjected to harmful academic research practices. Key examples include Indigenous peoples, Black people and People of Colour, disabled people, and people living with severe socio-economic poverty. And while we, as researchers who seek to deepen the commitments of the academy to meaningful and useful social justice work, are (cautiously) encouraged by the recognition of the value of community-engaged work, we are concerned about the concomitant pressures on researchers to not only provide low incentives, but also to act as agents of neoliberal surveillance for both the university and the state.

Our Experiences

Our reflection below draws primarily on our work together with people experiencing homelessness and poverty in urban and rural settings in Ontario. Tobin works extensively on the continuities and changes of institutionalization in the lives of disabled and Mad people in Canada. Laura also studies participatory democratic processes in Canada and the United States, working with racialized, low-income, and sometimes undocumented residents. We suggest three ways institutional practices in relation to incentives limit our ability to facilitate inclusive, respectful, and reciprocal community-engaged research practices. First, institutional incentive reporting requirements fail to consider the unique and overlapping structural vulnerabilities of people experiencing poverty, disability, and/or Madness, people who are Indigenous, and people who are undocumented. Second, institutional incentive guidelines do not recognize the significance of research contributions from lived experience constituencies and encourage inadequate payments to participants with lived experience. Finally, the primacy accorded to the enforcement of tax law and CRA guidelines in practice often outweighs institutional obligations to safeguard participant confidentiality.

Institutional incentive reporting requirements fail to consider the unique and overlapping structural vulnerabilities of people experiencing poverty by requesting legal names, addresses, and SIN numbers in situations where universities are not legally required to issue T4 slips. By applying a conservative standard to T4 requirements, institutions avoid any potential violation of CRA regulations.

This position, however, does not consider the unique structural vulnerabilities of constituencies overrepresented among those experiencing poverty and homelessness. In the case of Indigenous people in Canada, for example, there is a long, ongoing history of intrusive data requests from state institutions (Gupta et al., 2020; Monaghan, 2013), as well as experiences of policing and state violence (Crosby & Monaghan, 2018; Evans, 2021; Reece, 2020; Scribe, 2018). The Ownership Control Access and Possession (OCAP®) principles, which have been embraced by the Tri-Council as a foundation for just research with Indigenous people and nations, emphasize the autonomy of Indigenous people and communities over their own information. Demanding SIN numbers and addresses for the payment of modest honoraria seems a violation of these principles, and leads to refusals to participate in, and thus exclusion from, research. Moreover, without adequate understanding of multi-generational families or naming conventions, the involvement of administrative offices in research administration can lead to suspicion when payments are submitted for multiple participants with similar names or addresses. Similarly, when working with disabled people, in particular those with histories of institutionalization, it is necessary to recognize the long, disturbing history of research, in the form of experimentation, being carried out on the bodies of confined disabled and Mad people without their consent and without compensation (Simmons, 1990). In this context, telling research participants that sensitive personal information will be shared with a research institution creates a strong disincentive to participate in research, and consequent exclusion of a group of people whose voices are often neglected in academic spaces.

The following example from Laura's experience working on a community-engaged research project with Indigenous and non-Indigenous women illustrates these dimensions. Participants in the project were to receive a $75 payment, but financial services refused to provide this payment without the SINs of each woman. Nowhere in the informed consent document did it indicate that a SIN number would be required to receive payment, and our community partner indicated the women were not comfortable providing this information to the university. After much advocacy we received an exemption from the SIN requirement for this project but were required to still ask participants to provide a SIN number and then document their decline to do so. In future research, Pin has continued to have to advocate for an exemption from SIN number requests on a case-by-case basis. This example illustrates that institutional incentive processes are not designed with unique and overlapping structural vulnerabilities in mind. The SIN requirement was not seen as significant enough by the REB to merit note on the consent forms, yet was a strong enough disincentive that our participants would likely have declined participation if they had been required to provide this information. The pageantry of asking for and documenting a decline to provide this information was patronizing and confusing.

Despite securing an exemption for one project with the assistance of faculty advocates, Laura has continued to have to navigate SIN requests for other research projects with people receiving social assistance. With respect to people who receive social assistance, the mandatory request to share SINs or address information may be difficult to comply with: participants may not have a fixed address if they are without permanent stable housing. Moreover, for social assistance recipients, making an error in reporting the T4 income to their case worker can result in severe penalties, including the loss of necessary income support. As researchers in Ontario, where the Auditor General recently recommended intensified scrutiny of some social assistance recipients (Auditor General of Ontario, 2019), it is difficult to see the institutional demands for personal information as anything other than an expression of a deeply punitive approach to poverty in the province (Chouinard & Crooks, 2005; Dolson, 2015; Maki, 2011). People without immigration and citizenship status in Canada may not have a SIN number and may be wary of any type of institutional reporting of personal information and potential connection with immigration enforcement. The request for an address and SIN number, in and of itself, is a significant disincentive to participate in research, as the individual benefits of research participation do not outweigh potential risks, including loss of income, housing, and/or deportation.

A second issue with the current guidelines concerning research incentives stems from the previously discussed TCPS 2 (2018) directive to consider the socio-economic status of recipients in setting incentives to avoid coercion. This leads to additional pressure for researchers to justify incentive rates for low-income constituencies that would not be questioned for more affluent research participants. This practice also leads to equating income with the value of the knowledge that participants impart: the contributions of low-income constituencies are less valuable, and are thus compensated at a lower rate, contravening advice in the literature to set incentives for PWLE on an equitable basis to those with professional experience (Feige & Choubak, 2019). At the same time, low-income constituencies experience greater benefit from a robust incentive system, which is essential to equitable research participation, particularly in cases where full compensation is needed for missed work, or missed time that would ordinarily be spent meeting livelihood needs. We understand offering a robust incentive as a matter of enabling participation, and as crucial to a model of community-engaged research that seeks to subvert the typical researcher-participant hierarchy through collaborative and equitable research relationships. Offering robust incentives shows that we value participants' expertise. For constituencies that regularly experience structural marginalization or are treated as a social problem to "solve," the incentive is often part of relationship-building and assuring participants that we value their perspectives.

While recognizing the critical importance of voluntary and informed consent in research participation, we suggest that there are better ways to mitigate concerns of possible research coercion than offering low-income participants lower incentives. In our practice, we provide the incentive payment at the beginning of our interaction before any research begins. We then remind people that they may leave right at that moment and keep the incentive payment, and this will not affect their relationship with the research team; we will still inform them of future research opportunities if they wish. We also remind participants that they may ask that any information they have provided be excluded from the study and keep their incentive. Although most participants choose to complete the research process, these practices have occasionally produced situations where people will come, sign the consent forms, receive their incentive, and promptly leave without participating, or leave after a few questions without providing much information. This has happened with surveys, focus groups, and interviews. From our perspective, this is not a negative outcome, but evidence that we are effectively communicating the voluntariness of participation, in keeping with broader TCPS 2 directives concerning consent. Practices like offering payment upfront, repeated reminders of the voluntary nature of participation—including explaining that this means participants may leave at any time, and responding with neutral affect when participants choose to leave—are important components that reduce coercion without undervaluing the contributions of low-income research participants through a depressed incentive rate.

Finally, a third challenge of the existing regulatory regime concerning incentives is the greater emphasis placed on compliance with CRA guidelines over the protection of research participant confidentiality. Section 5 of the TCPS 2 states that researchers have an ethical duty to safeguard participant confidentiality and institutions should support researchers in maintaining participant confidentiality. Collecting and sharing legal names, addresses, and SINs for the purpose of issuing T4 slips *when not required to do so by law* is a violation of participant confidentiality, and moreover one that can lead to significant negative consequences for research participants, as outlined above.

In Tobin's work with disabled people, many of whom experience poverty, she was required by the REB overseeing the process to include language on the consent form regarding how the $100 honoraria is "taxable income" and it was the responsibility of the recipient to report it to the CRA. She was concerned that the language of "obligation to report" would be read as patronizing and threatening by participants, many of whom lived with poverty and/or were social assistance recipients. Nonetheless, Tobin was told by the institutional REB that this language was necessary to include. In contrast to the concern for CRA reporting, there was no recommendation from the REB to include information on consent forms about how receipt of incentives might impact social assistance or other benefits. Tobin independently researched how a $100 incentive would intersect with social assistance so people could make a fully informed decision about participation. As this example illustrates, the institutional incentives process was not designed for people who are experiencing poverty and/or accessing social assistance. While including a line on consent forms about reporting an incentive as income seems like a less pernicious practice than requiring SINs, once again it treats the research process as a moment to enforce state tax policy. It also is not legally required, as there are several institutions that neither require T4 slips for incentives under a set threshold nor this phrasing on the consent form. Our concern about this framing is the disciplinary and condescending nature of the statement when working with disabled people, many of whom have experienced institutionalization, and who, as a group, routinely navigate income assistance programs.

Recommendations and Conclusion

In this chapter, we have reviewed our experiences with the administration of incentives in a variety of research settings. Neither TCPS 2 guidelines nor institutional processes adequately consider the complexities of incentive payments within the framework of community-engaged projects working with people experiencing structural vulnerabilities (Cattapan et al., 2020). In this context, suggestions like reducing incentive payments when working with low-income constituencies (TCPS 2) or sharing personal information and SINs with universities (institutional processes), harm research participants and the research process itself. We have demonstrated how incentives work to facilitate the participation of PWLE of poverty in research processes by valuing their contributions as expertise and breaking down material barriers that can result in their exclusion. This, we contend, can deepen our ethical commitments to equity in and through research.

We would suggest that we are also at a hopeful juncture for developing more adequate practices for incentive payments in the context of community-engaged research with structurally marginalized groups. Increasingly, the importance of working with PWLE is being recognized in a variety of social science disciplines (Hayne Beatty, 2018) and by other institutional actors, including governments and policy makers (e.g., NHS). We also have encountered actors *within* institutions sympathetic to the role of incentives in facilitating more equitable research practices, who have heard our concerns and those of others and who are working towards making change. These changes are essential if we, as researchers, seek to facilitate the inclusion of PWLE in equitable ways. A rich literature drawing directly from the experiences of peers, frontline workers, and allies is developing best practices in relation to the respectful engagement of PWLE in research. There is an opportunity to bring institutional practices into better alignment with practices that respect participant autonomy and privacy. Some of these steps are relatively simple: individual institutions can set thresholds for the requirement of personal information at or near the $500 guideline set by the CRA. Rather than recommend that socioeconomic circumstances be considered in setting incentive payments, we suggest that TCPS 2 guidelines could advise on alternate steps that could be taken to mitigate concerns about possible coercion *in cases where the incentive could be perceived as coercive*. These might include steps similar to the ones we outline above, such as paying the incentive before research occurs and clearly communicating that participants may leave at any time.

Notes

1 Our review of a selection of publicly available guidelines around the administration of research incentives to participants shows slippage around the use of incentives and

honoraria. "Incentives" is always used to mean the small tokens (cash or gifts) given to research participants while "honoraria" is sometimes used as a synonym for incentives and sometimes used to mean token payments to people providing "voluntary" services to the university, such as guest speakers or Indigenous Elders. For the purpose of clarity, we use the term "incentives" throughout this paper.
2 In Canada, the Interagency Advisory Panel on Research Ethics establishes ethical standards for research involving humans. All university research in Canada is required to abide by these standards, with the Tri-Council Policy Statement: Ethical Conduct for Research Involving Humans (TCPS 2, 2018) being the most recent set of guidelines issued by the panel.
3 "Mad" is an umbrella term for a diverse group of people with experiences of psycho-medical pathologization and/or associated oppressions who are engaged in political struggles against saneism. For further reading, see Menzies, LeFrancois and Reaume (2013).
4 For example, the National Statement on Ethical Conduct in Human Research (Australia), the Research Governance Framework for Health and Social Care, 2nd edition (UK) and Title 45 Code of Federal Regulations, Part 46 (US) all apply broadly to researchers working with human subjects in the health and social sciences. For an overview, see Bracken-Roach et al., 2017.
5 TCPS 2 states that reimbursement of costs incurred for participation (for example, transportation to a research site) or compensation for injury incurred during the course of research is considered separately from incentives. See TCPS2 Article 3.1 for more details.
6 This administrative policy is stated in RC4157: Deducting Income Tax on Pension and Other Income, and Filing the T4A Slip, at p.2; Annotated Income Tax Regulations, C.R.C. 1977, c. 945, subsection 200 (2)—Remuneration and Benefits [T4A]. Available at https://www.canada.ca/en/revenue-agency/services/forms-publications/publications/rc4157.html
7 In our experiences, we have been required to provide this kind of information for as little as $50 but those guidelines are not publicly available. The amount of $76 reflects the University of Regina regulations.

References

Auditor General of Ontario. (2019). *Reports on value for money audits* [PDF file]. Office of the Auditor General. https://www.auditor.on.ca/en/content/annualreports/arreports/en19/v1_309en19.pdf

Block, S., Galabuzi, G.E., & Tranjan, R. (2019). *Canada's colour coded income inequality*. Canadian Centre for Policy Alternatives. https://www.researchgate.net/profile/RicardoTranjan/publication/337899061_Canada%27s_Colour_Coded_Income_Inequality/links/5df11c05a6fdcc28371a20a0/CanadasColour-Coded-Income-Inequality.pdf

Boilevin, L., Chapman, J., Deane, L., Doerksen, C., Fresz, G., Joe, D.J., Leech-Crier, N., Marsh, S., McLeod, J., Neufeld, S., Pham, S., Shaver, L., Smith, P., Steward, M., Wilson, D., & Winter, P. (2019). *Research 101: A manifesto for ethical research in the Downtown Eastside*. http://www.sfu.ca/content/dam/sfu/sfuwoodwards/PDF/CommunityEngagement/Research101_Manifesto.pdf

Bracken-Roche, D., Bell, E., Macdonald, M.E., & Racine, E. (2017). The concept of 'vulnerability' in research ethics: An in-depth analysis of policies and guidelines. *Health Research Policy and Systems*, 15(1), 1–18.

Cattapan, A., Dobrowolsky, A., Findlay, T., & Mandrona, A. (2020). Power, privilege, and policy making: Reflections on 'Changing public engagement from the ground up'. In L. Levac & S.M. Weibe (Eds.), *Creating spaces of engagement: Policy justice and the practical craft of deliberative democracy* (pp. 226–252). University of Toronto Press.

Cheff, R. (2018). *Compensating research participants: A survey of current practices in Toronto*. Wellesley Institute. https://www.wellesleyinstitute.com/wpcontent/uploads/2018/07/Fair-compensation-Report-.pdf

Chouinard, V., & Crooks, V. (2005). "Because they have all the power and I have none": State restructuring of income and employment supports and disabled women's lives in Ontario, Canada. *Disability & Society, 20*(1), 19–32. https://doi-org.ezproxy.lib.ryerson.ca/10.1080/0968759042000283610

Crosby, A., & Monaghan, J. (2018). *Policing indigenous movements: Dissent and the security state*. Fernwood Publishing.

Dingwall, R. (2008). The ethical case against ethical regulation in humanities and social science research. *Twenty-First Century Society, 3*(1), 1–12. https://doi.org/10.1080/17450140701749189

Dolson, M.S. (2015). Trauma, workfare and the social contingency of precarity and its sufferings: The story of Marius, a street-youth. *Culture, Medicine and Psychiatry, 39*(1), 134–161. https://doi.org/10.1007/s11013-014-9409-4

Ells, C., & Gutfreund, S. (2006). Myths about qualitative research and the tri-council policy statement. *Canadian Journal of Sociology, 31*(3), 361–373. https://doi.org/10.1353/cjs.2006.0053

Evans, J. (2021). Penal nationalism in the settler colony: On the construction and maintenance of 'national whiteness' in settler Canada. *Punishment & Society, 23*(4), 515–535. https://doi.org/10.1177/14624745211023455

Feige, S., & Choubak, M. (2019). *Best practices for engaging people with lived experience*. Guelph, Canada: Community Engaged Scholarship Institute.

Gazso, A., & Waldron, A. (2009). Fleshing out the racial undertones of poverty for Canadian women and their families: Re-envisioning a critical integrative approach. *Atlantis: A Women's Studies Journal, 34*(1), 132–141.

Gorman, S.M. (2011). Ethics creep or governance creep?: Challenges for Australian human research ethics committees (HRECS). *Monash Bioethics Review, 29*(4), 23–38. https://doi.org/10.1007/BF03351328

Government of Canada. (2017). *National housing strategy*. https://www.placetocallhome.ca/what-is-the-strategy

Gupta, N., Blair, S., & Nicholas, R. (2020). What we see, what we don't see: Data governance, archaeological spatial databases and the rights of indigenous peoples in an age of big data. *Journal of Field Archaeology, 45*(sup1), S39–S50.

Guta, A., Nixon, S.A., & Wilson, M.G. (2013). Resisting the seduction of "ethics creep": Using Foucault to surface complexity and contradiction in research ethics review. *Social Science & Medicine, 98*, 301–310. https://doi.org/10.1016/j.socscimed.2012.09.019

Haggerty, K.D. (2004). Ethics creep: Governing social science research in the name of ethics. *Qualitative Sociology, 27*(4), 391–414. https://doi.org/10.1023/B:QUAS.0000049239.15922.a3

Haley, T.L., Pin, L., Mussell, J., & Froese, R. (2019). *A picture of poverty in dufferin county, ON: A final report for poverty reduction grants*. Report prepared for the Ontario Trillium Foundation.

Hayne Beatty, S. (2018). *Institutionalizing community engaged scholarship at a research university: The organizational improvement plan at Western University*. https://ir.lib.uwo.ca/oip/46

Hedgecoe, A. (2016). Reputational risk, academic freedom and research ethics review. *Sociology (Oxford)*, *50*(3), 486–501. https://doi.org/10.1177/0038038515590756

James, F. (2020). 'Ethics review, neoliberal governmentality and the activation of moral subjects', *Educational Philosophy and Theory*, *53*(5), 548–558. https://doi.org/10.1080/00131857.2020.1761327

Jane Finch Community Research Partnership. (2020). *Principles for conducting research in the Jane and Finch community*. https://janefinchresearch.ca/research-principles

Jones, C. (in press). 'Wounds of regret': Critical reflections on competence and 'professional intuition' in research with intellectually disabled people. *Disability Studies Quarterly*.

Maki, K. (2011). Neoliberal deviants and surveillance: Welfare recipients under the watchful eye of Ontario Works. *Surveillance & Society*, *9*(1/2), 47–63. https://doi.org/10.24908/ss.v9i1/2.4098

Menzies, R., LeFrancois, B., & Reaume, G. (Eds.). (2013). *Mad matters: A critical reader in Canadian Mad Studies*. Canadian Scholars Press.

Monaghan, J. (2013). Settler governmentality and racializing surveillance in Canada's north-west. *Canadian Journal of Sociology*, *38*(4), 487–508.

Monaghan, L.F., O'Dwyer, M., & Gabe, J. (2013). Seeking university research ethics committee approval: The emotional vicissitudes of a 'rationalised' process. *International Journal of Social Research Methodology*, *16*(1), 65–80. https://doi.org/10.1080/13645579.2011.649902

Monahan, T. (2017). Regulating belonging: Surveillance, inequality, and the cultural production of abjection. *Journal of Cultural Economy*, *10*(2), 191–206. https://doi.org/10.1080/17530350.2016.1273843

Morris, K., Mason, W., Bywaters, P., Featherstone, B., Daniel, B., Brady, G., Bunting, L., Hooper, J., Mirza, N., Scourfield, J., & Webb, C. (2018). Social work, poverty, and child welfare interventions. *Child & Family Social Work*, *23*(3), 364–372.

Mosby, I. (2013). Administering colonial science: Nutrition research and human biomedical experimentation in aboriginal communities and residential schools, 1942–1952. *Histoire Sociale*, *46*(91), 145–172. https://doi.org/10.1353/his.2013.0015

O'Neill, P. (2011). The evolution of research ethics in Canada: Current developments. *Canadian Psychology/Psychologie Canadienne*, *52*(3), 180–184. http://dx.doi.org.ezproxy.lib.ryerson.ca/10.1037/a0024391

Queen's University. (n.d.). *Procedure for payments to research study participants*. https://www.queensu.ca/financialservices/sites/webpublish.queensu.ca.finwww/files/files/Procedure%20for%20Payments%20to%20Research%20Study%20Participants%20-%20July%2027%2C%202020%20v_4(1).pdf

Reece, R. (2020). *Carceral Redlining: White supremacy is a weapon of mass incarceration for indigenous and black peoples in Canada* (Policy Brief, Issue 68). Yellowhead Institute. https://yellowheadinstitute.org/wp-content/uploads/2020/06/carceral-redlining-r-reece-yellowhead-institute-brief.pdf

Scribe, M. (2018). Pedagogy of Indifference: State Responses to Violence Against Indigenous Girls., external link, opens in new window. *Canadian Woman Studies*, *32*(1–2), 47–57.

Simmons, H.G. (1990). *Unbalanced: Mental health policy in Ontario, 1930–1989*. Wall & Thomson.

Thompson, S. (1996). Paying respondents and informants. *Social Research Update*, 15 (Autumn). https://sru.soc.surrey.ac.uk/SRU14.html

Tri-Council Policy Statement, 2. (2018). *Ethical conduct for research involving humans*. https://ethics.gc.ca/eng/documents/tcps2-2018-en-interactive-final.pdf

Tri-Council Policy Statement, 2. (n.d.). *Interpretations*. https://ethics.gc.ca/eng/policy-politique_interpretations_privacy-privee.html

Tuck, E., & Yang, K.W. (2014). R-words: Refusing research. In D. Paris & M.T. Winn (Eds.), *Humanizing research: Decolonizing qualitative inquiry with youth and communities* (pp. 223–247). Sage Publications.

University of Regina. (n.d.) *Guide to honorariums*. https://www.uregina.ca/policy/assets/docs/pdf/honorariums.pdf

University of Regina. (2019). *Petty cash*. https://www.uregina.ca/policy/browse-policy/policy-OPS-010-040.html

University of British Columbia. (n.d.). *Guidelines*. https://finance.research.ubc.ca/policies-guidelines/guidelines

11
QUEERING PRIDE FACILITATION
An Autoethnography of Community Organizing

Amelia Thorpe

Introduction

"This is why we can't have nice things."[1] I've heard this a lot working in advocacy spaces. Recently, I was in an online meeting discussing virtual events for Pride NB, 2020, advocating for a greater diversity of content, participants, and performers. I wrote, "this is why we can't have nice GAY things" in the margins of my scrawled meeting minutes, referencing the disconnect I had been experiencing within local queer organizing spaces. My partner and I had been serving as co-chairs of Fierté Fredericton Pride (FFP) and recently entered a province-wide partnership with other Pride organizations in the wake of COVID-19 festival cancellations. In a conversation after the meeting, I struggled to articulate the discordant ideological and organizational priorities from my own ideals, ideals concerning sexually diverse identities that led to the above refrain.

I have been co-organizing Pride on Wolastoqiyik Territory in Fredericton, New Brunswick.[2] New Brunswick is small, socially and politically conservative, overwhelmingly white, and predominantly working-class province in eastern Canada with the distinction of being the poorest in the country (Burrill, 2019; Jones, 2019). With a population of just over 750,000 people, the province is half rural and half urban, with three major cities: Moncton, Saint John, and the capital city of Fredericton. This geographic context frames my autoethnographic reflection on my experiences in two community Pride organizations during the spring and summer of 2020 as both queer activist and FFP board co-chair, with attention to my privilege as a white, lower-middle class, queer, cis woman, and my position(s) of power.[3]

I use the phrase, "this is why we can't have nice things," to analyze my experiences of queer tensions and possibilities attempting to engage in queer, anti-racist facilitation within organizations that privileged homonormativity—manifestations

DOI: 10.4324/9781003199236-15

of queerness that align with dominant norms and as such, present less of a threat to hegemonic heterosexuality and hegemonic whiteness (Duggan, 2002; McCaskell, 2016; Warner, 1999)—and devalued queerness. Pride has grown out of a history of persecution, resistance, and solidarity. Despite its radical roots and potential as a site for social change, it is rife with tensions between homonormative ideals of progress and the possibility of political, intersectional queer futures. In line with Muñoz's (2009) conception of radical queer futurity, which invites us to be "attentive to the past for the purposes of critiquing a present," and to consider the possibilities of intentional, relational queerness and disruption, to work towards utopic futures of change, I argue that Pride is not queer (p. 18). Through my experiences of facilitation within queer community organizations, I consider how we might work to queer Pride in New Brunswick, through ongoing disruption, reconstruction, and reimagining in pursuit of radical, intersectional, inclusive, and anti-racist queer futures.

In this chapter, I discuss the notion of queering facilitation within Pride organizations by focusing on three concepts: inclusion, ownership, and progress. Guided by these interwoven concepts, I reflect on my experiences within Pride NB, using autoethnography as a form of writing that interrogates experience in conversation with dominant discourses of power and considers personal and political positioning (Jones & Adams, 2016). My approach to autoethnography is informed by queer theory, engaged as a critical approach to critiquing and reimagining our realities towards social and political change (Butler, 1993; Eng et al., 2005; Muñoz, 2009) and assemblage theory, mobilized as a tool to encourage expansive understandings of intersectional identities (Puar, 2012).

To develop context, I consider the concept of inclusion, or "we," as enacted in Pride organizations, emphasizing how oppressive boundaries are created through Pride organizing and programming. Further, I examine how the contested notion of "we" is informed through discourses of compulsory homonormativity, constructing racialized, disabled, poor, and gender and sexually diverse individuals as deviant, contributing to their marginalization from Pride spaces. Second, prompted by the assumption of possession ("we can't have"), I explore ownership, referencing my experience of community facilitation within Pride NB and probing the increasing corporate influence in Pride organizations. Third, I refer to the altered quote from my meeting notes: "this is why we can't have nice GAY things." to interrogate the concept of progress, in line with the homonormative and homonationalist (Puar, 2007) constructions of Pride. I demonstrate this by relating the tensions over the use of the progress flag for the Pride NB festival to the incongruence of homonormative conceptions of gay progress and critically anti-racist, and politically motivated queer futures.[4]

Theory and Method

As a reflexive and experiential form of self-writing, I engage in autoethnography to place my experiences in critical conversation with relevant social, political, and cultural contexts and influences (Jones & Adams, 2016). Autoethnography as a method unearths possibilities of meaning in a writer's experience (Bochner, 2000). The autoethnographic process of *recalling* is central to this chapter, as I analyse and reflect on my experiences of facilitation (Chang, 2016). I present myself, deeply entrenched in Pride organizing, as "a subject to look into and a lens to look through to gain an understanding of a societal culture" and to explore how dominant discourses of power have shaped these organizations and my experiences therein (Chang, 2008, p. 49). I engage autoethnography with attention to my positions of power and an awareness of how my experiences are both consciously and unconsciously shaped by this positionality. I seek to identify and disrupt the discourses of power that flow through me and limit my analysis.

I draw on queer theory as a mode of critical analysis that seeks to disrupt, destabilize, and deconstruct hegemonic discourses, norms, structures, and power relations that harm, oppress, or other any individual or group on the basis of prescribed alterity.[5] In this work, I draw inspiration from the works of Muñoz (2009) and Puar (2007) to take up queering, mobilizing queer theory as a method in my analysis to both critique the past and imagine future possibilities. Queerness rejects the insufficiency of the present and insists on the potentiality of socio-political change, motivating action towards queer utopian futures (Muñoz, 2009). In my particular context, Pride is not queer. To be queer is to be unfinished, to move critically between, within, and beyond, without isolating a singular or linear trajectory, in the direction of ever-expanding socio-political change (Ahmed, 2006; Butler, 1993). Queering Pride requires intentional and ongoing disruption of oppressive and exclusionary discourses and a commitment to queer, anti-racist, intersectional futures. I build on Crenshaw's (1991) concept of intersectionality and engage with assemblage theory, an analytic tool that acknowledges that the subjectivity is constituted by a fluidity of imbricated, intersecting identities which are neither fixed nor static (Puar, 2012). This theoretical framework informs my queer lens and my analysis of Pride as an organization that has long privileged aspects of identity, contributing to the erasure of other, intersecting identities (Greensmith & Giwa, 2013; Hinkson, 2021; Labelle, 2020; Lenon & Dryden, 2015; Ward, 2008).

Context

Fredericton is located on unceded and unsurrendered Wolastoq territory and has just under 60,000 inhabitants. Fredericton differs from other urban centres in New Brunswick as it is regarded as both a centre of government and a university town (Hempstead, 2017). Many employment prospects require advanced degrees or bilingualism, which shapes the socio-economic composition of the city, while a high transient student population further influences the local social, political, and economic context (Burrill, 2019).

Demographically, Fredericton is predominantly white, with an Indigenous population of roughly 4% and 10% racialized individuals (Statistics Canada, 2017).

Anecdotally, I've heard refrains that Fredericton boasts the highest 2SLGBTQ+ population per capita in the country, a statistic I have never been able to corroborate. I would argue that this longstanding myth of Fredericton as a queer city is perhaps connected to the student population enrolled in the colleges and universities, often lauded for bringing increased youth and ethnic diversity to the city.

Fredericton has a fraught history when it comes to 2SLGBTQ+ advocacy (Thorpe, 2021; Warner, 2002). Pride in Fredericton has long been predominantly white, middle class, cisgender, and Anglophone, demographics that mirror the capital city. When I became co-chair of FFP, I was unprepared for the intensity of this position and the challenges of facilitation within a community whose trust had been lost years prior. Fredericton's first Pride parade happened in 2010, 15 years following a debacle which saw the Mayor of Fredericton's refusal to read the Pride proclamation (Warner, 2002). I hoped to get involved with Pride upon moving to Fredericton in 2014 but found the organization to be insular and indifferent, focused predominantly on producing an annual festival. It took years to work my way into the organization and when I later became involved in 2018, I was struck by the board's resistance to change. In late 2018, the president, vice-president, and secretary retired collectively, instigated by heated meetings, and clashing politics and priorities.

2019 marked a season of change for Pride in Fredericton. Two local activists—Rebecca Salazar Leon and Indigo Poirer—formed BIPOC Pride, an organization committed to running Pride events by and for queer and trans* people of colour, in response to the longstanding exclusionary politics of Pride. I was elected co-chair of FFP in 2019, and our new team of volunteers began working to reimagine FFP with a radically inclusive and anti-racist agenda and build a collaborative relationship with BIPOC Pride. I was re-elected for the 2020 Pride season, when my partner joined me as co-chair. We wanted to distance ourselves from the previous board: rebranding, restructuring the board, engaging the community, developing policy, working to mend many a burned bridge, and developing new relationships with local organizations.[6] We collectively acknowledged that we were a predominantly white and privileged group of individuals working to reinvent an organization that has lost the trust of many in our community, particularly racialized queer and trans* individuals, knowledge that continues to inform all aspects of the organization's work.[7]

In our first year, racialized community members were wary of our motivations following years of programming that produced exclusionary spaces occupied by predominantly white, cis, able-bodied, middle class queers. Our 2019 board still did not represent the community we purported to serve, and as such, we were complicit in perpetuating the oppressive discourses of our predecessors. We worked to rebuild the organization through engaging in queer, anti-racist, community-focused facilitation and dismantling the hegemonic whiteness at work within this organization. We built a strong relationship with BIPOC Pride and began to gain the trust of long excluded community members. Our current board's makeup, which includes an array of ages, sexual orientations, gender identities, and socio-economic positions, races, ethnicities, and abilities, reflects our commitment to changing the narrative, politics, and priorities of FFP, as numerous community members previously excluded by the culture of the organization have chosen to get involved with the "new" board and participate in the ongoing queering of the organization.

Inclusion

Returning to the phrase that inspired this chapter, "this is why we can't have nice things," I seek first to interrogate the "we" in an effort to explore the human aspect of Pride organizations and queer the concept of inclusion within Pride NB—an organization that formed as a collaboration between FFP, Moncton's River of Pride, and Saint John Pride in Spring 2020 to create virtual events amidst the COVID-19 pandemic. It is necessary to further situate this work not solely within the unique context of a global pandemic but also during heightened calls for recognition of anti-Black racism within mainstream public discourse following the murder of George Floyd by police in Minneapolis (Self & Hall, 2021). Pride NB was the first province-wide Pride collaboration, and the organizing board was comprised of executive members of each committee. Aside from myself, my co-chair, and our third representative, the board consisted of white, gay, and cisgender men.[8] Both the transition to a virtual festival and the new aspect of collaboration presented new facilitation challenges, as our mandates, foci, and ideologies varied greatly. The debates changed and we found ourselves deflecting jokes we wouldn't dare to repeat, educating on respectful language, and calling out problematic statements during discussions of inclusion and representation. Our goals and values were regularly at odds and our diverging political and social locations created tension. Clashes on the patchwork board, quickly devolved into a toxic and verbally abusive environment, eventually culminated in the departure of one of the three participating organizations along with the abandonment of their responsibilities mere weeks before the festival began.

"This is why we can't have nice gay things," a comment spoken during a Pride NB board meeting, is symptomatic of a mindset I've encountered in advocacy spaces. I witnessed the pervasive and damaging us versus them dichotomy that privileges and prioritizes specific identities, politics, and ways of being. While the speaker sought to refer to our Prides collectively, and by extension, our local communities, I contend that they were inadvertently articulating a distinction between differing orientations to advocacy and conceptions of community, differences that speak to privilege. The individual, and by extension the organization, expressed a division that adhered to and reproduced a homonormative ideal of community that advances assimilationist desires, and demands compulsory whiteness and compulsory ability (Duggan, 2002; Warner, 1999). This narrow vision of gender and sexually diverse communities embodied in his use of "we" extended inclusion in Pride solely to select (white) identities and ways of being, thus reifying the construction of racialized, gender diverse, disabled, and poor queers as the deviant other. The homonormative work of establishing boundaries that delimit access to those considered deviant is well documented in Canadian Pride organizing through pervasive racism (Bain, 2017; Cole, 2020), colonialism (Greensmith & Giwa, 2013), and ableism (Peers & Eales, 2012; Piepzna-Samarasinha, 2018) among other axes of oppression. At the time I tried to articulate the exclusionary rhetoric inherent in the statement, but felt I wasn't being heard.

In Pride NB, we were tasked with facilitating fraught discussions of inclusion and representation within the board. While FFP members sought to focus on events that promoted advocacy, community-building, and knowledge-sharing, the lack of enthusiasm from most of our combined board was palpable. Our partner Prides desired a focus on elaborate, entertainment-orientated events, which was at odds with our vision of more diverse offerings designed to engage, empower, and spark discussions of social and political change. We argued that their desire to produce a smaller number of expensive, high-quality events, designed to garner increased attention, would not necessarily generate increased impact. Instead of impressing our communities with what some on this small board deemed "the best," paying for entertainers with bigger names, and pushing programming to satiate those who were missing clubs and drag shows during lockdown, we considered costs such as ASL interpretation and engaging a greater diversity of speakers and performers to be a greater priority in line with our values and mandate, notwithstanding the context of increased social isolation and renewed calls to confront the insidious social and structural anti-Black racism that persists within all institutions, including Pride.

Pride NB displayed hesitancy in engaging political topics and speakers for fear of what they might say and how this may reflect on the organization, which hampered our planning. Nonetheless, we forged ahead with as much programming as our organization could manage alone and extended a funded invitation to BIPOC Pride to produce events for racialized gender and sexually diverse individuals, which included a closed healing circle and a virtual coffee house. Further, we were heavily involved in the production of most events to ensure they were as inclusive as possible. Under the moniker of Pride NB, FFP produced several community-focused roundtables and teach-ins featuring an array of speakers, as well as an art show with an opening performance from a local non-binary, Two-Spirit electronic musician whose work engages with topics of identity, queerness, and decolonization (see Figure 11.1).

Despite our foci never truly aligning, FFP managed to both produce and co-produce events for Pride NB that reflected our prioritization of increased diversity and community engagement. These included our Strength and Support and Queer Experiences roundtables, a keynote address on Two-Spirit identities and histories, a screening of the "Pay It No Mind" documentary on the life and legacy of Marsha P. Johnson, and a performance by non-binary, Two-Spirit musician M3D14, among other events. The exclusionary conception of "we" put forth in a meeting of Pride NB and reflected in planning process epitomizes the rise

FIGURE 11.1 Pride NB programming posters.

of homonormativity within many Pride organizations across Canada, perpetuating oppressive discourses that restrict inclusion and representation to select queer subjects (Bain, 2017; Da Costa, 2020; Greensmith & Giwa, 2013; Labelle, 2020; Trevenen & DeGagne, 2015). This internal discord was further complicated by the involvement of an in-kind sponsor, retained by one of the partner Prides before the pandemic began. In what follows, I will problematize this external influence in connection with queering the concept of ownership.

Ownership

To complement this discussion of inclusion and exclusion, it is vital to question who holds the power to control and delimit access. I consider the implication of ownership inherent in "this is why we can't have nice things." Our hastily formed Pride NB board reflects the dominance of white organizers, specifically the queer patriarchy (Nast, 2002) of white gay men, the discourses of power that shape these organizations, and their resultant perpetuation of compulsory whiteness, ability, and homonormativity. In the early days of organizing the collaborative festival, FFP advocated to that we reach out to engage and consult smaller organizations in more rural areas across the province to explore ways we could increase accessibility, participation, and collaboration, a proposal met with hesitance and a counter suggestion that perhaps we could request a financial contribution in exchange for a seat at the table.[9] I interpreted both this exclusory idea and the aversion to more diverse and varied programming to reflect both a fear of losing power and control and a sense of possession of this new organization, as evidenced by the attempt to dictate whose voices were present in the planning and programming, thus creating parameters of who belongs.

In facilitating community involvement related to Pride NB programming, we encountered this sense of ownership of Pride from the white, gay patriarchy in numerous instances. Following the promotion of one virtual event, intended to intentionally decentre narratives of whiteness, we were contacted by a white, cis, gay man advocating combatively that unless we secured the participation of a speaker aligned with a specified positioning (a Black trans* woman), the panel should be cancelled.[10] I questioned the impetus for this assertion, which I read as invalidating to the racialized participants involved that did not necessarily fall within these specifications. As predominantly white organizers, we did not consider it our place to impose a hierarchy among racialized gender and sexually diverse speakers to decide whose voice was privileged above others, nor demand this affective labour from individuals who were not comfortable sharing their experiences. While we acknowledged our event was not fully representative, we considered the choice between privileging one voice deemed valid by a white gay man (implying a hierarchy of oppression) or taking space from Two-Spirit, queer, and trans★ speakers of colour to restrict valuable opportunities for knowledge-sharing and disrupting the social and structural privileging of whiteness within Pride, which raised further questions of how diversity is taken up within predominantly white organizations (Collins, 1990).[11] We went forward with the event, which resulted in a generative discussion of white privilege within purportedly queer spaces, welcoming the discomfort and disruption that our commitment to queer, anti-racist facilitation would cause.

These questions of ownership cannot be analyzed solely through the power dynamics of individuals within the organization; it is necessary to consider external factors which may exert power over both individuals and institutions, including the influence of neoliberal politics and corporatization. When we agreed to collaborate on a digital festival, we were made aware that involvement of one partner Pride's previously retained in-kind sponsor was non-negotiable.[12] We were berated for questioning the sponsor's control over the festival's appearance and publicity and warned against engaging in criticism or programming that might negatively reflect on the sponsor. This experience reflects the increasing corporate influence in white-dominated Pride organizations that wield their self-appointed ownership and positions of power to delimit access and uphold oppressive discourses, both in New Brunswick and beyond, facilitating a homonormative and homonationalist shift in queer politics towards depoliticization and respectability (Warner, 1999). Pride festivals in particular have facilitated this growing imbrication by trading corporate visibility and community access for monetary support and sponsorship, as evidenced by the displacement of the longstanding Blockorama stage at Pride Toronto in 2007 to facilitate a stage sponsored by TD Bank which proceeded to appropriate Black culture (Bain, 2017), the renaming of Edmonton's Pride Parade in 2009 to "TD Canada Trust Pride Parade and Celebration in the Square" (Spade, 2011); and the (overturned) ban enacted by Pride Toronto against Queers Against Israeli Apartheid in 2010 to appease local government and corporate sponsors (Awwad, 2015; Hatoum & Moussa, 2018).

The increasingly mainstream, heavily sponsored festivals mark a move away from the early political roots of rebellion against police violence led by queer and trans★ people of colour (Da Costa, 2020; Ferguson, 2019). This shift is reflected in Bain's (2017) work on systemic anti-Black racism within Pride Toronto, in which she cites the gradual evolution of Pride as "a big party" coincided with the increasing erasure of racialized queer and trans★ bodies (p. 82). The waning political focus and increased commodification of Pride as a spectacle for consumption is intimately tied to the rise of homonormativity. Returning to the implied possession in "this is why we can't have nice GAY things," I contend that white gay men's privilege in Pride organizing is tied to this sense of ownership, which (re)constructs Pride as a depoliticized space both by and for "respectable" gayness, prioritizing assimilationist desires and homonormative ideas of progress that contribute to the ongoing exclusion of queer and trans* others and reinforce discourses of racism and oppression.

Queering Progress

The third concept I explore as I reflect on engaging in queer, anti-racist facilitation within Pride in New Brunswick, progress, is deeply entwined with concepts of inclusion and ownership. This brief concluding observation connects a respectable, assimilationist, and homonormative understanding of progress to the narrow vision of inclusion perpetuated by the Pride organizers, who have wielded their sense of ownership to delimit access and invalidate bodies and identities that do not conform to compulsory homonormativity and hegemonic whiteness. In what follows, I draw on a final experience of facilitation and organization as a board member of Pride NB.

One of the first debates we encountered in Pride NB concerned the use of a new iteration of the rainbow flag, widely known as the progress flag. One of the partner Prides was less than keen, stating that the flag would confuse people, and that while the other two cities could fly whatever flag they chose, their organization did not want to be forced to. Reticent to consider the change, they argued that it wasn't necessary for their city to fly the more inclusive flag, citing that there were few people it would benefit. I contend that this hesitance, allegedly connected to the flag's increased recognition following decades of queer organizing, mirrors the normative goals of acceptance that have accompanied the increasing depoliticization of Pride, goals that hinge on the reproduction of oppressive and exclusionary discourses that seek to render racialized communities invisible by delimiting both participation and representation, goals that are inextricable from hegemonic whiteness and white supremacy. I recognized familiar refrains, concern rooted in homonormativity and the desire to occupy a space on the normative map (Muñoz, 2009). The partner Pride worried that acquiescing to the progress flag may risk the progress they had made to date. In this situation, the rainbow flag represented something that has grown legible, acceptable, and mainstream, in line with homonormative and homonationalist constructions of progress, and they felt it was being taken away. To revisit the opening quote of this article, I consider the rainbow flag to be an example of what might be considered a "nice thing," further, I would deem it a "nice GAY thing."

The rise of assimilationist discourses within Pride in the pursuit of normative rights and status reifies the ongoing oppression of racialized, disabled, and otherwise othered gender and sexually diverse individuals. Being asked to use the progress flag, intended to be more inclusive of gender minorities and racialized queer and trans* persons—identities that this board did not hold, was construed as a threat to the intelligible image their Pride had worked to achieve. Their position is reminiscent of white reactions to the perceived threat to homonormativity and homonationalism posed by Black Lives Matter Toronto [BLM-TO], who staged a sit-in during the 2016 Pride parade, to make visible the ongoing and systemic anti-Black racism of Pride Toronto (Cole, 2020; Keleta-Mae, 2020). This call to action was heavily twisted by white community members, resulting in the characterization of BLM-TO as the deviant other, responsible for "hijacking" a parade to which they had no claim (Greey, 2018; Tompkins, 2018).

In the meeting, I stated that the progress flag mattered, articulating the impact of this symbolic action in recognizing the immense diversity of gender and sexually diverse communities. Outvoted, they conceded. Several months later, as I watched the local flag-raising ceremonies live on Facebook, a kickoff to our collaborative week of events, I was heartened to hear a representative of the organization provide a bit of context and history to preface the raising of the progress flag (Figure 11.2).

While Pride in the province of New Brunswick is not yet queer, in this moment I recognized the fleeting effects of our commitment to queer, anti-racist facilitation in the near imperceptible disruption of hegemonic whiteness and white supremacy within the structure of the organization. I consider the impacts of this action of changing a longstanding symbol to represent a ripple of change and queering towards radically inclusive, anti-racist futures (Muñoz, 2009). The project of queering necessitates political and social movement with no singular endpoint and implementing changes such as this is integral to imagining a queer future. In the context of this work, I have employed a distinction between

FIGURE 11.2 The 2020 Flag Raising in Fredericton, New Brunswick.

queer, political orientations to Pride organizing and exclusionary, homonormative priorities of achieving assimilation into the mainstream, national discourse (Duggan, 2002; McCaskell, 2016; Warner, 1999).[13] I would argue that by embracing the progress pride flag, despite discomfort, the partner Pride initiated a partial acknowledgement of the homonormativity within the organization, a necessary step in working to queer the institution of Pride.

Conclusion

I have explored the concept of facilitating the queering of Pride in New Brunswick through three interconnected concepts: inclusion, ownership, and progress. Pride can never claim queerness, as queering requires continual disruption and remaking in response to the changing social, cultural and political milieu, relations of power, and new knowledges. The act of queering represents movement, the choice to abandon the stability of one's footing and embrace the fluidity and multiplicity of simultaneous and non-linear reflection, disruption, and construction, and a constant re-imagining of the future. Queering Pride requires a recognition of how facilitators are complicit in reproducing relations of power and systems of oppression, and re-imagining and re-defining this space, towards urgent political futures of queer, anti-racist inclusion (Muñoz, 2009; Walcott, 2012). To do so compels a commitment to listen, learn, and evolve, and actively work to recognize and resist perpetuating oppressive discourses.

As a queer individual deeply involved in an organization with a fraught history—one that has the potential to both disrupt and reinscribe homonormative and homonationalist discourses—I consider the project of queering to be a necessary action to identify, disrupt, and challenge these discourses internally and within Pride. My whiteness has enabled me to interrogate discourses and relations of power, and to speak politically of disruption and of queering. I must consistently examine how my attempts to queer Pride also serve to reinscribe discourses of compulsory homonormativity and hegemonic whiteness within Pride, discourses which are deeply embedded in my positionality.

Questioning, theorizing, and responding to how politics and power intersect in shaping understandings of inclusion, ownership, and progress within Pride organizing and community facilitation are necessary considerations in the Sisyphean project of queering Pride. The project of queering must extend to the individuals and external influences involved in the organization, the communities it seeks to serve, the spaces it creates, claims, and inhabits, and the discourses of power and oppression that shape its very existence. This work is ongoing, and I consider the project of queering, through reflection, disruption, and remaking, to be central in working towards critical political and social change within and beyond Pride and the imagining and pursuit of critically diverse, intersectional, anti-racist, and inclusive queer futures.

Notes

1 The origins of this idiom are unclear, but variations can be traced through the latter half of the 20th century in a variety of media. In the early 2000s it gained increasing popularity in reference to Internet trolling through the platform 4chan, intended to denote an individual that effectively ruins something for others (Phillips, 2015).
2 I capitalize Pride throughout this work to signal I am referring to an established group or organization, such as FFP and Pride NB, as opposed to "pride" as a noun or verb.
3 I use community singular to denote all queer, trans*, and non-binary individuals within this geographic region in order to increase legibility; however, I acknowledge there are numerous distinct queer, trans*, and 2SLGBTQ+ communities which may or may not overlap. Further not all individuals who identify as gender and sexual minority wish to be/feel included in this broad conception of community.
4 In 2018, artist Daniel Quasar developed the progress flag, a new iteration of the rainbow flag originally designed by Gilbert Baker, which includes white, pink, pale blue, brown, and black stripes in a right-facing chevron, intended to represent trans* individuals and people of colour (Lang, 2020).
5 By this, I refer to all persons that are othered (Ahmed, 2006; hooks, 1992) based on sexual orientation, gender identity, gender expression, race, ethnicity, ability, age, socio-economic status or other immutable ascriptive characteristics or identities deemed non-normative by dominant systems of power.
6 We adopted new core values of equity, diversity, inclusion, and intersectionality, that shaped the reimagining of Pride. For additional information about the organization, see http://www.frederictonpride.com/about
7 In late 2020, I took a leave from the board to work with our new sibling organization, ConneQT NB. I remain heavily involved as a liaison for ConneQT NB and collaborator.
8 Between us, we brought minimal diversity as a white, non-binary queer; a white, neurodiverse and chronically-ill, queer, cis woman; and a Latinx, gay, middle-aged, cis man.
9 This comment reflected the financial security of the Pride that suggested it, the only organization in the province that had significant, recurring financial support. Most organizations in the province, including FFP are run entirely by volunteers that fundraise tirelessly to fund their (primarily free) programming. Smaller rural organizations frequently reference a lack of access to both grants and sponsorship opportunities and are unlikely to be in a financial position to contribute as a condition of participation. FFP and the third partner Pride vehemently opposed this suggestion.
10 We were sensitive to demanding this labour of speaking openly about lived experience, when numerous individuals approached had declined due to the dangers associated with such a public event. These panels included numerous individuals with a diversity of intersecting identities, including Black, Latinx, Indigenous, Afro-Indigenous, Southeast Asian, white, Two-Spirit, immigrant, trans*, non-binary, disabled, and Jewish sexually diverse individuals.
11 In line with Walcott's (2012) work of futures of Black queer and trans* representation, I contend that true diversity is an impossibility within this context, rather it is an impetus to continually actively queering Pride spaces and organizations towards critically diverse futures. Both this work of critical diversification and representation and the decentring of whiteness are imperative foci in the project of queering Pride. The questions raised in this segment necessitate exploration beyond the scope of this chapter.

12 The Pride that retained this sponsor was fiercely protective of them, leading to one-sided communication that contributed to an uneven balance of power and control where the remaining board members felt their concerns were not being heard and the expression of criticism put their involvement at risk.
13 I note that this distinction, while presented in an oppositional manner, should not be understood as static and binary as it is significantly more complex, shaped and influenced by historical, socio-political, and economic contexts and discourses of power. This discussion merits further exploration beyond the scope of this chapter.

References

Ahmed, S. (2006). *Queer phenomenology: Orientations, objects, others.* Duke University Press.

Awwad, J. (2015). Queer regulation and the homonational rhetoric of Canadian exceptionalism. In O.H. Dryden, & S. Lenon (Eds.), *Disrupting queer inclusion: Canadian homonationalisms and the politics of belonging* (pp. 19–34). UBC Press.

Bain, B. (2017). Fire, passion, and politics: The creation of Blockorama as Black queer diasporic space in the Toronto Pride. In G.W. Kinsman, L.P. Rankin, & P. Gentile (Eds.), *We still demand! Redefining resistance in sex and gender struggles* (pp. 81–97). UBC Press.

Bochner, A.P. (2000). Criteria against ourselves. *Qualitative Inquiry, 6*(2), 266–272. https://doi.org/10.1177/107780040000600209

Butler, J. (1993). *Bodies that matter: On the discursive limits of "sex."* Routledge.

Burrill, F. (2019). Re-developing underdevelopment: An agenda for new histories of capitalism in the Maritimes. *Acadiensis, 48*(2), 179–189.

Chang, H. (2008). *Autoethnography as method.* Left Coast.

Chang, H. (2016). Individual and collaborative autoethnography as method: A social scientist's perspective. In S.L.H. Jones, T.E. Adams, & C. Ellis (Eds.), *Handbook of autoethnography.* Routledge.

Cole, D. (2020). *The skin we're in.* Doubleday.

Collins, P.H. (1990). *Black feminist thought: Knowledge, consciousness, and the politics of empowerment.* Routledge.

Crenshaw, K. (1991). Mapping the margins: Intersectionality, identity politics, and violence against women of color. *Stanford Law Review, 43*(6), 1241. https://doi.org/10.2307/1229039

Da Costa, J.C.R. (2020). Pride parades in queer times: Disrupting time, norms, and nationhood in Canada. *Journal of Canadian Studies, 54*(2–3), 434–458. https://doi.org/10.3138/jcs-2020-0045

Duggan, L. (2002). The new homonormativity: The sexual politics of neoliberalism. In R. Castronova, & D. Nelson (Eds.), *Materializing democracy: Toward a revitalized cultural politics* (pp. 175–194). Duke University Press.

Eng, D.L., Halberstam, J., & Muñoz, J.E. (2005). Introduction: What's queer about queer studies now? *Social Text, 23*(3-4), 1–17. https://doi.org/10.1215/01642472-23-3-4_84-85-1

Ferguson, R.A. (2019). *One-dimensional queer.* Polity.

Greensmith, C., & Giwa, S. (2013). Challenging settler colonialism in contemporary queer politics: Settler homonationalism, Pride Toronto, and Two-Spirit subjectivities. *American Indian Culture and Research Journal, 37*(2), 129–148. https://doi.org/10.17953/aicr.37.2.p4q2r84l12735117

Greey, A. (2018). Queer inclusion precludes (Black) queer disruption: Media analysis of the Black Lives Matter Toronto sit-in during Toronto Pride 2016. *Leisure Studies, 37*(6), 662–676. https://doi.org/10.1080/02614367.2018.1468475

Hatoum, N.A., & Moussa, G. (2018). Becoming through others: Western queer self-fashioning and solidarity with queer Palestine. In J. Haritaworn, G. Moussa, S.M. Ware, & R. Rodríguez (Eds.), *Queering urban justice: Queer of colour formations in Toronto* (pp. 169–186). University of Toronto Press.

Hempstead, A. (2017). *Nova Scotia, New Brunswick & Prince Edward Island*. Moon.

Hinkson, K. (2021). The colorblind rainbow: Whiteness in the gay rights movement. *Journal of Homosexuality*, *68*(9), 1393–1416. https://doi.org/10.1080/00918369.2019.1698916

hooks, b. (1992). *Black looks: Race and representation*. South End Press.

Jones, R. (2019). 'Tough to take': New Brunswick grabs unwanted title as Canada's poorest province. *CBC News*. https://www.cbc.ca/news/canada/new-brunswick/new-brunswick-poorest-province-equalization-payments-1.5400170

Jones, S.L.H., & Adams, T.E. (2016). Autoethnography is a queer method. In K. Browne, & C.J. Nash (Eds.), *Queer methods and methodologies: Intersecting queer theories and social science research* (pp. 195–214). Routledge.

Keleta-Mae, N. (2020). Black Lives Matter: Toronto sit-in at pride. In R. Diverlus, S. Hudson, & S.M. Ware (Eds.), *Until we are free: Reflections on black lives matter in Canada*. University of Regina Press.

Labelle, A. (2020). Intersectional praxis from within and without: Challenging whiteness in Québec's LGBTQ movement. In E. Evans, & E. Lépinard (Eds.), *Intersectionality in feminist and queer movements: Confronting privileges* (pp. 202–218). Routledge.

Lang, N. (2020, June 2). It's time Black and Brown people be included in the pride flag. *Them*. https://www.them.us/story/ipride-flag-redesign-black-brown-trans-pride-stripes

Lenon, S., & Dryden, O.H. (2015). Introduction: Interventions, iterations, and interrogations that disturb the (homo)nation. In O.H. Dryden, & S. Lenon (Eds.), *Disrupting queer inclusion: Canadian homonationalisms and the politics of belonging* (pp. 135–150). UBC Press.

McCaskell, T. (2016). *Queer progress: From homophobia to homonationalism*. Between the Lines.

Muñoz, J.E. (2009). *Cruising utopia: The then and there of queer futurity*. New York University Press.

Nast, H.J. (2002). Queer patriarchies, queer racisms, international. *Antipode*, *34*(5), 874–909. https://doi.org/10.1111/1467-8330.00281

Peers, D., & Eales, L. (2012). "Stand up" for exclusion? Queer pride, ableism and inequality. In M. Smith, & F. Jaffer (Eds.), *Beyond the queer alphabet: Conversations on gender, sexuality, and intersectionality* (pp. 39–41). Independently published.

Phillips, W. (2015). *This is why we can't have nice things: Mapping the relationship between online trolling and mainstream culture*. MIT Press. http://www.jstor.org/stable/j.ctt17kk8k7

Piepzna-Samarasinha, L.L. (2018). Toronto crip city: A Not so brief, incomplete personal history of some disabled QTPOC cultural activism in Toronto, 1997–2015. In J. Haritaworn, G. Moussa, & S.M. Ware (Eds.), *Marvellous grounds: Queer of colour formations in Toronto* (pp. 135–150). Between the Lines.

Pride NB. (2020, July 18). *Queer experiences: A roundtable*. [Video]. Fierté Fredericton Pride. http://www.frederictonpride.com/media/video

Puar, J.K. (2007). *Terrorist assemblages: Homonationalism in queer times*. Duke University Press.

Puar, J.K. (2012). "I would rather be a cyborg than a goddess": Becoming-intersectional in assemblage theory. *PhiloSOPHIA*, *2*(1), 49–66. https://www.muse.jhu.edu/article/486621

Self, R., & Hall, A.R. (2021). Refusing to die: Black queer and feminist worldmaking amid anti-Black state violence. *QED: A Journal in GLBTQ Worldmaking*, *8*(1), 123–130. https://www.jstor.org/stable/10.14321/qed.8.1.0123

Spade, D. (2011). *Normal life*. South End Press.
Statistics Canada. 2017. *Fredericton, New Brunswick and New Brunswick. Census Profile*. 2016 Census. Statistics Canada Catalogue no. 98-316-X2016001. Ottawa. Released November 29, 2017. https://www12.statcan.gc.ca/census-recensement/2016/dp-pd/prof/index.cfm?Lang=E
Thorpe, A. (2021). *Pride and (learned) prejudice: Education, activism, identity*. [Unpublished doctoral dissertation]. University of New Brunswick.
Tompkins, A. (2018). "Driving wedges" and "hijacking" pride: Disrupting narratives of Black inclusion in LGBT politics and the Canadian national imaginary. *Oñati Socio-Legal Series*, *10*(6), 1214–1241. https://doi.org/10.35295/osls.iisl/0000-0000-0000-1104
Trevenen, K., & DeGagne, A. (2015). Homonationalism at the border and in the streets: Organizing against exclusion and incorporation. In O.H. Dryden, S. Lenon (Eds.), *Disrupting queer inclusion: Canadian homonationalisms and the politics of belonging* (pp. 100–115). UBC Press.
Walcott, R. (2012). Black queer and Black trans: Imagine imagination imaginary futures. In M. Smith, & F. Jaffer (Eds.), *Beyond the queer alphabet: Conversations on gender, sexuality, and intersectionality* (pp. 28–31). Independently published.
Ward, J. (2008). White normativity: The cultural dimensions of whiteness in a racially diverse LGBT organization. *Sociological Perspectives*, *51*(3), 563–586. https://doi.org/10.1525/sop.2008.51.3.563
Warner, M. (1999). Normal and normaller: Beyond gay marriage. *GLQ: A Journal of Lesbian and Gay Studies*, *5*(2), 119–171. https://doi.org/10.1215/10642684-5-2-119
Warner, T. (2002). *Never going back: A history of queer activism in Canada*. University of Toronto Press.

PART IV
Art and Ethical Research Practices in Research Facilitation

12
FACILITATING QUEER ART IN THE CLIMATE CRISIS

Sabine LeBel

Introduction

The Queer Environmental Futures project is an ongoing creative and academic project that draws on histories of queer art and activism for strategies to respond to the ongoing climate crisis. We—myself and my long-term collaborator, Alison Taylor—imagine the project as a place to turn to, "tropes of science fiction where we can render the familiar unfamiliar and see it anew" (LeBel & Taylor, 2019, para. 3). We want to discover "the future as environmentalist and fuelled by a spirit of radical ethical experimentalism" (para. 3). We suggest that:

> Queering environmental futures means busting down the divisions between utopia and dystopia and asking: what can queering the future bring to the environmental crises of the current moment? ... Queering the future is about refiguring the paradigms of colonialism, capitalism, white supremacy, patriarchy and heteronormativity that have brought us to this environmentally precipitous moment.
>
> *(para. 1)*

The project includes a digital residency, collaborative videos, and other projects.

As part of this project, in May 2019, I co-facilitated a two-week Queer Environmental Worlds (QEW) residency at Anima Casa Rural, a permaculture farm in Jalisco, Mexico that holds art residencies and other activities.[1] The residency brought together queer artists from Canada, Mexico, and the United States, working in a variety of media, and culminated in a group show at Estudio Teorema in Guadalajara, the closest city. A small group of six artists participated in the residency, representing diverse identities including American, Canadian, Mexican, asexual, lesbian, gay, and non-binary folks. Most of the participants, including the facilitators are white, and only one is racialized. Although the primary language of the workshops was English, both English and Spanish were regularly spoken throughout the residency.

Anima Casa Rural, like most rural residencies, brought participants together in shared working and living spaces, with limited access to the outside world. Two critical factors that emerged were space and process. Queer methods "mak[e] space for what is" and this notion seems particularly apt for thinking through an ethics of queer facilitation (Love et al, as cited in Brim & Ghaziani, 2016, p. 18). The actual space of Anima Casa Rural created a place for the residency and shaped its trajectory. Facilitation during the residency required flexibility and creativity as we navigated a range of factors including studio schedules, shared languages, communal spaces, meals, and weather. The residency has shaped the larger, ongoing project in many meaningful and important ways.

This chapter is a reflection on the residency and as an opportunity to build on future discussions and methods for queer facilitation. In this way, the residency is the raw material from which I am drawing to imagine what an ethics of queer art facilitation can be. The first section of the chapter focuses on space. I examine how Anima Casa Rural is located in the larger context of the North American Free Trade Agreement (NAFTA) and how the neoliberalization of creative industries has shaped residency spaces in general. In the second section, I turn to the residency itself to argue for the importance of process in facilitation practices. The final section is a reflection on how facilitators enter spaces of facilitation, and the ways our own expectations inadvertently shape facilitation practices and expectations.

Space, Place, and NAFTA

The 1990s saw an explosion of artist residencies, fuelled largely by globalization and neoliberal policies aimed at further monetizing the culture industries (Elfving, Kokko, & Gielen, 2019). Artist residencies around the globe number in the thousands and have become crucial to global art infrastructures, offering artists career advancement through opportunities for networking, production of work, and venues to display work (Elfving, Kokko, & Gielen, 2019). Artist residencies vary greatly from smaller artist-driven spaces to larger institutional ones. Funded artist residencies are increasingly attached to major institutions, including airports, museums, universities, and businesses (Lithgow & Wall, 2017). There is a tension between artist residencies as part of the larger machinery of neoliberal globalization in which, on the one hand, increasingly impoverished artists are required to market and brand themselves, and at the same time as these same neoliberal policies reinforce and worsen North–South and other economic inequities. On the other hand, artist residencies can offer a reprieve from these pressures and many artists enjoy residencies as productive and collaborative spaces outside the 24/7 temporalities and pressures of late capitalism. In other words, artist residencies reproduce many of the contradictory aspects of globalization.

The Anima Casa Rural residency that I am reflecting upon must be located in this paradoxical global context. It exists in the neoliberal peculiarities of North America, including NAFTA that came into effect in 1994. NAFTA has directly affected patterns of work and migration in many parts of Mexico, including Jalisco (Quirk, 2007). On August 22, 2019, Julian Calleros, the Head of Development at Anima Casa Rural, gave a free public artist talk entitled "Community Engagement and Food Security" at Ryerson University in Toronto. In it, he located his creative practice as a queer artist and his work at Anima Casa Rural in the larger context of NAFTA (Calleros, 2019). He pointed out that family and community structures have been radically altered so that many local communities in the province of Jalisco are composed of the elderly, women, and children. Many local economies are now driven by remittances from migrant workers, mostly men, working in the US. Another change in Jalisco has been the development of agribusiness, notably the production of cash crops like sugar cane, cherry tomatoes, strawberries, and blueberries. These crops are not native to the area and are incredibly water-intensive. As a result, the water table in this arid region is being depleted. It is within this context that our small residency QEW took place.

Brim and Ghaziani (2016) draw from an interview with Judith Butler and Sara Ahmed to suggest that queer methods might "outline the conditions of queer worldmaking and to clarify, but not overdetermine, the conditions that 'make life liveable'" (Butler, as cited in Brim & Ghaziani, 2016, p. 6). This notion is apt for the aims of the residency where we were attempting to imagine liveable futures in the face of climate change. As facilitators, we saw Anima Casa Rural as an ideal place from which to create art and vision queer environmental futures because, as a functioning permaculture farm and artist residency, Anima is an island of economic and environmental experimentation in the midst of the realities of agribusiness and climate change. Anima's space includes a natural pool, studio, gardens, composting toilets, and a food forest, all of which are accessible to artists during the residency. In addition, because of uneven North–South dynamics at play for artists, Anima offers lower prices for Mexican artists and artists from other Latin American countries.

Anima is doing the work of making life liveable both through permaculture and fairer pricing for people attending residencies. Anima attempts to intervene in the uneven and destructive practices of global capitalism as they affect land, people, and their relationships. In this way, it is a place that is pushing back against dominant structures. My aim here is not to idealize Anima or to suggest that these small acts can necessarily make larger systemic changes. However, Anima intervenes into the spaces of globalization by creating a place for sustainable art, cultural exchange, and sustainable farming practices. It is, thus, fertile ground for a gathering dealing with and facilitating queer worldmaking.

Processing, Facilitation, and Art Making

The residency facilitators arrived a day before participants to get acquainted with the staff at Anima, the space, and to plan for the arrival of the participants. As facilitators, we needed to be flexible to accommodate the needs of Anima and participating artists. Mealtimes were set as artists were cooked for and fed by Anima and largely from the Anima permaculture farm, including fresh fruit, vegetables, and eggs. In terms of programming, each artist had their own project they were working on related to the larger theme of QEW. There was a day trip to Guadalajara planned, the closest city to the residency. As part of this trip, artists met with the director of Estudio Teorema, Fernando Garcia, to see the gallery space and plan for the final group show. In addition, Calleros taught many of the artists some rudimentary barro, a traditional Mexican pottery technique. Most of the artists worked in their own areas, which included writing, video, and painting, but also experimented with sculpture, barro, collage, and performance during their stay. We led four workshops over the two-week period: (1) Show and Tell: Objects from a Queer Future; (2) Storytime; (3) Wayfinding; and (4) Visitors from the Future.

Facilitation always involves meeting participants where they are at physically, politically, emotionally, and spiritually. My facilitation training and practice began through the Ontario Public Interest Research Group in Peterborough, Ontario, which drew heavily from the work of Paulo Freire (2005) and popular education techniques to lead high school and university students, as well as members of the public, in workshops on a variety of topics. This approach asks facilitators to understand participants as whole humans with their own existing knowledge base, and to meet them where they are (Freire, 2005). Other techniques include reflecting on shared strategies, visioning, and recognizing that everyone, facilitators, and participants alike, are both teachers and learners. Finally, popular education acknowledges that learning always involves power dynamics. For example, facilitators centre the knowledge, including lived experience, of participants in workshop and residency spaces. For white people, like myself and Taylor (one cis, one non-binary), this strategy enables facilitators to prioritize the experiences of racialized and non-English speakers whenever possible.

One of the ways that this training has translated into my approach to facilitation is to understand process as central. In art and activism, a focus on process can be a way of centring ethical ways of relating: a good process considers feelings, power dynamics, and resources. This focus on process is crucial to thinking about ethics especially when dealing with an art residency, and it might involve funding, technical skills, and the point the artist is at in the process of creating a work. And while process decentres the final product, our residency culminated in a group show, which necessarily influences how artists can engage with process as they are simultaneously trying to complete a showable piece. In other words, experimentation, a lovely and important part of process in art practice, might be curbed or limited to workshops and kept out of each artists' personal project.

Process during the residency meant keeping open lines of communication between artists and respecting the routines of staff. As facilitators, we regularly checked in with Anima staff in planning outings and workshops. In terms of the larger residency, process meant being flexible about where and when the workshops could happen. The workshop schedule was posted in the studio, and times varied based on weather and studio conditions, and were mutually agreed upon. Because the studio became unbearably hot in the late afternoon, we collectively opted to have workshops run during this time on the shaded, breezy veranda. This scheduling also enabled artists to make use of cooler mornings to work in the studio, and most evenings all the artists worked in the small space, including Calleros who was usually occupied with running the farm, cooking, and residency business during the daytime. We needed to let the artists, staff, plants, and animals at Anima dictate when, where, and how the rhythm of our days would unfold.

Part of the process of designing workshops is to build in contingencies. For QEW, this meant not making assumptions about what participants might bring to workshops and not to design them around a particular medium or skillset. Because we were unfamiliar with Anima before our arrival, it also meant keeping workshop materials basic and using paper, markers, and discussion as materials. Anima is rural and we did not have regular access to the local town, so process also meant working with the materials and facilities housed at Anima. Process during the workshops meant enabling a space for artists to come together and collaborate in some way on the residency theme of QEW. We followed the protocols of popular education and always began by asking participants to share what they knew. We would then work on finding commonalities and bringing in new information (Freire, 2005). This part of the popular education process is key to our facilitation practices, and we were able to successfully make this happen in three of the workshops.

The workshops were intended to punctuate the work of individual artists during the residency and to provide lateral inspiration and collaboration. As is typical of teaching and facilitation, the workshops were planned but required flexibility in their delivery. We decided to make the first workshop, Show and Tell: Objects from a Queer Future, low-stakes and it was intended to be where artists first engaged with the residency theme of QEW. Artists were asked ahead of time to bring with them an object from a queer future, either physical or virtual "that inspire[d] them or [came] from an imagined world, or represent[ed] a possibility. It [could] be a sketch, an idea, a stick, a spaceship, or a poem" (LeBel & Taylor, 2019, project materials). It was meant to happen on the first day as an icebreaker, but because artist arrivals were staggered over several days, it functioned as a wide-ranging discussion where artists were able to discuss their object, what it meant to them personally, and how it related to their work. In other words, the conversation flowed more towards our creative practices and histories, and less into how our objects might fit into notions of a queer future. We let participants determine the direction of discussion that was most meaningful to them. It also used the popular education technique of meeting participants where they are at, building on their knowledge base, and allowing them to determine the path of learning.

The second workshop, Storytime, involved sharing narratives in the form of short sci-fi videos and stories. Our intention as facilitators was to: "curate a short programme of environmental and queer science fiction… [and to] screen a few short films and read aloud a story or two – texts that we love that may provide inspiration to the artists" (project materials; personal communication). Here, again, artists were invited to share a text, and were prompted to do so before the residency. Because of different aptitudes in English and Spanish, and a somewhat unreliable Internet connection, this was perhaps the least successful workshop. Despite our intentions of building on the participants' interests and knowledge, in retrospect, it was the workshop that most used the "banking model" of education, or the assumption that participants are empty vaults to be filled with new information by informed educators (Freire, 2005). This method of facilitation undoubtedly contributed to this workshop being less fruitful.

We had described the third workshop, Wayfinding, as a place to consider what artists' imagined worlds brought to our own in terms of environmentalism. We were interested in exploring an "ethos of radical experimentalism" and a "place to journey between worlds and discover what they offer each other, and what art can bring to environmentalism" (LeBel & Taylor, 2019, para. 2). Because of the ways in which different artists interpreted the theme of queer environmental futures and the medium they were working in, individual artists were not necessarily working with an imagined world. For example, the barro artist was creating wonderful sculptures from doll heads and clay that were most certainly queer future objects, but they did not necessarily create or identify an imagined world as part of their process. This was perhaps the most successful workshop because it asked all of us to work outside our comfort zones and to collaborate as a group. It also used the popular education technique of visioning and built on our shared experiences and strategies from previous workshops.

We began with a set of collective brainstorming and discussions around a huge piece of paper, on which everyone wrote and drew in response to prompts about Wayfinding towards a queer future. Then, we asked each participant to go and create something inspired from our brainstorm. The results included sketches, photographs, collages, and a political banner. In Wayfinding, artists were at a stage in the residency where they were ready to engage in creative experiments outside their own media. Brainstorming provided a collective collaborative space from which to create new knowledge in the form of queer experimental technologies, concepts, and political campaigns intended to engage with sustainable environmental practices. In terms of the ethics of facilitation, it was an incredible lesson in letting participants guide the process. In certain moments during the workshop, I found myself wanting to insist that we discuss climate change directly and specifically. However, participants interpreted the prompt based on their own needs. In retrospect, this workshop is perhaps the richest when considered through the lens of environment because it encompassed such divergent topics from a designer genitalia catalogue to a tree spirit political campaign.

The fourth workshop, Visitors from the Future, was intended to "convene an interstellar, interspecies, queer gathering and see what conspiracies are hatched!" (LeBel & Taylor, 2019). This workshop landed towards the end of the residency when pressure to finish pieces for the final show was building. It was fun, low-stakes, and a break from the pressures of working towards the show. It was also one of the most intensely creative moments of the residency as artists spent most of the day assembling costumes. That evening, we gathered in the studio to drink beer, listen to music, and dance. While it was not necessarily productive as a workshop per se, it was a critical bonding experience—which is central to art facilitation processes. In that moment, a spirit of queer community, surely necessary for building queer environmental futures, was evident. It may seem strange to include a party in a discussion of facilitation, but queer parties have been central to our liberation, survival, and resiliency (Wortham, 2019). Whether gathering in houses, clubs, or Pride celebrations, queer parties offer space for LGBTQIA2S+ people to be ourselves, to dance out the microaggressions of the day, and to be celebrated as vibrant and sexy. As such, queer parties are important to queer organizing, theorizing, and art making.

Lesbian Processing, Queer Facilitation

Much of the existing literature on queer facilitation focuses on safer spaces training. My interest in queer facilitation is more global than safer spaces training, which, in my experience, often exposes LGBTQIA2S+ people, who typically do the training, to a myriad of microaggressions from workshop participants. While this training is clearly necessary, including within LGBTQIA2S+ spaces, can be too simplistic, in its approach to art facilitation in queer spaces. Safer spaces training often involves training cis and straight people how to use the correct language and be respectful to their queer and trans* colleagues or peers. Safer spaces training is perceived, at best, as learning to use respectful language, and, at worst, language policing. The vast and varied histories of queer organizing, activism, and art practice surely have more to offer the literature on facilitation. A key moment in queer activism is during the AIDS crisis in the 1980s, for example. Activists and artists mobilized to bring attention to the homophobia and neglect from the health care system for AIDS patients, including die-ins, kiss-ins, and the AIDS quilt. During this time, complex community support systems were created to feed, house, clothe, and care for sick community members. These practices demonstrate an ethics of care in activism that has much to offer facilitation practices.

Although leading artist workshops together was new for us as facilitators, as lesbians who have been out and artists for over 20 years, process is not. Drawing from Ahmed (2016), I have argued elsewhere (LeBel, 2021) that processing might be considered an innovation that comes out of histories of lesbian feminism. In that article, I am interested in how lesbian processing can be recuperated from more problematic aspects of lesbian feminist history, including transphobia and racism, and brought to bear on queer ecologies. In terms of facilitation, it means valuing process and using it to face difficult, contradictory, or downright problematic legacies. As discussed in the previous section, we see process as central to both creative works and facilitation. What might be specific about lesbian processing, as opposed to processing in other venues, is that it might be seen as an innovation that comes out of histories of lesbian feminism (LeBel, 2021). For me as a facilitator, especially a cis white Canadian, queer facilitation must attempt to make space for our various lived experiences and be attentive to culture, geography, age, and orientation. This means centring and amplifying the experiences and voices of racialized and trans* people, as well as people from the global South, in facilitation spaces and being attentive to what material conditions might make participation possible.

As I note in the introduction of this chapter, queer methods "mak[e] space for what is," and this includes making space for where workshop participants are at in terms of their sense of themselves and their art practice. In this third section, I process the residency from my perspective as a facilitator, using the example of language. I am particularly interested in how facilitators enter spaces, especially spaces that are not their own culturally. The following is a reflection on coming to terms with my own assumptions after the residency was over. Because I have lived and worked in a multicultural and intergenerational queer community contexts, I assumed that I understood aspects of the complex relationships between language and identity.

Positionality in the context of queer spaces means making space for both the coalition politics of the LGBTQIA2S+ acronym but also the specificity, especially intersectionality, of our individual identities and experiences. As Brown and Nash (2010) contend,

> ... queer rarely recognises its own location and how it travels. Much queer theorising originated in the Global North with its particular social and historical contexts and its uncritical engagement with gendered and sexual lives in other geographical locations is not necessarily appropriate or helpful.
>
> (Brown & Nash, 2010, p. 16)

Because of legacies of colonialism and white supremacy, Eurocentric notions of gender and sexuality as identity dominate globally.

In the context of our residency in Mexico, there were artists from the Global North and South. Latin languages, including Spanish, ascribe a gender (male or female) to everything. One of the real pleasures of QEW was listening to Calleros explain to cis Mexicans attending the art show the concepts of asexuality and non-binary gender, and doing so in a language that genders everything.

The small group chatting about what words to use in Spanish made me, a queer lesbian cis woman from Canada, think about my orientation to the United States, our neocolonial power house of a neighbour, and the ways in which this proximity influences my understandings of language, especially Spanish.

I had assumed that Mexican queers would not only embrace but also be knowledgeable about the term Latinx, but this was not at all the case. While the terms Latino, Latina, and Latin@ were all attempts to use language to disrupt histories of Spanish colonialism, and to unite communities and countries south of the United States, the term Latinx is fraught (Brammer, 2019; Gamio Cuervo, 2016). On the one hand, the term offers a gender-neutral term for those wishing to avoid gendered identity categories. On the other, it has been criticized for its linguistic imperialism. As Guerra and Orbea (2018, para. 3) note, "By replacing o's and a's with x's, the word 'Latinx' is rendered laughably incomprehensible to any Spanish speaker without some fluency in English" (quoted in Brammer, 2019). This critique takes issue with the recentring of English, particularly in the context of the United States.

Perhaps as facilitators, we also must make space for what we are—to paraphrase Love et al. (2012)—including and especially our own blind spots and failures. In my case, although we discussed the US and its colonial dominance in the context of North America throughout the residency, I assumed that understanding the language politics of Latinx people I had encountered would translate to all Spanish speaking regions. But as Brown and Nash (2010) (above) remind us, clearly this is not the case and I imposed ideas about queerness from the Global North onto the Global South. In terms of popular education, this experience enabled me, the facilitator, to learn from participants, both of the residency and of the art show. In terms of the ethics of facilitation, this experience is a reminder of the ways in which queer art facilitators, especially as white people who wish to be allies to racialized people, need to continually engage with the process and work of decolonizing our ideas and facilitation practices. Self-reflexivity is crucial to facilitation practices.

Theorist Gloria Anzaldua embraced the word *nepantla*, a Nahuatl word, that means in-between to deal with issues of language, colonialism, and identity. In North America, as elsewhere, colonialism has been tremendously violent to queer Indigenous practices and people. In English the terms Two-Spirit and Indiqueer function as pan-Indigenous concepts to unite Indigenous people who identify as LGBTQ+ but desire a more culturally appropriate term. In an episode of Wilbur and Keene's *All My Relations* podcast, Kim Tallbear notes that while queers have often been at the forefront of thinking through ethical nonmonogamy, we have not always understood the connections to larger colonial practices of family and community, and that limits our ability to fully realize the radical and decolonial potentials of polyamory (Wilbur & Keene, 2019). The legacies of colonialism include assumptions about how family is made and affect the radical potential for community building. Her discussion of family and community includes both humans and non-humans in Indigenous world views. It thus connects not only to the queer world and future-making in the face of global warming, but also to the ways that colonialism is insipid and ubiquitous in its reach.

In their introduction to the special issue on queer methods, Brim and Ghaziani (2016) discuss the slipperiness of the word queer, especially as it applies to an academic context intent on specificity. They explain their decision not to clarify their use of "queer/ing" as recommended by one of their peer reviewers:

> Such a comment [by the reviewer] reflects the impulse to find commonality and coherence where often there is none… These terms will not be clarified, as to clarify and define these terms is to limit their usage just to these understandings.
>
> (p. 19)

Bringing this approach to queer facilitation inspired by popular education that centres on process, once again, means meeting people where they are. This is a much more difficult task than simply policing language because it involves careful planning, deep listening, and allowing mistakes to happen. It also means having a process for mistakes, hurt feelings, and complete failures.

In *Queer Art of Failure*, Halberstam (2011) notes that queers are "very good at failure" (p. 3). If honouring process is a path towards queer facilitation, then honouring failures, or at the very least mistakes, should be part of it too. Of course, Halberstam is using the concept of failure to critique hegemonic notions of success:

> I argue that success in a heteronormative, capitalist society equates too easily to specific forms of reproductive maturity combined with wealth accumulation. … If the boom and bust years of the late twentieth century and the early twenty-first have taught us anything, we should at least have a healthy critique of static models of success and failure.
>
> (p. 2)

I suspect that this idea resonates deeply with many queer artists who are systematically kept out of many aspects of the economy, including arts funding structures and mainstream gallery shows. It also resonates with the ups and downs of teaching and facilitation because failures are so often a strange mix of mysterious and predictable, and often very productive. Clearly, I am pushing this concept to include the more banal and everyday aspects of queer life, and my interest in queer failure includes everything from meta-critiques to the basics of running a successful workshop.

Failure enables space for reflection (Halberstam, 2011). Processing can certainly be an active form of reflection. At worst, processing can be an endless circular conversation in which nothing changes, and existing power structures get re-entrenched. At best, processing can offer space for complaint and the possibility to shift power dynamics and critique institutional structures (See: Ahmed, 2016; LeBel, 2021; Rault & Cowan, 2021). If queer methods "make visible 'actual ways of working'" (Ghaziani & Brim, 2016, pp. 3–4), then queer facilitation must attempt to take the best aspects of processing at every stage.

Conclusions

As the Queer Environmental Futures project moves forward, we will continue to think about best practices for queer facilitation. Naturally, this practice involves paying attention to pronouns and language, and centring the needs and lives of LGBTQIA2S+ people. In many ways, best practices are inspired by the work of anti-racist, climate justice, and other activists who work to mitigate barriers to participation through ensuring that artists and facilitators are paid for their time, that childcare is made available, and that food and transportation needs are considered. Process involves considering the material conditions that make active and enthusiastic participation a possibility for all participants. In my experience, these can be the most difficult aspects to fulfil because of the neoliberal realities of shrinking arts budgets and assumptions about the free labour of artists and facilitators. Being attentive to the connections between whiteness and access to capital, including intergenerational wealth, is an important consideration in planning events. Several interested artists did not participate in QEW because they did not have the time or funds.

Processing has much to offer facilitation, especially with regards to art practice, because it can disrupt the product-oriented ways of working that sometimes limit our creativity as we attempt to meet deadlines. Paying attention to process can help understand how feelings, procedures, and money can affect group dynamics and our individual ways of working. It can help with the skills building and risk taking so necessary to making art and community. On the other hand, too much processing can lead to inertia, frustration, and bad feelings. It can stunt spontaneity and growth.

To a large extent, the artists in the QEW residency did not directly engage with climate change in the ways we originally envisioned, which was the stated aim of the workshop. This is perhaps a limitation of our facilitation strategies, that we did not make the aims of the residency clear, or that the workshops did not inspire participants to engage with the theme. On the other hand, it has also inspired me to think deeply about how the environment is defined, what issues are important to queers, and how these issues may or may not overlap. In many ways, it speaks to the larger issues that structure our shared environments. For example, many climate justice activists note that police brutality is necessarily linked to climate change (Thomas & Haynes, 2020). Another study suggests that climate anxiety is largely a white phenomenon because racialized people have lived with dystopic and uncertain futures for generations due to histories of slavery, genocide, and other colonial violence (Jaquette Ray, 2021). The larger spaces we occupy, from housing to communities to national contexts, matter.

The resilience and creativity of queer communities as evidenced through activism and art informs so much of my thinking about queer facilitation. Whether it is lesbian processing or queer dance parties, I hope that queer facilitation can draw from the collective practices of joy and sorrow nurtured across various queer communities. Two areas that queer histories can contribute to ethical facilitation are embracing lesbian processing and the queer art of failure. Both of these queer community strategies are instructive for ethical facilitation because they ask us to act both within the space of a workshop, from planning to delivery, and within the larger spaces of our communities, and our art and facilitation practices.

I have been very inspired by the work of adrienne maree brown (2017) who has brought me back to science fiction and other speculative genres as critical spaces of community building and imagination. Her book *Emergent Strategies* (2017) is deeply inspired by the late great sci-fi writer Octavia Butler, and brown uses her work as a tool for radical social change, including anti-racist and climate justice activism. As an activist, brown is interested in how we might go about imagining and enacting viable futures. She says, "science fiction is a way to practice the future together" (2017, p. 19). Her words speak to how I want to move forward with the Queer Environmental Futures project, and, how I see the overlapping roles of queer art and activism in creating viable futures in the context of neoliberalism, the COVID-19 pandemic, and climate change.

Note

1 My co-coordinator for the residency was Alison Taylor, a long-time creative collaborator. This paper considers my facilitation experience.

References

Ahmed, S. (2016). *Living a feminist life*. Duke University Press.
Brammer, J.P. (2019, May/June). Digging into the messy history of "latinx" helped me embrace my complex identity. *Mother Jones*. https://www.motherjones.com/media/2019/06/digging-into-the-messy-history-of-latinx-helped-me-embrace-my-complex-identity/
Brim, M., & Ghaziani, A. (2016). Introduction: Queer methods. *WSQ: Women's Studies Quarterly, 44*(3 & 4), 14–27. https://doi.org/10.1353/wsq.2016.0033
brown, a. m. (2017). *Emergent strategies: Shaping change, changing worlds*. AK Press.
Brown, K., & Nash, C. (2010). Queer methods and methodologies. In K. Brown (Ed.), *Queer methods and methodologies: Intersecting queer theories and social science research*. Routledge. https://doi.org/10.4324/9781315603223
Calleros, J. (2019, August 22). *Community engagement and food security* (artist talk). Ryerson University. https://www.ryerson.ca/jack-layton-chair/events/2019/08/ArtistTalkwithJulianCalleros/
Elfving, T., Kokko, I., & Gielen, P. (2019). *Contemporary artist residencies: Reclaiming time and space*. Antennae.
Freire, P. (2005). *Pedagogy of the oppressed*. (M. Bergman, Trans.) Continuum.
Gamio Cuervo, A.B. (2016). *Latinx: A brief handbook*. Princeton LGBT Center.
Guerra, G. & Orbea, G. (2018). The argument against the term "latinx". *Latino News Brief*. https://ucanr.edu/blogs/blogcore/postdetail.cfm?postnum=28867

Halberstam, J. (2011). *Queer art of failure*. Duke University Press.

Jaquette Ray, S. (2021). Climate anxiety is an overwhelmingly white phenomenon. *Scientific American*. https://www.scientificamerican.com/article/the-unbearable-whiteness-of-climate-anxiety/

LeBel, S. (2021). Lesbian processing at the end of the world: Lesbian identity and queer environmental futurity. *Journal of Lesbian Studies*, [Ahead of print], 1–15. https://doi.org/10.1080/10894160.2021.2000560

LeBel, S., & Taylor, A. (2019). Queer environmental worlds residency at Anima Casa Rural. *Akimbo*. https://akimbo.ca/listings/queer-environmental-worlds-residency-at-anima-casa-rural/

Lithgow, M., & Wall, K. (2017). Embedded aesthetics: Artist-in-residencies as sites of discursive struggle and social innovation. *Seismopolite* (19). http://www.seismopolite.com/embedded-aesthetics-artist-in-residencies-as-sites-of-discursive-struggle-and-social-innovation

Love, H. Crosby, C., Duggan, L., Ferguson, R., Floyd, K., Joseph, M., McRuer, R., Moten, F., Nyongo, T., Rofel, L., Rosenberg, J., Salamon, G., Spade, D. & Villarejo, A. (2012). Queer studies, materialism, and crisis: A roundtable discussion. *GLQj: A Journal of Lesbian and Gay Studies*, *18*(1), 127–147.

Quirk, M. (2007, April). The Mexico connection. *The Atlantic*. https://www.theatlantic.com/magazine/archive/2007/04/the-mexican-connection/305725/

Rault, J., & Cowan, T.L. (2021). Heavy processing part I — Lesbian processing. *Digital Research Ethics Collaboratory*. http://www.drecollab.org/heavy-processing/

Thomas, A., & Haynes, R. (2020). Black lives matter: The link between climate change and racial justice. *Climate Analytics*. https://climateanalytics.org/blog/2020/black-lives-matter-the-link-between-climate-change-and-racial-justice/

Wilbur, M., & Keene, A. (2019, March 19). Decolonizing sex. *All My Relations*. [podcast]. https://www.allmyreltionspodcast.com/podcast/episode/468a0a6b/decolonizing-sex

Wortham, J. (2019, June 6). The joy of queer parties: We breathe, we dip, we flex. *NY Times*. https://www.nytimes.com/2019/06/26/style/queer-party-safe-space.html

13
ETHNODRAMATIC INQUEERY

Patrick Tomczyk

Introduction

"Queering High School," is a queer ethnodrama that explores the lived experiences of sexual and gender minority youth with respect to homophobia, biphobia, and transphobia in an Alberta high school. This ethnodrama, conducted through a queer lens, which I refer to as an *ethnodramatic inqueery* considers participants as co-researchers, and data from ethnographic interviews are transformed into a script. The script is derived from participants' lived experiences and later performed to a live audience. To facilitate this inqueery, I drew on queer theory and critical pedagogy to position my research. The goal of critical pedagogy is what Freire (1970/1990) calls *conscientization*, the raising of awareness of oppression in systemic and structural forms. Through this queered method, participants are empowered to share their struggles, and thereby raise a queer conscientization to the larger 2SLGBTQ+ and school communities.

To "engender a queer conscientization," I utilize queer theory to "augment critical pedagogy" (Hackford-Peer, 2019, p. 77). Hackford-Peer (2019) explains that queer pedagogy "utilizes elements of critical pedagogy to engage in theoretically queer projects – projects aimed at naming, interrupting, and destabilizing normative practices and beliefs" (p. 76). At the root of this process is praxis, a combination of action and reflection that informs strategic action to enable social and structural/cultural change (Freire 1970/1990). Meyer (2019) states that

> in queer pedagogy, this reflection is focused on how patterns of what is 'normal' are created and reproduced in schools and asks [us] … to examine and question them to make space for other bodies and identities that have been marginalized.
>
> *(p. 47)*

These "normative" patterns and practices are most often defined by heteronormative and patriarchal attitudes and beliefs. With queer praxis, education has the potential to become a transformative and liberating practice for 2SLGBTQ+ youth through queer conscientization.

The intersections of critical and queer theory enable me to explore notions of ethics, equity, and justice, in ways that highlight oppression related to sexual identity and orientation, as well as gender identity. Queering the method exposes how "community" and "identity" are highly contested terms. Sullivan (2003) argues that identities are in a specific historical and cultural context, "as is the value accorded to particular identities" (p. 83). She further explains that "identities are continuously fracturing, multiplying, metamorphosing [and as such] identity is social, unstable, continually in process and to some extent, is both necessary and impossible" (Sullivan, 2003, p. 149). One of the highlights of the inqueery was to consider how identities and communities intersect. Facilitating this work required a sensitivity to multiplicity, and I sought to create space to explore participants' identities.

Intersectionality

All people carry multiple intersecting identities within larger social systems as identity is not singular. In defining ourselves, we use physical and biological markers, as well as socially and politically constructed identifiers. Gorman-Murray et al. (2010) identified that one of the challenges in queer research is "the difficulty in effectively communicating and achieving understanding across an increasingly wide range of sexual [and gender] subjects, each with their own experiences, practices, relationships and subjectivities" (p. 99). It is important to consider the multiple dimensions of identity and social systems at play and how they intersect with one another and relate to inequality.

Throughout my research, I often refer to the queer community or 2SLGBTQ+ community, and what I mean by this is "a group of individuals, with significant degrees of commonality in identities, interests, and culture, who socialize, provide mutual support, share resources, and engage in action to benefit one and all" (Grace & Wells, 2015, p. 258). Nevertheless, I am mindful that each individual 2SLGBTQ+ person within the larger queer community has a unique identity and this plays a significant role in our understanding of someone. Equally, each of these ways of identifying, whether it's gay, lesbian, trans*, and so forth, carries certain implications and assumptions around inequality and oppression.

In Hill Collins's (2000) understanding, "intersectionality refers to particular forms of intersecting oppressions, for example, intersections of race and gender, or of sexuality and nation" (p. 18). For Meyer (2019), "engaging in real-life work also demonstrates intersectionality—that gender and sexuality issues are always connected to other communities' struggles for justice" (p. 52). It is essential, therefore, to understand that every person has a unique identity and lived reality; it cannot be assumed that all members of a certain group have the same issues, experiences, or even face the same oppression. With this uniqueness comes multiple and intersecting identities and "intersectional paradigms remind us that oppression cannot be reduced to one fundamental type, and that oppressions work together in producing injustice" (Hill Collins, 2000, p. 18). This is important because "ignoring differences within groups contributes to tension among groups" (Crenshaw, 1993, p. 1242). I had to acknowledge my unique position within this group. I was intentional in trying to avoid avoiding what Binnie (2007) describes as homonormativity:

> The increasing visibility and power of affluent white gay men has been accompanied by the marginalization of the politics of both lesbian feminism and sex radicalism, and has highlighted the exclusions within queer communities on the basis of race, class, gender and disability.
>
> *(p. 34)*

Positioning myself in the study, I note my insider/outsiderness as a white gay cisgender male who experienced bullying and harassment in high school. I was drawn to this project as a former theatre student, and as a teacher who has felt powerless to help 2SLGBTQ+ youth as I witnessed ineffective policies and practices in schools.

As a student, I attended 13 years of Catholic education. I was a son of two working class parents who espoused conservative and homophobic values. I was a refugee to Canada who experienced poverty and had to learn English. Despite the age difference between myself and the participants, I positioned myself as someone with a vested interest in championing 2SLGBTQ+ rights, with the privilege and means to take on this project, and as someone who seeks to make a difference. Muñoz (2010) critiques that "queer sensibilities are theorized and understood through lenses that are largely academic, Western, white, and privileged" (p. 57). To disrupt queer sensibilities, I forefronted the fact that the participants were the experts in their lives. I facilitated through my multiple roles as an arts-based researcher, queer activist, educator, doctoral student, and drama practitioner.

In facilitating this research, I centred queer realities and identities. As Gorman-Murray et al. (2010) note,

> those who variously identify as homosexual, gay, lesbian, bisexual, trans or otherwise non-heteronormative [or gender diverse] share a range of common experiences around legal, political, and social constraints, there are also significantly different lived experiences of oppression and exclusion between these groups.
>
> *(p. 99)*

Therefore, queer is, as Halperin (1995) suggests, a unifying term that suggests a positionality that can be appropriated by varying marginalized gender and sexual minorities. "In many ways, queer intersectionality is simply the necessary tautology:

intersectionality is inevitably disruptively queer, and queer must be analytically intersectional" (Rahman, 2010, p. 956). Queer theory inserts positionality within identity construction, along the matrix of domination that intersectionality identifies.

I deliberately ensured that the participants I worked with represented as many various identities of 2SLGBTQ+ persons as possible (age, sexual orientation, gender identity, location of school, etc.). It was vital to consider the various points of identity intersections of the 22 participants from the two urban areas where I completed my research. Ignoring these differences would have excluded a full understanding of their lived experiences. Participants were between the ages of 16–22 and had differing high school experiences. Some participants were still in high school, others had graduated, a couple had entered the workforce, and some were studying at post-secondary institutions. Some of the participants went to high schools in affluent neighbourhoods, while others went to schools in communities that were historically disadvantaged. The participants I worked with used diverse terms to identify who they were: male, female, cis, lesbian, non-binary, gender fluid, gay, trans*, and queer. While I did not specifically ask anyone about their social economic status, religion, or race, a few disclosed the following identifiers: bi-racial, Chinese, Christian, Catholic, Muslim, Métis, and middle class. It was the uniqueness of each participant that contributed to the creation of characters in the ethnodrama.

Facilitating Ethnodramatic Inqueery

I began this work by facilitating dialogue with 2SLGBTQ+ youth to understand what, in their view, contributes to homo/bi/transphobia in their schools through semi-structured interviews. By analysing the data with the participants, we identified several overarching thematic categories that had emerged, including: identity, gender sexuality associations (GSAs), bullying, gendered spaces, systemic issues, Catholic school, coming out at school, and social media. These categories further led to several realizations: the existence of a reductive model of identifying 2SLGBTQ+ students, ineffective anti-bullying school policies, stigma associated with inclusive bathrooms, (mis)use of pronouns and gender identification, systemic and pragmatic issues around GSAs, heteronormative and cisnormative assumptions and microaggressions based on systemic failures. Finally, heteropatriarchal and cisnormative ideologies and practices compose the root cause of 2SLGBTQ+ oppression, which manifest differently within various systems. Through a participant-facilitated analysis process, we co-developed a script that was then rehearsed and presented on two separate occasions to public audiences. We facilitated a post-performance discussion about the calls to action raised in the performance. Audience members completed a post-performance questionnaire to offer insight on how an ethnodramatic inqueery might be a tool for inclusive practices in schools.

Facilitating ethnodramatic inqueery opens avenues for the audience to learn, question, explore and reflect on their own practices, by considering how heteropatriarchal and cisnormative school cultures can be the greatest source of oppression for 2SLGBTQ+ youth who long to feel safe. The audiences indicated that to create more inclusive schools, unpacking multiple layers of heteropatriarchal and cisnormative school cultures was essential. In reference to policy implications, our queer ethnodrama identified how safety and inclusion should be defined in ways that significantly impact majority school cultures, in addition to programs and procedures that respond to homo/bi/transphobia.

Ethics of Transparency and Representation

From the beginning of the study, new participants would ask me, "Are you gay?" This question struck me as my mistake from the beginning of the recruitment process: I had not disclosed my queer identity in my call for participants, and yet I was asking them to out themselves. I realized how important disclosing my identity was in facilitating ethical research with the participants. In relation to her research, Rooke (2010) asked, "are we willing to risk relinquishing our often-unspoken attachment to the categories that offer us a sense of ontological security" (34)—in my case, my authority as a doctoral candidate/researcher. She explained that while queer ethnographers are often "deconstructing the discourses and categories that produce ... informants' subjectivities, [they] might consider the extent to which [they] are willing to be pulled apart or undone [themselves]" (p. 34). My insider status in the 2SLGBTQ+ community, gave me credibility, relatability, and trustworthiness. Rooke (2010) states that queer field work:

> demands that the ethnographer work from an honest sense of oneself that is open and reflexive, rather than holding on to a sense of self which provides an ontologically stable place from which enter into the fieldwork and subsequently come back to.
>
> *(35)*

The politics of location are complex, and our backgrounds contain so many intricate layers. While I was cognizant not to make the study about centring my queer identity, I did need to disclose some of my experiences with the participants to build relational trust. Being vulnerable and transparent permitted me to develop a bond with the participants. This self-revelatory process helped reduce the power imbalances that I held as an older, white cisgender, gay male researcher. It wanted participants to feel ownership of the project for the study to be successful. O'Toole (2006) indicates that:

> an understanding of power relationships operating within the research will enable ... an exploration of the relationship between power and knowledge, and of the value systems involved in the research.
>
> *(p. 16)*

This act of de-powerment was part of "the unearthing of my own personal history" (Conrad, 2003, p. 50). Facilitating radical transparency, created a shift which acknowledged the participants as co-researchers. "Queer reflexivity" required that I draw attention to the central issue of my work—forms of heteronormative and cisnormative oppression, and I had to acknowledge to my participants that I was in and of the culture I was writing about (Rooke, 2010). O'Toole (2006) explains that in "developing a bond of trust" researchers need to reconcile two "important destabilizing factors": curiosity and fear (p. 94). Therefore, it was important to explain who I was, what I was seeking to understand, and why.

Within my facilitation practice, I was careful to address the authenticity of ethnodramatic representation. Richardson (1993, 1994) suggests that "transgression" occurs when writing ethnography as a drama because of the ethics of representation. Richardson questions if the piece is somewhat inauthentic if the participants' narratives are presented in an "ideal-typic" way or not. Here, Richardson wonders if the ethnographer must recreate the narrative word-for-word to remain authentic, or if artistic license may be taken within the process. It is through the continual processes of participant validation that Mienczakowski (1995) addresses this transgression, and with reference to authenticity, he argues, "text can achieve vraisemblance and appear truthful" (p. 371) even when it is fictionalized. Mienczakowski (1995) believes that vraisemblance, an authentic and realistic dramatization, is one of the main goals of ethnodrama. Furthermore, it seeks "to evoke belief by representing (perceived) social realities in terms that mask the cultural influences affecting the constructors of the report" (p. 264). Ackroyd and O'Toole (2010) affirm that a central challenge is being aware that their own positions, as researchers, influence the performance, despite their intention to foreground participants' experiences. Belliveau and Lea (2016) describe "ethic/aesthetic tensions" as they suggest that "when using empathic artistic research forms like ethnodrama ... it is as important to work aesthetically as it is ethically [and] the complexity lies in the fact that both aesthetics and ethics are subjectively defined" (p. 70). As an artist and a researcher, I had an obligation to my participants and the audiences to balance artistic expression with research integrity and authenticity. Saldaña (2011) indicates that these "tensions are not anomalies but givens ... [and] the resolution is not to shy away from these matters but *how* you deal with them" (p. 40).

The participants and I came to this work with different life experiences, different access to experience of privilege and oppression, and diverse world views. Our interpretations through the processes guided our artistic choices which informed aesthetics and representation. It was vital that the participant validation process addressed these tensions so that we could collaborate on what was put into the script or left out, what was fictionalized, how much verbatim text was adjusted, how composite characters were developed, and so forth. As the facilitator, I needed to navigate the interests of the participants, of the research, and the audience, as these informed artistic choices throughout.

The ethics of representation is a tension in research-based theatre (Saldaña 2011). Saldaña (2011) offers advice on how to navigate these tensions when he states, "rather than needlessly navel gaze about ... whether you are or aren't representing your participants fairly and ethically, collaborate instead with your participants on how it can best be done" (p. 39). When facilitating this type of research, it is imperative to address issues of representation by collaborating with participants from the beginning of the inqueery.

One of the concerns in retelling negative outcomes, such as incidents of homo/bi/transphobia, is that they can possibly trigger and re-traumatize someone. Regarding how theatre can navigate possible trauma, Salverson (1996) questions "what it means to speak and listen to difficult histories" (p. 183), and for whom. Questioning the different narratives that were presented, how they could be understood, who the intended audience was, what the expectations were, and how the existence of trauma might affect the reception of the performance, were all important considerations within my facilitation processes. For example, in one of the interviews a participant shared a graphic account of a time when they were physically assaulted, and the hate speech that was used during the assault. This story left us feeling unsettled. For the ethnodrama, the participants felt that it was important to tell this story to the audience, but not to re-enact it. In this case, the participant indicated that it was important that audiences know about the perpetuation of gender-based and homophobic violence, but that it had to be weighed against reproducing violence on stage. Through a dialogical process, we decided that there would not be any physical depiction of violence on stage, but that the story would still be told. Balancing, aesthetic, research, and participant agency was important in coming to a consensus. Attention to aesthetic distance was also important in this process to mitigate any risk to the audience as it includes a "protective function" so that the audience could observe and participate without being vicariously traumatized (Jackson, 2007, p. 140). The dialogical nature of ethnodrama facilitated opportunities to explore potentially traumatic spaces and address these important questions with the participants.

Ethnodrama can have "strong influences and affects [sic] on audience members, each one with a particular set of background experiences and values, attitudes, and beliefs" (Saldaña, 2011, p. 42). Saldaña (2011) asks, "what is our ethical responsibility toward our audiences?" (p. 43). I felt that it was my ethical responsibility to inform the audience about what they were about to see, and to caution them about possible triggers. At the beginning of the performance, I described the process of creating the ethnodrama. I warned the audience about the homophobic terms that were included in the ethnodrama, and that an experience about physical violence would also be shared. I believe my responsibility in ethically facilitating the performance ended there, "for I cannot control or monitor what every single audience member will think and feel during the performance" (Saldaña, 2011, p. 43).

Saldaña (2011) proposes one principle to resolve this conundrum of ethical representation and audiencing: "participants first, playwrights second, and audiences third" (pp. 42–43). Within my ethical facilitation practice, my first responsibility

Ethnodramatic Inqueery   **215**

was to the participants, their experiences, and their performance. My second responsibility was to maintain my own integrity as an artist-researcher. Lastly, I felt responsible to the audience. Without the audience there would be no ethno-theatre, no post-performance dialogue, queer conscientization, or the possibility of enacting change through the enthodrama.

One uncertainty I had about moving forward with the performance was the fact that the participant-actors did not have all their lines memorized. As O'Toole (2006) attests, "it is natural that we should try to manage our research 'elegantly' and aesthetically" (158). I had produced many plays as a high school teacher, and I always strive for my version of perfection. I felt that not having the script memorized was taking something away from the performance, and I was concerned if we were going to perform in front of an audience in a few weeks' time. Saldaña (2011), recommends a reader's theatre style performance with "binders containing the script in the actors' hands [and] if this is the case, directors should compensate for fewer hand properties with more whole-body movements throughout the performance" (137). I had to decide to postpone or be comfortable with a reader's theatre style performance. I was concerned that the performance would not live up to what I had envisioned, and I did not want to do disservice to the youth who had contributed so many countless hours to the whole process. I worried about how the audience would respond to this choice, and that the audience would pay more attention to the fact the participant actors were holding their scripts in hand during the performance, rather than to their actual words.

I asked participants about their thoughts, and one stated that my concern about adapting to a reader's theatre type performance "… has nothing to do with it. It's a queer play. Why are you worried about applying traditional norms and beliefs about theatre and aesthetics on this?" The actors all responded that they were comfortable—and even relieved—to be performing with the scripts in hand. These confirmations made my decision that a script would not take away from the value of the work.

Throughout this rehearsal process I had to negotiate my own multiple roles again. As an artist, I sought perfection. As a director, I was forward with what I wanted on stage. As an educator and researcher, I was more diplomatic and open to discovery, and as an activist, I wanted to ensure the message was heard loud and clear. I knew the first performance would be a practice run, and what really mattered was the final public show. It is one thing to write a research report and put it out there for an academic audience. It is something different to prepare an ethnodrama and then perform it to a public audience and then open the stage for discussion. I learned that there was something to be said about my vulnerability as a researcher through this process. Ethnodrama married my roles as artist and director and as researcher, and they were all up for scrutiny.

Performances

The first presentation was for a small, invited audience, which allowed the actors a chance to become familiar with performing for an audience before we presented to a larger group of strangers. The second performance was at an annual provincial GSA conference. The conference was attended by 2SLGBTQ+ students, educators, professionals, and allies from across the province. While we followed the same process for both performances, the second performance started off in a bit of a frenzy—one of the participant-actors was an hour late. With ten minutes to go before our presentation time, I was worried that we would be short one performer. I asked one of the participants who held the role of co-writer and co-creator, if she would consider taking on the acting role, as she was so familiar with the script, but she politely declined saying, "acting is really not my thing." One of the other participant-actors offered to ask a friend of theirs, a conference attendee, if they would consider reading the lines at the last minute. Faced with this uncertainty, I debated if I should take on the role or if this volunteer would suffice. I opted to remain out of the performance as it was important that the youth had the voice and agency in this performance. The optics of being the researcher, co-writer and then performer did not sit well with me. Fortunately, as we were about to enter our presentation space, the late participant-actor arrived.

Given that the second performance was at a high school, I assumed that we would be performing in a classroom. I was anticipating rows of desks, so I decided that we would assume that the characters were barging into a classroom. Unfortunately, the room was used by other conference presenters in the prior time slot, so we had only a few moments to setup before our time to begin and I was faced with a second dilemma. We were to perform in a science lab, with big square-shaped lab worktables secured to the floor and stools all around. Since the second performance also had a larger audience, this also reduced the amount of space in the room left to move about. The science lab minimized the participant-actors' capacity to be able to move around the space as freely as they had in rehearsal and for the first performance. For the most part, they were stuck in between workbenches and stools. Saldaña (2011) acknowledges this type of venue limitation as "ethnodramatic performances at conference most often occur in whatever room has been assigned for the session by the conference organizers" (p. 134). This less-than-ideal performance space was another example of needing to adapt my expectations of the performance.

Enthnodramatic Inqueery and Aesthetics

Saldaña (2011) describes the responsibility of ethnographic performances is to entertain ideas and entertain spectators by "creat[ing] an entertainingly informative experience for an audience, one that is aesthetically sound, intellectually rich, and emotionally evocative" (Saldaña, 2005, p. 14). An ethnodrama is successful in so far as the performers feel that their story has been told and audiences offer a response. Saldaña (2011) purposefully avoids providing a definitive argument about ethnotheatrical aesthetics. I reflect on Saldaña's assertion that "an ethnotheatre aesthetic emerges from the theatre artists' creative approaches to stage productions of natural social life" (p. 204). While the performance adhered to real stories based on real experiences, they were not depicted in a stereotypical performance about school—there were no desks, or lockers, the actors did not wear backpacks, we did not have a school bell, and there was no teacher character. The intention was to keep the audience engaged throughout the entire piece, and this was done through chanting, calls to action, and breaking down the fourth wall. Other elements that we engaged in the production included: not following a singular chronological linearity and moving the performance in amongst the audience. Honouring the participants' stories did "not paralyze [me] from thinking about [the] research study's staging potential" (p. 207). As Saldaña pointedly states, "ethnodramas are ... essentialized fieldwork reformatted in performative data displays" (p. 206). The nuances between truth and truthfulness within the narrative presented are central to ethnodrama (Saldaña, 2011). One of the guiding principles in this ethnodramatic inqueery was participant validation to maintaining integrity to the truth and honouring the voices of the 2SLGBTQ+ participants at every phase of the process. Another guiding principle was to maximize the amount of verbatim text included in the script, while not losing sight of our perspectives and the artistic choices that informed the script and performance. Even though most of the text within this ethnodramatic inqueery was verbatim, there was some room to fictionalize, omit, and enhance, if collaborative participant validation occurred.

To find a right balance between research and art, I employed "dramaturgical coding" (Miles et al., 2014, p. 76; Saldaña, 2013, p. 123), by employing the language of theatre to qualitative data to begin "thinking theatrically" (Saldaña, 2015, p. 130). Thinking theatrically is "not just about creating a written script out of your research but imagining it realized as performance" (p. 130). The goal of this ethnodramatic inqueery was always to perform in front of a live audience, and the magic of theatre began to take shape in the script writing phase as scenes and characters started to materialize out of the interviews, until it finally came to life in front of the audience. Finally, Saldaña's (2011) last assertion on an ethnotheatre aesthetic is that it "emerges from theatre artists' production and publication of research and creative activity in the genre to advance the field and to encourage dialogue among its practitioners" (211). I certainly aspired to move the field forward by merging queer theory with ethnodrama and articulating an ethnodramatic inqueery.

This ethnodramatic inqueery aesthetically engaged audiences in a live performance and in a post-performance discussion about the lived realities and experiences of 2SLGBTQ+ youth. Through the discussion and the responses to the questionnaire the audience indicated that they had become aware of the issues that 2SLGBTQ+ students experienced in school. While all the audience members worked with 2SLGBTQ+ individuals, most identified that the ethnodramatic inqueery was a powerful call to action based on the new information it offered.

Based on the post-performance data, ethnodramatic inqueery was an engaging research method that presented data creatively, effectively, and with a visceral impact. Unlike traditional forms of research, the performance caught the attention of the audience, and they felt empowered and motivated to begin conversations and make changes in their own classrooms and GSAs. The audiences indicated that it was essential to unpack the layers of school culture—and its relations to heteronormativity and cisnormativity—to create more inclusive schools. In reference to policy implications, this queer ethnodrama identified that safety and inclusion must be defined in ways that significantly impact school culture in general, not just defined by programs and procedures that are followed in response to bullying and harassment. The audience voiced a desire for this ethnodramatic inqueery to be shared at other venues, so that other educators could learn about the lived experiences of 2SLGBTQ+ youth so that they too could engage in praxis by querying and reflecting on their contexts and their schools. Raising queer conscientization through ethnodramatic inqueery is realized by a combination of two factors. The first, it holds up a critical mirror for participants to see themselves in what is typically a hetero/cisnormative world. Of equal importance, ethnodramatic inqueery opens a window for others to witness queer lives and realities and the accompanying oppression of living in a straight world. These two factors fostered voice and acknowledged the agency of both 2SLGBTQ+ youth and the audience.

Impact of Ethnodramatic Inqueery

The ethnodramatic inqueery found that based on the lived experiences of the participants, heteronormative and cisnormative school structures constitute serious and direct threats to participants' queer realities and identities. I understand Grace's (2015) statement that "it is the hetero-patriarchy itself that is to blame, inculcating heterosexism, sexism, genderism, and homo/bi/transphobia as everyday dangers for [sexual and gender minority] youth" (p. 22). These negative systemic forces fuel HBT oppression in various forms. This was evidenced throughout the script with a protest, chanting, and nine calls to action, whereby the actors exposed the nature of oppression for the bystanders/rally attendees (i.e., audiences for our performances) and demanded change. It became evident that a queer ethnodrama can be an effective pedagogical tool to disrupt heteropatriarchy entrenched in schools. This ethnodramatic inqueery aesthetically engaged audiences in a live performance and in a post-performance discussion about the lived realities and experiences of 2SLGBTQ+ youth. Through the discussion and in responses to a questionnaire, the audience indicated that they had become aware of issues that 2SLGBTQ+ students experienced in school. Grace (2015) indicated "the way forward begins with institutional knowledge building, understanding, and transformation that abet youth development and their transformation through recognizing, respecting, and accommodating their personal differences" (p. 22). Heteronormative and cisnormative oppression is traditionally silenced in discourse, and this performance empowered the audiences, comprised mostly of educators, to explore and challenge hegemonic normativity that includes power and privilege and to consider their complicity in what are perceived as normative sexual and gender identities. Our performance empowered the audiences, comprised mostly of educators and allied professionals, to explore and challenge hegemonic normativity that includes power and privilege and to consider their complicity in what are perceived as normative sexual and gender identities in school and social structures. Additional themes that emerged for the audience were the following:

- Ethnodrama is a powerful vehicle that can raise issues that lie beneath the surface in an engaging manner.
- Ethnodrama has the ability to maintain authenticity of real-life issues that are relevant to youth by giving the participants voice and agency.
- Ethnodrama has the capacity to cause a visceral experience that asks the audience to reflect on their understanding of the issues, which in turn, can lead to conversations about actions that need to occur to move issues forward.

What I have learned through the process of ethnodramatic inqueery is that for the audience, the participants, and myself, it is the unique stories that will live in our memories, not statistics. Being moved by the participants' stories encourage school-based change. Ethnodramatic inqueery as a pedagogy reinforces this point, as it holds the potential for participants and audience members to locate themselves in the world to witness themselves and others. In so doing, they can begin to see their role and the role of others in oppressive systems. Ethnodramatic inqueery is a powerful pedagogical tool that can disrupt, destabilize, and deconstruct heteronormative and cisnormative school culture and policies, and the normalizing practices of the hidden curriculum, teaching, and learning. This queer method unearths the contributing hetero/cisnormative forces in school that lead to the continued oppression of sexual and gender minority youth.

References

Ackroyd, J., & O'Toole, J. (2010). *Performing research: Tensions, triumphs and trade-offs of ethnodrama*. Trentham Books.
Belliveau, G., & Lea, G. W. (2016). *Research-based theatre: An artistic methodology*. Intellect.
Binnie, J. (2007). Sexuality, the erotic and geography: Epistemology, methodology and pedagogy. In K. Browne, J. Lim, & G. Brown (Eds.), *Geographies of sexualities: Theories, practices and politics* (pp. 29–38). Ashgate.
Conrad, D. (2003). Unearthing personal history: Autoethnography & artifacts inform research on youth risk-taking. *The Journal of Social Theory in Art Education, 23*, 44–58. https://sites.ualberta.ca/~dhconrad/PDFs/UnearthingPersonalHistory.pdf
Crenshaw, K. (1993). Mapping the margins: Intersectionality, identity politics and violence against women of color. *Stanford Law Review, 43*, 1241–1299. https://doi.org/10.2307/1229039
Freire, P. (1990). *Pedagogy of the oppressed* (M. B. Ramos, Trans.). Continuum Publishing Corp. (Original work published in 1970).

Gorman-Murray, A., Johnston, L., & Waitt, G. (2010). Queer(ing) communications in research relationships: A conversation about subjectivities, methodologies and ethics. In K. Browne, & C. Nash (Eds.), *Queer methods and methodologies: Intersecting queer theories and social science research* (pp. 97–112). Ashgate.

Grace, A. P. (2015). *Growing into resilience: Sexual and gender minority youth in Canada (Part I)*. University of Toronto Press.

Grace, A. P. & Wells, K. (2015). *Growing into resilience: Sexual and gender minority youth in Canada (Part II)*. University of Toronto Press.

Hackford-Peer, K. (2019) "That Wasn't Very Free Thinker": Queer Critical Pedagogy in the Early Grades. In C. Mayo, & N. M. Rodriquez (Eds.). *Queer pedagogies: Theory, praxis, politics* (pp. 75–92). Springer. https://doi.org/10.1007/978-3-030-27066-7_6

Halperin, D. M. (1995). *Saint Foucault: Towards a gay hagiography*. Oxford University Press.

Hill Collins, P. (2000). *Black feminist thought: Knowledge, consciousness, and the politics of empowerment*. (Revised 10th ed.). Routledge.

Jackson, A. (2007). *Theatre, education and the making of meanings: Art or instrument?* Manchester University Press.

Meyer, E. J. (2019) Ending bullying and harassment: The case for a queer pedagogy. In C. Mayo, & N. M. Rodriquez (Eds.). *Queer pedagogies: Theory, praxis, politics* (pp. 41–58). Springer. https://doi.org/10.1007/978-3-030-27066-7_4

Mienczakowski, J. (1995). *The application of critical ethno-drama to health settings* [Unpublished doctoral dissertation]. Griffith University.

Miles, M., Huberman, M., & Saldaña, J. (2014). *Qualitative data analysis: A methods sourcebook* (3rd ed.). Sage.

Muñoz, L. (2010). Brown, queer and gendered: Queering the Latina/o 'street-scapes' in Los Angeles. In K. Browne, & C. Nash (Eds.), *Queer methods and methodologies: Intersecting queer theories and social science research* (pp. 56–67). Ashgate.

O'Toole, J. (2006). *Doing drama research: Stepping into enquiry in drama, theatre and education*. Drama Australia.

Rahman, M. (2010). Queer as intersectionality: Theorizing gay Muslim identities. *Sociology, 44*(5), 944–961. https://doi.org/10.1177/0038038510375733

Richardson, L. (1993). Poetics, dramatics, and transgressive validity: The case of the skipped line. *The Sociological Quarterly, 34*(4), 695–710. https://doi.org/10.1111/j.1533-8525.1993.tb00113.x

Richardson, L. (1994). Nine poems: Marriage and the family. *Journal of Contemporary Ethnography, 23*(1), 3–13. https://doi.org/10.1177/089124194023001001

Rooke, A. (2010). Queer in the field: On emotions, temporality and performativity in ethnography. In K. Browne, & C. Nash (Eds.), *Queer methods and methodologies: Intersecting queer theories and social science research* (pp. 25–39). Ashgate.

Saldaña, J. (Ed.) (2005). *Ethnodrama: An anthology of reality theatre*. Altamira Press.

Saldaña, J. (2011). *Ethnotheatre: Research from page to stage*. Left Coast Press.

Saldaña, J. (2013). *The coding manual for qualitative researchers* (2nd ed.). Sage.

Saldaña, J. (2015). *Thinking qualitatively: Methods of mind*. Sage.

Salverson, J. (1996). Performing emergency: Witnessing, popular theatre, and the lie of the literal. *Theatre Topics, 6*(2), 181–191. https://doi.org/10.1353/tt.1997.0012

Sullivan, N. (2003). *A critical introduction to queer theory*. New York University Press.

14

ROUND AND ROUND THE CAROUSEL PAPERS

Facilitating a Visual Interactive Dialogue with Young People

Catherine Vanner, Yasmeen Shahzadeh, Allison Holloway, Claudia Mitchell and Jennifer Altenberg

One evening in June 2019, in a kitchen in Treaty 6[1] Traditional Métis Territory, Jennifer Altenberg, a Michif teacher and community scholar living in Treaty 6, and Catherine Vanner, a white settler researcher visiting Treaty 6, finalized the details of the participatory workshop taking place the following day with adolescent girls connected to the Young Indigenous Women's Utopia (YIWU). We needed a meaningful activity to open the workshop's research component. Drawing on her background as an educator and community organizer, Jennifer proposed the carousel paper method. Carousel papers are a cooperative learning strategy that strengthens student engagement by allowing them to participate more actively in discussion and knowledge production (Hunter et al., 2018).

This chapter describes the carousel paper as data collection method used in the *Time to Teach about Gender-Based Violence in Canada* (hereafter *Time to Teach*) project. We seek to understand how secondary school teachers can enhance the critical consciousness of Canadian youth about gender-based violence (GBV) issues, through student and teacher narratives. The overarching research questions guiding the student workshops were: How do young people learn about GBV in schools? How would they *like to* learn about GBV in schools? Carousel papers were used in three participatory workshops with secondary school students in Saskatoon on Treaty 6 Territory, the traditional homeland of the Métis people, in Halifax on the ancestral unceded territory of the Mi'kmaq people, and in Ottawa on the traditional unceded territory of the Algonquin Anishinaabe people. We identify carousel papers as an effective mechanism for engaging young people in participatory research, as they foster a space for visual interactions between participants, laying the groundwork for rich discussions.

Research Team Positionality

We reflect diverse perspectives and life experiences, as well as differing relationships to this project. The project was initiated by Catherine as her postdoctoral research, under Claudia's supervision. Claudia is a white queer settler and professor at McGill University—located on unceded Kanien'keha:ka lands in Tiohtia:ke/Montreal, Quebec. A grant to study the project's methodological approach enabled us to hire two research assistants: Allison Holloway and Yasmeen Shahzadeh. Allison identifies as a white able-bodied settler Canadian woman. Yasmeen identifies as a cisgender woman, born and raised in Jordan. During data collection, Yasmeen and Allie were graduate students at McGill.

Jennifer and Catherine's pre-workshop brainstorming initiated the carousel papers for the first workshop. Had the methodology been developed without Jennifer's contributions, the team likely would not have thought to use carousel papers. The analytical process and subsequent workshops were driven primarily by Catherine, Allie, and Yasmeen with guidance from Claudia. The following thus reflects the evolution of the method as it encountered different scholars.

Participatory Research with Young People

Participatory research is a combination of research, education, and action that seeks to empower marginalized voices, democratize research, and challenge power dynamics between researchers and participants (Hall, 1992) by inviting participants to become more involved in knowledge creation and mobilization. Increasingly, researchers advocate for including children and youth within collaborative research where they can contribute to data collection, analysis, and knowledge dissemination (Liebenberg et al., 2020). Youth Participatory Action Research (YPAR) "aims to engage youth in as many aspects of the research process as possible ... [giving them] more voice, choice, and power," (Bozlak & Kelley, 2015, p. 72). YPAR makes research more engaging for participants and enhances researchers' ability to identify young people's needs (Foster-Fishman et al., 2010), to dismantle social injustices and hierarchies within research and academia (Bozlak & Kelley, 2015), and to engage youth in change-oriented research focusing on social justice and political activism (Wright, 2020).

YPAR can foster "intergenerational partnerships between youth and adults" that are valuable for research, advocacy, and action (Wright, 2020, p. 35). Flicker et al. (2014) describe collaborative approaches, especially those involving art, "in which the contents of the research (product) and its interpretation (process) belong to the participant and his or her community" (p. 28). Cahill stresses that research with young people should encompass collective data collection *and* analysis as "one of the most critical contributions of a PAR process" (2007, p. 308). But how to engage young participants remains elusive as—like data collection—it should use engaging, flexible, and youth-oriented processes (Liebenberg et al., 2020).

Participatory Visual Methodologies

Many YPAR approaches utilize Participatory Visual Methodologies (PVM), defined as "methods that actively engage participants in creating and analyzing visual media (e.g., photography, video, or drawings) as part of the research process" (MacEntee & Flicker, 2018, p. 352). As a participant quoted by Flicker et al. remarked: "You talk so much you don't really remember, but if you do art you are going to remember it all" (2014, p. 23). PVM can be especially useful in researching distressing topics, which young people often struggle to speak with researchers about (MacEntee & Flicker, 2018). In a GBV study, Christensen (2019) found that photovoice helped young participants illustrate problems, enabling them to "disrupt, reorganize, activate, recover, restore, reclaim, and/or represent their perceptions and experiences so that they no longer feel trapped, victimized, imprisoned, defined by, or contained by the violence" (2019, p. 488). PVM are open-ended, enabling participants to determine the direction of the conversation more than traditional methods that are based more on researchers' questions and priorities (MacEntee & Flicker, 2018). Participant engagement in data analysis is an important means of assessing validity (Liebenberg et al., 2020), and points to the value of multimodal analysis. Jewitt (2017) describes multimodal analysis as attending to the relationship between images, texts, and other forms of expression, and the environment they are produced in. Participant involvement in data analysis—and consideration of the research's social function and context—prevents the misinterpretation of creative works.

As one of our workshops addressed education about Missing and Murdered Indigenous Women and Girls (MMIWG), we were strongly influenced by Indigenous perspectives, although we do not claim that the carousel paper method itself is inherently decolonizing. Dei (2019) describes decolonization as purposeful, intentional, and action-oriented, seeking to resist and transform all forms of exploitation and oppression derived from colonization. He writes that decolonization marks "an attempt by Indigenous and colonized bodies to take control of our own thought processes and to act in concrete ways to address colonialism, patriarchy and other forms of social oppression," (para. 2). Multiple Indigenous scholars (e.g., Coulthard, 2014; Duarte & Belarde-Lewis, 2015; Simpson, 2017; Tuck & Yang, 2012), have criticized surface-level or tokenistic movements to reconciliation by settler governments and individuals while the same bodies perpetuate colonial systems of exploitation and appropriation that oppress Indigenous peoples in new ways. These scholars instead connect decolonization to Indigenous-led cultural resurgence, political reclamation, radical activism, and the redistribution of territory and resources. The YIWU's decolonizing philosophy and practices are most closely inspired by Marie Battiste's (2013) work. YIWU often describes its work as encouraging its members to resist colonial and gender-based violence through self-love and Indigenous knowledge systems, reflecting Battiste's claim that,

[s]ome of the most important work being done by young people is found in the self-reflective narratives that help them to understand their own situation and what has held them there, and reframing what has been cast as negative into more positive ways

(2013, p. 71).

She also explains that part of the process of Indigenous Renaissance can involve a struggle of *collaborative conscientization* that invites settler Canadians to learn respectfully with Indigenous peoples about their unique knowledge and relationships, *without* appropriating that knowledge and experience.

As Indigenous communities in Canada have long had violent and damaging experiences with research (Battiste, 2013; Tuck, 2009), when engaging with Indigenous communities, it is essential for researchers—particularly non-Indigenous researchers—to ensure that the research experience and its outcomes have a positive impact on the participants and their communities. Collaboration with Indigenous leaders from the same community as the participants is critical for making research activities relevant and rewarding for Indigenous participants. Participatory action research has positive potential for Indigenous communities and participants, although this potential is dependent on the degree to which relationality, process, and content are respectful of Indigenous knowledge-building traditions and utilize a "critical reflexive lens that acknowledges the politics of representation within Indigenous research" (Kovach, 2009, p. 33). While recognizing that Indigenous knowledge systems are highly diverse and no single methodology reflects all Indigenous cultures, many Indigenous cultures share knowledge through art and storytelling (e.g., Starblanket & Hunt, 2020) that have traditionally been unwelcome in academic work (Kovach, 2009). Flicker et al. (2014) explain that Indigenous youth may engage most strongly with art that resonates with their traditional cultural practices. Considering the sensitive nature of discussions of GBV, and the high prevalence of violence against Indigenous women and girls, a visual approach, particularly when rooted in Indigenous art specific to the history of a given place, can root conversations about GBV in cultural resurgence (Wuttunee et al., 2019). We recognize the critique of scholarly and activism work that loosely uses the term decolonization as synonymous with social justice, arguing instead that decolonization must involve an active dismantling of colonial systems (Tuck & Yang, 2012). We do not assert that PVM is inherently decolonizing; of the three workshops we conducted, only the Treaty 6 workshop may be appropriate to describe in this way, as explained further below.

Carousel Papers

Large flip chart papers are set up around a room, each with a different prompt. Participants rotate in groups between different papers, spending several minutes at each. They read and respond to a different prompt on each paper and write their answers onto the paper before moving to another and building upon what others have written there and/or adding entirely new responses (Hunter et al., 2018). In English and Social Studies classrooms, carousel papers have been identified as an effective way to brainstorm, scaffold, and engage different types of learners (Yuli & Tiarina, 2013; Yusmanto et al., 2017). Carousel papers are a cooperative learning strategy that strengthen student engagement by allowing them to participate in discussion and knowledge production more actively (Hunter et al., 2018). Carousel papers can also be useful in helping students to better communicate and resolve conflicts (Randick & Gardner, 2016). Further benefits include motivating students to reflect on prior knowledge, encouraging collaborative groupwork, and facilitating movement by creating a fun and active process (Hunter et al., 2018; Yuli & Tiarina, 2013).

Using Carousel Papers in the *Time to Teach* Project

The three groups that participated in the workshops were identified by reaching out to community organizers known to do social justice-oriented work with young people. These community leaders included Jennifer as well as Morris Green, who facilitates guys groups and workshops on positive masculinity in Halifax, and Laura Riggs, who facilitated the 12th Ottawa Rangers Unit. These community leaders acted as gatekeepers (McAreavey, 2013), sharing information about the project with the participants and parents before they consented to participate. Workshops looked different in each context, but maintained a common formula: introduce the project's objectives, team, and workshop agenda, a presentation covering key GBV concepts, an art-based activity to help process the information received, the carousel paper activities, a focus group during which participants reviewed and discussed the carousel papers with the researcher(s), cellphilms—short videos recorded using basic technology (MacEntee, Burkholder, & Schwab-Cartas, 2016)—that recorded messages for teachers, and a screening of the cellphilms. Our ethical protocol emphasized that our discussion focused on participants' experiences *learning about* GBV, and not their experiences with GBV itself, in order to minimize disclosures. We did stipulate that an exception to our confidentiality clause in our consent form was disclosures of abuse, and that, were such a disclosure to arise, a path forward that was in the best interests of the participants would be determined with the group's leader (Jennifer, Morris, or Laura). The intent of this plan was that, if abuse was disclosed, the best way of addressing it would be determined with the group leader, who was trusted by the participants and intimately connected to their communities. While participants described some experiences of sexual harassment and discrimination in school, there were no disclosures that were deemed necessary to consider reporting. The following describes the use of carousel papers in each workshop, followed by a description of the analytical protocol for the data derived from all the workshops.

YIWU Workshop

The first workshop took place over two weekends in June 2019 with a group of 10 Indigenous girls ages 11–17 in Treaty 6. Half the participants were members of YIWU and each brought a friend who was not a member. There were three objectives: to bring the YIWU members together again; to enhance YIWU members' knowledge about GBV and methods of resistance to it; and to leverage the voices of Indigenous girls about teaching practices surrounding GBV as a means of decentring Western hegemonic ways of knowing in relation to this subject. It was essential that the workshop be centred on Indigenous worldviews within lasting, localized systems of support. The workshop was organized with the assistance of Dynelle Wolfe, then an intern with YIWU. Dynelle is from Mistawasis Neheyiwak, has two sons, and describes herself as a social worker, an advocate for change, and a determined, strong *Iskwew*. The workshop opened with the blessing of an Elder, followed by an introduction on gender, healthy relationships, colonial violence, and GBV that was led by local Indigenous community leaders. These elements were all organized by Jennifer and Dynelle. After discussing these difficult topics and the disproportionate rates at which Indigenous women and girls experience GBV, the girls undertook an art-based activity. Dynelle, who spearheaded the art project (Figure 14.1), described it as tying,

> together art, expression, culture and personal messages for any other person that may have been subjected to gender-based violence … [It] consisted of a large piece of deer hide, a large branch to hang the hide from, and ribbons chosen by each member of YIWU. Personal handprints and a written message from YIWU were added to the hide to mark as a statement to others: that their voices will no longer go unheard, they are not alone, and the unacceptable actions of GBV will no longer be tolerated…

We believe that this workshop illustrated the decolonizing potential of the carousel method, not because of the nature of the facilitation, but because of the Indigenous-led context in which it was implemented, and that it was used to respond to the objectives of the YIWU leaders and participants. To reflect YIWU's decolonizing objectives, many parts of the workshop were designed and facilitated entirely by the YIWU leaders and the Indigenous guests they invited to participate. The methods we used were designed to respond to the YIWU's objectives for building self-love and Indigenous knowledge to enhance their members' ability to challenge colonial and gender-based violence. The workshop also provided funding for girls to gather and to experiment. The workshop sought to strengthen the YIWU community, including through the paid participation of local Indigenous leaders to teach about GBV within Indigenous knowledge frameworks and unpack the intersections of colonial and gender-based violence. This collaboration was possible due to the trusting relationship that had been established between Jennifer and Catherine through pervious work

FIGURE 14.1 Artwork created in YIWU workshop.

together outside of the *Time to Teach* project, which also had objectives of leveraging the voices of YIWU members to disrupt, unsettle, and dismantle the status quo of colonial and patriarchal institutions (YIWU et al., 2021).

During the carousel paper activities, participants were asked to describe how they learned about GBV in and out of school. Then, we asked how they would like to learn about GBV in schools, by addressing four themes: spiritual, intellectual, physical, and emotional. In the Treaty 6 workshop carousel papers, participants demonstrated deep engagement with the prompts,[2] explicitly building on each other's points while also diverting to share their own experiences and suggestions. They referenced their lived experiences as Indigenous young women and their experience of the violence directed at them by white people, including teachers, for example through the written comment that Indigenous youth know that "there is a 'target' on our people." They used images, such as thumbs up signs and checkmarks, to indicate their agreement and solidarity with each other, as seen in Figure 14.2.

All 12 participants contributed to the carousel papers, but only four opted to participate in an audio-recorded focus group. That many participants opted out of the focus group demonstrates the ability of the carousel papers to provide a forum for participants who want to share their perspectives within the research but may not want to be audio-recorded. The focus group enabled Catherine to ask participants to clarify their meaning and build upon each other's analysis.

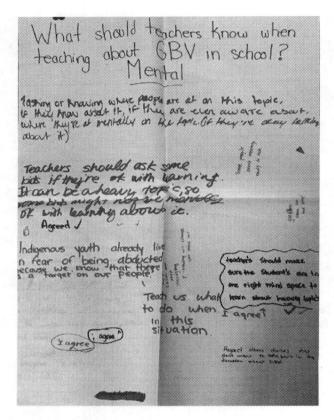

FIGURE 14.2 A YIWU carousel paper.

For example, they reflected upon how some participants wrote that they had learned about MMIWG as a form of GBV in school, without addressing the connections to colonial and gender-based violence:

PARTICIPANT 1: I was taught about situations involving gender-based violence without knowing that it was gender-based violence like [MMIWG]… I feel like the teachers don't want to go right out and say like "oh that's gender-based violence.' Like they just teach you about it without telling you that that's what it is.

PARTICIPANT 2: Yeah, it's like going to a doctor all your life and them not really telling you what's wrong with you… they're just like telling you the symptoms but not telling you like, 'You have this disorder, you have this certain type of disease.'

The carousel papers provided the freedom for participants to take the questions in directions driven by their experiences, while the focus group provided an important form of data verification and a means of engaging participants directly in initial analysis.

Adaptations

Following analysis of the YIWU data and reflections on the workshop between Catherine and Jennifer, the team planned the next workshops and considered what would remain and what might change. A major difference with the subsequent workshops was that they did not involve Indigenous participants or organizers, nor did they have the same decolonizing focus, although they did discuss the disproportionate rates of GBV towards racialized and Indigenous women and girls in Canada. As the Indigenous knowledge at the first workshop was taught by local Indigenous leaders, we did not think it would be appropriate to try to replicate these teachings without Indigenous facilitators. Instead, we worked with local leaders attached to these groups to identify ways of introducing knowledge and perspectives about GBV that would be most relevant to the participants.

We maintained the same steps for the carousel papers that had worked well in the YIWU workshop. After finding that participants seemed to struggle with classifying how teachers should teach about GBV, we reflected on how to simplify what we were asking. We hoped participants would suggest ways in which teachers could address the topic from a content perspective, from a pedagogical perspective, and from a student well-being perspective. Thus, we kept the initial prompt, "What do you think your teachers should know when teaching about GBV?" and created sub-questions on three different carousel papers that read: "What should I learn about?" (content); "How should teachers approach it?" (pedagogy); and "What should teachers consider in terms of student well-being?" (well-being). A further adaptation was to have participants choose one coloured marker for the activity's duration. By keeping the same marker, we could follow a participant's thought process throughout while maintaining a degree of anonymity.

Rangers Workshop

The second workshop was organized in coordination with the Ottawa Rangers 12th Unit (a Girl Guides program) for girls ages 15–17. Five girls were members of the unit but four chose to participate. Catherine had not worked with the Rangers group before and needed to build trust with the group. The community leader agreed to the introductory portion of the workshop, involving the overview of key concepts followed by a collage as the art-based activity to speak back to GBV, before asking the girls and their parents to decide whether to proceed with the research. This enabled the Rangers to establish a comfort level with the team and their objectives before agreeing to participate further in the research. We met the Rangers three times, beginning in November 2019, while the research activities took place in early March 2020. The majority of the group was white and one participant was of South Asian descent. Race did not appear to be a subject that the group discussed.

The Ottawa group's carousel papers reflect a distinct dynamic as participants had varying levels of knowledge about GBV. This dynamic is illustrated

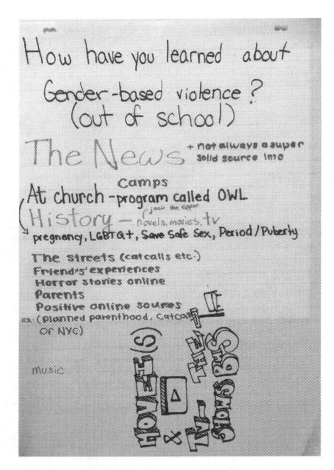

FIGURE 14.3 A Rangers workshop carousel paper.

in Figure 14.3, where one participant comments on another's statement that she learned about GBV from the news, observing that the news is "not always a super solid source."

Discrepancies between the participants' critical thinking is also evident in the differences between comments about what they wanted to learn: all wanted to learn about prevention, but one participant associated GBV prevention with things that girls can do to protect themselves, "like avoiding dark alleys," while others called for education "directed toward boys as well" and about "the history of it within the legal systems (the failure of it)," demonstrating critical thinking about how GBV is often addressed. Here, there is peer conversation and dialogue on the page without identifying who is, enabling difficult dialogues in a way that may minimize embarrassment that could have arisen should the same dialogue have occurred aloud. The activity also prompts participants to comment, whereas a focus group may have been dominated by the participants who were more familiar with GBV issues. By prompting responses from all participants in this semi-private space, the carousel papers highlight differences, while providing a forum in which peers can learn from each other. Finally, in both the Treaty 6 workshop and the Ottawa workshop, the participants reflected not only on times that they had learned about GBV in school, but also times that they had experienced GBV in schools. The following is from the Ottawa workshop:

CATHERINE: I find this really interesting, "harassment in the halls," so you're actually experiencing [GBV] in schools in some cases…?
PARTICIPANT 1: Yeah.
CATHERINE: And how does that get taken up or responded to?
PARTICIPANT 1: … there's been maybe two or three assemblies about it in our school but, the thing is, it doesn't really prevent it from happening… it'll happen to most girls and when it's happened two or three times you just kind of learn to ignore it and live with it, in a way? I know that sounds kind of bleak…And then they get mad at you because you're making a big deal…
CATHERINE: Who gets mad at you?
PARTICIPANT 1: Like the people that are doing it and the administration just kind of [sigh].
PARTICIPANT 2: They'd say like "Oh it's just a joke". It sucks, it's not funny, it's not a joke. A lot of the times I've noticed like some of my friends come forward about it and nothing's happened.

Because they first worked independently with the written prompts, participants interpreted the question in ways that aligned with their experiences but were unanticipated by the researchers, creating discussions that may not otherwise have emerged.

Guys Group Workshop

The third workshop occurred in December 2019 over two weekday mornings with a group of seven African Nova Scotian boys, aged 15–17, in Halifax. Race and gender were significant backdrops for the conversation about GBV education. Black masculinity in North America has been constructed to be associated with violence, aggression, and hypersexuality (Bowleg et al., 2017). Historically, these constructions were based on claims of biological difference and more recently have been based on descriptions of Black culture; in both iterations, they have been a means by which dominant white male identity has been naturalized as superior (Ferber, 2007). Halifax is a city characterized by a long history of racial segregation and discrimination towards Black people, as well as an illustrious legacy of Black activism, leadership, and community dating back centuries (Pachai & Bishop, 2006).

The workshop was organized by Catherine, Allie, and Yasmeen with input from the community leader and a former guys' group member. Catherine and Allie travelled to Halifax to lead the workshop together. The participants attended the same nearby high school and joined the workshop during school hours with their principal's encouragement. We worked with the community organizers to develop a program and an art-based activity that would be engaging for the participants, inviting them to develop TikTok videos that spoke back to GBV, and adapting the Ottawa workshop's introductory presentation to use more examples oriented towards men/boys, including examples of Black men (Pharrell Williams and Terry Crews) challenging GBV norms and behaviours. The participants split into smaller groups for the carousel papers and the same prompts were used as in the Ottawa workshop. All the groups proceeded smoothly through the prompts and participated in subsequent focus group discussions. In this group's workshop, a sense of camaraderie emerged from shared experiences acquired through their guys group, yet participants also spoke to their experiences learning about GBV issues individually (See Figure 14.4).

In a subsequent focus group discussion, we asked if the person who had referenced learning from their mom would share more about that and there was silence, showing that the participant was comfortable disclosing this information in the semi-anonymous carousel paper but not to speak about it aloud in the

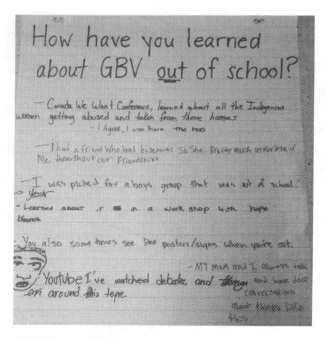

FIGURE 14.4 A Halifax workshop carousel paper.

group. By contrast, there were some topics that generated enthusiastic discussion, for example, the value of a caring teacher:

PARTICIPANT 1: ...if you have that like mother figure teacher teaching stuff like this, you know like that it's coming from like deep down place and she actually cares for the students because she's showing her students that she cares for them... I know when certain teachers speak I listen better than others.
CATHERINE: What do the teachers you listen to do? You talked about they show that they care?
PARTICIPANT 1: Oh, like they're engaging.
PARTICIPANT 2: Yeah, and they ask you how you're doing in general at home, at school, how's your grades going, they don't just care about this class they care about how you're doing until later.
PARTICIPANT 3: Yeah, they wanna know about your life. They wanna know about your sports, about stuff like that. It's just good to have, like, it's pretty much like a friendship, just someone to talk to.

In both the Guys Group and the YIWU workshops, participants sometimes wrote informally using slang, like writing "Yessir" to indicate agreement, that they did not use when speaking with us, and papers from all three workshops have doodles scrawled in the margins or in responses, giving them youthful vibes. In the Guys Group focus group, we asked participants whether they thought that race was a factor in their experiences and suggested that it could be problematic that the majority of teachers are white women like us (Allie and Catherine), but the participants did not respond to or expand upon these points—possibly because they did not feel comfortable discussing them with us given our race and lack of prior relationship with them—so we moved to other areas that they chose to speak with us about.

Data Analysis

Data analysis began in focus groups following the carousel papers at each site. Participants read aloud from the papers and the researchers asked verifying and follow-up questions. Such discussions allowed participants to elaborate on their points and to agree or disagree with their peers. This self-analysis process enabled participants to represent themselves and reiterate or clarify their thoughts (Cahill, 2007). After engaging the youth in a preliminary review of the data, the carousel papers and focus groups were transcribed by Allie and Yasmeen. To analyse these multimodal papers, the research team documented not only the comments but also the interactions between them. This process was challenging, given the papers' non-linear nature and the importance of reflecting the energy and interactions between the participants that the papers captured (Jewitt, 2017). The team developed a table with four columns to transcribe each paper. The first column summarized the text; the second summarized the ways participants responded to

234 Catherine Vanner et al.

Linear text	Reactions / Comments	Observations (process, flow, interactions, narrative, interpretation)	Illustrative screen shots (Shift+Command+4)
teacher's should give a warning or a warning in general	+ → + → + → (pointing from this comment to three other comments)	This comment seemed to generate a lot of interest. There are four separate reactions to this comment: two arrows connecting previous comments to this comment, a checkmark that both validates and gives agreement to the original writer, and a writer who emphatically wrote 'I agree!' This comment provoked a strong reaction from the group who saw similarities in this comment and their own understanding of the issues explored.	

FIGURE 14.5 Analytical table.

other comments through text and drawings; the third described the researcher's observations on the process, flow, interactions, and main message; and the fourth included a screenshot to display each comment and its reactions (See Figure 14.5).

We prepared one table for each paper and, at the end, the researcher wrote a memo to reflect the main themes emerging from each paper. We offer Allie's example, describing the Treaty 6 workshop paper depicted in Figure 14.2:

> This poster, at first glance, looks big and loud. Comments are generally written in large writing, almost every inch of the poster is filled, and although it starts off structured, as comments start building off of each other it becomes increasingly more chaotic. This poster seems to be dominated by a single writer who builds upon her initial comments and takes up ⅓ of the poster. She outlines the main themes that will come to play in the rest of the poster: the idea that teachers need to be sensitive to the students' needs while teaching about GBV, that students require a "heads up" before a teacher can launch into the subject, and that teachers themselves need to be better supported/instructed in how to approach these subjects with

their students. Although the majority of these comments are in collaboration – most agree that students should not be forced to participate, should be given the choice of participating, and should be informed ahead of time about course content – one writer, in yellow, in small writing at the center of the paper lends her voice. YES, BUT she writes. She is in agreement that young people should not be forced 'emotionally' to learn about GBV, but her understanding is that to "know about the topic" will allow a person to "call it out." She struggles with the idea of the individual's right to extricate oneself from the conversation and how she feels that knowing about GBV can help others. Her comment is quickly swallowed by others who reiterate that they, students, should decide.

The memo constitutes a second step of analysis of the paper (the first being the focus group), including the conversations among the participants on the page, attending not only to the text itself but also reflecting the social context and research environment (Jewitt, 2017).

Reflections

The carousel papers were introduced to respond to the objectives of the YIWU workshop. We continued using them because, as observed regarding their pedagogical use (Hunter et al., 2018; Yuli & Tiarina, 2013), we found that they encouraged participants to communicate knowledge and ideas in a way that seemed comfortable for them. Participants who preferred working independently had the space to do so, while others who preferred brainstorming collectively could do so during and after the activity. The papers allowed participants to engage in the research, particularly those who did not feel comfortable being audio-recorded, as demonstrated in the YIWU workshop. They further provided a vehicle for participants to share things that they would not say out loud in front of their peers and/or the researchers, as demonstrated in the Guys Group workshop, but enabled a collaborative and conversational dynamic that facilitated peer education, demonstrated in the Rangers workshop, that would not have been possible in individual interviews.

Our use of carousel papers was shaped by our team's racial and socio-economic positionalities, as well as by our relationships to research, education, and our participants. The carousel papers were initiated as a result of Jennifer's deep relationship and extensive prior work with the YIWU participants, combined with her teaching experience, which led to the design of a method that provided a means of collective reflection among participants *before* they were invited to discuss their thoughts with Catherine. That some participants decided against joining the subsequent discussion but gave permission for the carousel papers they created to be used suggests that the method provides a mechanism for participants to engage with the research without having to speak directly to outsider researchers. Switzer (2020) connects the advocacy of Indigenous communities, scholars, and activists for the refusal to participate in research (Simpson, 2014; Tuck, 2009) to young people's refusal to engage. She makes the case for non-participation as a "conceptual tool to disrupt, complicate and/or refuse hegemonic, linear theories of change" (2020, p. 3). Particularly for communities with extensive destructive research experiences, this ability to participate (or not) on their own terms is essential (Battiste, 2013). Another possible act of non-participation was observed in the decision from participants in the Guys Group workshop to decline to respond to focus group discussion questions related to their personal relationships and the influence of race on their learning experiences. We decided to continue using the carousel papers partly because the challenge of the outsider researcher(s) remained with the other groups. We were mindful of the differences between the adult, mostly white and settler academic research team and our young participants. We believe participants' deep engagement was achieved partly because the carousel papers enabled them to first connect with the prompts among themselves before discussing them with us.

We note the limitations of our methodological approach, particularly in relation to decolonization. While we are proud of lessons learned from the Treaty 6 workshop to advance the decolonizing objectives of the YIWU, we recognize the tension between those objectives and the practices of publishing about the experience for the benefit of white settler scholars. Because we were limited in time and our lack of prior relationships with the participants in the Rangers and Guys Group workshops, we did not forefront race in our discussions with these groups. Notably, in follow-up focus groups, we asked the African Nova Scotian participants of the Guys Group workshop whether race may have been a factor in shaping their experiences, but did not ask the same question in the focus group discussions in the Rangers workshop, where the majority of the participants were white. This discrepancy points to our own subconscious acceptance of hegemonic whiteness as normative and thus unlikely to shape the experiences of the Rangers participants but more likely to have been influential for the Guys Group workshop participants, although it had not been raised by the participants in either workshop. We recommend, where possible, moving towards the model taken in developing the YIWU workshop, which was built upon pre-existing partnerships that enabled trusting relationships to develop, planned for a full two days together, deeply integrated local knowledge systems, and had decolonizing and anti-racist intentionality. The carousel paper process could also be made more participatory by involving participants in research design, for example, in creating the prompts that they would then respond to. We also sought to validate the results of the more formal data analysis with the participants, but none of the groups opted to pursue this step, although they expressed gratitude for the opportunity.

Carousel papers enable young participants to speak to, support, and educate each other. The use of slang and doodles show that they are spaces that participants can make their own. While this does not remove the power dynamics created by having a mostly white research team conducting research with adolescents, including groups of Indigenous girls and African Nova Scotian boys, carousel papers decentre the researchers and provide a space for young people to engage with each other and the prompts before researchers ask follow-up questions in a conversation that participants can decline to join. Recognizing the legacy of damaging research with Indigenous people (Tuck, 2009) and a history of adult-centred research with young people (Wright, 2020), carousel papers provide a valuable method for countering some of these risks within research, while creating an active approach that leaves a written testimony of experiences, recommendations, and relationships.

Notes

1 Treaty 6 refers to the agreement signed between representatives of the British Crown and the Cree, Assiniboine, and Ojibwa peoples governing use of the lands extending across central parts of present-day Saskatchewan and Alberta (Filice, 2016).
2 The prompts for the initial workshop were: How have you learned about GBV in/out of school? What do you want your teachers to know when teaching about GBV? (Spiritual) (Intellectual) (Physical) (Emotional).

References

Battiste, M. (2013). *Decolonizing education: Nourishing the learning spirit*. UBC Press. http://ebookcentral.proquest.com/lib/mcgill/detail.action?docID=5652479

Bowleg, L., del Río-González, A.M., Holt, S.K., Pérez, C., Massie, J.S., Mandell, J.E., & Boone, C.A. (2017). Intersectional epistemologies of ignorance: How behavioral and social science research shapes what we know, think we know, and don't know about U.S. Black men's sexualities. *The Journal of Sex Research*, 54(4–5), 557–603. https://doi.org/10.1080/00224499.2017.1295300

Bozlak, C.T., & Kelley, M.A. (2015). Participatory action research with youth. In Hal A. Lawson, J. Caringi, L. Pyles, J. Jurowski, & C. Bozlak (Eds.), *Participatory action research* (pp. 67–89). Oxford University Press.

Cahill, C. (2007). Doing research with young people: Participatory research and the rituals of collective work. *Children's Geographies*, 5(3), 297–312. https://doi.org/10.1080/14733280701445895

Christensen, M.C. (2019). Using photovoice to address gender-based violence: A qualitative systematic review. *Trauma, Violence, & Abuse*, 20(4), 484–497. https://doi.org/10.1177/1524838017717746

Coulthard, G.S. (2014). *Indigenous Americas: Red skin, white masks—Rejecting the colonial politics of recognition*. University of Minnesota Press.

Dei, G.J.S. (2019). Forward. In A. Zainub (Ed.), *Decolonization and anti-colonial praxis* (pp. vii–x). Brill/Sense.

Duarte, M.E., & Belarde-Lewis, M. (2015). Imagining: Creating spaces for indigenous ontologies. *Cataloging & Classification Quarterly*, 53(5–6), 677–702.

Ferber, A. (2007). The construction of black masculinity: White supremacy now and then. *Journal of Sport & Social Issues*, 31(1), 11–24. https://doi.org/10.1177/0193723506296829

Filice, M. (2016, October 11). Treaty 6. The Canadian Encyclopedia. https://www.thecanadianencyclopedia.ca/en/article/treaty-6

Flicker, S., Yee Danforth, J., Wilson, C., Oliver, V., Larkin, J., Restoule, J.-P., Mitchell, C., Konsmo, E., Jackson, R., & Prentice, T. (2014). "Because we have really unique art": Decolonizing research with Indigenous youth using the arts. *International Journal of Indigenous Health, 10*(1), 16–34. https://doi.org/10.18357/ijih.101201513271

Foster-Fishman, P.G., Law, K.M., Lichty, L.F., & Aoun, C. (2010). Youth ReACT for social change: A method for youth participatory action research. *American Journal of Community Psychology, 46*(1), 67–83. https://doi.org/10.1007/s10464-010-9316-y

Hall, B.L. (1992). From margins to center? The development and purpose of participatory research. *The American Sociologist, 23*(4), 15–28.

Hunter, W.C., Maheady, L., Washington, C., Christopher-Allen, A., & Jasper, A.D. (2018). Effects of carousel brainstorming on student engagement and academic performance in a summer enrichment program. *Journal of Evidence-Based Practices for Schools, 17*(2), 220–244.

Jewitt, C. (2017). Multimodal discourses across the curriculum. In S.L. Thorne, & S. May (Eds.), *Language, education and technology* (pp. 31–43). Springer International Publishing. https://doi.org/10.1007/978-3-319-02237-6_4

Kovach, M. (2009). *Indigenous methodologies: Characteristics, conversations, and contexts*. University of Toronto Press, Scholarly Publishing Division. https://proxy.library.mcgill.ca/login?url=http://search.ebscohost.com/login.aspx?direct=true&db=nlebk&AN=682652&scope=site

Liebenberg, L., Jamal, A., & Ikeda, J. (2020). Extending youth voices in a participatory thematic analysis approach. *International Journal of Qualitative Methods, 19*, 1609406920934614. https://doi.org/10.1177/1609406920934614

MacEntee, K., Burkholder, C., & Schwab-Cartas, J. (Eds.). (2016). *What's a cellphilm? Integrating mobile phone technology into participatory visual research and activism*. Sense Publishers.

MacEntee, K., & Flicker, S. (2018). *Doing it*: Participatory visual methodologies and youth sexuality research. In S. Lamb, & J. Gilbert (Eds.), *The Cambridge handbook of sexual development* (1st ed., pp. 352–372). Cambridge University Press. https://doi.org/10.1017/9781108116121.019

McAreavey, R. (2013). A delicate balancing act: Negotiating with gatekeepers for ethical research when researching minority communities. *International Journal of Qualitative Methods, 12*, 113–131.

Pachai, B., & Bishop, H. (2006). *Historic Black Nova Scotia*. Nimbus Pub.

Randick, N.M., & Gardner, E. (2016). Creating connections: Using art in school counselling. In *The therapist's notebook for children and adolescents: Homework, handouts and activities for use in psychotherapy* (2nd ed.). Routledge/Taylor & Francis Group.

Simpson, A. (2014). *Mohawk interruptus: Political life across the borders of settler states*. Duke University Press.

Simpson, L.B. (2017). *As we have always done: Indigenous freedom through radical resistance*. University of Minnesota Press.

Starblanket, G., & Hunt, D. (2020). *Storying violence: Unravelling colonial narratives in the Stanley trial*. ARP Books.

Switzer, S. (2020). "People give and take a lot in order to participate in things:" Youth talk back – making a case for non-participation. *Curriculum Inquiry, 50*(2), 168–193. https://doi.org/10.1080/03626784.2020.1766341

Tuck, E. (2009). Suspending damage: A letter to communities. *Harvard Educational Review, 79*(3), 409–428.

Tuck, E., & Yang, K.W. (2012). Decolonization is not a metaphor. *Decolonization: Indigeneity, Education & Society, 1*(1), 1–40.

Wright, D.E. (2020). Imagining a more just world: Critical arts pedagogy and youth participatory action research. *International Journal of Qualitative Studies in Education, 33*(1), 32–49. https://doi.org/10.1080/09518398.2019.1678784

Wuttunee, K.D., Altenberg, J., & Flicker, S. (2019). Red ribbon skirts and cultural resurgence. *Girlhood Studies, 12*(3), 63–79. https://doi.org/10.3167/ghs.2019.120307

Young Indigenous Women's Utopia (YIWU), Moccasin, C., McNab, J., Vanner, C., Flicker, S., Altenberg, J., & Wuttunee, K. (2021). Where are all the girls and indigenous people at IGSA@ND? *Girlhood Studies, 14*(2), 97–113. https://doi-org.ledproxy2.uwindsor.ca/10.3167/ghs.2021.140208

Yuli, R.F., & Tiarina, Y. (2013). *Teaching reading comprehension by using carousel brainstorming strategy at senior high school.* [Dissertation, Universitas Negeri Padang]. Universitas Negeri Padang Repository.

Yusmanto, H., Soetjipto, B.E., & Djatmika, E.T. (2017). The application of carousel feedback and round table cooperative learning models to improve student's higher order thinking skills (HOTS) and social studies learning outcomes. *International Education Studies, 10*(10), 39. https://doi.org/10.5539/ies.v10n10p39

15

SCREENING STORIES

Methodological Considerations for Facilitating Critical Audience Engagement

Caterina Tess Kendrick, Katie MacEntee and Sarah Flicker

Introduction

The electronic backbeat of Cardi B's *Drip* plays as a viewer discretion advisory appears on the screen. Viewers are transported to a snowy streetcar while a voiceover introduces the *Celling Sex* research project.[1] In the first minute of the film, audiences learn that 15 young women who trade sex in Toronto wanted to share their experiences through a compilation of cellphilms (or videos made with cellphones). Through their voices, drawings, montages, and bodies, the viewer learns how different people define their trading practices, motivations, challenges, and strategies for harm reduction. The overarching message of the *Celling Sex* film is clear: young women who trade deserve dignity and respect.

The *Celling Sex* film was a culminating output from the community-based participatory research project led by Drs. Katie MacEntee, Ciann Wilson, and Sarah Flicker, in partnership with two community health centres, with support from Caterina Kendrick (who was Sarah's master's student at the time). The project engaged young women to share their harm reduction practices, challenge stigma, and offer peer-led advice for youth and the service providers who support them. Stigma surrounds people who trade sex, and this stigma has been shown to have detrimental impacts on health and well-being (Benoit et al., 2018; Kendrick et al., 2021b). The *Celling Sex* film sought to directly challenge stigma. Creating the film required careful facilitation. First, participants were individually guided through one-on-one interviews and cellphilm making workshops. Participatory analysis meetings followed: cellphilms were screened and participants used summary handouts to jot down key themes. Sticky notes were used to create a thematic mural wall. Katie drew on these themes to produce *Celling Sex*—a composite film that stitched together clips from the original cellphilms with audio voiceovers, music, and b-roll footage (MacEntee, Kendrick, & Flicker, 2021).

DOI: 10.4324/9781003199236-20

When researchers and participants gathered to watch a rough-cut of the video, the group expressed a clear desire to share the work. This enthusiasm prompted another surge of facilitation as we organized community screenings of the *Celling Sex* film (Kendrick, MacEntee, Wilson & Flicker, 2021a).

Here, we explore how participants and research team members co-facilitated screenings of the composite film. Outside of conventional disciplinary fields, audiencing, or the act of sharing products, and analysing engagement among audience members (Fiske, 1992), is a relatively understudied area. Consequently, screening the *Celling Sex* film became an opportunity to share our findings, challenge stigma, and think through the mechanics of audiencing. We use this frame to critically examine four screenings and the role of facilitation in these encounters.

Participatory Visual Methodologies, Cellphilming, and Audiencing

Several scholars have explicated the potential of arts-based and participatory visual methods (PVM) to catalyse social change (Boydell et al., 2012; Liebenberg, 2018; Mitchell, de Lange, & Molestane, 2017; Walsh, Rutherford, & Crough, 2013). Making and sharing participatory visual products can have a positive impact on community-based producers across a variety of contexts (Botfield et al., 2017; de Jager et al., 2017). Flicker et al. (2019) have outlined how digital stories have also been used to shift conversations at the community-level, and influence public health decision-makers.

Cellphilming mobilizes cellphone technology to support novice filmmakers to creatively tell their own stories (MacEntee, Burkholder, & Schwab-Cartas, 2016). Cellphilming has been celebrated for its use of local, accessible technology to democratize the research intervention process (Fine & Barreras, 2001; MacEntee, Burkholder, & Schwab-Cartas, 2016).

Numerous ethical issues arise in the process of creating participant visual products. These include blurred boundaries between participants and researchers, navigating ongoing consent for dissemination, and challenges related to confidentiality (Clark, Prosser, & Wiles, 2010; Gubrium, Hill, & Flicker, 2013). Researchers may engage in a range of reflexive practices to facilitate open and critical discussions of participation and risk to reduce potential harms (Gubrium, Hill, & Flicker, 2013).

Studies of audience engagement with products of PVM are still nascent. In line with Mitchell, de Lange and Molestane's (2017), thinking, "if we are to take seriously the potential of this work to influence social change, we are obliged to go full circle to study the idea of engaging audiences" (p. 22). They go on to describe a tiered framework for engaging audiences critically. The framework includes "political listening" (considering the politics that come with sharing and listening across power differentials) and reflexivity (p. 25). Taken together, the possibility of community and policy dialogue may be realized.

Other scholars have explored the tensions associated with sharing PVM-generated media for social change agendas. MacEntee and Mandrona (2015) documented the productive possibilities of discomfort for cellphilm producers when screening their work, as well as the dialogic space which opened between the producers and the audience. Kindon, Hume-Cook and Woods (2012) trouble assumptions that "traveling with such products is inherently empowering for those involved in their production" (p. 360). MacEntee (2016), builds on this critique by acknowledging that audiences will read participatory visual products in unpredictable and sometimes problematic ways. Similarly, Burkholder and Rogers (2020) argue project facilitators have ethical obligations to their participants to engage audience members who react either superficially or who respond to the visual outputs from PVM in ways that reinforce hatred. This paper builds on this body of work by reflecting on how co-facilitators negotiated screenings and diverse audience discussions of the *Celling Sex* film.

Methods

Studying audience engagement was a sub-study of the Celling Sex research project, which engaged 15 racially diverse cis- and gender queer young women in cellphilming to share their experiences of trading sex (Kendrick et al., 2021b; MacEntee, Kendrick, & Flicker, 2021). In this article, we focus exclusively on the data collected during the composite video screenings.

Audience Engagement Data Collection

To organize screenings, we contacted colleagues and organizations who assisted with recruitment. Our pitch included information about the research, film, and the request to hold a one-hour screening. When venues were secured, we shared promotional posters to circulate information in advance on community listservs and with drop-in groups (see Figure 15.1).

Each 60–90-minute screening was co-facilitated. On average, there were 1–3 academic team members and 2–4 peer researchers (the Celling Sex participants) present. Audiences volunteered to participate in the research and received a $5 gift card. When audience members did not want to participate, we divided into groups so that their contributions would not be recorded.

We used non-verbal and verbal data collection methods to document the audiences' reflections to the *Celling Sex* film. Index cards distributed at the outset invited audience members to share their demographics on one side (age, ethnicity, gender, sexuality, and profession/area of study) and to write or draw their initial ideas about transactional sex on the other (see Figure 15.2).

Alongside capturing demographic data, the cue cards were an opportunity for audiences to begin reflection and give our team some insight into who was in the room.

Screening Stories   243

FIGURE 15.1 A poster advertising the screening event.

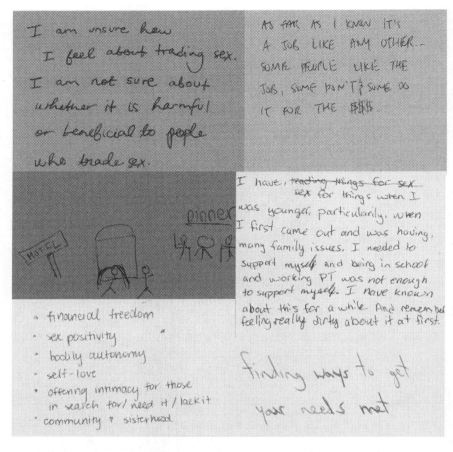

FIGURE 15.2 Index cards with viewers' first impressions of transactional sex.

After showing the film, both a brochure highlighting key messages and a handout was distributed. The handout asked audiences to jot down their thoughts on the following questions:

- What did you think about the video? What were its key messages?
- What questions remain about trading sex or sugaring for you?
- How does the video compare with the brochure?
- How does the video impact you in your personal or professional life?
- How does your impression now differ from your initial thoughts you jotted on your cards?

Responses to these questions were recorded in semi-structured group discussions. Recordings were transcribed verbatim for analysis. Caterina took copious fieldnotes to represent dynamics not captured by the audio-recorder. Her notes included sidebar conversations with screening hosts, perceptions about feelings in the room, body language, and facilitator debrief sessions after each showing. Here, we revisit these screenings using a reflexive frame—paying attention to personal reactions and the socially situated, co-constitutive dynamics, to examine the role of facilitation (Finlay, 2002).

In total, 30 organizations and ten professors in the fields of health, education, and social work were contacted, and 16 screenings took place. This paper focuses on four exemplar screenings that highlight a diversity of experience, considerations, ethical issues, and challenges related to facilitation and its interpreted impact on different audiences (see Table 15.1).

Following Mitchell (2011), there was something about these four screenings that was "haunting" (p. 199). The lingering impacts of these screenings were signposts for us to pause and deeply reflect on the role of facilitation to support critical audience engagement.

Facilitating the Screenings

No matter the venue, our facilitation team followed the same screening procedure. When a screening venue was secured, details were circulated on a team WhatsApp group. Participants chose to co-facilitate when their schedules and interests aligned. Facilitating peer researchers were provided a $20/hour honorarium for their time.

On the day of the screening, facilitators met at the venue 20 minutes before showtime. During this time, we set up our technology and discussed presentation

TABLE 15.1 Background of the four screenings and key considerations raised

Audience	Organizing the Screening	Key Takeaways
Underhoused youth group 6 attendees	Organized via email Posters were shared via listserv and on location	(non) Participation of audience members Attendance, advertising
Young parent's group 9 attendees	Referred to by another community organization Communicated via email and telephone	The "echo chamber" effect Challenging stigma in the moment Facilitation roles
Sex shop customers 4 attendees	Organized via telephone, email Poster shared on social media Registration on community partner's webpage	Risks of sharing "insider" information Registration versus turnout
HIV+ youth support group 5 attendees	Organized via telephone, email, and in-person meetings Poster shared on location	Having partners who go the extra mile Investment of time, resources

roles. Peer researchers were encouraged to lead when comfortable. To begin, everyone would introduce themselves and Caterina or Katie would provide background on the Celling Sex project and audience research. Following the collection of signed consent forms, peer researchers would sometimes introduce the film or transactional sex. Caterina outlined the index card activity. Then, the composite film was screened. Once the film ended, viewers were given the thematic brochures and the question handout. Using the handout as an initial guide, the research team co-facilitated group discussions. As peer researchers co-facilitated more screenings their comfort level responding to audience questions and participating more actively seemed to increase.

Facilitators met immediately after each screening for a quick 10–15 minute debrief. These debriefs were informal conversations that focused on how we felt the screenings went for us as individuals, and as a team. For instance, we would discuss audience questions, our responses to those questions, our perceived reception, and moments that were touching, important, or awkward. Our team of nine regular co-facilitators built a kind-hearted and supportive rapport that enhanced our ability to be honest and open with one another. Afterwards, brief updates and notes of thanks were shared with our WhatsApp group.

A Tale of Four Screenings

To protect the anonymity of locations and the audience members, we address the audiences in general terms (see Figure 15.3). However, the demographic information collected about the four audiences reported here shows that they were diverse in terms of gender (59% women, 37% men, and 4% as non-binary), race (41.5% identifying as Black, 37.5% white, and 21% South Asian or Asian), and age (ranging between 18–46).

Underhoused Youth Group

This screening was set up with an organization which provides shelter, transitional housing, and programmes for youth navigating homelessness. It was scheduled during a weekly drop-in programme focused on harm reduction. Planning went smoothly. We did, however, encounter a few logistical challenges upon arrival. That evening, only one woman came for the drop in. The programme lead canvassed the building to see if other youth would be interested in joining. Another three youths and a staff member arrived. The predominant themes that arose from this conversation included the transferability of the harm reduction strategies portrayed and how we might all re-think the meaning of transaction(s). One service provider confided that she was a former sex worker and appreciated how the screening offered an opportunity to reflect on how her programming could be more inclusive of those who might trade. Some audience members were quieter throughout the conversation.

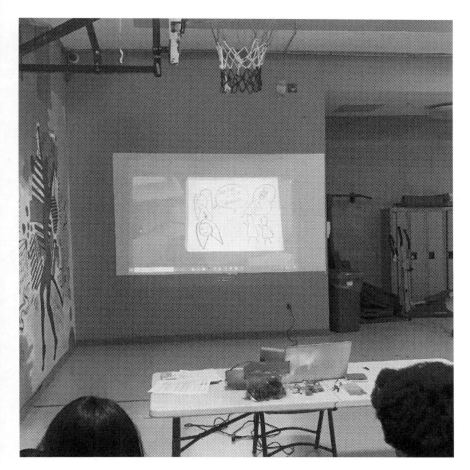

FIGURE 15.3 A Celling Sex screening in action!

Young Parents Group

Several perplexing miscommunications relating to date, time, location, and preferred audience hindered the planning of this screening. When the screening finally took place, our group introduced the project and were met with rude comments about trading sex from the convened audience of young parents and staff. Part way through screening the film, one of the staff members approached us and whispered that a programme participant wanted to know why we were teaching them to "become *whores*." Programme participants and staff continued to use derogatory and insulting language throughout. We quickly realized that our follow-up discussion needed to unpack assumptions and challenge negative stereotypes of women who trade sex. This was a difficult (and somewhat hostile) audience for the co-facilitating group.

The complexity of this screening was compounded by the racial makeup of the audience and research team. Seven of the attendees and four of the Celling Sex peer facilitators were women of colour. When loaded and judgemental questions were directed to the peers, Caterina and Katie (both white women), felt uneasy about speaking for, or over, our racialized co-facilitators. When Caterina and Katie did respond to questions, we sought to reiterate the peers' remarks and support their lead. While this strategy strengthened our shared sense of solidarity as co-facilitators, it did not dissolve the tension around the stigmatization of trading sex. The conversation lasted 45 minutes and ended somewhat abruptly reflecting the discomfort that all parties were feeling. Right before our departure however, one of the women in the group asked if we could return to share the film with members of their group who were absent that evening.

Our team spent an hour debriefing after this screening. Many felt disrespected by the audience and were frustrated with how the event had unfolded. We debated our responses and asked ourselves whether we successfully challenged stereotypes. The racial dynamic was raised by Katie and Caterina, and peers noted their appreciation for moments when we stepped back. They felt it respected their agency however, peers also pointed to moments where we might have stepped forward, such as putting an end to conversations that ran on for too long. Following the screening, we sent an email to the organizers thanking them for the opportunity and invited them to continue the conversation over the phone. We did not receive a response.

Sex Shop Customers

This screening took place at a sex shop where people of all genders, sexualities, and desires are welcomed. It often holds educational events to explore and learn about sexuality. Together, we decided to advertise the screening as a "movie night" on their web event calendar, alongside the Celling Sex social media pages. Fourteen people pre-registered. At showtime however, only one person was present. Eventually four more people arrived, and we started.

The conversation began by answering questions about the research project and methodological approach. Harm reduction strategies were shared including tips not covered in the film. There was an odd question from a man about whether we knew any "horror stories" which involved sex workers. From there, the conversation shifted to highlight the structural invisibility of women who trade sex and the dehumanization they face. After the screening, we spent 15 minutes debriefing. We generally felt good about the event. All of us remarked that we felt strange with the man's question about "horror stories." A peer researcher remarked that from the start, this person gave them "bad John vibes." Given the prevalence of narratives that sensationalize and normalize violence against women who engage in sexual work in the media (Strega et al., 2014), the comment suggested a certain morbid fascination or fetishism of violence against sex workers that made us all uncomfortable.

HIV+ Youth Support Group

This screening was held at a community organization that offers diverse programming to people living with HIV. Prior to the screening, we were warmly invited to tour the space. Immediately, there was a good feeling about the partnership.

Once we set up, we began our screening with an intimate group of five gay men. Our team was moved by the vulnerability, openness, and honesty of audience members. People shared very personal moments in their lives and articulated how the young women's stories impacted them. Thoughtful reflections were shared by audience members who connected the film's themes with their own experiences. When it came time to debrief, we all felt appreciated and valued. A contributing factor to the affirmation we felt was the group of people we were with. The organization explicitly embraces a diversity of sexual and gender identities. Through connecting with people who also experience stigmatization, we were able to let our guards down and feel warmly welcomed.

What Can Be Drawn from These Experiences?

These four vignettes demonstrate the range of contexts and reactions to our work. They are a starting point to explore key issues that may be useful for other facilitators, especially as they engage in audiencing participant-produced films.

Dialogue and Echo Chambers

In all four screenings, discussion following the film was important, albeit for different reasons. In all but the Young Parents' screening, most attendees expressed their appreciation for the film's content. Audience members who had experience trading were particularly excited to see authentic representation. They were further grateful for a non-judgemental space to discuss their experiences with a knowledgeable facilitating team. Others, who did not disclose lived experience of trading sex, made connections between the subject matter and their personal and/or professional lives (Kendrick, MacEntee, Wilson, & Flicker, 2021a). These reflections point towards the productivity of supporting audiences to make personal connections with participant-produced visual media.

The reception of the visual media, however, was not always obviously generative. We were left wondering if the reception of the composite video by the male audience member at the Sex Shop Screening somehow missed the mark. Furthermore, while the reception at the Young Parents' group was not interpreted as a positive experience, we felt it was important. Given the judgement that was encountered, we were challenged to respectfully engage while debunking stereotypes. Scholars have written of the dangers that come with echo chambers, a phenomenon whereby content shared online within networks of people with similar political leanings are reproduced to reinforce polarization across differing viewpoints (Garimella et al., 2018; Quattrociocchi et al., 2016). While the Young Parents' screening was the least comfortable, it was perhaps the most important for meeting our goal of trying to challenge stigma. Being asked to return by one audience member as we were packing up demonstrates that there were elements of value or resonance in the screening and discussion, despite their personal views of transactional sex. This willingness to dialogue with each other is a promising gesture when considering the aims of challenging stigma.

Sharing with outside audiences should be carefully measured next to the potential risk of distributing information that might best be kept within a limited circle of knowers. For example, in the *Celling Sex* film, discrete strategies were presented as advice for safeguarding against bad dates. The apprehensiveness that our team felt with the audience member who was interested in "horror" stories motivated us to reflect on the gravity of publicly sharing harm reduction practices. Some of these strategies work because they are covert; they could potentially be undermined if shared with people who wish to perpetuate violence. Project teams should think very carefully about the knowledge being represented and shared through visual outputs. Sharing insider information with outsiders could open communities to very real physical and emotional harm. While it is not always possible to control who is in the room at every screening, this cautionary moment became a contributing reason for why we never publicly posted our film online.

Facilitator Roles and Identities

At most screenings, peer researchers felt degrees of affirmation by engaging audiences on matters that are important to them. These positive receptions were one of the reasons they continued co-facilitating. But the Young Parents' Group posed a lasting challenge. This experience raised an ethical concern about the safety and emotional tax on the peer facilitators who were the target of vitriolic stigma. We were caught off guard. Realizing we did not discuss how we would address harmful or judgemental remarks, in our post-screening debrief we strategized tactics for future reference. These included leaving the room or taking a break, redirecting questions back to the film's content, and demanding respectful language.

We continue to grapple with the tensions of facilitating as a diverse group where multiple social power dynamics were simultaneously in place. The peer facilitators were mostly racialized young women (Black, Indigenous or Asian) who were precariously employed. All had lived experience of trading that was made visible by their role in the project. The white researchers–facilitators (whose experiences of trading were not publicly acknowledged in the film) tended to be older and positioned as experts. At the Young Parents' screening, the simultaneous visibility and invisibility of whiteness (Britton, 2019) and other forms of privilege that shaped the interaction were particularly potent. As Burkholder and Rogers (2020) argue, Caterina and Katie—as representatives of the research team—had an ethical responsibility to ensure the safety of the co-facilitators. However, we also wanted to support the growing capacity of peer researchers to take the lead when they felt comfortable. Caterina and Katie were not ignorant to the potential harm to the co-facilitators in this instance. We sat with a great deal of discomfort and uncertainty regarding if/when/how we should respond and what it would mean to not respond. Our actions were informed in part by the recognition of what it means to conduct anti-racist research that advocates researchers "move out of the way" as part of the process of building "non-hierarchical and ethical research relationships" (Goddard-Durant, Sieunarine, & Doucet, 2021, p. 191). Our negotiation of these tensions relied on our relational commitment to the project and our trust that we had built through facilitating together as a team for several months. Our experience at this screening pushes the ethical responsibilities of the researcher outlined by Burkholder and Rogers (2020). The intersectional dynamics contributed to an uncertainty about the most productive way to challenge stigma while creating space for peers' agency and knowledge to lead. Our thwarted attempts to follow up with the host to address the event were part of our ethical responsibility to the project and participants, and an action that felt instinctively right. As we know from community-based participatory research, the ethics of decision making is contextually dependent, shifting from moment-to-moment (Flicker et al., 2007; Israel et al., 2005). Facilitating audience engagement with participant-produced media also requires contextual agility. While it is difficult to measure how our positionalities—both real and assumed—impacted audience engagement, our team benefited from openly, honestly, and vulnerably, addressing the tensions that accompany the shape-shifting manifestations of power within our facilitation group. Maintaining a reflexive engagement when revisiting complex moments with peer investigators can provide insight into what actions might be more or less appropriate.

Another consideration that arose was representing differences in personal definitions of trading amongst peer facilitators. During public discussions, some vocal peers equated trading sex with sex work, while others chafed at that categorization. Those who felt they were misrepresented flagged concerns. PVM offer the power of representation to participants: it is less clear how to uphold individual representation within a group context. When misrepresentation arises, who should moderate? Would moderation sideline particular voices? These concerns elicit further questions about the role of participants as co-facilitators—are they present for themselves? For the researchers? Or for the audience? Jacobs (2010) critically assessed the concept of participation in community-based participatory research and examines tensions between participation for empowerment, participation as important to academic quality, and participation's practical usefulness to the goals of the project. These motivations can be happening all at once in sometimes competing degrees. At screenings, there were regularly questions of who amongst our group had experience trading. Audiences wanted to know that we were doing research *with* and not *on* people. Our approach to navigating this tension was to highlight the nuance and continuum which exists with transactional sex without singling anyone out.

Facilitating (non) Participation

How audience feedback is captured is a key consideration for researchers. For our project, discussions happened in groups. This was an effective method for breaking the silence surrounding trading sex and hearing a diversity of perspectives in a short time. However, it can limit the participation of audience members who are uncomfortable speaking in front of a group. Discussing stigmatized subject matters, with strangers or with peers and colleagues, can raise feelings of discomfort or apprehension.

At the Underhoused Youth screening, conversation sometimes stalled. Facilitating through silence was a challenge: we attempted to balance inviting people into the conversation, while respecting their chosen level of engagement. Though, it meant there were awkward silences—staff would jump in to fill the space and subsequently, their reflections dominated. Kitzinger and Farquhar (1999) describe hesitation and awkwardness in focus groups as illuminative sites that can push boundaries of conversation. Despite signing consent forms, two people in the Underhoused Youth group did not actively participate; their body language seemed to indicate disengagement. Perhaps, the youth were enticed by the modest ($5) honoraria? Or what Fisher (2013) describes as the compromised voluntariness due to social, economic, and political contexts as "structural coercion" (p. 355). While there was no straightforward way to navigate the tension of ambiguous participation, we take inspiration from Milne (2012) who encourages researchers to "make publicly visible the absences, silences, and resistances that are currently (not) present in the literature" (p. 258). Research participants are not powerless. Choosing non-participation can be a way for participants, especially youth, to exercise their power in the research dynamic (Switzer, 2018). Following Switzer (2018), facilitators should create space for participants to set the terms of how they want to participate. Being mindful of expectations of participants and adapting engagement strategies as needed is recommended.

Attendance and Advertising

Across screenings there were varying levels of attendance and participation. We never quite knew who or how many people would show up. Organizing screenings required a significant investment of time and resources: communicating with screening hosts, our facilitating team, travelling to and from the venues, preparing engagement resources and honorarium, set-up, tear-down, and follow-up. We learnt that the deep level of commitment to research partners (Strand et al., 2003) extends to include the process of audience engagement with host organizations. Therefore, when audience attendance is low, it can be a blow to the facilitator's morale and cast doubt on the project's worth. Though, in some cases (e.g., HIV youth group), incredibly rich conversations were facilitated alongside small turnouts.

Facilitating greater public interest was a challenge. We advertised screenings on social media and through the host organizations. While social media outlets, such as Instagram, TikTok, and Twitter, are important tools in spreading awareness of issues and events, it is easy to become digitally saturated; particularly in the time of the COVID-19 pandemic where realms of work, health, social interactions, and community building, are virtually subsumed. Virtual worlds can be sites for conversations and change-making, though online engagement may not be enough to translate into off-line presence (Highfield, 2016). Facilitators could include trailers of the film, biographies of the presenters, or the event programme, to promote longer-lasting impressions.

Current social media trends increasingly rely on brief sound bites. Tailoring visual outputs to better coincide with online engagement—for instance, creating several one-minute clips showcasing findings—could be another way to engage a wider group of people. Low turnout at community organizations can also be associated with barriers of time and access. Service providers and youth alike have identified systemic barriers that young people navigate in accessing health supports: an absence of youth-friendly spaces, encountering stigma, and not knowing about what services are available, are just a few barriers that are exacerbated by economic vulnerabilities and institutionalized racism and sexism (Flicker et al., 2009). Low turnout at the youth drop-in programmes that we visited may reflect the barriers that young people encounter in being able to show up in the room to access services and support.

What Does This Mean for Other Community-Based, Participatory Visual Researchers?

We return to Mitchell, de Lange and Molestane's (2017) framework for critical audience engagement. Some of the questions that we raised—balancing individual and group representation, participants' roles, and audience participation—can be addressed by political listening, reflexivity, and training opportunities.

Political listening, a process of attuning oneself to the unfolding layers of power, in each moment, is a way to clarify tension. Dedicating training time for facilitators to discuss strategies for responding to judgemental feedback, balancing divergent views, and encouraging personal reflections, can be a valuable practice to assist in responding productively in stressful situations. Practice can also help teams refine key messages. While training does not prepare for every situation, it can build confidence and provide tools for responding in-situ.

Taking time to establish the team's pedagogical approach is recommended. There are a range of engagement strategies that facilitators can employ (see Table 15.2).

In Table 15.2, we capture the steps in our screening process alongside other engagement strategies for researchers to consider. Our use of cue cards,

TABLE 15.2 Screening checklists and suggestions

Before	During	After
Determining direction of media dissemination	Peer researchers and academic team present for event	De-briefing with facilitation team
Editing, group screenings for feedback, final cut	Independent engagement: Cue card activity, handouts	Following up with screening partners
Creating advertisements	Providing take home brochures with key findings	Reflective note taking
Community outreach	Screening the film	Monitoring emails
Preparing technology and screening materials	Group discussion	Social media posts sharing event photos
	Other Strategies to Consider	
Rehearsal/drills for the facilitation team	Pair-share, mural walls, interactive online polls/word clouds, booths for responding back	Setting up accountability measures with community partners

brochures, handouts, and discussion groups were popular education interventions that allowed us to raise consciousness and challenge stigma. These activities allowed audiences to choose their level of participation and engagement. Mural walls, interactive online polls, word clouds, pair-share, or responding booths are other strategies that can allow a range of responses that are anonymous, low risk, and may better address challenges of silence or judgemental remarks.

Follow-up measures are equally important. De-briefing was integral to our group process. Following up with community partners provided further opportunity for relationship building and held potential to be an accountability measure when events soured. We received resource requests via email and direct message on Instagram from screening attendees to share with other people in their lives. These were important channels in our goal of making the research findings accessible beyond one-time screening events.

Conclusion

In this paper, we have made visible the challenges and opportunities associated with facilitating community-based screenings of the *Celling Sex* film. The logistical organization, environment, and power differentials which existed across audience members and the research team, all impacted how the visuals were consumed, as well as the resulting conversations. The choices around *who, how, when,* and *where* this work takes place are central features of facilitation consideration. For this project, the process encouraged us to reflexively lean into discomfort, seek out diverse audiences, deeply listen and engage with differing ideals, values, and social codes. We found returning to our community partners after screenings integral to building relationships and opened the door for continued reflection. Power differentials amongst our team of academic and peer researchers, as well as with our audience members, became an opportunity for us to critically engage with how we were approaching the facilitation process. The process of taking a dissemination strategy—screenings—typically the end point of research, and seeing it as another beginning, was fertile ground for exploring the complexities of facilitating audiencing strategies.

Acknowledgements

This project was funded by CANFAR and the Social Sciences and Humanities Research Foundation. We want to thank the entire Celling Sex team including: Mesha, April, Friesa, Crystal, Daisy, Sophia, Halimo, Erica, and Ciann. Audience engagement could not have happened without all of the host organizations who welcomed us—thank you.

Note

1 The project obtained ethics approval from York University in Toronto, Canada.

References

Benoit, C., Jansson, M., Smith, M., & Flagg, J. (2018). Prositution stigma and its effect on the working conditions, personal lives, and health of sex workers. *The Journal of Sex Research*, 55(4–5), 457–471. https://doi.org/10.1080/00224499.2017.1393652

Botfield, J.R., Newman, C.E., Lenette, C., Albury, K., & Zwi, A.B. (2017). Using digital storytelling to promote the sexual health and well-being of migrant and refugee young people: A scoping review. *Health Education Journal*, 77(7), 735–748. https://doi.org/10.1177/0017896917745568

Boydell, K., Gladstone, B.M., Volpe, T., Allemang, B., & Stasiulis, E. (2012). The production and dissemination of knowledge: A scoping review of arts-based health research. *Forum: Qualitative Social Research*, 13(1). http://dx.doi.org/10.17169/fqs-13.1.1711

Britton, J. (2019). Being an insider and outsider: Whiteness as a key dimension of difference. *Qualitative Research*, 20(3), 340–354. https://doi.org/10.1177/1468794119874599

Burkholder, C., & Rogers, M. (2020). Screening participatory videos and cellphilms (cellphone + film production) in live-audience and online spaces. *Visual Methodologies*, 8(1), 1–15. https://doi.org/10.7331/vm.v8i1.12

Clark, A., Prosser, J., & Wiles, R. (2010). Ethical issues in image-based research. *Arts & Health*, 2(1), 81–93. https://doi.org/10.1080/17533010903495298

Fine, M., & Barreras, R. (2001). To be of use. *Analyses of Social Issues and Public Policy*, 1(1), 175–183. https://doi.org/10.1111/1530-2415.00012

Finlay, L. (2002). Negotiating the swamp: The opportunity and challenge of reflexivity in research practice. *Qualitative Research*, 2(2), 209–230. https://doi.org/10.1177/146879410200200205

Fisher, J.A. (2013). Expanding the frame of 'voluntariness' in informed consent: Structural coercion and the power of social and economic context. *Kennedy Institute of Ethics Journal*, 23(4), 355–379. https://doi.org/10.1353/ken.2013.0018

Fiske, J. (1992). Audiencing: A cultural studies approach to watching television. *Poetics*, *21*(4), 345–359. https://doi.org/10.1016/0304-422X(92)90013-S

Flicker, S., Flynn, S., Larkin, J., Travers, R., Guta, A., Pole, J., & Layne, C. (2009). *Sexpress: The Toronto teen survey report*. Planned Parenthood Toronto. https://utgaap.files.wordpress.com/2019/10/tts_report.pdf

Flicker, S., Travers, R., Guta A., McDonald, S., & Aileen M. (2007). Ethical dilemmas in community-based participatory research: Recommendations for institutional review boards. *Journal of Urban Health*, *84*(4), 478–493. https://doi.org/10.1007/s11524-007-9165-7

Flicker, S., Wilson, C., Monchalin, R., Restoule, J.P., Mitchell, C., Larkin, J., Prentice, T., Jackson, R., & Oliver, V. (2019). The impact of Indigenous youth sharing digital stories about HIV activism. *Health Promotion Practice*, *21*(5), 802–810. https://doi.org/10.1177/1524839918822268

Garimella, K., De Francisci Morales, G., Gionis, A., & Mathioudakis, M. (2018). Political discourse on social media: Echo chambers, gatekeepers, and the price of bipartisanship. *18: Proceedings of the 2018 World Wide Web conference*, 913–922. https://doi.org/10.1145/3178876.3186139

Goddard-Durant, S., Sieunarine, J.A., & Douce, A. (2021). Decolonising research with Black communities: Developing equitable and ethical relationships between academic and community stakeholders. *Families, Relationships and Societies*, *10*(1), 189–196. https://doi.org/10.1332/204674321X16104823811079

Gubrium, A., Hill, A.L., & Flicker, S. (2013). A situated practice of ethics for participatory visual and digital methods in public health research and practice: A focus on digital storytelling. *American Journal of Public Health*, *104*(9), 1606–1614. https://doi.org/10.2105/AJPH.2013.301310

Highfield, T. (2016). *Social media and everyday politics*. Cambridge & Malden: Polity Press.

Israel, B.A., Eng, E., Schulz, A.J., & Parker, E.A. (2005). *Methods in community-based participatory research for health*. San Fransisco: Jossey-Bass.

de Jager, A., Fogarty, A., Tewson, A., Lenette, C., & Boydell, K.M. (2017). Digital storytelling in research: A systematic review. *The Qualitative Report*, *22*(10), 2548–2582. https://doi.org/10.46743/2160-3715/2017.2970

Jacobs, G. (2010). Conflicting demands and the power of defensive routines in participatory action research. *Action Research*, *8*(4), 367–386. https://doi.org/10.1177/1476750310366041

Kendrick, C.T., MacEntee, K., & Flicker, S. (2021b) Exploring audience engagement and critical narrative intervention with the Celling Sex film. *Health Promotion Practice. Critical Narrative Intervention Collection* https://doi.org/10.1177/15248399211040492

Kendrick, C.T., MacEntee, K., Wilson, C.L., & Flicker, S. (2021a). Staying safe: How young women who trade sex in Toronto navigate risk and harm reduction. *Culture, Health & Sexuality*, 1–15. https://doi.org/10.1080/13691058.2021.1900603

Kindon, S., Hume-Cook, G., & Woods, K. (2012). Troubling the politics of reception in participatory video discourse. In E.J. Milne, C. Mitchell, & N.D. Lange (Eds.), *Handbook of participatory video* (pp. 349–364). Alta Mira Press.

Kitzinger, J., & Farquhar, C. (1999). The analytical potential of 'sensitive moments' in focus group discussions. In R.S. Barbour, & J. Kitzinger (Eds.), *Developing focus group research* (pp. 156–172). London, Thousand Oaks, New Dehli: SAGE Publications Ltd. http://dx.doi.org.ezproxy.library.yorku.ca/10.4135/9781849208857

Liebenberg, L. (2018). Thinking critically about photovoice: Achieving empowerment and social change. *International Journal of Qualitative Methods*, *17*(1). https://doi.org/10.1177/1609406918757631

MacEntee, K. (2016). Facing constructions of African girlhood: Reflections on screening participant's cellphilms in academic contexts. In K. MacEntee, C. Burkholder, & J. Schwab-Cartas (Eds.), *What's a Cellphilm? Mobile digital technology for research and activism* (pp. 137–152). Rotterdam: Sense Publishers.

MacEntee, K., Burkholder, C., & Schwab-Cartas, J. (2016). *Whats a Cellphilm? Integrating mobile phone technology into participatory visual research and activism*. Rotterdam: Sense Publishers.

MacEntee, K., Kendrick, C.T., & Flicker, S. (2021). Quilted cellphilm method: A participatory visual health research method for working with marginalized and stigmatized communities. *Global Public Health*, 1–13. https://doi.org/10.1080/17441692.2021.1928262

MacEntee, K., & Mandrona, A. (2015). From discomfort to collaboration: Teachers screening cellphilms in a rural South African school. *Perspectives in Education*, *33*(3), 42–56

Milne, E.-J. (2012). Saying 'no' to participatory video: Unraveling the complexities of (non)participation. In E.J. Milne, C. Mitchell, & N.D. Lange (Eds.), *Handbook of participatory video* (pp. 257–268). Lanham: Alta Mira Press.

Mitchell, C. (2011). *Doing visual research*. London, Thousand Oaks, New Dehli: SAGE Publications Ltd.

Mitchell, C., Lange, N.D., & Molestane, R. (2017). *Participatory visual methodologies: Social change, community and policy*. London, Thousand Oaks, New Dehli, Singapore: SAGE Publications Ltd.

Quattrociocchi, W., Scala, A., & Sunstein, C.R. (2016). Echo chambers on Facebook. Preprint, https://ssrn.com/abstract=2795110 or http://dx.doi.org/10.2139/ssrn.2795110

Strand, K., Marullo, S., Cutforth, N., Stoecker, R., & Donohue, P. (2003). Principles of best practice for community-based research. *Michigan Journal of Community Service Learning*, *9*(3), 5–15. http://hdl.handle.net/2027/spo.3239521.0009.301

Strega, S., Janzen, C., Morgan, J., Brown, L., Thomas, R., & Carriére, J. (2014). Never innocent victims: Street sex workers in Canadian print media. *Violence Against Women*, *20*(1), 6–25. https://doi.org/10.1177/1077801213520576

Switzer, S. (2018). 'People give and take a lot in order to participate in things': Youth talk back—Making a case for non-participation. *Beyond the End or the Means: Co-theorizing Engagement for HIV Programming and Service Provision*. [Doctoral Disseratation, York University].

Walsh, C.A., Rutherford, G., & Crough, M. (2013). Arts-based research: Creating social change for incarcerated women. *Creative Approaches to Research*, *6*(1), 119–139.

16
"BECOMING I/WE" TOGETHER AS CRITICAL PERFORMANCE PEDAGOGY

Facilitating Intra-Actions and Metissage from Inhabiting/Living Practice

Genevieve Cloutier, Alison Shields, Lap-Xuan Do-Nguyen, Samira Jamouchi and Yoriko Gillard

Introduction

During the International Society for Education through Art World Congress in 2019, Geneviève Cloutier and Alison Shields co-curated and co-facilitated an exhibit titled *Inhabiting/Living Practice*. In it, 18 PhD students from around the world came together to engage in artistic inquiry. Here, five of those participants want to share an aspect of the collaboration focusing on critical performative pedagogy (Boal, 1979; Freire, 1970; Huber, 2013; Pineau, 2002). Lap-Xuan Do-Nguyen, Samira Jamouchi, and Yoriko Gillard were the artists whose practices came together for the opening of the exhibit. Geneviève has a socially engaged and performative practice, and was honoured to participate in their provocation to inhabit the space through critical performative pedagogy together.

Born from Paulo Freire's (1970) work about critical emancipatory practices in *Pedagogy of the Oppressed* along with Augusto Boal's (1979) *Theatre of the Oppressed*, we work towards critical performance pedagogies that challenge hierarchy. Boal (1979) believed that performance could be a site for action, liberation, and justice. More recently, researchers in the field of education assert that "Critical Performance Pedagogy implements critical pedagogy in a humanizing manner that allows the purpose, content, and methods of performance to bring us closer to the goal of liberation" (as cited in Tintiangco-Cubales, Daus-Magbual, Desai, Sabac, & Torres, 2016, p. 1313). In this chapter, we work through facilitation practices that honour the transformative potential of performance (Fischer-Lichte, 2008; Huber, 2013) through métissage (Hasebe-Ludt & Jordan, 2011; Hasebe-Ludt, Chambers, & Leggo, 2009; Lionnet, 1989).

We share our experiences through métissage as a creative assemblage. Deleuze and Guattari (1980/2019) state that an assemblage "is a *collective assemblage* of enunciation, of acts and statements, of incorporeal transformations attributed to bodies" (p. 88). Our positionalities reveal our embodied sense of research ethics and hold us accountable "to the specific materializations of which we are a part" (Barad, 2007, p. 91). We consider how our métissage and assemblages of performative intra-actions (Barad, 2007) and dialogues emerge as a feminist and artistic research methodology alongside critical performance pedagogy.

Françoise Lionnet (1989) created a framework to work through the ethical, feminist, and decentralized concept of métissage: a braided methodology of oral, visual, and written narratives which transcended genre, language, and politics. Speaking to relational pedagogy, "métissage encourages genuine exchange, sustained engagement, and the tracing of mixed and multiple identities" (Hasebe-Ludt & Leggo, 2018, p. xxii). We employ métissage as an assemblage of artistic research voices while we work through Karen Barad's (2007) concept of intra-action. We do this to unsettle hegemonic understandings of identity, difference, and relationality. We seek to disrupt hierarchical research practices in favour of alternative ways of coming to know difference and relationality. In this chapter, each collaborator takes up space to express their ways of knowing and being in the world. These dialogues and the liminal spaces therein generate intra-action while honouring our differences. Intra-actions also offer lessons for thinking about how ethical facilitation requires us to adopt relational processes that honour these differences. For us, this happened through critical performance pedagogy.

Intra-action is observed and employed through relational *métissage* as we reflect on critical performance pedagogy—an individual and collective practice that "attends to the relational nature of difference" (Barad, 2007, p. 72). Thinking through critical performative pedagogy allowed us to consider the body as a place of learning and experience (Pineau, 2002); one that recollects experiences (Morawski & Cloutier, 2016) with co-inhabiting practices. We consider the collaborative *affected* spaces of Inhabiting/Living Practice. As such, we contend that collaborative artistic research necessitates facilitation that holds space for "Becoming I / We," together. We begin with Alison's reflection.

Alison Shields: The purpose of the exhibition was to give doctoral students the opportunity to share and extend their arts-based research through "making" alongside and in collaboration with other students, conference attendees, and the general public (see Figure 16.1). The title of the exhibition, *Inhabiting/Living Practice*, was developed as a way of viewing the exhibition as emergent and interconnected. We imagined the gallery as a living body: an embodied space that we inhabited for the week with material, affect, and relationality. We propose that inquiry occurs with and through ongoing encounters, and we invited attendees to participate and collaborate in this emergent exhibition.

The exhibition was conceived around the premise that arts-based and artistic research are a performative practice. Through this lens, we ask, what can art *do*? Barbara Bolt (2016) argues that artistic research is ontologically performative in its capacity to provoke and generate experiences. A performative lens emphasizes

FIGURE 16.1 Performance by Samira Jamouchi. Photo credit: Alicia Arias-Camison Coella.

engagement with art making as an embodied, affective, sensory, experiential, and emergent learning process. Bolt (2004) describes this process:

> In the heat of practice, the body has the potential to become language and the work may take on a life of its own. Through process, the outside world enters the work and the world casts its effects back into the world.
>
> (p. 190)

Karen Barad (2007) similarly argues that to focus on the performative rather than the representationalist means focusing on "practices or doings or actions" (p. 28). Barad makes a distinction between interaction and intra-action. She proposes that individuals exist because of interactions. As such, entities are in a constant state of becoming in relation to encounters with other entities in a process of intra-action. This performative lens views the world as constantly changing.

We viewed the exhibition as an intra-active process. Entering the space, we asked what would happen as we brought together 18 arts-based researchers to allow their artistic processes to intra-act as exhibitors engaged in dialogue and formed connections and relationships with each other's practices. As a co-curator/co-facilitator of the exhibition, I learned that for a collaborative and emergent exhibition to work, this intra-active process must be embraced by all involved. Participants need to enter the space with an openness and a responsiveness to viewing and engaging with their work through the work of others. It is an ongoing process of letting go and building trust. And as curator and facilitator, I too had to be open to this emergent process.

As a facilitator, I sought to create the conditions for relationships to emerge. These relationships emerged between artworks and participants as each student's artistic research process inhabited the space alongside, through and within the artistic process of the other participants. This project challenged my view of facilitation. I had thought that the facilitation of an exhibition meant to step back and allow participants take the lead in bringing the exhibition into fruition. However, I realized throughout this project the tension that existed between my idealized understanding of facilitation and the reality of working with 18 arts-based researchers. While I struggled within this tension, I realized that embracing the intra-active process also included embracing tensions between art materials and practices. Intra-action meant that artists and artworks emerged in and through each other. These tensions allowed for the emergence of a deeper level of trust as artists and facilitators had to relinquish control and allow for new processes to emerge. As a facilitator, I came away from this exhibition recognizing that to embrace emergence meant giving space to dwell within this intra-active process where relationships form between materials, artists, and space. I had to let go and enter a space of not knowing.

The opening performance discussed in this chapter was an exercise in practicing this process. Relationships had formed between Yoriko, Lap-Xuan, and Samira, but I did not fully know their plan. I went into the conference space and did a brief presentation about the exhibition's intentions. Then I invited the conference attendees to follow me across campus to the Hatch gallery. I was anxious as conference attendees gradually followed me. Although I had co-curated the exhibit, I did not know exactly what I was inviting them to see. In this moment that I embraced the emergent process of facilitation. I was struck by Samira, Lap-Xuan, and Yoriko's bravery, honesty, and openness. They had entered the space two days earlier from three different areas of the world, with three separate artistic practices. In the performance that evening, they developed a conversation through words, actions, and material engagement that resonated with gallery visitors. Through this intra-active encounter, these artists set the tone for an open, responsive, and trusting emergent exhibition.

Geneviève Cloutier: In her master's thesis, Yoriko Gillard (2014) asks, "How can we trust each other through art and its practice?" This question anchors our reflections as Alison and I endeavoured to facilitate trust-based, collaborative encounters. While we initially curated the group of artists based on their willingness to work collaboratively, we identified as facilitators to acknowledge and disrupt the power imbalances between curators and artists. For us, creating trust necessitated a willingness to give up power and share space. Within this conception of facilitation as flexibility, space cannot be inhabited without other participating bodies, voices, and differences working together.

Freire's (1970) work on critical pedagogy provokes us to destabilize established models of authority in favour of decentralized processes of radical education, whereby all participants—curators/facilitators, artists, and gallery-goers—can learn from each other. Curation becomes a form of facilitation that creates and shares decentralized space. Augusto Boal's (1979) theatrical and performative work about a "rehearsal for revolution" (p. 122) comes into dialogue with Freire here and illuminates radical collaboration within institutions, whereby every participant who experiences a production is responsive to one another. Freire and Boal alongside feminist poststructuralist Karen Barad (2007), Patti Lather (1992), and Elizabeth Ellsworth (1997, 2005) who remind that positionality also impacts facilitation practices. Political and social justice-informed facilitation can only occur through responsiveness to others.

Decentralized space is intra-active. It opens possibilities. It is through the performance of our social and political positioning that I move through this shared space, because "just as bodies produce oppression through specific performances, bodies also produce transformative possibilities through performance" (Huber, 2013, p. 423). As a facilitator, I look towards the emergent possibilities of "becoming I / We," together.

My experience here was embodied through the interwoven roles of researcher, artist, curator/facilitator, and participant, and as such, I work through a liminality of encounters (Gillard, 2019) and ethical responsibilities. Honouring "I" necessitates invitational spaces that are open, generative, and based on dynamic forces and relational encounters that allow us to trust, heal, shift, acknowledge, be flexible, and let go. The felt "I" becomes a part of each of us all, simultaneously.

I signed a consent form to partake in Yoriko's cut hair piece. In doing so, I agreed to be "a piece of wood" for the work. I could not speak. I could not move. This was about trust. My long hair, extending down to my back, was to become material for a sculpture: a symbol of trust in the wake of traumatic histories. As co-curator and co-facilitator, it felt meaningful to volunteer. I wanted to give up power, to be a piece of wood for the development of reconciliation and togetherness, to consider others' space and be willing to support and adapt.

Yoriko told me that she would take my hand when she was ready. I welcomed the conference attendees and asked them to remain quiet while Lap-Xuan began the performance. I walked with conference attendees as Samira and Lap-Xuan performed, guiding everyone through their critical performance practice. That's when Yoriko took my hand. When it was over, Yoriko touched my face gently, as if a new relationality had been built. She took my hand and brought me to the bathroom so that I could see myself, but I did not really care what it looked like. I was ready to part with as much hair as she believed I should lose for a trust-based encounter. For me, this was not about taking up space, it was about working with those inhabiting it with a willingness to shed aspects of myself to exist in the present.

I did not know Yoriko before the performance—in the performance, our trust-based encounter resulted in a closer relationality. It was not about taking up space. It was about moving with those who inhabit it. Trust, the disruption of "I" in favour of relationality, necessitates that we sometimes volunteer to become

Becoming I/We Together   263

FIGURE 16.2 Performance by Samira Jamouchi and Lap-Xuan Do-Nguyen. Photo credit: Alicia Arias-Camison Coella.

a piece of wood; that we embody the willingness to be sculpted into something new, emerging in relation to others.

I will never forget how the multiple sounds and textures of "I" transformed the exhibition space into something else altogether. Lap-Xuan's voice resonated throughout the gallery as Samira shared and facilitated a collaborative experience with gallery attendees (Figure 16.2). I was walking alongside everyone as Yoriko guided me to a chair beside Samira's felt process. Lap-Xuan's voice resonated as I felt my hair fall to the ground.

Lap-Xuan Do-Nguyen:

I.

What was I thinking before the event that afternoon? I was imagining myself sitting at UBC's Hatch Gallery, alone, performing amongst a big crowd. In that scene, my voice was soundless. But as the real day arrived, I was not alone, I was with Samira, Yoriko, Geneviève, and many others.

II.

The exhibition underlined the intention of provoking, emerging, and collaborating in a shared space. I realized we had very little knowledge about each other's practices, thus our aspiration to collaboratively develop an exhibition and organize participatory elements confronted how we "practice" the exhibition. I am reminded of Kemmis, Wilkinson, Edwards-Groves, Hardy, Grootenboer, and Bristol (2014)'s definition of the term practice as "a form of socially established cooperative human activity that involves characteristic forms of understanding (sayings), mode of action (doings), and ways in which people relate to one another and the world (relatings), that 'hang together' in a distinctive project" (Snepvangers & Mathewson-Mitchell, 2018, p. 6).

Expanding on Kemmis et al.'s (2014, pp. 155–156) idea of "practice," I believe saying, doing, and relating is at the core of an emergent collaborative practice of togetherness. To "relate" is to face the conflict of personal benefit as the fear of losing presence in a community while having to contribute to building that community. How do we practise hanging together if we don't loosen up? For me as a performance artist, I am often particular about what I wish to imply in my art. This includes my ideal plan for the installation and its arrangement so that the viewers could experience the entire concept. But I am also a researcher about participatory practice, thus I am concerned with developing an equality structure. I wonder: how do I maximize the autonomous presence of the participants during the artistic experience that I designed? I try to be aware that viewers might be overwhelmed by the artistic imposition and the atmosphere which may cause them to hesitate in participating. I also wonder about the differences between a participatory project—where the participants are predetermined, and a participatory performance—where the participants encounter their engagement by-chance.

The more I consider the exhibition as an experimental project, the more challenging it is to think through the ways that different practices might co-exist, respond, and transform within the specific site and time. According to Kemmis' idea of the site (2009) that "practices arise in relation to one another in a particular site," in this case, 18 practitioners were aware that they were producing a living assemblage. The willingness to inquire in others' actions generated meaningful engagements, objects, images, and happenings. Learning about others' artistic medium gave me the time to reflect on my own and embrace the surprising interference. I removed my assumptions, to learn by "being" with this community.

Samira and Yoriko and I had an affinity which encouraged us to intertwine our individual performances at the exhibit's opening. We carried our personal pieces separately in a shared space and time, and in conversational nature with each other. The collaboration set out to be emergent. We did not script how we were going to interact. We were led by our instincts. We invited each other and the public to their journey of the "I"—power, identity, otherness, and trust.

III.

I embarked on a contemplative journey where I had to limit my speech to a single phoneme: the self (I) and the other (who). I spoke the sound /ai/ at different levels, durations, and emotions. I walked around the room, humbling, speaking, shouting to myself, to my peers, other performers, and to the audiences.

My performance titled "Speaking piece" used a single sound to interrogate the polysemy of language; and by/to activate participation and made visible the lessons of co-presence during a participatory event. The phonemes: /ai/ resonated with different meanings to the speaker and the listener. Most English speakers in the room might have assumed the sound /ai/ to mean "I" or the "ego." The most intrinsic sense of the /ai/ sound to my Vietnamese ear is "who." In other languages such as Chinese or Japanese, /ai/ means "love." In Korean, /ai/ is "little children," and in Indonesian, /ai/ is "water." There may also have been hidden meanings that I did not know.

On my journey, I spoke to Yoriko's "wood," but she could not answer me because of the confines of her performance. In becoming "wood," Geneviève was unable to perceive her own image, yet she witnessed my sounded presence. My voice was the extension of the sentence: because of /ai/, and thus /ai/, doing /ai/ to /ai/, and /ai/ for /ai/.

On my journey, I sat down by Samira's felting group (Figure 16.3). The fabric joined our hands, and the sound /ai/ connected our voices. The multitude of utterance suddenly took its shape paralleling the appearance of the felt on the floor. The conversation became intimate and coded within the visual. Our voices emerged like a choir with the sound of drenching materials under our constant steps.

FIGURE 16.3 Performance by Samira Jamouchi and Lap-Xuan Do-Nguyen. Photo credit: Thu-Nhi Vo.

On my journey, I brought my voice to spectators, and without prompting, some responded with their own /ai/ sound. We exchanged the /ai/. Responses were individualized, and yet we were sharing a moment of affinity. Audience members became collaborators, in the making of togetherness: only /ai/ can speak and cannot speak.

While we were contemplating these voices, we seemed to also witness "I"(s) becoming witnesses in "a zone of indistinction in which it is impossible to establish the position of the subject, to identify the 'imagined substance' of the 'I' and, along with it, the true witness (Agamben, 2017, p. 841)."

IV.

That afternoon, the event created an aesthetic encounter including action, sound, and characters. Some were mandatory, some were not. They were not separate or blended, but contiguous. As I started with my voice, I engaged in a performative duration of emotion, and thus, encountered unanticipated ways of knowing amidst the private and the public. These encounters acted as both the material and the condition that constituted agency and change. After my performance, I spoke with a Japanese audience member, with whom I shared a very intimate connection during my performance of /ai/. I asked her if I scared her since I was speaking aggressively while her reply was so gentle. Her answer moved me: "No, I wasn't scared, it was 'love'" (see Figure 16.4).

FIGURE 16.4 Performance by Lap-Xuan with Geneviève as silent sculpture "wood." Photo credit: Alicia Arias-Camison Coella.

Diverse creative processes can inhabit and inform each other. The event surprised me with many beautiful moments; and affirmed my belief on my socially-engaged practice: making the possibility for participation to emerge autonomously. Practising encounters for me, hence, is not just the meeting, but the making-of-the-meetings.

That day, while Yoriko and Samira played a direct role to me, as we initiated our collaboration, Geneviève's position seemed more modest. By being Yoriko's silent sculpture, Geneviève ceased her voice, making her the ultimate listener of others. As the familiar sound rang, Samira, Yoriko, Geneviève, and I were both invisible and visible partners in each other's presence. And we did that whilst we were altogether letting go.

Samira Jamouchi:

Prelude

I came to the exhibition space with a wish to encounter others, both professional artists and the public. My material was a large amount of wool, which I brought from Norway. I did not intend to make a product, or plan to hang a finished piece of art on the gallery walls. I did not anticipate the encounters which emerged from our gathering. Lap-Xuan and I discussed our practices in an early phase of the process. This led us to a close working process, both in the gallery and on the shore, not long from the University of British Columbia. My intention was to open myself to the impulses and to what could occur. A feeling of affinity emerged.

Symbolically, wool fibres encourage us to become porous to others and otherness. Felting wool is a sensory and aesthetic experience of the porosity of the material. When we pour water on wool fibres, they open and expand.

Becoming an Assemblage

This gardening, that afternoon, with all the artists was like an event. It generated an assemblage (Deleuze & Guattari, 1980/2019) created by our intra-action emerging from a flow of agency in a state of constant becoming. The relationship of the parts, or co-components, of an assemblage are not fixed. They are intensities, thoughts, touches, voices, sounds, movements, and gestures that spread in the room. The room is not only a metric dimension measured and determined by its width, length, and height. The space is dynamic and relational.

I felt the space of the gallery as my senses became attuned to others and their otherness. Time and elements became liquid. I felt that the elements in the space, human and non-human, entered a state of "liquidness." Time became simultaneously in-motion and vibrant. I felt that this set the base for what was to (be)come in the exhibition.

Entanglement, Togetherness, and Intra-Action

The day before the opening of the exhibition, I placed a large amount of black and white wool on the floor in the shape of a long, narrow, white rectangle placed in the middle of a larger and wider back rectangle. The design of those several layers of wool recalled ancient geometric patterns. That form also recalled the letter "I" (from Latin alphabet) or "Aleph" (from Arabic alphabet).

Felting wool is one of the most ancient textile techniques (Figure 16.5). It has been performed for centuries. I often think about the act of felting as a linkage connecting me to other times and spaces. Putting a large amount of wool on the floor and starting to felt it with others is more than a collaboration. I think about this performative act as a co-making or an intra-action (Barad, 2014). I theorize the practice as co-making because it is more intimate than collaboration. Co-making implies the idea of a common sensory action, beyond cognition. Intra-action describes an event, or a phenomenon, as a relationship that emerges between entities from within their relationship while the event takes place, not prior to or outside it. The event takes us further in the intra-active process, more than if we were to anticipate the final product.

The performance is generated by each component present in the room: participants' bodies and actions, the water and its fluidity, the wool fibres and their transformability, the fragrance of pine tree soap, the durations in that moment, the flux of movements, the space, the voices, echoes, the silences, and the rhythms and re-iterations of frictions between our feet and the wool. We use our hands and rub the wool to entangle the loosen fibres on the floor. We roll the enmeshed fibres forth and back. We walk on it to filter it even more.

Our relationship as co-makers evolves as our bodies in motion change the loose fibres of the wool into an entangled and large piece of felted wool. The entanglement of the wool fibres mirrors the entanglement of the people in the room. We shape the event, as much as the event shapes us. Above all, we are *feeling* a sense of togetherness under the process of *felting* wool (see Figure 16.6).

We lifted the piece of wool and held it a moment before letting it go and fall with all its weight on the floor. Each fall brings us closer to a completely entangled piece. Both the wool fibres and the participants became entangled. In this process, we were creating a sort of community. We created a moment of togetherness.

The Performative Power of an Encounter: From "I" to "WE"

It is difficult to pinpoint a particular moment that could describe the transformation from "I" to "WE" in the collaborative felting piece. Nevertheless, I can sense how "WE" became the event/performance. Through the process, we were not a group of separated individuals, but a diversity of entangled "Is." During the piece, the tautophony[1] of the single personal pronoun "I," pronounced by Lap-Xuan fills the room. Sometimes Lap-Xuan spoke loudly, sometimes whispered,

FIGURE 16.5 Setting for Samira Jamouchi's performance. Photo credit: Monica Klungland.

FIGURE 16.6 Performance by Samira Jamouchi. Photo credit: Alicia Arias-Camison Coella.

FIGURE 16.7 Gallery attendees and Samira Jamouchi felting wool together. Photo credit: Samira Jamouchi.

sometimes next to me while looking into my eyes, and sometimes from the other side of the room. The public became a collective we as she spoke "I." I felt a powerful encounter between Lap-Xuan's utterance and the iterative gestures within the felting piece, as several persons from the public joined me in the felting process (see Figure 16.7).

The "we" loosened up, and people started to talk to each other or walk around in the art gallery. The event moved me. In it, my relation to others shifted. I left the room and came back after a moment. I saw Geneviève sitting on a chair and Yoriko cutting her hair. I saw wool fibres on the floor and Geneviève's hair on the floor. I saw these too as a kind of weaving, an intra-action between the pieces.

Yoriko Gillard:

愛 *feel you,* 愛 *hear you, and* 愛 *see you...*

> a time you learned something almost
>
> always begins with letting go
>
> — *Carl Leggo (2018)*

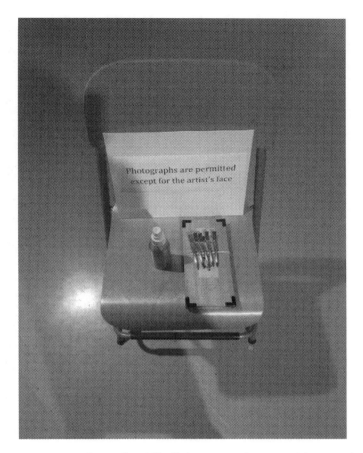

FIGURE 16.8 A setting for Yoriko Gillard's haircut performance. Photo credit: Yoriko Gillard.

I felt fortunate to be invited to the exhibition. Each artist's individual practices inspired me to feel their emotion during my haircut performance. Lap-Xuan's performance reflected in my ears as 愛 (ai)—love in English—and Samira's beautiful sculpture warmth and care. Geneviève was the very first person who agreed to become my "wood" sculpture and her courage and trust in me reflected in my heart as comfort one can seek in a relational world. All of us became one by performing 愛 (ai) to feel, hear, and see 愛 (ai) through the act of co-creation by trusting each other. This haircut performance was an extension of my own arts-based research practice, *Kizuna* to connect with people in a meaningful way (see Figures 16.8 and 16.9). My poetry 愛 (ai) emerged after reading my co-creators'

272 Genevieve Cloutier et al.

FIGURE 16.9 Artwork by Yoriko Gillard. Photo credit: Yoriko Gillard.

reflections. I envision my poetry 愛 (ai) as a thank you note that has been echoing in my mind. It is with this poem that we close the chapter.

愛 *(ai)*

I see you

my 愛
your 愛
our 愛

you see me

inside
outside

emergence of 愛

see us all

your beauty
your desire
your dignity
your courage
your fear
your joy
your regret
your hopes
your care
your trust
your 愛

you act 愛

I feel you
I feel you

you trust 愛
you give 愛

愛 see you…
Geneviève
愛 see you…

cut cut cut   cut cut cut   cut cut cut   cut cut cut
cut   cut   cut cut cut
cut cut cut

do you hear my 愛?
let me reveal
let me trust
do you hear my 愛?

you say 愛

I hear you
I hear you

you meant 愛
you desire 愛

愛 feel you…
Lap-Xuan
愛 feel you…

cut
cut cut
cut
cut cut   cut
cut
cut
cut
cut
cut cut cut cut   cut
cut cut cut
cut cut   cut cut   cut

do you see my 愛?
let me reveal
let me trust
do you see my 愛?

You WEave 愛

I see you
I see you

you care 愛
you know 愛

愛 hear you…
Samira
愛 hear you…

cut cut cut cut cut cut cut cut cut cut cut cut cut cut cut cut cut cut
    cut cut cut cut cut

do you feel my 愛?
let me reveal
let me trust
do you feel my 愛?

Note

1 Tautophony = the repetition of the same sound.

References

Agamben, G.(2017). *The omnibus homo sacer.* Stanford University Press.
Barad, K. (2007). *Meeting the university halfway: Quantum physics and the entanglement of matter and meaning.* Durham, North Carolina: Duke University Press.
Barad, K. (2014). Diffracting diffraction: Cutting together-apart. *Parallax, 20*(3), 168–187.
Boal, A. (1979). *Theatre of the oppressed.* New York: Theatre Communications Group.
Bolt, B. (2004). *Art beyond representation: The performative power of the image.* London: I.B. Tauris and Co. Ltd.
Bolt, B. (2016). Artistic research: A performative paradigm? *Parse Journal, 3,* 129–142.
Deleuze, G., & Guattari, F. (1980/2019). *A thousand plateaus: Capitalism and schizophrenia.* London: Bloomsbury Academic.
Ellsworth, E. (1997). *Teaching positions: Difference, pedagogy and the power of address.* New York: Teachers College Press.
Ellsworth, E. (2005). *Places of learning: Media architecture pedagogy.* New York: Routledge Falmer.
Fischer-Lichte, E. (2008). *The transformative power of performance.* New York: Routledge.
Freire, P. (1970). *Pedagogy of the oppressed.* Harmondsworth, Middlesex: Penguin Education.
Gillard, Y. (2014). Trust through art and its practice: A/r/tography study. MA thesis, the University of British Columbia.
Gillard, Y. (2019). Living with a liminal mind. *Artizein: Arts and Teaching Journal, 4*(1), 31–47.
Hasebe-Ludt, E., Chambers, C., Leggo, C. (2009). *Life writing and literary métissage as an ethos for our times.* New York: Peter Lang.
Hasebe-Ludt, E., & Jordan, N. (2011). "May we get us a heart of wisdom": Life writing across knowledge traditions. *Transnational Curriculum Inquiry, 7*(2). https://ojs.library.ubc.ca/index.php/tci/article/view/2035
Hasebe-Ludt, E., & Leggo, C. (2018). *Canadian curriculum studies: A métissage of inspiration / imagination/interconnection.* Toronto: Canadian Scholars.
Huber, A.A. (2013). Documenting a present: Coming to performance studies. *Text and Performance Quarterly, 33*(4), 422–424.
Kemmis, S. (2009). Understanding professional Practice: A synoptic framework. Chapter 2. In B. Green (Ed.), *Understanding and researching professional practice* (pp. 19–38). Rotterdam: Sense Publishers.
Kemmis, S., Wilkinson, J., Edwards-Groves, C., Hardy, I., Grootenboer, P. & Bristol, L. (2014). *Changing practices, changing education.* Singapore: Springer.
Kleinman, A. (2012). Intra-actions: Interview with Karen Barad. *Mousse Magazine, 34,* 76–81.
Lather, P. (1992). Post-critical pedagogies: A feminist reading. In C. Carmen (Ed.), *Feminisms and critical pedagogy* (pp. 120–137). New York: Routledge.
Leggo, C. (2018). Holding fast to H: Ruminations on the ARTS preconference. *Artizein: Arts and Teaching Journal, 3*(1), 15–25.
Lionnet, F. (1989). *Autobiographical voices: Race, gender, self-portraiture.* Ithaca; London: Cornell University Press.
Morawski, C., & Cloutier, G. (2016). Memories, crossings, and station stops: Displaced pasts into present teaching of language and art. *Journal of the Canadian Association for Curriculum Studies, 14*(1), 55–65.
Pineau, E.L. (2002). Critical performative pedagogy. In E.L. Pineau, E. Lamm, N. Stucky, & C. Wimmer (Eds.), *Teaching performance studies* (pp. 41–54). Carbondale & Edwardsville: Southern Illinois University Press. Research Networks.

Snepvangers, K., & Mathewson-Mitchell, D. (2018). *Beyond community engagement: Transforming dialogues in art, education, and the cultural sphere.* Common Ground.

Tintiangco-Cubales, A., Daus-Magbual, A., Desai, M., Sabac, A., & Torres, M.V. (2016). Into our hoods: Where critical performance pedagogy births resistance. *International Journal of Qualitative Studies in Education, 29*(10), 1308–1325.

17
WHAT WE THINK WE KNOW FOR SURE

Some Concluding Thoughts on Facilitation

Casey Burkholder, Funké Aladejebi and Joshua Schwab-Cartas

Introduction

What do we think we know for sure about ethical research facilitation in community-based research? In this chapter we summarize the key contributions of our edited collection, provide major methodological takeaways, and explore the possibilities of future work. In addition, we highlight several lessons for application, taken from the chapter contributions. By spotlighting key challenges and concerns, we hope to help the reader/researcher situate examples featured in this volume within the existing literature, understand contributors' choices, and also consider how we can expand the larger field of research facilitation.

Established Problems in Research Facilitation

We begin by highlighting some established problems in research facilitation, and weave arguments and takeaways from contributors to the book together.

Compensation

In Tobin LeBlanc Haley and Laura Pin's chapter on working with people experiencing poverty as well as in Sadie Godard-Durant, Andrea Doucet, and Jane-Anne Sieunarine's chapter with young Black mothers, scholars advocate for compensating participants with honoraria before the research begins. Emma McKenna and Ryan Conrad's chapter discussing the experiences of sex workers during COVID-19 highlighted that most of their research budget funds—65%— were allocated and redistributed to sex worker participants. In their chapter on non-participation with 2SLGBTQ+ youth in Atlantic Canada, Brody Weaver and their colleagues highlight the need to redistribute resources—in their case

DOI: 10.4324/9781003199236-22

art supplies—directly to queer, trans*, and non-binary participants by sending art materials and research prompts in the mail each month for a year (July 2020–July 2021). Contributors encourage us to think through the ways in which funding and economic limitations create barriers for research facilitation. They also consider the ways in which power gets inserted through institutional requirements and assess how researchers might disrupt and create new opportunities for participants. Central to this review is a way of valuing research participants as knowledge producers whose expertise is critical to research projects. These authors consider their own positionalities (and the rewards of academic affiliation) to redistribute, albeit with constraint, meaning making and economic support back to research participants. While these compensation measures continue to stand as an important challenge in research facilitation, authors in this volume encourage us to consider compensation at every stage of the research process, rather than simply through the lens of institutional ethics requirements. As such, ethical research facilitation for social change must reckon with the ways that compensation not only serves as a mechanism to support participants, but one that embeds broader social, political, and economic circumstances in ways that create inequality. The economic conditions that research participants might encounter often confront the parameters and definitions of what academic institutions consider worthy of compensation. As LeBlanc Haley and Pin remind us, these parameters create tensions that structurally and systemically leave marginalized communities at a disadvantage. In essence, contributors in this volume suggest we foreground compensation that not only meets institutional definitions but prioritizes the material realities of our research participants as an ongoing commitment to bridge divides between diverse communities and the academy.

Surveillance by Government Agencies

In both Tobin LeBlanc Haley and Laura Pin's chapter on working with people experiencing poverty as well as in Sadie Godard-Durant, Andrea Doucet, and Jane-Anne Sieunarine's chapter with young Black mothers, we see the impact that government agencies and institutional structures have on research participants, and how these influence research facilitation—this includes the monitoring of funds (honoraria) by Social Services and the surveillance of mothers by Child and Youth Services. Each of these systems provide barriers to ethical research facilitation. In Emma McKenna and Ryan Conrad's chapter, we see how government surveillance of sex workers' income leads to further inequalities, including ineligibility for wage subsidies during the COVID-19 pandemic—further complicating their inclusion and exclusion from research. In these instances, particular attention must be paid to confidentiality, encouraging researchers to push against predetermined rules and requirements that do not consider the diverse range of participants' lives. Scholars must not only be attuned to these considerations but must also be prepared to challenge their research institutions to provide ethical frameworks for research facilitation.

Collaboration

Scholars in this volume recognize the histories and ongoing focus of academic institutions and the potential for research facilitation to create ruptures within these spaces. Through researcher transparency and vulnerability, Helen Yeung suggests that feminist research collaboration might disrupt structures of white supremacy, including within academia. In Molade Osibodu's chapter on facilitating critical mathematics education with South Saharan African youth studying in the US, and in Tenzin Butsang's chapter highlighting research within Indigenous non-profit organizations—both authors reframed the researcher/researched relationship, queried a researcher-led approach to their studies, and refocused on a collaborative approach to facilitation as a mode of disrupting white supremacy and settler colonial logics anchored in traditional research methods. Facilitating community-based research through this lens considers the radical potential of collaboration by emphasizing the ways it shifts the gaze of Western knowledge and white supremacist practices of othering to instead create methodological approaches co-created by diverse communities of thought and people.

Racial Dynamics

The role of white researchers in research with Black, Indigenous, and other racialized participants is highlighted in Tess Kendrick, Katie MacEntee, and Sarah Flicker's chapter on screening sex workers stories. Exploring the spaces where white facilitators should step in—and when they should step back—in responding to audience questions at a screening of a composite film on harm reductions strategies for people who trade sex demonstrates that there's no one size fits all approach to doing this work ethically: it must be contextually located, guided by participants' needs and desires, and responsive to participants' well-being. Considering the social and systemic contexts that create environments of distrust of white researchers, ethical facilitation may mean that white researchers should not enter fieldwork spaces when working in and with communities of colour—as Sadie Godard-Durant, Andrea Doucet, and Jane-Anne Sieunarine's chapter with young Black mothers highlighted when Doucet—the white member of the research team—decided to not enter the fieldwork space. As such, when considering race as an identifying marker in research facilitation, researcher positionality and confrontations about the ways race is understood in varying social contexts is critical.

More pointed in this discussion of race is how researchers can understand and interpret silence—a key contribution of Brushwood-Rose, Low, and Salvio's chapter. Research facilitation that notes when and why silence occurs, as well as infuses methods for non-participation within research creation offer opportunities to consider the intersections of race, power, and access. As such, race does not become a factor that participants must address, but a dynamic that the researcher considers at multiple levels, including one's own positionality. These scholars ask: for whom are you researching and why? In our work as early career scholars, we see the benefit of using our privilege to redistribute resources and wealth. We try to model this in our scholarship and activism. We see value in engaging our institutional access to write grants, and with funding, hiring and training Black, Indigenous, racialized, queer, and disabled facilitators and students to collect data. We work with these facilitators and students to disseminate the work in the media, in academic venues, and with the larger public as an attempt to disrupt anti-Black racism, abelism, homophobia, and transphobia in heteropatriarchal white supremacist scholarly processes including who has access to scholarly funding, who has the right to collect knowledge, and who has the authority to disseminate knowledge produced (Weiland, 2020).

In Catherine Vanner and colleagues' chapter, they note that in one of their workshops in Treaty 6 Territory (Saskatoon, Canada), white facilitators needed to take a minimal role, and instead provide resources, tools, and support for Indigenous girls and community members themselves to facilitate the workshop. Intentional discussion and facilitation placed at the hands of Elders and community members modelled consideration around mutual respect and collaboration. In Amelia Thorpe's chapter, she describes using her positionality as a white middle class queer to disrupt hegemonic whiteness within the facilitation of Pride in New Brunswick. However, Thorpe also recognized the contradictions in this approach for the ways her positioning simultaneously reinscribed notions of homonormativity and hegemonic whiteness. In Sabine LeBel's chapter on queering facilitation in art residencies, we also see a tension between positionality and culturally informed facilitation. In this instance, ethical research facilitation explores the effect of mistrust on research participation, and ground this framework in histories of racial discrimination, colonialism, and exploitation to situate it as an important factor in decision making and information given during research processes.

Culturally Responsive Facilitation

As Tang and Gube suggest in their chapter, it is important to try to ensure that insiders are included in all aspects of facilitation and project development. Being an insider can be advantageous in some research contexts, however the language that the facilitator uses in their approach has the potential to be politically charged. Within the context of working with ethnic minority participants in Hong Kong, they describe the ways in which they facilitated through the choice of language for their studies—English and Cantonese—and highlighted,

> Choosing to speak in English – one of the official languages of Hong Kong which could be understood by most – may appear to be favorable. However, defaulting to English may reinforce the assumption that a non-Chinese person is not considered a 'local' Hong Konger and hence not expected to be fluent in the local language. Similarly, if it is deemed more inclusive to

speak Cantonese, should it turn out that they are not fluent, [the researcher] may be equally at risk of othering [their] interlocutor by highlighting their lack of proficiency and creating an isolating experience for them.

Tang and Gube's chapter demonstrates that facilitating in a culturally responsive manner is complex, unexpected, and nuanced because participants are also complex, unexpected, and nuanced. Participants are not a monolith and while it is critical to include an insider in aspects of research development and facilitation, Tang and Gube remind us that researchers can't assume that insiders will always be prepared to navigate the socio-cultural and socio-political complexities that exist in any city, community, culture or in relation to individual participants.

Querying Decolonial Claims in Community-based Research

In both Molade Osibodu and Tenzin Butsang's chapters, they suggest that research calling itself "decolonial" must thoroughly disrupt white supremacy and settler colonialism. Beginning with research design, to the facilitation of the studies, to the dissemination of the results (including a reframing of who benefits most from the study), researchers are asked to create a purposeful shift away from the academy and towards communities. As Butsang acknowledges in their chapter, taking up Tuck and Yang's definition of decolonization as the "repatriation of Indigenous land and life" (2012, p. 1)" many supposedly "decolonizing" projects fail. Instead, Butsang suggests, "it is difficult to reconcile the academic project as anything but inherently extractive and exploitative." Osibodu also considers this framing by critically taking up ethical facilitation that moves away from Western ideals of knowledge to encourage co-learning. As Osibodu contends, a commitment to decolonial research facilitation can (and must) include joy, shifting the gaze away from damage-centred research to disrupt power relationships from within the academy. As Butsang and Osibodu consider, ethical facilitation of community-based research needs to centre the goals of community-participants and perhaps, a connected sense of political, cultural, social, and environmental communities. These authors ask us not to assume that community-based research is inherently decolonial, but instead infuse the *doing* in research to open new (and in some instances old) ways of knowing. As PhD Candidate Sara Tenamoeta Kahanamoku (2021) remarked on Twitter, "Been seeing a lot of 'decolonizing' talk in academia lately. You can't decolonize without returning Indigenous land, resources, lifeways. Making an aspect of the university more equitable is great, but isn't decolonizing. You can't decolonize unless you re-Indigenize."

However, Catherine Vanner and her colleagues' chapter suggest that there is something worthwhile in framing research as decolonizing, particularly when working with asset-informed approaches with Indigenous girls. To this end, contributors evaluate ways scholars can move beyond the simple insertion of "decolonizing" in research facilitation, to actively practice decolonial work through a series of ongoing methods that support the needs and goals of community-participants. While these scholars indicate that this work remains fraught and complex, they provide concrete examples for how researchers can add this level of reflexivity into their work. Perhaps more pointed in their critiques is a reflection that community-based research must be dynamic and allow for a series of processes to exist within individual research projects. This dynamism allows for projects to react, respond, and revisit approaches in ways that prioritize communities and shift the potential extractive nature of research work.

Confronting Whiteness

Authors in this volume consider confronting whiteness not only as a practice of reflexivity, but as an interrogation of biases, values, and ideas shaped by the historical and social construction of race (Vadeboncoeur, Bopp, & Singer, 2020). In order for ethical facilitation to take place, whiteness is not assumed to be neutral or normative, but a category that has undergone a series of social and systemic practices in opposition to racialized populations (Johnson & Aladejebi, 2022). In MacEntee et al.'s chapter, Jennifer Thompson reflects on the role of emotion and trust in facilitating research as a white woman in Cameroon,

> Potentially uncomfortable emotions can be present when doing anti-racist and decolonising facilitation, and how they are addressed (named, given space, or ignored) have implications for trust. If trust is important in order for participants and researchers to believe in the research process together, what is the role of transparency in naming the specific injustices like racism, colonisation, and patriarchy within this work?

A conscious engagement with this fact serves to consider how whiteness affects research facilitation and practice from a conceptual and methodological level.

Listening as a Key to Facilitation

Listening is much more difficult than it sounds. It requires, as Stó:lō scholar Jo-Ann Archibald, notes

> Patience and trust are essential for preparing to listen to stories. Listening involves more than just using the auditory sense. Listening encompasses visualizing the characters and their actions and letting the emotions surface. Some say we should listen with three ears: two on our head and one in our heart.
>
> *(Archibald, 1997, p. 10)*

In Brushwood-Rose, Low, and Salvio's chapter, they discuss the value of listening deeply to participants' and researchers' experiences and realities in facilitating research for social action. The way researchers can truly understand the role and importance of a participant's non-participation is by listening. Brushwood Rose, Low, and Salvio argue that listening is a key intersubjective process with social, ethical, and affective dimensions. Some strategies for thoughtful listening within research for social change includes listening that is informed by curiosity rather than expertise, aesthetic listening, and listening that can tolerate discomfort and ambiguity. As Tang and Gube suggest in their chapter, negotiating insider and outsider dynamics within research facilitation can offer opportunities for deeper listening, and require researchers and research assistants to think carefully about how they both speak and listen to participants, including the language choices and practices used within the research space. Making space to listen to perspectives beyond one's own, and to disrupt the need for researcher control of what is heard (and how it is heard) is key to listening deeply within research facilitation. This type of deep listening is about asking questions to ensure what was said was understood and to ensure the person or community has truly been heard.

Non-Participation

How might we facilitate through non-participation and refusal in research processes? As Tuck and Yang argue (2014, see also Tuck, 2009), respecting refusal is an important component of community-engaged research. Within our volume, we see multiple examples of theorizing non-participation and refusal. For example, in Brody Weaver and their colleagues' chapter on facilitating non-participation with 2SLGBTQ+ Atlantic Canadian youth amidst the pandemic, they argue that facilitating research in the digital realm requires an attentiveness to modes of non-participation, including leaving a Zoom call, keeping cameras off, and participating in some art activities, but not others. In Tess Kendrick and her colleagues' chapter, they argue that, "Research participants are not powerless. Choosing non-participation can be a way for participants, especially youth, to exercise their power in the research dynamic (Switzer, 2018)." (p. 16). As Brushwood-Rose, Low, and Salvio's chapter demonstrates, researchers must take non-participation seriously, by disrupting researcher assumptions, and by listening deeply to participants' words and silences. Non-participation is a form of participation that considers participant choice and decision making (see also Milne, 2012; Switzer, 2020). In other words, non-participation is equally important in the research process, and scholars can consider this as an expression of individual autonomy, agency, and confrontation, as well as a way to address the parameters of the research project itself.

Facilitating through Trauma and through the Unanticipated

Trauma for those who have experienced it will tell you that it does not discriminate against race, gender, age, or socio-economic backgrounds. It is experienced and manifests differently within each individual and/or communities. Patrick Tomczyk's chapter underscores this very issue and makes us as researchers aware how facilitation and facilitators need to be cognizant of participants' trauma or the potential to "trigger and re-traumatize someone" with negative stories. Tomczyk argues that when working with ethnodrama, being mindful of a person's trauma does not end with participants themselves, but also needs to be extended to consider one's audience and how they could potentially be affected. Tomczyk's chapter describes how an unanticipated space disrupted the intention for the performance of a queer youth-produced ethnodrama in ways that represented moments of violence and trauma rooted in participants' school-based histories. In Kendrick and colleagues' chapter, unanticipated audience discomfort with their composite film describing harm reduction strategies for people who trade sex created a challenge for peer facilitators. In MacEntee, Thompson, Nyariro, and Mitchell's chapter, they argue that within participatory research projects, "Research facilitation is an embodied, relational, and contextual practice that must be continually examined with an appreciation for the local research setting, intersecting social identities, and the global system of knowledge production." Facilitation through the unanticipated can also indicate a relinquishing of power and give way to not just collaboration but co-making as Coultier and their colleagues indicate.

Facilitating Community through COVID-19

In the Weaver et al. chapter working with 2SLGBTQ+ youth in Atlantic Canada as well as in Yeung's chapter exploring Instagram and art production with migrant women of colour in Aotearoa (New Zealand) during the COVID-19 Pandemic, Yeung reminds us of the power of facilitating research for social change while participants and researchers are "digitally together, yet physically apart." Facilitating through and amidst the Pandemic provides an opportunity for people to build communities within research spaces, to form trusting relationships and to confront the instability of changing public health mandates, while navigating losses, and creating new solidarities. We see key theoretical and methodological opportunities to this time, amidst the challenges of the Pandemic. As the COVID-19 pandemic lingers and its impacts are ongoing, facilitation and adaptation around global shifts remains an important factor by which researchers can better understand participants and their experiences.

We also see facilitating through trauma as a significant issue for further research. How might facilitators think through facilitation practices that centre and make space for trauma-informed practices? What might it look like to teach research methods courses with trauma-informed practices or a trauma-informed focus? Given the collective traumas experienced during the ongoing COVID-19 Pandemic, we have seen opportunities for facilitation that meets people where they are at, including, sometimes, within their homes. We believe that more research needs to be undertaken to understand facilitation through the shift from virtual to in person participation in a post pandemic context. How might we take some of the lessons from Pandemic research practices—for example, encouraging participant safety, changing what participation could look like—be maintained or even bolstered? We wonder: how more people could participate in projects, and attend conferences and talks without the same financial responsibility? We also think that more needs to be known about the stressors of engaging in research from home contexts (see also, Switzer, 2021).

Future Sites of Inquiry

Although the contributions in the book have offered deep reflections on facilitation, we also seek to highlight some future sites of inquiry for researchers who wish to explore theories and pedagogies of research facilitation. We seek to highlight the need to understand more about facilitating the redistribution of resources from the academy into the communities in which we work. We believe that more sustained inquiry into processes where grants accessible only from the academy are redistributed to communities. We seek to understand the ethical affordances and challenges to facilitating this kind of engaged practice.

Building on the critiques from Eve Tuck and K. Wayne Yang (2014), we see value in exploring the ways that researchers engage in research practices that are allegedly decolonizing. We believe that more work needs to be done to trouble facilitation that calls itself decolonizing, in particular when practiced by settler researchers on stolen land (see also: Held, 2019). We also think that there is a great value in resisting extractive practices in relation to the ways in which community-engaged researchers facilitate working with data (and archiving participant knowledge, see Burkholder et al., 2021) over time. We think that more work needs to be done in terms of redistributing this knowledge, including thinking about ways of making archives of data accessible to the communities in which we work, as well as facilitating the dissemination of the work to be in modes and formats that will be useful for these communities.

As authors in this work take note of research facilitation for social change; we conclude this chapter by exploring future possibilities for how facilitation can support rest as a mechanism for reciprocal relations between researcher and participant. To this end, drawing on the activism and public scholarship of Black feminists, (e.g. community activist Tricia Hersey's the Nap Ministry; Dr. Katherine McKittrick's academic and public scholarship through Twitter), we think that it is important to resist business-as-usual academic structures and expectations by encouraging and facilitating rest, including resisting the neoliberal demands of the academy (e.g. increasing demands on scholarship and facilitation practices). As the Nap Ministry suggests, "Disrupt and push back against a system that views you as a machine. You are not a machine. You are a divine human being. WE WILL REST!" (2021, para. 1). What might it look like for researchers to facilitate rest with the communities in which they work? What might this look like, including redistributing resources (financial and time) to facilitate more reciprocal relations? What might it look like to redistribute time—even waste time—as a critical facilitation practice? As Saul and Burkholder argue,

> While it is true that when considering waste in its material forms it is hard to imagine how its willful production could support a sustainable project of emancipatory protest or critique, in the case of *temporal waste*, waste need not be conceived of as pejorative, need not exist on the other side of value, but could instead assume its own structure of values in ways that contest the excesses of late stage capitalism. In a society that fetishizes efficiencies, making temporal waste can be seen as an important critical intervention, a subversion of what neoliberal logics value most.
>
> *(2020, p. 9)*

We see exploring rest and redistributing (and even wasting) time as important inquiries into the future of research in community-engaged research facilitation.

We see such value in facilitating reflexively, over long periods of time, and by building reciprocally beneficial research relationships. Resisting extractivism is a clear component of this work (Flicker & Nixon, 2018; Pain & Francis, 2003; Switzer et al., 2019; Tilley, 2017), and we suggest that more thinking on facilitating longitudinal practice (e.g. facilitating with the same people for a long period of time, and negotiating participation / non participation over time) is necessary for future thinking.

Through this collection, we have aimed to make clear that research facilitation is an important methodological work. It is clear that thinking through facilitation in community-engaged research is a rich and productive space of methodological inquiry. We argue that the incremental decisions made within research processes matter and must be theorized deeply. We draw inspiration from the contributors to this volume who engage in thoughtful facilitation in multiple geographical contexts, including New Zealand, Canada, and the United States. We conclude this chapter with one thing that we know for sure about research facilitation: that it needs to be fluid, adaptable/flexible, never static, and recognizant of community goals and objectives. Research facilitation must be conscious and willing to adapt to the ever-shifting socio-political and socio-cultural ethnoscapes of the present moment to uphold and fight for social justice and marginalized populations' rights and freedoms.

References

Archibald, J. (1997). *Coyote learns to make a storybasket: The place of First Nations stories in education*. [Unpublished doctoral dissertation]. Simon Fraser University.

Burkholder, C., MacEntee, K., Mandrona, A., & Thorpe, A. (2021). Coproducing digital archives with 2SLGBTQ+ Atlantic Canadian youth amidst the COVID-19 pandemic. *Qualitative Research Journal*. ahead-of-print. https://doi.org/10.1108/QRJ-01-2021-0003

Flicker, S., & Nixon, S.A. (2018). Writing peer-reviewed articles with diverse teams: Considerations for novice scholars conducting community-engaged research. *Health Promotion International*, *33*(1), 152–161.

Held, M.B. (2019). Decolonizing research paradigms in the context of settler colonialism: An unsettling, mutual, and collaborative effort. *International Journal of Qualitative Methods, 18*, 1609406918821574.

Johnson, M., & Aladejebi, F. (Eds.). (2022). *Unsettling the great white north: Black Canadian history*. University of Toronto Press. 9781487529178.

Kahanamoku, S.T. [@sara_kahanamoku]. (2021, August 16). Been seeing a lot of "decolonizing" talk in academia lately. You can't decolonize without returning Indigenous land, resources, lifeways. Making an aspect of the university more equitable is great, but isn't decolonizing. You can't decolonize unless you re-Indigenize [Tweet]. Twitter. https://twitter.com/sara_kahanamoku/status/1427351035589251099

Milne, E. (2012). Saying 'NO!' to participatory video: Unravelling the complexities of (non)participation. In E. Milne, C. Mitchell, & N. deLange (Eds.), *The handbook of participatory video*. AltaMira Press. https://rowman.com/ISBN/9780759121133

Nap Ministry. (2021, August 3). How will you be useless to capitalism today? *The Nap Ministry*. [Blog]. https://thenapministry.wordpress.com/2021/08/03/how-will-you-be-useless-to-capitalism-today/

Pain, R., & Francis, P. (2003). Reflections on participatory research. *Area, 35*(1), 46–54.

Saul, R., & Burkholder, C. (2020). Making waste as a practice of freedom: On temporality and time wasting in the academy. *Taboo: The Journal of Culture and Education, 19*(3). Retrieved from https://digitalscholarship.unlv.edu/taboo/vol19/iss3/2

Switzer, S., Chan Carusone, S., Guta, A., & Strike, C. (2019). A seat at the table: Designing an activity-based community advisory committee with people living with HIV who use drugs. *Qualitative Health Research, 29*(7), 1029–1042.

Switzer, S. (2018). What's in an image?: Towards a critical and interdisciplinary reading of participatory visual methods. In *Creating social change through creativity* (pp. 189–207). Cham: Palgrave Macmillan.

Switzer, S. (2020). "People give and take a lot in order to participate in things:" Youth talk back—making a case for non-participation. *Curriculum Inquiry, 50*(2), 168–193.

Switzer, S. (2021). Community engagement in COVID-19: Exploring online and remote pedagogies amongst practitioners: About. *Beyond the Toolkit* [Website]. https://www.beyondthetoolkit.com/about

Tilley, L. (2017). Resisting piratic method by doing research otherwise. *Sociology, 51*(1), 27–42.

Tuck, E. (2009). Suspending damage: A letter to communities. *Harvard Educational Review, 79*(3), 409–428.

Tuck, E., & Yang, K.W. (2012). Decolonization is not a metaphor. *Decolonization: Indigeneity, Education & Society, 1*(1), 1–40.

Tuck, E., & Yang, K.W. (2014). Unbecoming claims: Pedagogies of refusal in qualitative research. *Qualitative Inquiry, 20*(6), 811–818.

Vadeboncoeur, J.D., Bopp, T., & Singer, J.N. (2020) Is reflexivity enough? Addressing reflexive embodiment, power, and whiteness in sport management research. *Journal of Sport Management, 35*(1), 30–43.

Weiland, A. (2020, June 28). Black Lives Matter Fredericton teams up with UNB on Black history resources for teachers. *CBC News*. https://www.cbc.ca/news/canada/new-brunswick/black-lives-matter-fredericton-unb-1.5665954

INDEX

2SLGBTQ+ 1, 3, 7, 10, 12, 127–141, 181, 189, 208–218, 277, 283–284; *see also* LGBTQIA2S+

ability 4, 97, 134, 157, 167, 169, 182, 184; *see also* disability
accountability 17, 26, 118, 125, 165–166, 254
action research 54, 129, 130, 224
activism 7–9, 24, 34, 39, 67, 88, 96, 98–102, 127–130, 134, 195, 198, 200, 206, 222–224, 231, 280, 285
aesthetics 7, 113, 115, 118–123, 125, 213, 215–218, 266–267, 283
African 53; communities, 54; contexts, 51, 52; countries, 55; diaspora 50; Indigenous knowledges 49, 56, 54, 59; people of African descent 17–21, 27–28, 231, 236; ways of knowing 50, 57; women 51, 52, 54
youth 5, 48, 51, 52, 279
Afrocentric, 18, 20–21, 49–51, 59, 62
Ahmed, Sara 96, 104, 109, 124, 180, 197, 201, 204
American Educational Research Association (AERA) 76, 78–79, 81–85
Anima Casa Rural 195–197
anti-Black racism 1, 17–21, 26, 27, 68, 182, 183, 185–187, 280
anti-racist 17, 22, 23, 78, 83, 88, 148, 177, 179–182, 185–188, 205, 206, 236, 251, 282
Aotearoa; *see also* New Zealand 6, 95–109, 284
archives 100, 128–130, 133, 135–138, 285

art 4, 7–11, 99, 104, 107, 118, 127–138, 183, 195–198, 200–206, 217, 222–226, 229, 232, 258–261, 264, 267, 270, 278, 280, 283, 284; practice 10, 134–136, 138, 198, 201, 202
arts-based research 3, 9, 10, 78, 131, 259
assemblage 179, 180, 258, 259, 264, 267
Atlantic Canada 6, 7, 127–131, 134, 167, 277, 284
audience engagement 10, 121, 123, 136, 240–243, 245, 251–255
autoethnography 6, 8, 9, 76–80, 88, 90, 178–180

Barad, Karen 11, 28, 259, 260, 262, 268
binaries: gender 189, 190, 202, 211; rejection of 96, 100, 190; researcher / researched binary 5
Black Lives Matter 88, 153, 187
Black Canadian 3, 4, 17–31, 35, 76, 163, 176, 183, 190–192, 237, 287
Black communities 17–28; *see also* African descent
Burawoy, Michael 6, 76, 79

Canada 1, 5–8, 17, 18, 20–23, 25–28, 34, 35, 37, 39, 64–65, 69, 70, 74, 76, 77, 80, 85–87, 89, 90, 112, 123, 161–163, 165–167, 169–171, 174, 178, 184, 195, 203, 210, 221, 224, 229, 280, 284, 286
Canadian Criminal Code 34
Canadian Emergency Response Benefit (CERB) 34–36, 39, 40

Canadian Social Sciences and Humanities Research Council (SSHRC) 21, 28, 43
capitalism 68, 166, 195, 197, 286; surveillance capitalism 101
care 37, 38, 41, 99, 108, 201, 205, 233, 240, 271, 273, 274; caregiving 33; community care 134; radical care 107; self-care 107
the Caribbean 17, 18, 21–27
case study 4, 17, 118
cellphilm 2, 3, 10, 76–79, 87, 88, 131, 134, 225, 240–242
class 4, 20, 67, 134, 210; middle class 24, 33, 38, 88, 97, 101, 163, 178, 211, 280; working class 33, 101, 120, 163, 178, 210
climate change 58, 197, 200, 205, 206
coercion 18, 162, 171, 173
collaboration 5, 33, 34, 37, 39, 54, 58, 69, 80, 96, 113, 152, 182, 184, 199, 224, 226, 258, 259, 262, 264, 267, 268, 279, 284
collage 21, 87, 103, 107, 128, 134, 136, 198, 200, 229
colonialism 5, 6, 19–21, 35, 48–50, 52, 53, 56, 63–72, 83, 89, 95, 97–99, 130, 166, 183, 195, 202–205, 223, 224, 226–228, 279–281; hidden colonialism 151; neocolonialism 79; *see also* decolonial
community 2, 3, 33, 49, 50–52, 54–59, 63, 67, 72, 77, 78, 88, 90, 96, 97, 100–102, 107, 112–118, 132, 134, 136, 149, 151–156, 162, 169, 181, 183–185, 189, 203, 205, 208–210, 222, 225, 226, 231, 242, 245, 250, 253, 254, 268, 278, 278, 283, 284; academic community 39; Black communities 19–27; community activism 34, 285; community organizing 5, 9, 18, 95, 98, 99, 178, 188, 221, 232, 249; disabled 33; engagement 120, 197; Indigenous communities 64, 66, 72–74, 235, 236, 280, 281; marginalized 49, 148; media 114, 124, 125, 241; minoritized 151–156; queer communities 127–129, 131, 179, 182, 186, 201, 202, 206, 208, 224; racialized communities 181, 186; researcher relationship within 70, 85, 108, 130, 156, 157, 212, 225, 264, 285; sex work communities 34, 37, 38, 42; solidarity 133
community-based research 1–4, 6–8, 10, 11, 36, 37, 41, 69, 71, 76, 78, 89, 95, 114, 118, 132, 162–166, 169–173, 240, 241, 251, 253, 279, 281–283, 286
compensation 22, 24, 40, 164, 167, 170, 171, 174, 277, 278
confidentiality 162, 166
consent 5, 19, 23, 40, 41, 57, 101, 121, 133, 137, 146, 170–172, 225, 241, 246, 252, 255, 262

co-production 156, 158
Cote d'Ivoire 51
COVID-19 3, 4, 6, 7, 9, 12, 13, 33–37, 39, 40, 42, 43, 72, 80, 87, 88, 89, 107, 109–111, 127, 131, 134, 178, 182, 206, 253, 277, 278, 284, 286, 287
criminalization 5, 34, 35, 39, 40, 42, 45, 46
critical 35, 40, 79, 107, 129, 188, 189, 240, 262, 286; analyses 71, 251; audience engagement 240, 241, 245, 253; consciousness 68; engagement 78, 89, 255; facilitation 76, 80, 285; learning 76; mathematics 5, 48, 50, 51, 61, 279; methodologies 67, 97, 256; praxis 96; pedagogy 10, 11, 208, 261; reflection 73, 76; research 33, 63, 67, 162; self-reflection 90; theoretical orientations 70, 100, 130, 132, 133, 180, 209; thinking 3, 37
Critical Race Theory 21, 97
culturally responsive facilitation 280, 281

damage-centered research 3, 17, 23, 49, 51, 59, 71, 166, 238, 281, 287
decolonization 5, 51, 53, 56, 63, 67, 68, 166, 183, 223, 224, 226, 229, 236, 281; decolonizing facilitation 83, 88, 203, 281; decolonizing methodologies 6, 49, 58, 69, 71, 224, 285; decolonizing research 6, 26, 49, 57
desire-based research 3, 5, 49, 53, 100, 106, 279
digital archive 7, 12, 127–129, 135–138
digital storytelling 97, 114, 115–118, 121
disability 34, 39–41, 109, 169, 210; *see also* ability
disclosure 73, 146–150, 168, 225
discomfort 6, 7, 11, 57, 58, 76, 78, 80, 85–90, 98, 132, 136, 188, 242, 248, 251, 252, 254, 283
discourse 9, 35, 50, 61, 87, 98, 99, 104, 129, 179, 180–182, 184–188, 190, 212, 218, 238, 256
disruption 50, 51, 54, 55, 179, 180, 185, 187, 188, 190, 262
DIY 97, 99, 100, 106, 132, 134, 136, 138
drawing 10, 77, 85, 87, 115, 136, 173, 223, 234, 240

editing 70, 102, 133, 254
education 10, 20, 28, 38, 80, 86, 87, 119, 121, 128, 146–149, 153, 154, 158, 169, 199, 200, 203, 204, 209, 210, 222, 230, 235, 245, 261, 286; community 112; critical mathematics 5, 48, 51, 279;

decolonizing 12; land-based 2; sexual health 78
embodiment, 87; *see also* embodied
embodied 6, 9, 57, 77, 83, 85, 88, 89, 96, 135, 182, 259, 260, 262, 284
emotions 83, 100, 103, 106, 124, 135, 138, 265, 282
engagement 72, 89, 101, 114, 121, 122, 125, 127, 129, 132, 136, 164, 173, 183, 197, 202, 221, 225, 227, 236, 240–242, 254, 259, 260, 261; audience engagement 10, 11, 240–242, 245, 251, 252, 255, 282; civic engagement 113; critical 77, 78; ethical 70, 123, 124; participant 77, 223, 264; virtual engagement 134, 253
epistemology 10, 20, 21, 27–30, 52, 61, 63, 64, 67–69, 89, 109, 154, 157
equity 4, 9, 15, 61, 86, 99, 145, 147, 153, 156, 158, 163, 173, 189, 209
ethical dilemma 10, 146, 148, 154, 156, 157
ethical research 1–5, 11, 17, 19, 25–27, 145, 150, 151, 156, 157, 160, 161, 164, 212, 238, 251, 277, 278, 280
ethical practice 73, 130
ethico-onto-epistemology 5, 21, 28
ethics 1–4, 8, 9, 12, 13, 17, 24, 26–28, 36, 40, 45, 46, 57, 63, 70, 72–74, 90, 121, 126, 143, 146, 149, 150, 151, 156, 159–163, 165, 166, 174–176, 198, 200, 201, 203, 207, 209, 212–214, 251, 255, 256, 259, 278; *see also* Institutional Review Boards, Research Ethics Boards
ethnodrama 208, 211–219, 284; ethnodramatic inqueery 10
ethnography 3, 10, 13, 152, 213
Eurocentrism 18, 56, 95, 98, 202
exhibition 121, 128, 129, 130, 132, 137, 258–264, 267, 268, 271
exploitation 18, 34, 43, 37, 64, 72, 73, 151, 164, 223, 280, 281
extractivism 73, 164, 281, 282, 285, 286

facilitator 7, 9, 11, 72, 78–79, 85–90, 95, 112–125, 127, 129, 135, 188, 196–203, 205, 229, 242, 245, 246–253, 260, 262, 279, 280, 284
failure 1, 11, 12, 168, 203, 204, 206, 211, 230
feelings 9, 68, 98, 117, 204, 205, 245, 252
feminism 6, 28, 33, 35, 50, 77, 89, 96–109, 202, 262; Black feminism 20, 21; fourth-wave feminism 97, 99, 100; Indigenous feminisms 67–72; intersectional 41; and research 17, 128, 130, 133, 140, 259, 279
fieldwork 3, 8, 23, 145, 157, 158, 212, 217, 279

First Nations 27, 65, 72, 73, 74
food security 125, 197, 206
Freire, Paolo 198, 199, 200, 208, 258, 261, 262

the Gambia 51
gender 1, 4, 5, 7, 10, 41, 63, 65, 68, 74, 77, 80, 85, 87, 90, 97, 98–104, 113, 119, 128, 130, 131, 134, 163, 179–189, 202, 203, 208–212, 214, 218, 219, 221–223, 226, 228, 231, 242, 248, 249, 283
generalizability 38, 41, 64, 70
globalization 3, 97, 112, 125, 196, 197

Halifax 129, 221, 225, 231, 232
homeless 163, 164, 169, 246
homonormativity 9, 178, 179, 182–184, 186–188, 210, 280
Hong Kong 8, 95, 97, 145–158, 280
honoraria 8, 38, 40, 41, 161, 167–174, 252, 277, 278; *see also* incentives
hooks, bell 67, 96, 107
human rights 21, 28, 31, 33, 45, 113

identity 9, 20, 25, 41, 50, 63, 71, 74, 95–97, 103, 104, 107, 114, 115, 121, 125, 149, 155, 180, 183, 189, 190, 202, 203, 209, 211, 212, 231, 259, 264
images 25, 54, 79, 80–85, 87–90, 101, 104, 107, 118, 122, 132, 136, 137, 154, 187, 223, 227, 264, 265
immigrants 29, 115, 116, 120, 147, 189
incarceration 25, 64, 65, 66, 69
incentives 8, 161–174; *see also* honoraria
Indigenous 33, 35, 38, 65, 71, 166, 168, 180, 189, 203, 221, 224, 226, 235–237, 250, 256, 279–281, 287; Elders 174; feminisms 68, 69; girls 10, 221, 223, 227; health 63, 73; knowledges 49, 56, 59, 67, 229; research 17, 64, 70, 133; parents 6; peoples 3, 27, 66, 163, 169, 170; practice 2; women 65, 66
Instagram 6, 95–102, 104, 106, 108, 109, 128, 136, 253, 254, 284
Institutional Review Boards 24, 146, 165, 256; *see also* ethics, Research Ethics Boards
intersectionality 7, 20, 33, 41, 69, 77, 82, 97, 99, 106, 128, 138, 179, 180, 188, 189, 202, 210, 211
Inuit 27, 65

joy 48–50, 53, 55–57, 59, 89, 102, 107, 206, 207, 273, 281

knowledge creation 6, 49, 66, 70, 96, 97, 100, 102, 104, 119, 138, 222, 279
knowledge mobilization 38, 47, 128, 180, 222
knowledge production 3, 6, 8, 56, 60, 77, 88, 89, 97, 98, 100, 104, 107, 138, 145, 151, 154, 158, 163, 183, 216, 221, 225, 255, 262, 284
Kovach, Margaret 64, 69, 224
Kuti, Fela 5, 48–50, 55, 60

labour 8, 34, 35, 43, 89, 138, 165, 185, 189, 205
Lacks, Henrietta 19, 31
language 2, 8, 9, 34, 39, 42, 73, 104, 121, 125, 140, 147, 149–151, 153–155, 158, 159, 167, 172, 182, 196, 202–205, 217, 247, 252, 259, 260, 265, 275, 280, 283
lens 53, 71, 79, 180, 201, 208, 210, 224, 259, 260, 278, 279
LGBTQIA2S+ 201, 202, 205; *see also* 2SLGBTQ+
listening 7, 9, 12, 20, 49, 60, 66, 69, 88, 112–126, 131, 134, 140, 202, 204, 241, 253, 282, 283
lived experience 5, 10, 17, 19–21, 40, 71, 85, 96–98, 102, 103, 109, 121, 162, 169, 172, 202, 205, 208, 211, 217, 218, 227, 249, 250

Madagascar 51, 59
Māori 71, 109
materiality 86, 217, 259
memory 6, 7, 100, 109, 121, 129
mental health 23, 28, 42, 107, 125, 240, 253
Métis 27, 65, 211, 221
#MeToo 101
Mexico 195, 197, 202, 207
microaggressions 106, 153, 201, 211
migration 41, 45, 97, 100, 103, 104, 112, 116, 197
Mitchell, Claudia 6, 10, 76, 90, 128, 221
mobile phones 6, 95, 97, 99, 101, 102, 257
Montreal 7, 30, 80, 112, 113, 120–123, 125, 222
mothers 5, 17, 18, 21–26, 28, 50, 65, 69, 85, 96–99, 103, 104, 114–117, 124, 163, 233, 277–279
multimedia 7, 112, 113, 118, 126
multimodal 99, 223, 233, 238

NAFTA 196, 197
narrative inquiry 18, 71, 138, 259
New Brunswick 128, 130, 163, 168, 178–180, 185–188, 280

New Zealand 6, 27, 95, 284, 286; *see also* Aotearoa
New York 7, 112, 113, 118, 125
non-binary 5, 10, 98, 129, 131, 139, 183, 189, 195, 198, 202, 246, 278
non-participation 7, 8, 127, 129–141, 236, 238, 252, 257, 277, 279, 283, 287

OCAP (Ownership, Control, Access and Possession) principles 27, 72–74, 170
objectivity 4, 36, 63, 69, 89, 90, 119, 125, 225–227, 229, 235, 236, 286
ontology 18, 28, 63, 64, 67–69, 212, 237, 259
oral history 1, 3, 28, 70, 113
Ottawa 29, 34, 36, 39, 40, 44

pandemic 3, 4, 6, 7, 9, 12, 34, 35, 37, 39, 40, 42, 44, 72, 88, 89, 99, 109, 110, 127, 131, 134, 135, 182, 184, 206, 253, 283, 284
participation 7, 8, 12, 18, 22, 23–25, 29, 38, 79, 101, 118, 119, 126–140, 162, 163, 165, 167, 170–174, 184, 186, 202, 205, 226, 236, 238, 245, 251, 252–254, 265, 267, 277, 280, 283–287
participatory analysis 10, 240
participatory action research 54, 130, 131, 133, 139, 222, 224; *see also* youth participatory action research
Participatory Cultures Lab 76, 85
participatory media 112, 113, 121
participatory video 113, 132, 133, 140, 256
participatory visual research 1–4, 6, 7, 9, 12, 26, 76–79, 127–138; *see also* visual research
pedagogy 7, 10, 11, 60, 77–79, 85, 87–90, 113, 118, 125, 126, 208, 219, 229, 239, 258–261
performance 6, 11, 76, 78–88, 90, 183, 198, 211, 213–219, 258–266, 268, 269, 271, 284
photography 25, 77, 85, 87, 91, 101, 103, 115, 200, 223
photovoice 77, 85, 87, 131, 223
poetry 59, 199, 271, 272
policy 8, 17, 22, 24, 27, 28, 39, 42, 43, 99, 102, 118, 123, 128, 130, 147, 161, 168, 172–174, 181, 212, 218, 241
positionality 1, 8, 36, 44, 52, 79, 83, 85, 95, 98, 104, 145, 151, 152, 154, 156–158, 180, 188, 202, 210, 211, 222, 235, 251, 259, 262, 278–280
postcolonial 69, 79
poverty 8, 33, 40, 42, 44, 112, 133, 161–164, 168–173, 210, 277, 278

power 2, 3, 5, 8, 9, 11, 13, 18, 20, 23, 26, 30, 49–51, 54, 58, 59, 64, 67–71, 85–87, 95, 97, 98, 101, 102, 104, 106, 107, 109, 118, 131–133, 140, 145, 151, 152, 154, 155, 164, 178–180, 183–185, 188–190, 198, 203, 204, 208, 210, 212, 213, 217–220, 222, 236, 241, 250, 252–255, 261, 262, 264, 268, 270, 278, 289, 281, 283, 284, 287
practitioner 4, 77, 130, 138, 148, 149, 210, 217, 264
precarity 35, 175
praxis 6, 11, 67, 96, 97, 100, 104, 191, 208, 209, 218, 220
Pride 9, 178–190, 201, 280
Pride/Swell 7, 127–138
process 2–12, 17–28, 38–41, 48–53, 56–59, 63, 64, 66–69, 71–73, 77–81, 83, 85, 89, 90, 96, 99, 102–104, 106, 107, 112, 113, 115–118, 121, 125, 128, 133, 136, 137, 143–145, 146, 148, 149–152, 162–164, 167, 169, 170, 172, 173, 176, 180, 183, 196, 198–205, 211–217, 219, 222–225, 229, 233, 234, 236, 241, 251–255, 259–261, 263, 268, 270, 278, 280, 282, 283, 285, 286; lesbian processing 206–209
public health 33, 54, 55, 65, 71, 72, 241, 256, 284

qualitative research 12, 21, 36, 37, 41, 78, 91, 98, 131, 151, 175, 217
queer 33, 96, 101, 203–206, 208–219, 222, 242, 280, 284; activism 178–190; art 10, 242; community 7, 127–137, 201; environmental futures 195–200, 202–206; methods 9, 196, 197, 198

race 2, 4, 5, 7, 12, 20, 21, 23, 41, 44, 49, 63, 68, 83, 88, 95, 97, 101, 103, 106, 134, 139, 170, 182, 189, 203, 209, 210, 211, 218, 229, 231, 233, 236, 246, 249, 260, 261, 264, 279, 282, 283
reflexive revisiting 6, 76, 83, 85, 88, 245, 251
reflexivity 2, 3, 23, 26, 63, 64, 71, 78, 85, 89, 91, 124, 125, 155, 156, 203, 213, 241, 253, 282
refugee 64, 113, 121–123, 126, 210
relationality 67, 68, 113, 125, 224, 259, 262
relationships ,11, 13, 18, 22–26, 37–39, 50, 64–68, 70, 72, 73, 76, 82, 87, 89, 90, 96, 99, 103, 105, 110, 114, 115, 123–125, 129, 134, 151, 152, 163, 164, 166, 181, 197, 202, 226, 233, 235–237, 254, 255, 260, 261, 267, 268

researcher/participant 7, 8, 13, 17, 21, 49, 131, 132, 154, 168, 171, 212, 251, 281, 286
research assistants 8, 36, 40, 66, 85, 145–158, 222, 283
research participants 21, 29, 172
research practice 71, 153, 157, 163, 164, 255, 271
research processes 4, 5, 8, 17, 18, 19, 21, 23, 26, 27, 38–40, 48, 53, 71, 72, 77, 164, 167, 172, 173, 222, 261, 278, 282, 283
Research Ethics Boards 27, 161, 164, 165, 170, 172; *see also* ethics, Institutional Review Boards
rest 285, 286
Riot Grrrl 100
Rwanda 122, 123

Sankofa 48–52, 54–58
Saskatoon 221, 280
school 8, 10, 11, 20, 43, 51, 55, 56, 60, 74, 85, 113, 118, 120, 121, 128, 130, 137, 147, 152, 153, 166, 198, 208, 210–212, 215–219, 221, 225, 227, 228, 231–233, 237, 284
screenings 10, 78, 115, 183, 225, 240–243, 245–255, 279
settler colonialism 64–71, 97–99, 110, 130, 176, 223, 224, 228, 279, 281, 287; *see also* colonialism
sexuality 4, 39, 86, 97, 128, 131, 134, 179, 202, 209, 211, 231, 242, 248
sex workers 5, 33–44, 246, 248, 277–279
Simpson, Leanne Betasamosake 2, 68, 133, 233, 236
Smith, Linda Tuhiwai 64, 71
social change 1–4, 6, 9, 10, 42, 50, 69, 71, 76, 77, 80, 87–90, 96, 108, 179, 188, 206, 241, 242, 278, 283–285
social media 7, 36, 39, 60, 99, 101, 102, 130, 137, 138, 153, 211, 245, 248, 253, 254
social science 2, 25, 43, 64, 98, 106, 146, 165, 173
solidarity 10, 36, 71, 88, 102, 108, 109, 128, 130, 133, 136, 179, 227, 284
South Africa 52, 60, 87
space 1–12, 49, 50, 52, 54, 56–60, 69–72, 77–79, 81–83, 89, 96–102, 104, 107, 109, 112, 114, 115, 117, 119, 120, 122, 125, 127, 129–132, 135, 136, 145, 149, 150, 156–158, 169, 170, 178, 179, 181, 182, 185, 186, 188, 189, 196–206, 208, 209, 211, 214, 216, 221, 231, 235–237, 242, 249, 251–253, 258–264, 267, 268, 279, 282, 283, 284, 286

Index

storytelling 7, 69, 99, 100, 103, 106, 112–119, 125, 224
structural violence 25, 97, 185, 249; *see also* violence
Sub-Saharan Africa 5, 48, 51, 52, 85
supervisor 36, 65, 66, 73, 76
surveillance 42, 45, 101, 162, 168, 169, 278
Switzer, Sarah 4, 77, 78, 89, 127, 133, 135, 252, 283, 285

TCPS 2, 8, 17, 22–28, 161–167, 170, 172–174; *see also* Tri-Council Policy Statement
teachers 1, 5, 8, 20, 49–51, 53, 59, 78, 90, 118, 120, 121, 125, 128, 130, 137, 146–149, 153–155, 198, 210, 215, 217, 221, 225, 227–229, 233, 234, 237
technologies 6, 89, 101, 107, 115, 225, 241, 245, 254; digital technologies 4, 101
thesis 37, 67, 261
Tiohtià:ke 222; *see also* Montreal
Tkaronto 5, 130; *see also* Toronto
Toronto 5, 7, 65, 66, 70, 73, 112–115, 118, 125, 164, 185, 187, 197, 240, 255; *see also* Tkaronto
trans★ 10, 33, 38, 98, 101, 128–133, 163, 181, 184–189, 201, 202, 210–213, 218, 278; *see also* transgender
transactional sex 242, 244, 246, 250
transcripts 72, 78
transgender 130, 134, 163; *see also* trans★
transphobia 130, 202, 208, 211, 212, 214, 218, 280
trauma 64, 96, 98, 100, 103, 109, 124, 125, 214, 262, 283, 284
Treaty 6 221, 224, 226, 227, 231, 234, 236, 237, 280
Tri-Council Policy Statement 8, 17, 22–28, 161–167, 170, 172–174; *see also* TCPS 2
Tuck, Eve 1, 3, 64, 68, 71, 73, 166, 281, 285
Tuskegee experiments 18, 31
Twitter 99, 101, 128, 253, 281, 285
Two Spirit 6, 66, 73, 183, 185, 189, 203

Ubuntu 48–54
Uganda 51
United States 17–21, 51, 104, 169, 195, 203, 286

video 53, 77, 97, 100, 101, 113, 118, 132, 133, 135, 137, 138, 195, 198, 200, 223, 225, 232, 240–244, 249

violence 25, 35, 40, 42, 99, 166, 248, 250, 284; colonial violence 97, 109, 205; domestic violence 65, 99, 102; gender-based violence 10, 85, 87, 214, 221, 223–231; police violence 185; sexual violence 79, 101; state violence 42, 64; structural violence 25, 71
visual research 1–4, 6, 7, 9, 12, 26, 76–79, 127–138; *see also* participatory visual research
vulnerability 33, 35, 3, 8, 58, 96, 121, 122, 124, 125, 162, 166, 169, 170, 173, 212, 215, 249, 253, 279

waste 285, 286
Wet'suwet'en Nation 88
white privilege 19, 68, 88, 178, 180–182, 185, 210, 250, 280
white supremacy 1, 19, 53, 57, 68, 186, 187, 195, 202, 279, 281
whiteness 23, 55, 59, 70, 109, 179, 181, 182, 184–189, 206, 236, 250, 280, 282
Wilson, Shawn 64, 68
women 38, 80, 98, 99, 102, 104, 112, 170, 197, 246; Asian Migrant 6, 7, 95–109, 284; Black 19–28, 50, 51, 54; Indigenous 65–67, 71, 170, 226, 227; incarcerated 65; Missing and Murdered Indigenous Women and Girls 223; newcomer 112, 114–116; of colour 248; queer 242; racialized 250; shelters 35; violence against 224, 229; white 101, 163; who trade sex 247; young 77, 87, 90, 227, 233, 240, 242, 249, 250
workshops 10, 41, 42, 77–79, 81, 82, 85–89, 100, 114–116, 121, 122, 196, 198–206, 221–237, 240, 280

Young Indigenous Women's Utopia (YIWU) 222
youth 1, 5, 7, 10, 18, 28, 48, 49, 51–55, 57, 59, 64, 65, 80, 86, 90, 103, 113, 120, 121, 127–134, 138, 181, 208–212, 215–219, 221, 222, 224, 227, 233, 240, 245, 246, 249, 252, 253, 277–279, 283, 284
Youth Participatory Action Research (YPAR) 222, 223

Zimbabwe 51, 122
zines 95, 99–100, 103, 104, 106, 108, 128, 131, 134, 136

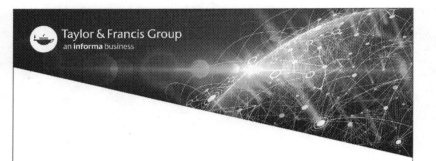

Printed in the United States
by Baker & Taylor Publisher Services